THE CLAMOUR OF NATIONALISM

Manchester University Press

The clamour of nationalism

Race and nation in twenty-first-century Britain

Sivamohan Valluvan

Manchester University Press

Copyright © Sivamohan Valluvan 2019

The right of Sivamohan Valluvan to be identified as the author of this work has been asserted by him in accordance with the Copyright, Designs and Patents Act 1988.

Published by Manchester University Press
Altrincham Street, Manchester M1 7JA
www.manchesteruniversitypress.co.uk

British Library Cataloguing-in-Publication Data
A catalogue record for this book is available from the British Library

ISBN 978 1 5261 2614 6 hardback
ISBN 978 1 5261 2612 2 paperback

First published in hardback by Manchester University Press 2019
This edition first published 2020

The publisher has no responsibility for the persistence or accuracy of URLs for any external or third-party internet websites referred to in this book, and does not guarantee that any content on such websites is, or will remain, accurate or appropriate.

Typeset
by Deanta Global Publishing Services
Printed in Great Britain
by TJ Books Limited, Padstow

For Uncle

Contents

Acknowledgements — viii

Introduction: mapping the nation — 1
1 Theorising the nation — 28
2 Notes on two red herrings: progressive nationalism and populism — 57
3 Valuing the nation: liberalism, Muslims and nation-state values — 68
4 Conservatism and mourning the nation — 89
5 Unholy alliances: the neoliberal embrace of nation — 121
6 Left problems: the left and welfare state nationalism — 155
Conclusion: absences and futures — 184

Notes — 208
Index — 267

Acknowledgements

There might at first glance appear to be little pleasure to be had in working through the numbing misery that is contemporary nationalist politics. One stolen joy, however, of exploring a question as expansive and live as nationalism is how readily and expertly those around me have been willing to offer their insights. Many gentle souls have tried in their affectionate wisdom to rescue for this book a clarity, purpose and precision that often elude me. I remain, of course, warmly indebted to these many generous people.

For helping me retain a voice and perspective not entirely obscured by hopelessly grandiloquent intellectualising, particular gratitude is owed to Virinder Kalra and Nisha Kapoor, dear friends whom I now also have the very good fortune of calling colleagues.

For forensically scrutinising my prose, Kausikan Rajeshkumar has gone well beyond the duties ordinarily expected of a younger cousin, even a Sri Lankan one. His capacious but effortlessly relaxed intelligence remains astonishing.

For readings of select chapters, I extend my thanks to Luke de Noronha, David Evans, Nisha Kapoor, Jamie Matthews, Sara Salem, James Rhodes and Gavan Titley. Tom Dark too has been an invaluable reader as well as scholarly ally, exceeding any going understanding of what a 'senior commissioning editor' notionally is. The copy-editing efforts of Andrew Kirk were also much appreciated. Working with an author who struggles even with the basics of harmonising spelling formats is no enviable task. The labours, however, of Malcolm James were of a particularly heroic order. Malcolm, having already treated me to years of caring friendship, worked through the drafts of this book in painstakingly loving detail. I can only hope that the final contents are in some approximate keeping with his deeply humane commitment to quiet and careful scholarship. I also note that much of Chapter 6 was borne out of an essay co-authored with Malcolm for the magazine *Salvage*. I remain herein doubly grateful to Malcolm for allowing me to reproduce in this book various passages from that original essay.

Appreciation is also extended to friends from the sociology departments of both Warwick and Manchester universities, friends who have been such encouraging but also spirited interlocutors during the writing of the book. It has been my typically good fortune to have somehow uncovered, amid the otherwise burgeoning ruins of a decimated higher education sector, a corner of academic life that is everything I could have hoped it would be. A corner where learned conversation is always in good supply and where I am continuously reminded by better people than me of the importance of maintaining a caring but firm political resolve. This is also a corner of academic life where the restless effervescence of students renders each year a giving as well as entertaining experience. These are, in other words, the joys of work that have rendered the otherwise solitary craft of book life far from lonely.

When they do arise, however, the strains of book writing fall most heavily on those closest to us. It is accordingly the enduring patience of Grace for which I remain most grateful. It is also to my family – scattered across Colombo, Jaffna, Stockholm, London, Amsterdam and even California – that any semblance of quality as found in the book is ultimately attributable. It is after all the painful complexity of their experiences, but also the colourful wisdom of their tales, that courses quietly across its pages.

And, as always, to *Mama*. I share with my mother a bond that has been marked and shadowed, from the very beginning and at every turn, by the merciless spectre of nationalism. Any thought worth having on the subject, I have learned from her.

***

Some select passages of this book have featured in essays and articles previously published. I am thankful to all the following sources for allowing me to reproduce relevant material. The Introduction includes some excerpts from a 2017 essay published in the now defunct magazine *Juncture*: 'Defining and challenging the new nationalism', *Juncture* 23:4, 232–9. Some very brief excerpts from Chapter 5 also appeared passingly in a short article, co-authored with Eleanor Penny, for the online magazine *Red Pepper* ('The new undesirables', 20 October 2018). Chapter 6 includes fairly extensive excerpts from an essay, co-authored with Malcolm James, which appeared in the Autumn 2018 issue of the cultural criticism periodical *Salvage*: 'Left problems, nationalism and the crisis', *Salvage* 6, 165–74. And finally, the Conclusion includes some excerpts from a 2019 article published in the journal *Sociological Review*: 'The uses and abuses of class', *Sociological Review* 67:1, 36–46.

Introduction: mapping the nation

No event in recent British political history has produced the level of despondency, exhilaration and chaotic scramble such as that which accompanied the result of the 2016 EU referendum. Brexit, in the course of generating a historically unique standard of sociopolitical uncertainty and constitutional intrigue, tore apart the two-party compact that had defined the parameters of political contestation for much of twentieth-century Britain. The allure of nationalist assertion in the form of exiting Europe seemed to cross and confound the distinctions of class, geography and ideology that had underpinned so much of recent British and, truth be told, western European politics writ large.

Cutting through the already too narrowly defined divide of Labour and Conservative, the Brexit vote represented the formal consolidation of a new electoral coalition: middle-income conservatives dotted across the green shires and provincial towns of England hitched to huge swathes of previously Labour-voting working-class Britain. Copious ink has been subsequently spilt trying to account for the different motivations and socioeconomic circumstances that aligned to produce this new political pivot, where 'Middle England' meets the 'left behind'; a political reconstitution that has emphatically put paid to the two-party system definitive of post-war European politics.

Amid the all-pervasive public commentary, disagreement prevails about whether the underlying cause of such politics is economic, cultural or actually the result of a much wider technologically mediated collapse of trust in a liberal establishment. But regardless of how commentators contest the underpinning causal factors, the one consensus is that Brexit, and other comparable trends elsewhere, has been principally framed, in its overt sense, by issues of immigration, race and difference.[1] This consensus becomes most starkly apparent in how those wrongfooted by the rise of the new right are now scrambling to parrot much of its politics. This scenario is encapsulated in Hillary Clinton's painfully tautological nostrum that the only way to repel the rise of nationalist populism in Europe is in fact to concede to its key ambitions: that is, to 'erect the barricades' vis-à-vis immigration.[2] Various critics skewered with relish the hollowness of this distinctly centrist brand of non-politics. As Jan-Werner Müller observed, '[Clinton's] underlying idea appears to be that one can defeat one's political adversaries [only] by imitating them.'[3] Or as Atossa Abrahamian drolly noted, 'Clinton evidently came out of her 2016 "deplorables"[4] gaffe with the wrong lesson: instead of pinning populist discontent to a range of easily identifiable social and economic ills, her takeaway was to start speaking like the deplorables.'[5] Such mocking of the centrist guard's spluttering is certainly warranted. Capitulation on immigration and complementary race-coded anxieties is not, however, solely a trait of the now panic-stricken centre. With regard to the ostensibly *left-wing* iteration of this same surrender, left 'realists' such as Slavoj Žižek, Angela Nagle and Wolfgang Streeck have been eager to reinterpret anti-capitalism so that it may more fluently dovetail with the communitarian and bordering principles so prized by the new nationalists. The premise that is accordingly shared by many *across* the political spectrum is that recent political events represent, in their most fundamental sense, a desire for a reconsolidation of the nation vis-à-vis immigration, multiculturalism and broader understandings of community.

Of course, amid all such talk of curtailing immigration, restoring the border, 'white shifts' and returning dignity to the 'left behind' working class, it is important not to discount the various other themes that surfaced during the Brexit campaign and its aftermath – issues pertaining to unaccountable bureaucracies, democratic deficits, the crisis tendency of the Euro, the steady drive towards centralised EU federalism, and even, admittedly from fairly fringe leftist factions, the EU as an unapologetically neoliberal single-market body that undermines the possibility of locally progressive politics. Yet in spite of these no doubt significant themes, it is not conjecture to observe that an assortment of more overtly xenophobic, race-baiting issues was 'wot won the referendum'; issues relating to immigration, refugees,

Muslims, the spectre of Turkey, the Roma, and the tyranny of political correctness, a tyranny allegedly magnified by the ECHR-sanctioned human rights restrictions that supposedly impugn and castrate the British character. The fact that populist firebrands across Europe, not least Marine Le Pen (perhaps *the* archetypal populist politician of our era), received the result with a flurry of enthusiasm is no mere footnote to the Brexit episode. It was instead an exemplary expression of the very political reality that has come to define contemporary Europe. Similarly well documented, of course, are the transatlantic dimensions of this new political stage, best embodied in Nigel Farage, the former leader of UKIP and charismatic lynchpin of the Brexit cause, decamping to the United States in order to bolster Donald Trump's own nationalist assertion. This affinity was mirrored in Prime Minister Theresa May's happy 'normalisation' of Trump while also enthusiastically ventriloquising Farage in her own electioneering, repeatedly asserting that Brexit, in terms of what remains non-negotiable about it, must represent the end of free movement.[6]

It ought be noted in this context that the much-celebrated recent collapse of UKIP is mostly pyrrhic. It is not the case that UKIP was defeated; it had simply been successfully absorbed into the fold of the mainstream Conservative Party. The initial consolidation of UKIP's political prominence, culminating in the Brexit outcome, certainly constituted one of the more overt instances of the new nationalist trend within the UK context.[7] Brexit represents, however, only one (albeit spectacular) milepost of this trend. Indeed, the issues constitutive of new nationalism, and the demagoguery intrinsic to it, only seem to have intensified in the wake of the referendum result, having worked themselves deep into the contemporary political mainstream: issues such as the purported 'refugee crisis' and immigration concerns more generally; the 'War on Terror' and related anxieties regarding the integration of British-born Muslims; the more diffuse disenchantment with any multicultural commitment and associated fears about cultural integrity, liberal values and white space; and the sudden but perhaps not entirely insincere outpouring of nativist concern regarding the plight of a disenfranchised 'white working class'. All of these are themes that intertwine to produce a densely knotted pivot of concerns conducive to nationalist solutions, solutions that escape any neat sense of party-political divides and constituencies.

Defining nationalism

Many arguments have been advanced in an attempt to develop an analytic schema that can account for this nationalist consolidation, a consolidation that consigns both the social democratic and liberal left to the ignobly hapless position of bystander, a mere observer of history dramatically unfolding. This opening chapter adds to that body of writing, advancing an argument that trades on two claims – the first, diagnostic, the second, political.

Nationalism's long historical arc in Europe has, by my reckoning, been punctuated by two bouts of intensity: first, the era of Romantic expressionism[8] and the major nationalist yearnings it sponsored, culminating perhaps in the mid-nineteenth-century 'Spring of Nations', when various revolutionary movements of 1848 coalesced around the popular desire for the formalisation of respective European nation-states;[9] second, the early twentieth-century era of protectionist mercantilism as tied to fading imperial influence and economic instability which suffused two global wars, fascism, and the subsequent not unrelated crafting of the welfare state contract.[10] This book argues that the West is in the midst of a third such nationalist moment. It is clear that the idea of nation has recovered today the lustre that had momentarily subsided[11] – a hiatus during the late twentieth century that fed much hubristic speculation about the 'end of history' and the teleological triumph of liberal, 'post-ethnic' democracy.[12] This hubris has proven spectacularly misplaced in light of today's nationalist resurgences, leading to hurried if equally hapless repudiations by Fukuyama and company of their original confidence.[13]

The nationalist politics of today has not gone entirely unchallenged, as was evidenced in the 2017 electoral success delivered by Labour's rehabilitation of a social democracy-cum-urban liberalism pivot; it remains, however, uncontroversial to observe that the idea of nation currently gallops across Europe with a distinct sureness and purpose. But what actually renders any such recourse to nation, nationalism? Nationalism can, of course, be read through any number of postulations. Such a significant feature of modernity, perhaps even modernity's most enduring programme, will always have many dimensions: culture and unity, territoriality and borders, sovereignty and democracy, the popular and the vernacular, alongside the 'invention of tradition' and monumentalised elite history. In short, nationalism pertains to the manner in which modernity frames the entire aspiration for peoplehood, community and the attendant expression of political sovereignty. But if one basic principle about what constitutes Western nationalism is to be advanced, one simple premise from which all else follows, it is the relationship between political discourse, ideology and nation that is the most helpful. Namely, nationalism might be initially understood here as the set of framings by which primary culpability for significant sociopolitical problems, whether real or imagined (depending on one's political leanings), is attributed to various 'alien' ethno-racial communities. Put differently, Western nationalism can be read as the formation by which a self-appointed normative community attributes its putative sociopolitical, cultural and security concerns to the excessive presence, influence and allowances made to those understood as *not belonging*. Those who comprise the relevant field of non-belonging include the variously constituted insider minorities, but also various foreign peoples and/or international forces, some of which intertwine with and reinforce the pathologies attributed to internal, generally non-white groups. (For instance, the intensification in anti-EU sentiment in the run-up to Brexit made extended reference to how the refugees massing in Calais and elsewhere in Europe threatened to replenish the already vilified internal minority groups with whom the potential refugees share an ostensible commonality – via Islam, skin colour or country of origin.)

The contemporary certainly constitutes one such moment where much political discourse projects a significant nationalist orientation. Increasingly shrill populist debates traffic in a number of core anxieties that hinge on certain iconic figures of non-belonging. Anxieties written upon the figure of the migrant, a figure who is articulated via multiple guises – as the labour migrant, as refugee, as asylum seeker and, less frequently, as rapacious, uncouth foreign capitalist. Anxieties associated with the nihilist materialism of the black inner city, and the young black male in particular. Anxieties stemming from the purported vulgar incivility of Eastern Europeans (with the Roma becoming a particularly visceral signifier of this) stemming from their unsolicited arrival in the towns of provincial Britain as well the labour threat they pose to the white working class. And, of course, the increasingly trenchant, nigh world-historical anxieties tied to the figure of the Muslim – as patriarchal, indolent, violent, fanatical, sectarian and, perhaps most deviously, as protean and unpredictable.

It seems uncontroversial to note that the entire democratic landscape in Europe is being remade by the increased prominence of these anxieties, anxieties that ask for harsh, uncompromising responses to the threats that these multiple but often overlapping outsiders represent. Relatedly, solutions that project a nationalist tenor increasingly obtain a panacean value in the popular imagination, suggesting that various significant challenges – be they economic, security, social or cultural – will be magicked away through the emasculation of the significant Others in the nation's midst.

For instance, in Scandinavia, that timeless beacon of reasonable social democracy, rabidly nationalist parties proudly sit in government, agitating for measures that can only be described as a macabre (partial) reprise of the continent's darkest twentieth-century chapter. Consider how in Denmark, at the peak of the 2016 'refugee crisis', it was reported that those waiting to file an asylum application were stripped of any valuable possessions on their person. This aggressive spectacle of state power, which was nominally claimed as intended to finance the costs of processing an asylum application, meticulously laced the racial horror of nationalism with the deference to legal procedure that has always been the unique province of European modernity. See also Denmark's recent announcement of a 'ghetto' policy that singles out people of non-Western origin for a whole suite of specialist remedial justice and state re-education measures, a policy programme that represents a remarkably overt entrenchment of nation-state racism – whereby populations, already characterised as undesirable and deficient, are subjected to a state-orchestrated public humiliation, while also being corralled into a formal two-tier citizenry based on ethnic background (with urban geography operating partially as a thinly veiled proxy).

In Sweden, the party once known for street-level neo-Nazi violence now entertains credible hopes of a 20 per cent electoral return. The sustained political presence of the Swedish Democrats (SD) has indeed rendered them the self-satisfied arbiters of the democratic discussion, the entire political class now at their mercy; Sweden, many months having lapsed since the 2018 election, remains at the time of writing unable to form a government, owing to a complete party-political paralysis about how to cope with the SD challenge. Austria, in its characteristically understated way, was in 2016 a whisker away from winning itself a far-right president, only to successfully include the far-right Freedom Party in the ruling government the next year.

In France, the Front National (now operating under the presumably less toxic name, National Rally), until recently a Holocaust-denying, largely *verboten* political outfit, threatens to claim executive power and has already engendered electoral havoc at the parliamentary and regional level. The party trades heavily in a demagoguery of Islam and immigration, often concomitantly, and has made a virtue of claiming that the 'nation-state is back' – an analytic point that escaped many sociologists but was seemingly perfectly well understood by Marine Le Pen. Similarly, in Germany, the first sustained challenge to the unfussy reign of Merkel was posed by Alternative for Germany, an uncompromisingly xenophobic, straight-talking new arrival to German politics. In Finland, a country whose immigrant and Muslim populations are very low, a quixotic party devoted to these very themes has become parliamentary kingmaker. In Hungary, the prime minister, a self-styled defender of Christendom, raised a razor-wire fence buttressed by water cannons along the country's southern border with the Balkans, contravening any number of EU regulations regarding free movement but playing acutely well to a citizenry increasingly distressed by the brown and black 'poison' drifting out of the Mediterranean. And in Italy we have seen a man called Salvini, until recently presiding over an increasingly irrelevant separatist party (Lega Nord), establish himself as the country's most prominent politician. Having restyled himself as an unapologetic nationalist, putting aside previous separatist pretensions, Salvini is now in all but name the most significant player in Italian politics – making particularly strong play of an uncompromising anti-immigration position that received major international coverage when Italy refused permission to humanitarian refugee rescue ships to dock at Italian ports.

These assorted rampages across the continent by avowedly populist new right outfits are indeed legion. They must *not*, however, be read in isolation. There is a prevailing analytic danger that the quickening march of nationalism is solely and exclusively attributed to these groups, absolving in turn the other, more established political and cultural players. Put simply, such a reading risks suggesting that new right groups operate in a vacuum of their own making, when, in actuality, they merely represent the coarser edge of formations already sanctioned by the established political parties themselves and the broader press cultures[14] and thinktank industries that sustain them – not least, the various centre-right governments that have enjoyed an extended spell of power over the past decade. A nascent nationalist consensus across the centre-right was perhaps best attested to by the three most influential European leaders of the early 2010s (Cameron, Merkel and Sarkozy) all assuming a strident anti-multiculturalism position. This populist play to the 'crises of multiculturalism' narrative, expertly chronicled by Lentin and Titley in 2011, can retrospectively be remembered as merely a harbinger of nationalism's full consolidation as the decisive contemporary arbiter of European electoral power.[15] There has been, in short, a continued oscillation over the last decade or so between the new right and what Richard Seymour succinctly captured as being 'the soft racism of the hard centre' — each doing the other's work.

By drawing these preliminary emphases, I do not mean to exhaust the explanatory role of racialised outsiders when accounting for the rise of nationalist projects across the West; my purpose is simply to reconfirm the disproportionate importance of race (and as the far as the UK is concerned, imperial nostalgia) to any credible account of that project. As this book will periodically argue, complementary analyses, in explaining the rise of nationalism, would include an account of the prevailing post-welfare, 'austerian' neoliberal consensus that provides the socio-economic context against which to situate the enhanced appeal of nationalist assertion;[16] they would include an account of the party-political *centrist* compact alongside the increased tendency of the EU towards opaque technocratic governance that jointly engineered substantial democratic deficits and attendant feelings of entrenched political exclusion; they would include a speculative attempt to map the emergent circuits of social media political communication that have allowed various, more rabidly populist-nationalist information campaigns to obtain a heightened historical intensity; and they would include an account of the broader fatigue with supposed liberal social equality commitments as propagated by outlets such as *Spiked* and the plethora of online Men's Rights Activists (MRA)-inspired material that has nurtured a sense of pronounced victimhood and grievance, particularly among allegedly disaffected men.[17] But, significant themes as these no doubt are, a meaningful analysis would also certainly recognise the *central* role of racialised anti-minority assertions in anchoring contemporary European nationalisms.

From the brief scan of the European political moment just offered, we can slowly begin to glimpse the importance of nationalism in shaping the contemporary, an electoral power that was, of course, realised in particularly profound ways during the 2016 US election. To quote the *New Yorker*, in the context of Trump's seemingly *carte blanche* and largely improvised political programme, 'voters are willing to tolerate [various seemingly unpopular personality details and political measures] in exchange for the rest of Trump's ethno-nationalist ideological agenda'.[18] Indeed, in the wake of Brexit and Trump, it seems banal to assert the contemporary importance of nationalism. Even *The Economist* pithily entitled its 19 November 2017 issue, 'The New Nationalism'.

This assertion does, however, remain necessary only because nationalism has not been afforded the social science attention that it warrants. Left to the already isolated field of race and racism sociology, mainstream social science, including its nominally critical theory traditions, has had until now impressively little regard for the nationalist ructions that are remaking the society it is putatively tasked with studying. Even more egregiously, when critical attention is given to the rising nationalist mood, sociologists and seasoned pundits alike tend towards a lazy economic reductionism. These accounts ascribe to nationalism some basic illusory properties that merely deflect or manage economic struggle, uncertainty and inequality. This frustratingly thin thesis seems to understand the fundamental allure of the nation as only being applicable to momentary crisis resolution and as temporarily deflecting more pressing questions about economic stagnation.[19] Accordingly, nationalism is *not* entertained as being a force of modernity that exerts its own momentum, needs, desires, fears and anxieties which cannot be contained or understood solely through reference to material determinants.

Beyond economistic explanations

Economic factors are certainly integral to the emergence of this new nationalism, given that they undeniably cultivate certain nationalist desires. Hostility towards national governments' transfers to the European Union or through international aid, claims over the financial largesse extended to refugees and comparably 'recalcitrant' Others, or competition for the diminished and seemingly diminishing resources that insecure and low-skilled labour affords, all operate as grist to the nationalist mill. The fact that nationalism has been emboldened at the very moment when economic inequalities are widening across advanced industrial nations and as economic deregulation and recession have engendered deeper senses of insecurity – which if not directly experienced is widely felt – cannot be a coincidence. Indeed, as Shatz argued in relation to the 2016 US presidential election, 'Trump is inconceivable without the 2008 financial crisis.'[20] Inconceivable, that is, without the wider economic hardships and uncertainty resulting from deindustrialisation, outsourcing, rising living costs, the casualisation of labour and the depletion of public services and social security provisions.

However, I argue – with Shatz – that such economistic explanations only get us so far, and that in fact to see nationalism simply as epiphenomenal of economic factors misses the way in which nationalist appeals find resonance through both busts and booms and across stark economic divides. It may not be that the economic organises nationalism, but that ideas of nation itself shape how material forces are comprehended and responded to.

There are in turn three brief observations I would like to make here that help situate the economic in a manner that avoids attributing to it an exhaustive, reckless and/or misrepresented causality. First, despite regular intimations to the contrary, it is not just the 'white working class' that has experienced hardship as a result of the broader neoliberal consensus, most acutely experienced in the wake of the 2008 recession. In Britain, as elsewhere, minority ethnic groups remain disproportionately worse off across a range of indicators in the areas of employment, housing, health and poverty, and have been severely impacted by both the recession and subsequent state austerity. The play to class as being the preserve of white people is, therefore, at best naive, at worst, an incendiary racial nativism.[21] While it remains understandable that the economic hardship encountered by working-class people who happen to be white is presented as a contextualising factor vis-à-vis recent politics, this foregrounding needs to be sensitively handled, so as not to obscure the shared if not worse working-class penalties endured by many racialised minorities.

Second, the voter base for the new nationalist politics is not simply or exclusively this oft-invoked 'white working class'. This nationalism is in fact more electorally reliant on the middle and lower middle classes, those who inhabit the provincial towns of Middle England, as well as capturing a not insignificant share of the affluent conservative vote – appealing here to a shared hectoring around moral decay, multicultural excess and welfare dependency.[22] This important acknowledgement helps us better understand that it is not simply acute economic abjection that is fuelling these recent political turns. Needless to say, the appeal of new nationalism confounds traditional class distinctions and, for that matter, always has. A defining hallmark of fascism was, after all, its ability to rescue from the ruins of industrial exploitation and *fin-de-siècle* alienation an invigorating, putatively unifying ethnic ecology. Similarly, one simple context that immediately compromises the economic thesis regarding new nationalism is the case of Norway.[23] Norway has seen over the past decades the slow emergence of the very same nationalist political discourse and electoral capture that is now being rehearsed elsewhere. The reality that Norway famously enjoys some of the highest living standards in the world and has witnessed steady economic growth across the last thirty years, premised on its well-managed petro boom, seems to do nothing to dispel the nationalist anxieties around immigration, Muslims and multiculturalism that are definitive of the nationalist formation.

Third, some try to equate nationalist populisms with certain new left, anti-capitalist agitations – reading the nationalist rise as a misrecognised and/or deformed critique of contemporary neoliberalism, and constituting in turn a disjointed expression of solidarity against a global elite; a critique and yearning that is said to otherwise sit more naturally within the supposedly equally prominent left-wing agitations. If only. This wilfully optimistic reading of the political spectrum bundles the newly emboldened, often youth-driven leftist movements' *desire* for change with the *actual* change and brokerage of power already exercised by nationalist factions. This is therefore not the age of populisms *sui generis*, as is suggested by John Judis and others.[24] It is instead the age of *nationalist* populism. This adjectival specification is not a minor quarrel. It instead fundamentally alters how we, as analysts and critics, diagnose the present.

Only one brand of politics and mobilisation has successfully claimed the mantle of power – democratic, media (mainstream and digital) and otherwise. That brand is nationalism. Brexit belongs to the real, while left-wing movements such as Occupy and Momentum still remain essentially gestures of hope. The National Rally belongs to the general, the *Nuit debout* and *gilets jaunes* protests and Mélenchon to the particular. (Mélenchon is doubly interesting here, as his subsequent attempt to obtain wider popular appeal has resulted in him pursuing at times a more explicitly nationalist position.) The People's Party and the Progress Party, both long-term Nordic stalwarts of xenophobic alarmism, are *in* government, not merely aspirants. (Podemos in Spain and Syriza in Greece represent powerful counter-examples but remain by my reckoning exceptions that prove the rule, and are also buffeted by historical and present circumstances that render both contexts substantially different to the broader northern European clustering, and the place of Britain in particular, that is the direct focus of this book.)

Closer to home, Theresa May did not try to secure her otherwise absent mandate as premier through an appeal to the virtues of class solidarity, scrutiny of capitalist alienation and an end to boom-and-bust crisis cycles. Rather more prosaically, May tried to shore up her legitimacy through an unambiguously nationalist interpretation of Brexit as having constituted a straightforward proxy referendum on immigration: her pilloried attempt at negotiating a Brexit deal boasted only one red line, this being the absolute end to free movement. Similarly, in her inaugural party conference speech as PM, May tried to cement this nation-making ploy through pointed appeals to 'putting the power of government squarely at the service of ordinary working-class people'. In claiming this platform for herself, she proceeded to excoriate the establishment: 'They find your patriotism distasteful, your concerns about immigration parochial, your views about crime illiberal, your attachment to your job security inconvenient.'[25] All these are different ways of conjuring the same normatively majoritarian constituency while affirming their putative concerns about immigrants and/or various racialised minorities. This broader positioning was a proactively nationalist gamble that – according to Kenneth Clarke, the resident dissident of the Conservative Party – would have made even Enoch Powell blush.[26]

Which nationalism?

There is, however, an underlying validity to the argument that the contemporary populist form is not merely right-wing and conservative. Herein lies the distinctive analytic emphasis of my intervention, which accordingly constitutes the *second* observation upon which this opening argument turns. Namely, it is not that populisms of all different constitutions are currently competing in a largely unresolved contest for cultural ascendancy. It is rather that new nationalist populism, as *the* ascendant form, absorbs and rearticulates a wide variety of political constitutions – constitutions that traverse, crudely put, the 'Left–Liberal–Right' spectrum. Put differently, much of what poses today as populism is in actuality just nationalism, but, importantly, nationalism's current appeal and vitality lies precisely in its ability to draw upon an assortment of opposing ideological traditions, meanings and symbols.

A passing glance at the historical theorisation of the nation-state helps situate this important claim. As Hobsbawm and Ranger memorably clarified, nationalism hinges on the 'invention of tradition' that establishes a polity's preferred historical bearing and its entrenching of what Anderson described as a 'simultaneous temporality' – a conception of peoplehood that ties the present to a particular imagining of the past but also the future.[27] These narrative mechanisms culminate in engendering a profound sense of a timeless 'we', a 'deep horizontal comradeship'[28] that placates other social divisions and inculcates a continuous desire for cultural and political integrity – an ever-present but insatiable appetite for closure and wholeness.[29] The nation consequently offers modernity the fundamental lens through which it renders *community*, as the appeal to a shared entity of belonging beyond those whom we know and congregate with at any given moment. This fundamental sociological concern regarding communal membership, framed in classical sociology as the question of *Gesellschaft*, is therefore, when properly drawn vis-à-vis modernity, a concern with the nation.[30] No other modern social formation has been able to generate the communitarian taxonomy and feeling that is, in any historical context, so central to how a society manages and expresses its sociopolitical transactions and ambitions.

It is now certainly a truism, in the time after Anderson, Hobsbawm and Thompson, to assert the historicity of the nation, the idea of nation finding its proper expression via the waves of Romantic nationalism and the subsequent 'mass society', state-centralisation periods that succeeded it. This historical contingency of the nation is perhaps made most beguilingly apparent in Massimo d'Azeglio's 1861 exhortation, as an ambivalent observer of Italian unification, that 'we have made Italy, now we must make Italians'.[31]

Less well understood, outside of the shamefully neglected canons of postcolonial and anti-racist scholarship, is that this construction of the national 'we' is not in any sense benign. Rather, as scholars attuned to the nuances of racism's centrality to colonial modernity have observed, nation-states do not simply reflect pre-existing framings of ethno-national membership.[32] It is in fact states that actively produce and entrench ideas of nation, conceptions of the national subject (what Balibar calls 'fictive ethnicity')[33] that are, in turn, necessarily *exclusionary*. To revisit an elementary structuralist observation, in the making of the nation, definitional emphasis is placed on who is *not* part of that nation. And crucially, this process of national self-definition through relational negation has always found ideas of ethno-race and broader civilisationist constructs of the 'West and the rest' to be its most instructive typology.[34] As Gilroy and Goldberg have regularly noted, that the European nation and ideas of race both began to find their proper definition at the same historical moment is no coincidence.[35] It is instead the fundamental constitutional interplay that the very premise of European modernity regarding its sense of community and peoplehood rested upon and continues to rest upon.

This brief theoretical digression regarding the historicisation of the nation – which in the next chapter will be expanded upon in much more detail – is necessary here only in order to clarify an understanding of nationalism's relationship to the more general concern of political ideology. Simply put, the nation, which is at its plainest a constitution of the normative 'we', has no inevitable political complexion other than that of its own exclusionary ethno-racial desires. Contrary to the often assumed propinquity of the nationalist to the crudely pictured conservative, a more watchful analysis will note that nationalist sway at any given historical moment requires a particular kind of racial Othering that is able to assemble an ideologically disparate collage, comparable to what Solomos and Back have called, in the course of summarising George Mosse's important commentary on racism's elasticity, 'a *scavenger ideology* which gains its power from its ability to pick out and utilise ideas and values from other sets of ideas and beliefs in specific socio-historical contexts'.[36]

I accordingly posit that any real reckoning with the current nationalist moment must better locate its mooring within very different and at times contradictory ideological clusters. This diffusion is in fact central to its current triumph. This might be phrased even as the nationalist *overdetermination* particular to the present historical conjuncture. The ability of nationalist affirmation to find its *sense* amid contrasting ideological vocabularies and symbols plays a vital role in accounting for the intelligibility of contemporary nationalism to so many different factions and recesses constitutive of Britain's current political scene.

To give this claim a little more initial definition, of interest here is the ability of contemporary nationalist discourses to appropriate and occupy a number of prominent political platforms, each of which have had a substantial role in shaping the recent political history of western Europe. These multiple discursive heritages that have become susceptible to nationalist expression include:

1 The *liberal* – as the self-arrogated and ethnically weaponised European claim to values of tolerance, free speech, secularism, the rule of law, alongside the more indefinite sense of liberal civility and everyday etiquette.
2 The *conservative* – as the nostalgic appeal to the moral and aesthetic clarity of the provincial, the imperial and the rustic.
3 The *neoliberal* – as the symbolic premium placed on a moral distinction between the deserving, self-reliant and entrepreneurial capitalist self ('homo economicus') on the one hand, and, accordingly, the work-shy dependency of others.
4 The *communitarian left* – as the collective, as the welfare state, as the critique of market individualism, and as anti-capitalist and anti-globalisation sentiment.

Across these basic contours also lurk more finely tuned political movements and lexicons, not least the nominally feminist rhetoric of gender equality and sexual liberation, the conservationist feeling for and visualisation of bucolic environmentalism, and even certain speculations about ideal urban life – in terms of regeneration, leisure consumption and habitation. It is in turn these distinctly different and often contradictory ideological traditions and the manner in which they have all been made to bend to the service of nationalist imperatives that will be the focus of the chapters that follow in this book.

Labour (the left) and contesting nationalism

Recognising this expansive ideological map accordingly prevents the all too convenient attribution of the current malaise to an allegedly vulgar, largely emotive rump of fear and bigotry. Instead, any attempt to resist nationalism must first involve properly addressing its sophisticated affinity to multiple ideological forms, some of which we mistakenly consider to be inured from such trends. Importantly, I am not simply arguing that all political repertoires are capable of racism: that is, the left too can be racist or the liberal too can be nationalist. This is already very well understood and I have no wish to rehearse such truths. Rather, I am merely positing that nationalism, in order to become ideologically overdetermined, requires all these various repertoires. And part of the resistance to this nationalist wave, as much as it involves a critique of the economic conditions that render populist nationalisms more likely, is also about clawing away at these ideological contradictions that comprise European nationalisms.

This argument also constitutes a particular reminder to those with left or left-of-centre leanings that nationalism cannot be opportunistically gamed for other political ends. Nationalism is itself the contemporary populist play – all else is merely marshalled in its service. Of course, as Maya Goodfellow comments, to realise a popular politics without appealing to the totems of anti-immigrant xeno-racism might seem a Sisyphean task.[37] But it is the challenge that must be reckoned with, as otherwise one merely gives further succour to the nationalist call, a call that might absorb other ideological positions but is ultimately promiscuous, only committed to its own ethno-racial exclusion and nativism.

It is within this context, and as the Corbyn movement started to find some serious momentum, that the observant Ash Sarkar despaired via Twitter, 'I asked last year if it was possible to do leftist populism without nationalism, and Labour apparently cba [can't be arsed] to even try.'[38] Sarkar's frank frustration was warranted. There are increasingly vocal summons that ask the left, via Corbyn or otherwise, to bargain with the nationalist case. Thankfully, the dignified and unapologetically social democratic policy vision set out by Labour for the 2017 election did seem mostly to decline the nationalist invitation. Labour does, however, remain frustratingly silent, even conflicted, on actively rebuffing the anti-immigration consensus. Relatedly, it remains largely non-committal on Brexit and the particular issue of migration that is most emblematic of the Brexit debate. But transposed to the context of this book's argument (the discussion of the left's relationship to nationalism becoming particularly prominent in the book's two final chapters), it is hoped that Labour can continue to perform credibly without emulating nationalist impulses. If it succeeds in doing so, it might then obtain the base and time to pursue a sustained spell of coherent and confident opposition that might in time allow for a political template to take root that constitutes a distinctive and substantial left-wing alternative to nationalist politics. Or seen inversely, it remains clear that a mangled attempt to ventriloquise nationalist motifs, as some of the current Labour Party and its commentariat are attempting, will only prove counter-productive. Doing so will only sow further confusion while still conceding relevant territory to those outfits, not least the established right, that already boast a well-defined anti-immigration and racialised law and order line. These outfits will accordingly always outmanoeuvre Labour if offered these terms.

Labour must then recognise that any attempt to recycle nationalism has become a fool's errand. Nationalism is not a viable vehicle towards other political ends, not least leftist collectivism. Nationalism is, in the final instance, primarily about its own exclusionary racisms – anything else is largely a convenient bedfellow co-opted to make its appeal more likely. Or, as was put analogously by Nesrine Malik, 'you cannot outflank the [nationalist] right by adopting its promises, that way you only end up as its handmaiden'.[39] This reflection is important. The deep affect of nationalism, once galvanised, is not easily reversed, diluted or repackaged. By working to its tune, it remains hopelessly naive to assume that one can 'strategically' opt back to a more orthodox left-wing programme, should that even be the ultimate intention. Any friend of the left who wishes to realise a politics that finally escapes the demands of nation would do well to remember this.

The structure of this book

The far-ranging and cacophonous ideological scope that characterises contemporary nationalist thinking requires both recognition and theorisation – an understanding of how multiple major political rationalities simultaneously converge around the idea and politics of nation. Put differently, I posit in this book that a comprehensive contemporary analysis of new nationalism must acknowledge the ideological multiplicity animating it and the deeply hostile whiteness that suffuses much of this expansive terrain.

Any such understanding of the wider ideological underpinnings of new nationalism also allows us to repudiate the simplistic complacencies currently prevalent among many commentators about what nationalism is. Nationalist populism is not just a base appeal to fear and hatred, lacking any broader conceptual and affective loading.[40] This book will instead make apparent the complicity of multiple political rationalities in conceptually *anchoring* and symbolically *sustaining* the nationalist wave. Recognising this expansive ideological map accordingly prevents the convenient attribution of the current nationalist malaise to a pool of unreconstructed racists, whose only impulse is one of base fear and parody parochialism. Instead, any attempt to resist nationalism must first properly address its sophisticated affinity to multiple ideological forms, some of which – such as various leftist, feminist and liberal political repertoires – are mistakenly seen as being largely inured from such trends. Conversely, any attempt to draw out a reading of ideological multiplicity also necessitates commentary and analysis of the respective ideological platforms themselves. Hence this book, as much as it purports to constitute a reckoning with new nationalism, is also about the respective ideological threads relevant to contemporary Western life – not least, classical value liberalism, left socialism and/or social democratic ideals regarding the welfare state, neoliberalism and conservatism. For instance, one of the key ambitions of this book is to disentangle conservatism from neoliberalism, a conflation that is otherwise endemic to contemporary critical analysis.

A cultural-studies-inspired analysis of ideology proves to be particularly useful for working through the political multiplicity that contemporary nationalism comprises, a theoretical tradition steered magisterially by Stuart Hall and those who worked around and after him. Of these later theorists, a particular interest arises for me in the analysis offered by Wendy Brown on the complex and ostensibly unlikely intertwining of neoliberalism with neoconservatism in American political culture. Brown, in the course of her exposition, makes a number of highly helpful clarifications that she sources in the Hallsian reading of ideology.[41] First, she observes that it might be best to see ideology as 'political rationality', insofar as ideologies bestow on the public and its different fragments a particular but active way of *thinking* about the world around it. Or, as follows the oft-circulated definition of ideology offered by Hall himself: 'By ideology I mean the mental frameworks – the languages, the concepts, categories, imagery of thought, and the systems of representation – which different classes and social groups deploy in order to make sense of, figure out and render intelligible the way society works.'[42] This is a salutary insight central to my own book's argumentative emphasis. In terms of considering the contemporary nationalist capture of the political, I am interested in how the different ideological traditions it sources offer denizens a whole assortment of symbols, values and rationales with which to think through. Hereby, nationalism's contempt for the racialised minority and/or the racialised foreigner cannot be reduced to some derivative notion of ideological deception, but rather must be read as being *actively affirmed* through the conceptual tools and symbolic repertoires available. It becomes, in short, the *sense-making* schema via which we reckon and respond to our social and political horizons. This process of making sense (thinking) therefore captures an understanding of ideology that goes beyond ideas of a passive and impressionable subject, but instead incorporates a whole circuit of desires, anxieties and overlapping political solutions that the subject actively navigates.

Relatedly, Brown reminds us that any significant historical moment is best understood in terms of how it grafts and cobbles together very different traditions. A 'dreamwork', Hall's coinage (via Freud) for how all ideology rests on setting a fantastical horizon against which it orients itself, is not 'monological' or 'coherent'.[43] On the contrary, it is most efficient when multiple, often contradictory, traditions manage to converge around it. It is in this manner that a conjuncture can become overdetermined towards a particular political orientation, whereby many different political tendencies all become susceptible to the same resolution – in our case, the nationalist resolutions that aspire to stymie, defuse, obstruct or exclude the relevant minority communities (e.g. Muslims), their foreign equivalents (e.g. Middle Eastern refugees) and/or their alleged facilitators/enablers (e.g. the liberal establishment). The rest of this book then seeks to map these multiple, contradictory traditions, interrogating the various formations through which contemporary nationalisms are advanced – specifically focusing on

Britain, but also considering other European discourses, a broader regional context within which the British case is no exception.

The opening chapter offers a wide-ranging picture of the different theoretical accounts relevant to addressing nationalism. I reprise here the various canonical debates over how the nation-state emerged as a concrete historical force. In so doing, particular clarifications about how best to understand the constitutive elements of nationalism will be offered. This argument will involve, among other things, a reappraisal of the early modern circumstances germane to the formalisation of the nation-state; it will distinguish the idea of nation from the politics of nationalism; it will more properly define the terms by which nationalism is to be understood by its specifically *exclusionary* mechanisms; and it will situate the colonial context within which the nation-state as an idea and practice became fundamentally imbued with meanings of race.

Chapter 2 will briefly repudiate the increasingly common attempts to read contemporary politics through the lens of populism. It will be argued that a notion of populism, if overstated, risks analytically obscuring the racial nationalisms that in fact underlie any such populist politics. The notion of 'progressive nationalisms', as often attributed to certain trends within contemporary Catalonia and Scotland, will also be critically addressed here. Having established these two clarifications, as regards populism and progressive nationalism, the following chapters will substantively situate contemporary nationalist discourse within the respective and contrasting political traditions that it calls upon.

Chapter 3 explores the assertion of 'muscular liberalism' and civic nationalism. A sustained trend in academic political discourse over the last two decades, as led by figures such as Ignatieff and Habermas, contended that a national community need not be demarcated by its ethnic origins but by its civic, liberal principles (what is sometimes called the 'post-ethnic' nation or 'constitutional patriotism'). That is to say, it was asserted that what determined an inclusive European polity was its adherence to liberal and democratic principles. While this did open certain interesting progressive possibilities regarding visualisations of the democratic polity, it is also apparent that an aggressively white, anti-minority nationalism has been very successful in publicly capturing this liberal position and the broader legacy of Orientalist civilisationism that sits within such affirmations. An anecdotal primer of this capture was evident in the then Prime Minister David Cameron's notorious call for a 'muscular liberalism' in the context, and this is important, of a speech on Muslims, terrorism and integration – signalling how many ideas of liberal virtue become ethnically coded during the course of centrist populist demagoguery. More broadly speaking, it is important to consider here the intensity with which many ethnic minorities are popularly presented as lacking the cultural disposition to assume these prized liberal virtues, virtues that are foregrounded as constitutive of the national self.

The argument of Arun Kundnani and his concept of 'values racism' is also helpful here, certainly in relation to liberal demagoguery vis-à-vis European Muslims.[44] This is the basic postulation that Muslim culture is said to be uniquely adversarial to a liberal value base, the base that defines the nation. The opportunistic recourse to certain putatively feminist themes regarding gender and sexuality in propagating an ethnically aggressive civic nationalism becomes a uniquely telling site of analysis here in terms of scoping the full, sophisticated reach of a racialised liberal nationalism, particularly in relation to the public demagoguery around European Muslims. Most pertinently, in the British context, Gargi Bhattacharyya's *Dangerous Brown Men* constitutes a particularly generative opening deconstruction of this densely knotted political terrain.[45] Sara Farris's concept of 'femonationalism' also offers a particularly helpful recent reworking of some of these themes.[46]

Such 'faux-feminist'[47] positioning also becomes allied to wider understandings of a Muslim assault, under the auspices of multiculturalism's governmental hold, on consecrated liberal values – not least, a particularly disingenuous weaponisation of free speech and secularism.[48] The chapter will accordingly assert that what ultimately materialises here is a particular kind of self-satisfied liberalism, one that is expertly steered by *The Times* and other such bastions of Middle England political propriety – an aggrandising and racially marked liberal civilisationism that in turn does a great deal of work in terms of how nationalism attains a degree of popular validity, particularly in terms of its attractiveness to certain middle-class constituencies.

Chapter 4 examines more traditional, conservative appeals to racialised notions of blood, territory, purity and tradition as a means of reclaiming the nation. Popularly seen as the direct antonym of a liberal position, the conservative flank of contemporary nationalist assertion is perhaps the most obvious to parse. I explore here a set of conservative nostalgias – a pastoral and imperial nostalgia, or what Gilroy famously called 'postcolonial melancholia' – that has become particularly pervasive of late.[49] These nostalgias are seen, for instance, through the rehabilitation of monarchy and its recurring spectacles of reproduction and weddings; the revival of Edwardian and interwar period drama; the Help for Heroes campaign in terms of how it relates to the valorisation of the soldier both past and present; and also the all too explicable popularity of the television programme *Countryfile* and other cultural phenomena that sponsor a similarly provincial ideal. All these instances speak to a conservative cultural nostalgia and the deeply seated imperial mythology that underpins it. It is a nostalgic formation that remembers greatness and a genteel whiteness necessary for that very greatness.

However, what is often elided or misunderstood in existing analysis of conservative nostalgia is that much of this commentary and cultural performance does in fact pivot off a critique of unbridled free-market capitalism. This critique is often expressed via a conservationist, pastoral, Christianist and/or culturally elitist mould. It becomes necessary therefore to disentangle this particular formulation of nationalist desire from neoliberalism, a line of thought that it is often but wrongly bundled together with. Doing so helps capture another constituency and tradition, significant as it is, in the broader flurry of voices that animate the nationalist cry.

Chapter 5 examines how neoliberalism, through its recourse to discourses of meritocracy, entrepreneurial self and individual will, alongside its exaltation of a 'points-system' approach to the ills of immigration, engineers its own unique rendition of the nationalist crisis. A traditional concern of the neoliberal right posits that a market-society ideal is hampered by cultures of welfare dependency and the absence of individual responsibility. This neoliberal position individualises outcomes of success and failure, muting in turn issues of structure and access. But, again, important questions arise regarding the imperative of this neoliberal frame to also racialise conceptions of failure, dependency and national crisis. It is imperative to understand here that neoliberalism is not only an economic or legislative programme but that it is also fundamentally a cultural and moral programme. So while it is on one level quite obviously about the retreat of the redistributive and interventionist state in favour of the market and its internal mechanisms, it is also a cultural category that foregrounds particular value sets and motifs, including the modelling of the ideal individual as the aspirational, responsibilised, self-reliant subject.

This modelling of nation and enterprise generates a particular anxiety as regards immigration; an anxiety that can only be resolved through a particularly aggressive 'points-system'-led streamlining of how migration into the country is to be managed. It is also the case that the symbolic mediation of these ideals draws upon established racial representational frames in asserting who is *not* the ideal neoliberal subject — for example, the black 'welfare queen', the lazy, deceitful 'immigrant' leeching on the largesse of the welfare state, or the 'Muslim' denizen and her unproductive proclivity for family, religion and custom. These are what we might call the racialised subjects of the neoliberal. Indeed, even when some white working-class figures are brought into the fold of a general capitalist shaming, they are often judged by their proximity to the pathology of blackness. An obvious but nonetheless telling instance was when the ubiquitous Tudor historian David Starkey claimed in the wake of the 2011 riots that the 'whites have become black'.[50] Or simply consider the racial implications of the term 'white trash' or consider why the term 'chav' is seen as the preserve of poor white people — signalling a reaffirmation of whiteness, when properly realised, as the marker of neoliberal success.

Similarly, the neoliberal imperative's prizing of urban consumerism, and the remaking of cities and their inner cores as havens of experience shopping,[51] also bring about a series of racialised anxieties, whereby certain bodies, languages and tastes become antithetical to the ideal consumer space and, in turn, the ideal consumer citizen.[52] These bodies become repulsive and disruptive to pleasurable consumption, adding a further significant layer to how the neoliberal rallies a particular anxiety about the outsider, the new migrant, and the urban poor more broadly. Put bluntly, if Roma people show up on your carefully curated consumer street, it poses a challenge to neoliberal, hipster aesthetics.

Moving accordingly to the converse political flank, the final substantive chapter examines how amid the historical advance of the neoliberal orthodoxy, an influential counter in 1990s public commentary was the communitarian position — a left-driven critique of the increased normalisation of the market society, globalisation and its attendant neoliberal individualism. It was argued that an altruistic, progressive society that might operate beyond the terms of solipsistic self-reliance and provide meaningful solidaristic reference points for its polity requires a common community bond. Considerable emphasis was placed here on the 'thick affective ties' (as opposed to the 'thin abstract altruism' of humanism and/or cosmopolitanism)[53] necessary for a defence of a redistributive welfare state ideal.

However, this line of argument did not merely entail that a sense of the public good was unviable without a sense of community to undergird it, but, rather, that it was only via the realisation of *ethno-national* community that this very idea of the ethical, as being accountable to something beyond oneself, could materialise. Within this context, it is vital to observe how this communitarian critique of global capitalism's excesses is straightforwardly appropriated by nativist discourses. For instance, there is increased talk of how a defence of the welfare state is only possible if we can rekindle an idea of a unitary ethnic community. The emergence of a tendency called Blue Labour, a communitarian school within the pre-Corbyn Labour Party, and also the general ubiquity of David Goodhart's writing and political influence all speak to this ideal of ethnic homogeneity. Goodhart's famous 'Too Diverse?' paper was, I contend, particularly formative for a whole spate of nationalist left-leaning commentary. I argue in turn that this putatively progressive understanding of community, as a critique of market individualism, has been reduced in prominent public analysis to a concern with normative *ethno-national* community. Indeed, it is interesting here that the putatively far-right parties across Europe exhibit a very assertive but racially coded defence of the welfare state, workers' rights and collective solidarity, a defence that is presented as a central plank of their nationalist aspirations. This move is now finding some qualified rearticulation among certain new left parties, not least the high-profile breakaway attempt in Germany to launch a left party led by Sahra Wagenknecht that intends to more formally assert an anti-immigration position.[54]

This nationalist frame has obtained particular ubiquity in Britain in the wake of the Brexit referendum, whereby numerous public intellectuals have centred their analysis on the notion of a 'left behind'.[55] This constituency is made to figure prominently across many of the above ideological frames, not least the populist left platform. The left behind alludes to a white working class that is understood as uniquely marginalised, and looks, accordingly, to rehabilitate certain anti-migrant and anti-minority attitudes that are discursively attributed to this constituency. An extensive matrix of populist left-wing motifs – for example, anti-establishment, anti-metropolitan elite, anti-globalisation – is in turn folded into a much broader, symbolically aggressive nationalist attachment to a notion of authentic white working-class consciousness and history. Herein, in unpacking the left formations that have become susceptible to contemporary nationalist articulation, particular critical attentiveness must be given to how this 'left behind' framing of the white working class manifests itself, and the ideological work it is called upon to perform.

My conclusion advances a few notes on how resistance to the new nationalist wave would in part involve prising open these ideological contradictions as they sit within the nationalist position. The chapter reserves its primary attention, however, for the alternative sociocultural energies coursing through Britain that, if formally harnessed, offer a ready-made platform to check and subvert the long march of nationalism. A particular emphasis is inevitably devoted here to the Corbyn left position, warts and all. This concluding chapter is accordingly where this book's own political orientation is worn most publicly. It is an orientation that believes, as a point of departure but also of faith, that it is the organised left that is best-placed, of the respective ideological traditions discussed, to put a more forceful anti-nationalist political project into play.

Complementary attention will be given to the theme of 'everyday multiculture' as an important reference point: an interactive and expressive circuit that, if properly harnessed, can do much of the symbolic but also practical work relevant to the shaping of a popular but substantially anti-nationalist popular collectivism. 'Everyday multiculture' refers to the highly casual, nigh banal, interactive practices that emerge in spaces characterised by ethnic and other diversities, practices that undemonstratively cultivate dispositions less prone to nationalisms and other forms of overtly communitarian claim-making on space, culture and politics. It is not that the people living in such areas, generally working- or lower middle-class, are any less likely to assert identifications as premised on ethnic and racial difference. It is only that such myriad identifications alongside the complementary iterations of migration in and out of a particular space become normalised as being a given and natural feature of social life. In the habituation of such features of shared space and interaction, many people, including the many white people who call such places home, increasingly find the political appeal to nation to be summarily anachronistic, uninteresting and, frankly, wrong. The cultural and political energies that flow accordingly from such everyday practices offer a very useful and underappreciated indication of how an alternative, post-national popular politics might be envisaged as well as pursued.

This conclusion will also engage certain empirical themes relevant to an account of nationalism's rise that this book has otherwise not addressed at any great length – not least, the role of social media and the related phenomena of what is called the alt-right, the particular parallel role of a male resentment culture, and also the more explicitly *global* dimensions of nationalism's newfound confidence.

A note on style and method

I aspire here for a mostly generalist and perhaps even lively mode of writing and argument – one that might invite the general reader disposed to critical cultural commentary on the one hand, while still being worthwhile for the academic specialist of nation, race and ideology on the other. This might ultimately prove to be a hopeless ambition for which I lack the required skill, but it is an ambition that I have nonetheless tried to pursue. There are certainly moments when a slightly heavier theoretical style does prove necessary – for this, I apologise. But such moments are, I believe, mercifully infrequent. My penchant for long sentences is, however, an affliction that I cannot shake off and for which there is seemingly no cure. But to quote from the ever-wonderful mission statement of the ever-giving magazine *Salvage*: '[We] do not believe the first, last and only word with regard to prose style was passed down on a stone tablet by Orwell in one overrated essay.' To always eschew complex language in the interests of clarity and simplicity is not necessarily a virtue and not necessarily consistent with the aspiration to provide sufficiently searching argumentation.

Relatedly, in order to ensure a more engaging style that might elicit enough moments of interest to the reader, because moments are all that really happen in text, I wish to position this work within a more avowedly essayistic tradition. Easier said than done, yes, but it is a tradition that I find, if done well, to be the most generative of the approaches available to an academic writer. One implication of this approach is that I will not be engaging this wider discursive field and political commentary in a *systematic* manner. I will instead be *folding in* select instances of popular discursive output in the course of mapping and commenting on the respective ideological forms that simultaneously comprise the contemporary nationalist position. This 'folding in' is certainly impressionistic, whereby such output will not be intricately weighted or neatly tabulated. My discussion throughout the following chapters will instead centre on various pieces of public commentary as well as political and cultural events that are noteworthy by their prominence, influence, novelty and/or ideological complexity.

It is ultimately up to the reader to find the ideological impressions that I put forth here to be a reliable and familiar account of the world of ideas that they too encounter. Sadly though, this is not a given. Some will likely find in this book an unrecognisable, all too distorted reading of the broader public conversation that currently prevails. Put differently, this book is primarily argumentative, not descriptive. That is not to say that it is the work of a polemicist. But it is an argument that will trade on summoning a realm of ideas that I believe to be apparent; I therefore cannot guarantee that everybody else will be in agreement that this is in fact the world that we currently share.

1

Theorising the nation

Few political terms loom as large as 'the state'. In critical analysis, the state is everywhere identified as the agent of any number of modern sins. The multiple effects of the state's existence provoke, in turn, agonised laments about modern power, its immanence, and its uniquely *perpetual* violence. It is, however, telling that the actual form in which the state has been concretised within modernity is often summarily neglected. This disregard has in fact become intellectual habit, as if the modern state is merely an abstraction that can then be summarily affixed to the preferred intellectual and political emphasis of the author.

It is instructive to note that the engine of governance we most concern ourselves with, in the course of these various critiques, is, in fact, the *nation*-state. At its simplest, such a clarification amounts to the basic acknowledgement that the state in its contemporary iteration represents the political and legal framework that governs a territorially demarcated community defined as a nation.[1] The nation is hence not some gratuitous prefix optional to how the state seeks to operate or draw its legitimacy. It is instead the very specific basis by which the modern state has been operationalised, whatever its other mandates and manifestations. Whole swathes of cutting theoretical commentary – spanning various Marxist theories of bourgeois hegemony, Foucault's understanding of the transition from power over death to 'power over life', various iterations of feminism's deconstruction of how womanhood and femininity are socialised and dominated – have bequeathed traditions of critical thought regarding the state that can at times remain strangely oblivious to its most immediate formal presentation and cultural anchoring.

While these multiple concerns are all equally germane to critical commentary, the state's specific manifestation in the *nation* guise surely ought to have featured more prominently as the authoriser of modern governmental power. At the risk of over-claiming, it is worth noting that the nation remains the most pervasive mode of sociopolitical organisation in the modern world. As David McCrone reminded us, more presciently than he dared imagine: 'We inhabit a ... world in which many of the old nostrums and doctrines have withered. Socialism has gone; fascism has gone. Nationalism [however] has survived and prospers.'[2] Or, as was put in *The Economist*'s celebrated Christmas essay, 'Whither nationalism?':

> Nationalism is an abiding legacy of the Enlightenment. It has embedded itself in global politics more completely and more successfully than any of the Enlightenment's more celebrated legacies, including Marxism, classical liberalism and even industrial capitalism. It is not an aberration. It is here to stay.[3]

The nation remains not only the most entrenched imaginative form but also the most concrete institutional arrangement through which most moderns have been invited to consider and enact their sociopolitical lives. To deal with politics in the contemporary is therefore also to deal with claims to the nation, to either find further solace in its embrace or to unsettle its long reach.

Beyond historicisation, beyond nation as construct

The nation is still assumed in much commonplace Western intellectual and cultural production to be an automatic, timeless unit. In a thoroughly entertaining take on what he calls Netflix's 'nationalism problem', Kanishk Tharoor laments how the historical epics popular on the platform play into an easy sense of the nation, as we currently understand it, as always having existed.

> It is a pity that so many historical films feel so obliged to place the imagined nation at their emotional core. That not only distorts understandings of the past, but it suggests that the past can only be relevant and interesting if it supports conventions of the present [...] Nationalism becomes a kind of virtue that transcends time.[4]

The narrative conventions that abound in such shows and films are emblematic of the enduring perception that the nation is the most obvious container of the world's respective peoples – the unit that conveniently organises an otherwise teeming mass into discrete pools of humanity. This conception of the nation remains a legacy of the Romantic era's defining role in shaping nineteenth-century European conceptualisation, during which an emergent sense of popular peoplehood was yoked to the revolutionary upheavals that conclusively buried the formal and Church-ordained hierarchies characteristic of feudalism. It was, for instance, a canonical roll call of Romantic writers such as Goethe, Herder and Fichte who shepherded the *volk*-ish, *Sturm und Drang*[5] formulation of a German people – a formulation that allowed the initially disjointed, highly nascent sense of German peoplehood to gradually obtain the quality of having been present across human time and in possession of a shared cultural spirit.[6] This Romantic move, rehearsed across western and central Europe, allowed national peoplehood to become cast as quintessentially cultural in a unity that is also written into the very nature of the land[7] – the thick dense forest that is perceived in the Friedrichian visualisations of the Germanic self as husbanding the nation's most primeval Ur.[8]

As these various Romantic propositions were given further intellectual and cultural elaboration, alongside securing the institutional infrastructure of the nineteenth-century centralised state, the nation came to be apprehended as an ahistorical ontological fact. This is what is often designated as the *primordial* conception of the nation, as representing a particular ethnic, linguistic, religious or even genetic community that is both *natural and ancient*. The nation is seen within this framework as a timeless collection of people united in their ethnic commonality. The nation becomes, in short, a trans-historical truth.[9]

This primordial vision did once hold much intellectual sway, and some reconstructed, more refined versions still lurk in certain circles. Consider, for instance, the formative work of Anthony Smith and his 'ethno-symbolism' approach, which maintains that the myths and symbols of ethnic community that far predate the emergence of the modern state are equally important to understanding nationalism's duration and appeal.[10] In the main, however, the precise emergence of the nation is these days historicised with relative scholarly ease, whereby the vicissitudes and imperatives of early capitalism (intertwined with colonial expansion) and the aforementioned nineteenth-century era of cultural Romanticism are straightforwardly identified as the two defining stages.[11] Commonly dated to the 1648 Westphalian Treaty, the nation-state proper, as a form of centralised territorial sovereignty, is now seen as only emerging from the debris of the 'religious' wars that tore Europe asunder from 1517 onwards.[12] It is hence *modernity*, as a particular historical force, that is seen as incrementally promulgating a political belief that the legitimacy of government must always be vested in an idea of the national people that the territory comprises. It is this twinning of the territorial state to a spirit of national integration that leads the Catalan anthropologist, Josep Llobera – who harbours himself a qualified commitment to the nation form while also insisting on the nation's various pre-modern, *medieval* roots – to conclude that nationalism is 'the god of modernity'.[13] Or as Anthony Smith again observes, amid the seeming dissipation of religion's hold on society, it is the idea of nation that constitutes modernity's staging of the 'sacred' – this being a sacralised sense of community whereby nationalism becomes in practice 'a surrogate political religion'.[14]

To summarise, the nation was over an extended period understood by many academics and popular thinkers alike as something natural. But from the 1980s onwards, mainstream scholarship realised a more aggressive deconstruction of how nations are themselves specific outcomes of modernity, something that was summoned into existence by the confluence of various historical factors from the seventeenth century onwards. This culminated, in the wake of the cultural and linguistic turn in social theory, with the now famous conception of nation as 'narration', nation as 'discourse' and nation as 'a category of practice':[15] this being the notion that the idea of the nation – comprising its many myths, its symbols, its nominal values and also the historical events that it ritualises as iconic – becomes only something that is told, said, gestured and performed. Nation is only a narration, but a narration with formidable institutional backing and consequences.

Given this rather uncontroversial academic consensus, Rogers Brubaker, the contemporary authority on many things national, rightly notes that the primordialist claim to nation is scarcely worth repudiating any longer, and to insist upon doing so generally amounts to an intellectual gambit that enjoys the 'flogging' of straw men.[16] To probe the historical contingency of the nation, to reveal it as a historically specific sociocultural artefact, is hardly a taxing intellectual challenge. And it might be mooted that even the most hardened of nationalists themselves would be inclined to acknowledge the constructed form of their project. That is to say, nationalists too might understand the nation to have only emerged through a particular history. But even in the wake of such a concession, the nationalist might still plausibly posit this construction as a unique and ideal historical achievement.

This is, after all, precisely the kind of historical pride that is intimated in Ernest Renan's classic 1883 lecture, which extols the nation *without* attributing to it a timeless metaphysical status. Renan's 'What is a Nation?' remains one of the more maudlin accounts of the nation – a collective project that is sentimentalised by Renan as a 'daily plebiscite' that trades on the memory of 'having accomplished great things together and wishing to do so again'.[17] But recall here that Renan did also famously pen the prescient line that 'to be wrong about your history is part of becoming a nation'.[18] This is a sharp demystification of the nation's claim to transcendental history that complements Anderson's later argument about the nation's necessary compulsion towards 'selective' remembering – or selective forgetting, more properly put.[19] Apparent in Renan's claim is the disinterested recognition of the nation-state's historical specificity while, much like Weber and Durkheim, still seconding it as a worthwhile political project indispensable to modern life.[20] Put differently, the construction of nation, once real, becomes to its proponents something to be husbanded, protected, nurtured and further refined. The nation becomes here the crowning accomplishment of political history, a unique achievement with a particularly intoxicating and thickly textured sense of peoplehood around which an allegedly coherent and deeply rooted cultural legacy has been crafted. Also worth mentioning here is the parallel intimation, emerging through an International Relations disciplinary canon, that the nation-state arrangement remains the term along which politics is most efficiently realised – the template upon which sovereignty is best parcelled out across an otherwise anarchic realm of global contestations (see Chernilo and Wight for an instructive conversation about this form of 'methodological nationalism').[21] Consequently, owing to these twin assertions, one cultural and the other pragmatic, recognition of the historical contingency of various political categories (i.e. the nation) ceases to be the triumph that sociologists often presume it is.

In other words, even though a *made* communal category is historically contingent, it does not discredit the ordering hold of the 'idea'. That is to say, ideas constitute social reality. Historically constructed ideas posit a social ontology, a way of scripting the world by reference to certain entities, which are then rendered real in the lives of society's members and become insistent reference points against which social and political life is oriented. To evoke the oft-quoted 'Thomas theorem', 'If men [sic] define situations as real, they are real in their consequences.' As Gilroy has accordingly argued, to recognise an identity as a social construct, as pivoting off a historically specific 'idea', is not much of a theoretical critique in the final reckoning.[22] It would therefore be right to argue that the importance of an 'idea' should not be weighed by its ability to accurately 'reflect' a noumenal reality independent of human perception, but that its traction lies in the very constituting of a social reality (human perception) itself. Put differently, the 'making real' of a discursive 'fiction' is indeed the very stuff of societies.[23] To draw a distinction would be to miss the point of how it is that human societies manifest and reproduce themselves.

The more urgent and more credible critical intervention vis-à-vis the historical specificity of nationalism is accordingly to be had elsewhere. Namely, it is not the constructed nature of the nation but *how* it is necessarily constructed that is to be contested. It is the interrogation of the process of making in itself that is of more meaningful political value. It is not whether the nation has always existed but how it is that the nation exists that renders political critique viable but also tangible. The theoretical contestation that consequently remains of interest to me concerns the manner in which the 'making process' by which nations are realised, upheld and reproduced is, by definition, *exclusive*.[24]

Defining nationalism

It might admittedly seem too obvious, too tautological, to say here that the nation is committed to a series of exclusionary distinctions. To be something *particular* is, after all, to preclude itself from being something else. Put less abstractly, to go to one university (let's say Yale) also means one isn't going to a different university (let's say Harvard). Furthermore, to institutionalise a set of political rights via the nation-state – be it in the form of passports,[25] welfare rights[26] or voting privileges – is exclusionary against those who are not of the same nation-state. The exclusionary reality of the nation-state might in this context be said to be all too prosaically apparent in its very mechanical configuration, unworthy of any further analytic parsing.

It is true that, at its simplest, the exclusivity claim only amounts to the basic postulation that those who are identified as not belonging are necessarily naturalised as outsiders. For instance, as will be apparent in an example that will be discussed shortly, to say that we are Greeks would generally also mean that we are not Macedonians. But crucially, and perhaps counterintuitively, I maintain that this exclusivity is not summarily secondary to the foundational claim to nationhood and national belonging. On the contrary, it is to be proposed in what follows that it is in fact the claim to national belonging that is epiphenomenal to the initial exclusionary assertion – that is, it is because we are not Macedonians that we are Greeks, or it is because we are not Muslims that we are Danish. It is often through asserting a strong and substantive difference from somebody else that the subsequent claim to belong to something particular becomes more apparent and tangible. Put in more forceful terms, it is the generally pathologised identification of those who do not belong that acts as the container for the remaining entity of belonging.

It was, unsurprisingly perhaps, the fascist thinker Carl Schmitt who seemed to best understand this when developing his friend/enemy thesis – the declaration of targeted enmity being central to how the nation-state asserts itself as a *political* community.[27] Schmitt's emphasis on the *targeted* assertion of outsider status, what we might now call Othering, is important.[28] It is the case that, at any given moment, only very *particular* entities of non-belonging become the reference point against which the nation orients itself. And it is the specific characteristics of that particular Othering that determine to some significant degree and intensity the *interior* content of a nation's claim to being – content as derived through specific forms of present Othering that also overlay residual and/or dormant forms of Othering as relevant to the nation's previous historical instances of assertion.

Much of what is being said here might seem a little too abstract to be meaningful. One grounded example that is accordingly worth engaging might be Anna Triandafyllidou's piece on 'National Identity and the "Other"' in the context of Greece (albeit pre-crisis).[29] To summarise her reading of the Greek context, it is the antagonistic repudiation of Macedonia along its inland frontier (and, we might now add, the racialised non-white migrants lapping in from the sea on the other frontier) that gives Greek 'national identity' its particular substantive content. As she argues, it is the identification of 'significant others' that is necessary for a nation to meaningfully acquire a sense of selfhood.

This 'Macedonia Question' vis-à-vis Greece is vexed across multiple threads.[30] But the most symbolically interesting feature for Triandafyllidou is how a mythology of Alexander the Great has been folded into Greek narratives of integral historical continuity. Importantly, Alexander was *not* considered during the early nineteenth-century assertion of Greek independence as being party to the Greek imagination. Indeed, Alexander was generally narrated as being constitutive of a broader history of Greece's submission, stretching through to the Ottomans. But in the course of the Macedonia Question becoming a significant register of Greek Othering and frontier-making (upon the former becoming a nation-state after Yugoslavia's dissolution), Alexander has retrospectively become an iconic reference point for internal assertions of Greek belonging and folklore – what is described by Triandafyllidou as a reassertion of the 'Hellenicity of Alexander'.[31]

The example of Macedonians being the basis by which Greece acquires and asserts its national meaning is, of course, entirely peripheral to the specific remit of this book. But it remains helpful for making clearer what is ultimately a fairly simple point that is more immediately germane to my own arguments regarding contemporary western European nationalisms. Namely, to recall a contiguous observation from the previous chapter, it is not all frontiers, migrants and internal minorities that come to be concomitantly seen as (problematic) outsiders. Instead, it is specific assertions about particular, generally racialised figures that do this nation-making work. Only specifically mediated migrants (including those who are born, often over multiple generations, into the territorial fold of the relevant country) become here the objects of derision, fear and alarmism against whom the nation asserts itself.

Furthermore, and equally important to understanding the compositional specificity of nationalism, the exclusionary principle that the nation hinges on not only 'inferiorises' those who are defined as not belonging but also renders the excluded Other the overdetermined and outsized object of political discourse – determining in turn the character and content of putatively democratic deliberation writ large.[32] This remains, to those readers who are either by background and/or by intellectual training anti-racist in their temperament, the crucial play by which the nation becomes imbricated with politics. To be at the sharp end of a nationalist politics is to know yourself not only as an outsider, but also as an outsider who is actively and incessantly spoken of. This is a different kind of absence than traditional theorists of nation and nationalism would have you believe.

It is often intimated that a moderate nationalism is simply a desire for sovereignty, a desire for determination over one's own affairs – those not of that nation are therein presented as being a benign absence to whom one wishes no active harm. I wish to invert this assumption. Absence is not the condition of anonymity, of being elsewhere, or, at worst, of being denied access. It is instead the absence that is always acutely present. Nationalism, seen on these terms, is the making present of the iconic ethnic absence – an absence that, in the course of its active pathologisation, exercises an inflated hold on the anxieties of a country's political psyche. In other words, in restating here a recurring notion central to my argument, I note that while the nation is always an assertion of non-belonging, this in itself is not necessarily nationalism. Nationalism instead better denotes those particular moments when political discourse substantially *centres* the spectre of non-belonging when making sense of and reckoning with its various economic, cultural and security concerns, whether real or imagined.

It is in turn this book's key argument that nationalism, as opposed to being a claim premised primarily on active belonging, is principally a wager of non-belonging, an assertion of the nation's 'constitutive outside'. It is therefore a related and recurring assumption of this book that someone who does not feel any strong conviction of belonging – of feeling strongly English or Swedish or so forth – is just as susceptible to nationalist *politics*. This is less a question of being moved by desires about who we are and more a question of being agitated by concerns about who we definitely are not.[33]

This attunement also makes it possible to better appreciate how people who are not themselves white British, including those racialised as non-white or meaningfully off-white, can also credibly consent to certain nationalist talking points. Accepting the contention that nationalist politics is indeed best understood as the marshalling of certain rationales via which a wider sociopolitical, sociocultural or socio-economic malaise is attributed to the presence of various outsiders, it is then perfectly possible that many people, regardless of their own background, can comprehend the problems attributed to particular outsider groups and forces as something that ought be politically acted upon.

So while nationalism is, of course, to some significant degree always about belonging, it does also draw much of its purpose and sense through identifying iconic figures of non-belonging. As Malcolm James writes regarding the complex youth politics of whiteness and belonging in a borough of East London, many working-class subjects often fail in their attempts to competently perform a hegemonic and refined whiteness.[34] However, many such individuals, some of them not even white, do still become drawn towards an active demonisation of certain new migrants, repeating more pervasive claims about how such subjects are not deserving of the labour, welfare and social resources available.

Any such affinity with a nationalist hostility to outsider figures becomes all the more tenable given that nationalism itself trades on so many different rationales, the different objects of non-belonging multiplying for every new rationale played into the nationalist mix. So while an individual might feel far too exposed along one particular nationalist sensibility (e.g. Islamophobia), owing to the Muslim social identity that they might have been ascribed/assumed, they might still be able to credibly entertain a different nationalist position (e.g. anti-immigration and its particular emphasis on resource strain, overcrowding and cultural incompatibility).[35]

Any such understanding allows us to move away from the often lazy slurs about self-loathing, amnesia and worse that are often directed at those non-white subjects who parrot nationalist leanings. Nationalism, when seen in the above terms, is a social current that exceeds simple subject location. It is a form of apprehending the world, of making sense of its order and disorder, of trying to reckon with its frustrations. It is a form of attributing culpability for the world's wrongs that exonerates the self, spares the powerful and blames the weak. Indeed, at its crudest, it is a glorified and institutionalised form of communitarian *ressentiment* – [36] a form of politics that Twitter folk call 'punching down', while, importantly, absolving the self, wholly and nobly. When understood as such, it becomes clear that people of various constitutions, including women,[37] sexual minorities[38] and various non-white groups,[39] are all invited to participate in the nationalist consideration. It is, of course, the case that minoritised subjects remain more likely to subject nationalist canards to greater scrutiny compared with their majoritarian peers, given their acute experiences of being apprehended as ethno-racially inadequate according to certain considerations. It is, however, also the case that one's own subject location, of being minoritised, of not being read as the principal national subject, does not of itself entirely inure any such person from the nationalist rationale.

Having gestured at these various ways of thinking about exclusivity and nationalism, it is to be remembered that the oft-cited authority on the nation's historical specificity, Benedict Anderson, was himself tellingly blasé about the nation's exclusionary properties – intimating that the nation in itself is a benign entity. There are various moments in his *Imagined Communities* where it seems as if the making of the nation is simply a conduit via which to establish community – a structure of belonging that, though itself unique to modernity, is merely an iteration of a broader move central to all history, a move that attests to the comforts of fellow feeling and the realities of communal distinctiveness and even 'love'.[40] It is in relation to this ultimately sympathetic disposition towards the nation form that it should also be recalled that the distinctive daring of Paul Gilroy's *There Ain't No Black in the Union Jack* was not simply that it successfully grounded the centrality of a nationalist racism to everyday British political culture but, equally, that it spoke against so many implicit assumptions of the left too, including those taken-for-granted nostrums peddled by various stalwarts of a 'homely [British] Cultural Studies' such as E. P. Thompson and Raymond Williams.[41]

A recurring target of Gilroy's work was the British left's affection for the nation; an affinity that seemed oblivious to the hierarchical and often racialised exclusionary logics and practices so central to any such formation.[42] As Gilroy so witheringly put it: 'It is as if the only problem with nationalism is that the Tories have secured a near exclusive monopoly of it.'[43] The leftist naivety that Gilroy derides here stems from the intuition that the nation is a proxy for a popular working-class vernacular, constituting in turn a valid vehicle for left collectivism. The nation is in turn considered a progressive, even revolutionary, entity, whereby it is only an explicitly Tory version of nationalism that remains objectionable. There lingers here a cognate assumption that nationalism, unless extreme, merely attests to a healthy democratic appetite (see here discussions of patriotism)[44] for collective sovereignty.[45]

As has been argued above, any such complacency about the nation stems from a simple misunderstanding. It misreads the nation as a politics of belonging as opposed to a politics of enmity; a matter of strong collective feeling as opposed to a matter of strong aversion.

The nation conquers the state

Having proposed a particular attunement to the question of the nation, the following pages will engage further some of the more specific historical detail relevant to the nation's emergence and popularisation. But instead of tending towards a historical account of the nation-state's *constructed* specificity, this historical discussion will be further geared towards positing a more precise reading of the exclusionary principle that underpins the nation formation. To reiterate, it is not the nation's allegedly inauthentic form that is interesting, but instead it is its exclusionary structure and the specificity of that exclusion that commands both scholarly but also political relevance.

Much of the defining work on the nation-state's emergence spans a highly disparate set of disciplinary backgrounds: state-formation theory, Marxist social history and functionalist anthropology. It is accordingly helpful to start here with Etienne Balibar's 'The Nation Form: History and Ideology' – a piece that offers a critical phraseology generative for amalgamating these multiple approaches.[46] Balibar reminds us, as a point of departure, that the preliminary institutional work done to standardise language and legal administration across a territorial field was rendered during the seventeenth and eighteenth centuries. It was here that the monarchic and mercantile assertion of power over territory gradually became formally autonomous, whereby a centralised authority came to enjoy full exclusivity in the exercise of governance over the designated territory. This territorial exclusivity was unique to modernity, having had to free itself from the overlapping claims to authority previously advanced by competing powers such as the Vatican (and its domestic wings) and transnational merchant leagues and guilds (e.g. the Hanseatic League) while also ending the formal fealty of various fickle domestic nobilities to monarchies located elsewhere. This process of incrementally accrued territorial sovereignty (commonly denoted as 'territorialisation'), dating back to the tail end of the Middle Ages, accordingly set the foundations for a territorially centralised state formation *upon which* the nation would be subsequently produced.[47] Or, as Balibar clarifies with a far more becoming precision:

> Non-national state apparatuses aiming at quite other [for example, dynastic, monarchic and/or mercantile] objectives have progressively produced the

elements of the nation-state, or, if one prefers, they have been involuntarily 'nationalized' and have begun to nationalize society – the resurrection of Roman law, mercantilism, and the domestication of the feudal aristocracies are all examples of this. And the closer we come to the modern period, the greater the constraint imposed by the accumulation of these elements seems to be. Which raises the crucial question of the threshold of irreversibility.[48]

It is accordingly this reverse engineering of the nation upon the state that remains the crucial detail central to all subsequent critical reckonings with the nation-state, summed up in Hannah Arendt's characteristically uncompromising line – 'the nation conquered the state'.[49]

As the modern state, with a territory now exclusively in its possession, begins to solicit a *raison d'état* commensurate to that territory, it gradually secretes a mythology of alleged ethnic integrity from which the state is said to draw its legitimacy. It is necessary to reiterate that this was, of course, not apparent in the administration of the colonies, which were relegated to a formal dependency that privileged the imperial 'nation-state': this being indeed one of the principal violences of colonialism, whereby rule is pursued not through a principle of popular legitimacy but through a rationale of benevolent racism and rampant plunder.[50] Or, as Cedric Robinson phrased this absence of hegemony, this absence of a principle of mass legitimacy: 'In the peripheral and semi-peripheral regions of the modern world system, at least, Gramsci's hegemonic class rule was never to be more than a momentary presence.'[51]

In the core, however, the European populations were indeed being appealed to in the name of the nation, as would also later transpire in the decolonising Global South. This is an appeal that is set up discursively, through the institutional mechanisms central to what Bhabha calls the 'pedagogic' demonstrations of the nation-state's ethnic integrity.[52] This is realised, for instance, through the concerted standardisation of a common language, a standardisation that proved and continues to prove much more difficult than commonly presumed;[53] through the active intervention in the telling of an official history, particularly in school curriculums;[54] through the preferential institutionalisation of state Churches or, as in France, the sacralisation of a principle of *laïcité*, a principle that is said to be unique to the nation; through the oratorical tropes of figures of state; through the funding and commercial structures of popular culture productions but also academic research financing; and through the more ceremonial rituals that rehearse national unity and ethnic custom, constituting a set of seemingly banal practices that Michael Billig terms everyday 'flagging'.[55]

It is here that we begin to understand that it was the state that rendered the nation. It was the core features of the territorial state that appeared first – territorially contiguous trade zones free of tariffs and charter obligations and therefore receptive to domestic merchant expansion;[56] the universalisation of law, often Napoleonic; the standardisation of language and civil service administration; and the emergence of a mass print and commercial culture.[57] Only then is a nation-state 'personality' fully realised, through the active pursuit of a political programme of nationalism.[58] To somewhat clumsily transpose Gellner's axiomatic line, in which he understands nationalism primarily as the process through which the territorial state's claim to political legitimacy is made 'congruent' with the ethnic constitution of the polity: 'It is nationalism which engenders nations, and not the other way round.'[59] Interestingly, when critically following through with this reading, even minority secessionist movements become only an extension of this decidedly state-led nation-making process, despite it ostensibly seeming as if secessionist aspirations represent organically constituted nations in search of a state. Put differently, minorities only become meaningfully designated as such once a certain normatively majoritarian conception of nation claims the existing territorial state, leaving in turn this newly formed minority to understand itself as now a nation in need of a state.

We can hereupon conclude, however tentatively, that ideas of 'nation' and 'nationhood' are constructed and reproduced through the political, social and cultural discourses that *succeed* the formalisation of the territorial state. This basic observation allows us to enter in turn into the more familiar language of 'imagined communities'. As the modern territorial and centralised state became more and more embedded as a historically unique form of sovereignty, it gradually solicited an ideological rationale upon which it secured its legitimacy, a legitimacy that can engender and cement a notion of a people coterminous with its borders. As Steve Garner asks, how can such a substantial mass, 'divided [so acutely] by wealth, class, region, ethnicity, gender, political viewpoint, religion, language and cultural orientation', believe themselves to be part of the same 'community'?[60] The nation becomes in turn the most prevailing language by which this state formation becomes imaginatively anchored within modernity, superseding these other divides, while placating the broader alienating condition of mass anonymity said to be characteristic of modernity, to produce a textured commitment to a shared and unitary political entity.[61] This is the nation-making sequence in which 'ethnicity' becomes the primary 'political identity' in whose name governance is actioned.

Crucially, as Mahmood Mamdani observes, though in a rather different context, this is not the turbo-charged constructionist assertion that there was no notion of ethnicity prior to the nation-state/colonialism. Key here is the rather more precise claim that the nation-state actively centres ethnicity and communitarian identity in ways that are historically unique vis-à-vis governance. As Mamdani writes,

> I want to distinguish between ethnicity as a cultural identity – an identity based on a shared culture – from ethnicity as a political identity. When the political authority and the law it enforces identify subjects ethnically and discriminate between them, then ethnicity turns into a legal and political identity [...] To distinguish between cultural and legal/political identities is [therefore] to distinguish between self-identification and state-identification.[62]

This reading of ethnicity via a concept of 'political identity' is highly generative. Namely, the nation-state promotes ethnicised notions of community as the primary terms by which the state acquires its political meaning and purpose. Categories of ethnic belonging and exclusion become hereby politicised to extents unique in historical terms – insofar as the direct role of the state and its rationale for existing are concerned. This gives ethnicity, through a state-making process, a unique political centrality – and, more importantly, via its attendant conceptions of the ethnic Other, the nation-state renders ethnicity and cognate categories a key basis for legitimate exclusion. It is this exclusionary remit that will be the focus of the following section.

Exclusion, minorities and Hannah Arendt

There is a passage in *Origins of Totalitarianism* in which Arendt executes a typically irreverent reading of the French Revolution and its many illusory promises.[63] Drawing provocatively from Edmund Burke, the decidedly conservative debunker of revolutionary hubris, Arendt observes that the

European claim to peoplehood and collective liberation was in fact far more modest, far more specific and far more perfunctory. Revolution was, in short, a claim to the sovereignty of the nation, not the sovereignty of man (*sic*) – or, to revisit the damning indictment of Burke himself: 'The world found nothing sacred in the abstract nakedness of being human.'[64] The Revolutionary Era's assertion of radical freedom was, or became, merely the freedom of the nation – and that freedom moved fundamentally, as an operational freedom, on the unfreedom of those it deemed to be constitutively different and substantively Other. Akin to Césaire's haunting words on the subject – though Césaire has unsurprisingly a far more comprehensive understanding of the centrality of *colonial racism* to the rendering of European nation-state projects – the alleged excesses of twentieth-century fascism were therefore not seen by Arendt as exceptional.[65] On the contrary, they represented merely a logical continuation of the historical agreement that had already been cemented – a compact where the state exists for the nation:

> They thereby admitted – and were quickly given the opportunity to prove it practically with the rise of stateless people – that the transformation of the state from an instrument of the law into an instrument of the nation had been completed; the nation had conquered the state, national interest had priority over law long before Hitler could pronounce 'right is what is good for the German people.' Here again the language of the mob [national will] was only the language of public opinion cleansed of hypocrisy and restraint.[66]

It might be accordingly said that modernity, in spite of its mooted merits elsewhere, produces a particularly violent rupturing of the more humdrum and tumultuously pluralistic conceptions of peoplehood and shared space that characterised previous political eras. (See, for instance, some emergent writing on the Ottomans,[67] Moghul India, as well as the Mediterranean basin during Antiquity; or, for a more raucous diversion, see Boccaccio's medieval classic, *The Decameron*, which, through its collection of bawdy tales, indirectly reveals the simply dizzying array of ethnic backgrounds that was such an unremarkable, taken-for-granted feature of European urban life in the fourteenth century.) Through the nationalisation of the state – a *raison d'état* that hinges on the state acting only as a vehicle for the national ethnic community – it is only modernity that establishes a hierarchical and absolutist indexing of who, on the basis of their ethnic status, belongs where.

43

Again, this is not to be read as anything so crude as flatly denying the pre-modern realities of ethnic formation and difference. Rather, any such observation seeks only to bring into relief the unique relationship *between ethnicity and the centralised state* that modernity engenders. Modernity might promise and/or threaten to be many other things – a socialist utopia, say, or as is seemingly more likely, a bourgeois ecstasy premised on the full socio-legal triumph of liberal individualism. It is, however, Arendt's provocative but, to my mind, correct assertion that the formal parcelling of political legitimacy into discretely maintained nation-state forms renders nationalism, and its myriad complementary structures of ethnic Othering, modernity's primary and most tenacious logic. After all, if we follow through with the Aristotelian contention that we are, by the final reckoning, *political animals*, it is then the precise form(s) in which we understand our distinctly political lives and possibilities that most determines our social experience.

In reading some of Arendt's somewhat synoptic commentary through other more fully formed postcolonial critiques, not least Frantz Fanon and Edward Said, another contiguous line of critical thought emerges that raises some important but perhaps awkward paradoxes.[68] Namely, the violence of European modernity was not only that it enshrined an exclusionary racialised principle at the heart of its own collective politics, but that, perversely, it also normalised this national aspiration as the only valid basis for resistance by those who were in the first instance excluded – what Arendt, with atypical understatement, calls 'nationally frustrated populations'.

> The worst factor in this situation was not even that it became a matter of course for the [Othered minority] to be disloyal to their imposed government and for the governments to [exclude them] as efficiently as possible, but that the nationally frustrated population was firmly convinced – as was everybody else – that true freedom, true emancipation, and true popular sovereignty could be attained only with full national emancipation, that people without their own national government were deprived of human rights. [This was a] conviction which could base itself on the fact that the French Revolution had combined the declaration of the Rights of Man with national sovereignty.[69]

Central here is the proposition that, having been rendered a minority or 'subject race' that has to rely on the whim and munificence of the ruling national majority, the only worthwhile political goal that remains is to realise a nation-state for oneself.[70] The exclusionary chauvinism of nationalism was in turn rendered manifestly immanent, insofar as those who resist their marginalisation were obliged ultimately to commit themselves to their own chain of nation-making essentialisms and exclusions.

This is the sobering reality that has been so well attested to by much of the twentieth-century's postcolonial reality, the wider Zionist capture of Palestine being a particularly poignant witness, when the more specific legacy of Arendt's own intimate Jewish experience and politics is considered, to this bloody reality of endless nation-making; a bloody reality where one original suffering induces another suffering. As regards the case of Israel, we have seen how the enduring place of antisemitism for European nation-making projects resulted in the consolidation of dreams among many Jews for another nation-state elsewhere. And it is, of course, equally well documented that the actual pursuit and realisation of that elsewhere, that promised homeland, has itself been so constitutively reliant upon a variety of radically exclusionary principles and practices. This wider realisation of a confessionally Jewish state – one that trades on the 'erasure' of the Palestinians already there[71] – reached its logical apogee in the recent promulgation in Israel of the 'nation-state law', legislation that further underscored the overt ethnic supremacism of the state's existence, explicitly clarifying that 'only Jews have the right of self-determination in Israel'.[72]

The endemic violence particular to the Zionist imperative remains well known and hotly contested. But importantly, Israel, the unique scale of its Western backing notwithstanding, is not necessarily exceptional; it is to my mind only a particularly stark and visceral instantiation of how historical exclusion at the hand of one set of nation-state logics can itself often precipitate new nation-state exclusions. Achille Mbembe, though engaging issues that go well beyond nationalism, bravely elaborates upon this broader modernist trap regarding our contemporary political possibilities. This is the trap in which so much communitarianism seems only to beget more communitarianism, exponentially proliferating for every original exclusion. In the epilogue to his recent *Critique of Black Reason*, Mbembe sensitively observes how so much ostensibly progressive identitarianism that is racial and ethnic in form remains seductive, emboldening and even necessary. He notes, however, that any such liberation politics is also ultimately a conservative politics that leaves intact the broader normative moral economy and ontology that precipitates the political claim to difference in the first place. As he notes, 'often, the desire for difference emerges precisely where people experience intense exclusion. In these conditions the proclamation of difference is an inverted expression of the desire for recognition and inclusion.'[73]

Mbembe is, of course, addressing in his book the specific condition of blackness – as constituting a unique mode of exploitation and humanity denied that white supremacism has delivered so steadfastly. But his observation is also a delicate and affectionate way of capturing the general forms by which modernist communitarianism is not only an assault on the 'open world'. Perhaps even more cruelly, those who are excluded in this first instance are themselves denied an intelligible language that could prise open *another* future.

> These cuts and scars [left by history] prevent the realization of community. And the construction of the common is inseparable from the reinvention of community. This question of universal community is therefore by definition posed in terms of how we inhabit the Open, how we care for the Open – which is completely different from an approach that would aim first to enclose, to stay within the enclosure of what we call our own kin. This form of *unkinning* is the opposite of difference. Difference is, in most cases, the result of the construction of desire. It is the result of a work of abstraction, classification, division, and exclusion–a work of power that, afterward, is internalised and reproduced in the gestures of daily life, even by the excluded themselves.[74]

Mbembe mourns here the increasingly evident reality that when contending with exclusion from the normative political community, with all the viscerally material, bodily but also discursive charge of any such racialised governance, the excluded themselves are encouraged to settle for a political future premised on their own splendid isolation elsewhere. One accordingly senses here a complex but important note of caution against some of the more clichéd lionising of the 'liberation' knowledges and projects said to be intuitively available to the oppressed or marginalised. There is the profound risk that such putative liberation simply upholds the wider communitarian logic of culture, politics and space so central to colonial modernity, only that it is in certain instances presented from a position of marginality and ostensible resistance. After all, if we accept the contention that power rehearses its preferred form of resistance, then, as far as the assertion of nation-state power goes, the forceful cultural assertion of minority identitarianism is precisely the type of resistance that nation-state hegemony finds logically comprehensible and ontologically satisfying.

Returning to the finer specifics of contemporary Western discourse, the above reflections also get to the heart of what is ham-fistedly derided in many quarters as 'identity politics'. Much of what gets dismissed as the allegedly divisive and self-absorbed identity politics of minority racial groups trades on a misnomer, a result of critics wilfully misapprehending the present through a *camera obscura*.[75] Namely, such allegedly anti-identity politics voices actually end up reinforcing the underlying logic of identity that they otherwise purport to deride. In short, they take umbrage only with a caricatured reading of minority politics, happily absolving the underlying identitarianism of normatively white majoritarianism. Put in stronger terms, it is worth noting that the primary 'identity' game of real consequence in Europe is nativist white nationalism, with the various assertive (and, yes, sometimes sanctimonious) claims to minoritised identity in certain generally youth or campus circles simply a reactive attempt to recover a dignity, pride and sensitivity denied by that self-same white nativism. It is, after all, not minority ethnic groups that summon of their own volition the banner of identity; instead, it is their constitutive estrangement from the normative (white) identity politics of nation that results in frustrated attempts to re-centre their own identity on terms freed of white normativity.

It is in this context fairly understandable, predictable even, that some people adopt defensive racial formations as borne out of demonisation at the hands of white nationalist claims. We should, however, always bear in mind, in keeping with Mbembe, that it is indeed the original assertions of national normativity that forge defensive minoritised racial categories in the first instance. Assertive claims to minority difference, as a political end in its own right, obtain thereby a somewhat futile and circular tenor. This is what Gilroy, and more recently Haider and Olaloku-Teriba, have so creatively deconstructed as being the hopeless dead-end of endless identity making.[76] Or, to bring our discussion full circle, we might conclude with Arendt's own frustrated observation about the fallout that met the late nineteenth-century formalisation of nation-state logics across Europe: 'Since [the rendering of minorities through nation-state formalization], not a single group of refugees or Displaced Persons has failed to develop a fierce, violent group consciousness and to clamor for rights as — and only as — Poles or Jews or Germans, etc.'[77]

Nation and race

Much argumentation along the above lines, about both nationalism's historical specificity but also its distinctive political content, has been ably rejuvenated in the wake of recent political events across the West, not least in Brubaker's widely circulated 'Between Nationalism and Civilizationism'. The expansive argument advanced by Brubaker, emblematic of a recurring and currently popular critique, does, however, press a misleading nationalism versus civilisationism distinction — a confusion that principally stems from the need for a more precise clarification of the specific role of race proper in the charting of contemporary nationalisms.

Brubaker does start with a helpful definitional emphasis on belonging and non-belonging, wherein nationalism refers specifically to the multiplying political threats that become attributed to those who escape the threshold of belonging:

> [The] opposition is between insiders and outsiders: between 'people like us', those who share our way of life, and those on the outside who are said to threaten our way of life. This includes 'internal outsiders': those living in our midst who, even when they are citizens of the state, are not seen as belonging to the nation. The 'outside' also includes impersonal forces or institutions that are seen as threatening our way of life or our security: globalization, unfettered trade, the European Union, radical Islam, and so on.[78]

This diagnosis of the contemporary nationalist moment is, of course, highly complementary to my own book's own point of departure. But Brubaker, in order to situate the broader framework of this newly confident nationalist logic, proceeds to make a distinction between national and civilisational nationalism:

> The national populisms of Northern and Western Europe — especially those of the Netherlands, France, Scandinavia, Belgium, Austria, and Switzerland —

> constitute a distinctive cluster. They are distinctive, I shall argue, in construing the opposition between self and other not in narrowly national but in broader civilizational terms.[79]
>
> [...]
>
> In Northern and Western Europe, where the 'national question' in its classic territorial form is not on the agenda, the civilizational overlay of nationalist rhetoric is increasingly pronounced, and the semantics of self and other are rearticulated in broadly civilizational rather than narrowly national terms [...] This raises the paradoxical possibility that the ostensibly and even demonstratively nationalist populisms of Northern and Western Europe may not be all that substantively national or nationalist. Talk of 'the nation' is not disappearing, but 'the nation' is being re-characterised in civilizational terms.[80]

While much of this is again very well put, it is my hunch that it would be best to dissolve this distinction altogether, as both forms do similar, mutually dependent work. Brubaker is certainly right to note that the broader *civilisational* claim to secular liberalism – with its attendant symbolic weaponisation of free speech, gender equality, anti-antisemitism (the appellation of 'philosemitism'[81] used by Brubaker might be to overstate the trope), and a broader *de jure* deification of democracy as a symbol – does assume a powerful profile in the making of contemporary nationalist harangues.[82] This is indeed central to the argument that will be put forward in Chapter 3 of this book.

Two substantial issues do, however, arise with this reading. First, the nationalist form in western Europe is not exclusively or even primarily constituted by liberal secular posturing – intertwined as it is with neoliberal, social democratic and conservative rationales. Similarly, a disjuncture between the purported claim to liberalism and the actual mechanisms of liberal governance might also be noted here – insofar as the self-same demagogues of liberal civilisationism seem perfectly at ease with rolling back some of the liberal gains of the last two decades. Consider, for instance, the impassioned barracking *against* the Human Rights Act that is commonplace in British political theatre, or the increased recourse to 'states of exception' and opaque judicial and carceral measures provoked by the 'War on Terror' and 'hard bordering'.[83]

Secondly, and more importantly for this particular argumentative juncture, the nationalist is rarely ever 'narrowly national', excepting the high point of various intermittent wars; instead, nationalism has consistently assumed much more powerful pretences of European white civilisationism in order to generate its expansive conceptual and affective reach. Hall's 'The West and the Rest' offers perhaps the definitive statement here on how claims to national distinctiveness within the European fold manage to draw this wider civilisational differentiation, a differentiation with potent hierarchical frameworks.[84] It is the brand of racialised civilisationism that could hold together multiple different European nation-making mythologies:[85] a span of civilisationism that informed Montesquieu's assertion of Western republican rationalism contra Oriental despotism,[86] a distinction key to the later consolidation of French nationalism; Kipling's 'White Man's Burden' which provided the righteous moral mandate central to British imperial nationalisms;[87] and Weber's decidedly racial exhalation of German bureaucratic secularism as the triumph of history.[88]

In other words, I would maintain that a structure of national Othering in recent western European memory is rarely straightforwardly territorial. Again, except for the acute but generally temporary theatre of regional war, it is not apparent that a form of nationalism has been present in western Europe whose primary attempt at distinction work centred on purely national distinctions vis-à-vis other nations ('notably language and specifically national cultural particularities and traditions' as singled out by Brubaker), whether near or far.[89] Instead, I see a recurring racialised practice where the nation's claim to being maintains a scope decidedly civilisational in form and reach.

Attention to the place of internal minorities, and their frequently racial resonance, unlocks this nation-civilisation node in particularly helpful ways. Internal minorities, always central to how the nation obtains its definitional content, are often ascribed forms of threat and disruption that exceed any simply national and/or territorial encroachment; such threats represent instead an ordering of conflict or rupture that is *civilisational* in scope. I mean here the situation in which a relevant domestic minority becomes the most resonant local proxy for the broader civilisational divide along which the nation fumbles for definitional orientation. For instance, as European nations gradually found their symbolic and institutional footing in the nineteenth century, it was the Jew who came to represent this internal field of illegitimacy in particularly acute ways.[90] So while nationalisms in most nineteenth-century forms had always found a civilisational purpose as tied to emergent colonial ideas of whiteness and Europe's historic mission, they also managed to ground this purported civilisational purpose in certain agitations against the foul interior – the Jew, the gypsy, as well as the off-white status of the Irish in the British context.

The contemporary can be seen as another radical flaring of this well-documented joint pivot, a pivot where the nation is always civilisational in its conceits, and where the primary object of derision and alarm is in fact an *internal Other* that often obtains racial contours. While nationalism has always rumbled along relative to the vagaries of its respective countries, its most frenzied form (i.e. the early twentieth century and the contemporary) does seem to assert this more racialised civilisational remit as a central operational move. It is through the threading of a whole host of domestic minorities or imminent encroachers (e.g. refugees and migrants) through broader grids of racialised meaning-making that such inflections of a nation contending with pending existential crisis and in need of a robust revival can be expressed with a scope and urgency that goes beyond mere territorialism. This revival is directed through the imperatives of cultural recovery, fortification of borders and the broader neutering of the excessive rights and resources alleged to have been provisioned to inauthentic minority denizens.

This is a form of nationalist anxiety that borrows with renewed purchase from broader racial representational regimes as formalised during previous colonial-era assertions of civilisational purpose and distinction – regimes that are both Orientalising and animalising:[91] Orientalising, as in a culture-clash framework where those racialised as non-white are said to be bearers of cultures of unreason irreconcilable with the West;[92] and animalising insofar as the racialised become weighted as vulgar, dangerously fecund, primitive, violent, boorish, noisome, temperamental and, perhaps most fatally, ungrateful. Put differently, some reference to European civilisationism seems to me the shared constant that suffuses the more explicitly national nationalisms currently unfolding across Europe; but the strand of distinctly *civilisational* emphasis that is drawn becomes specific to the forms of race-making and immigration scaremongering applicable to the different national histories and contexts: the Christendom lore of Hungary and Poland, the secular militancy of France, the imperial nostalgia of Britain, the Germanic mourning of a fast-fading social democratic post-war golden age, alongside the *frontier* conception of civilisational invasion characteristic of certain Mediterranean countries' attempts at nationalist alarm vis-à-vis immigration across the sea.

Let us be more precise here. The claim to nation trades on a number of assertions about the outsider, but this outsider is already located *within* the confines of the territorial jurisdiction in question. Indeed, it seems to me that the nation's primary impulse is to take issue with an *internal* presence that is understood as having always-already penetrated the confines of the territory. What accordingly constitutes the difference between nation as nationalism in itself and nation as racialised nationalism is this civilisational insinuation that is necessarily Janus-faced. Racialised nationalism anxiously scans the border and the exterior only because it already takes issue with the interior and the many problematic minorities that are in some form already deemed excessive – excessive in the sense that they are simply too many, have been given too much allowance, wield too much power, or threaten to wield too much power if not pre-emptively stymied. This latter scenario is evidenced in certain Finnish new right groups' *pre-emptive* actions against the spectre of multicultural ruin, resulting in various politically potent references to the dystopia that must be averted despite the immigrant and/or Muslim community in Finland still being relatively small. The exterior is therefore rendered a threat partly because it is seen as replenishing, enhancing or emboldening the already problematic interior. Such an anxiety about the exterior even extends to certain seemingly impersonal international forces. For instance, supranational institutions such as the EU are in large part considered politically suspect precisely because they are construed as either allowing for the unchecked movement of refugees and Muslims (in the form of Turkish accession for instance) or because they more generally project certain moral orthodoxies ('liberal internationalism') that are said to hamper the ability of national majorities to check the excesses of particular minorities. In this specific context, the EU beast is objected to not because it is an external force *ipso facto*, but because its authority is seen as circumscribing the ability of the nation to check, contain and regulate the internal minorities about whom it already remains acutely anxious.

Or, seen through a rather more speculative psychoanalytic lens, the expansive and anarchic exterior – juxtaposed against the homely and 'hyggelig' hearth that the nation ideally insinuates – becomes cross-referenced against the interior and its multiple insider threats.[93] The multiple and irredeemable violences attributed to Islamist movements in the Middle East or even the widely held perceptions of black governmental dysfunction across Africa are seamlessly written back into the chronic significations of pathology that the corresponding domestic minorities already wear so easily. The *world out there* furnishes in turn the paranoid nationalist psyche with a form of spectacular and sublime doom, a doom that foretells the full emasculation of the home nation, these being external threats deeply scored into the internal Others already so tangibly and abundantly in our midst.

This scenario of the exterior informing the nation's agitated reckoning with the interior, and vice versa, need not be seen as exhaustive of all that nationalism is. Nationalism does at times certainly represent only a form of competing territorialism and border ructions: things like the cod wars and broader disputes over fishing zones,[94] contestations over water access privileges,[95] or comical attempts to stem the all-assailing sweep of Americanised global commercialism – what was humorously remembered by Hobsbawm and Kertzer as the fledgling and ultimately hopeless 1950s 'campaign against "coca-colonization"'[96] – or contemporary elite French paranoia about the full Anglicisation of online leisure consumption.[97]

The nation's mobilisation against a formidable international power's pursuit of self-serving gains represents another related form of territorial retrenchment of sovereignty that need not be seen as being driven by some corresponding anti-minority proposition. This is a form of nationalist politics where the primary threat is conceived of as being capitalist or geopolitical interventions that are foreign in origin (things such as trade wars, goods dumping and neoliberal 'structural adjustment' impositions) or simply straightforward neo-imperialist occupation. See, for instance, the various anti-IMF and anti-EU sentiments as tied to punitive economic impositions in Greece, Italy and comparable countries, or certain prominent strains of Palestinian, Pakistani or Venezuelan politics. Nationalist politics can also comprise a competing territorialism among neighbouring states, as seen for instance in Kosovo/Serbia, Russia/Ukraine and Azerbaijan/Armenia. But all such tendencies remain an increasingly uncommon and often transient form of nationalist politics. Whenever a political process becomes badged, over a meaningful duration, as one of nation, it does seem to reserve its greatest conviction for anti-minority politics, and only subsequently does it assume, if necessary, certain strictly xenophobic (anti-foreigner in its original and 'undiscriminating' sense) and/or anti-internationalist/anti-globalisation positions.

To reiterate, as far as western Europe is concerned, it is the renewed intimations of race that can best realise any such relationship of nation and Other that does not simply map onto self-explanatorily territorial notions of national self and foreigner. It is the figuration of race that has taken on the ontology that best scores the grooves that demarcate the extra-territorial separation of nation and Other. Or, seen inversely, it is the language and logic of nation that best hold together a contemporary political discourse that can invoke race but without naming it formally.[98] Gilroy, anticipating this broader consolidation of nationalism's relationship to a mastering of how we understand our 'collective political problems', noted how race becomes funnelled into the demons that agitate the nation – demons that are currently read as immigrants, Muslims, terrorists and criminals:

> Now, the exclusive attachment of [...] nationalist feeling to a definition of collective political problems in which war supplies the master trope and immigration constitutes the principal menace, is dangerous and destructive even when the language of 'race' seems to have disappeared altogether.[99]

As was hinted at before, taxonomies of race on the one hand and ethnic conceptions of the nation on the other emerged concomitantly, each generating complementary logics, vocabularies, symbols and affects as relevant to engendering structures of thick belonging and exclusion. Indeed, these twin languages of ethnic nation and race become co-dependent. As many formidable thinkers have noted, the rehearsals of race throughout the nineteenth and twentieth centuries endowed it with the most avowed clarity in allowing modernist ontologies of human distinction to be established and invested in, including those distinctions that become central to the national assertion of community (even if some foundational nation thinkers such as Herder remained greatly suspicious of the pretences of race itself).[100] But importantly, to retrace a definition previously deployed, this assertion has less to do with the racially generated clarity with which the national self can be visualised; the falsity of race all too often betrays any attempt at a strong substantive claim to belonging. Instead, this assertion proves more reliable in establishing a series of racially contoured *outsider* figures. As I have written elsewhere,[101] race rallies a variety of coordinates that allows for 'Othering' to carry a more pronounced reach not always available to ethnicity on its own terms: not least, it enjoys the not to be understated immediacy of *visual* signification; it marries with but also *thickens* the otherwise ethnically framed attributions of irreducibly different *cultures*, whereby differently grouped members are said to be bearers of absolutely different cultural repertoires; it is also able to generate a more visceral index of affective repulsion, tied to registers of hygiene, dirt, etiquette, noise, alongside the many titillations and excesses that are sexualised in form; and crucially, as has been the principal emphasis of this section, race is able to buttress, however spuriously, much more aggrandising historical distinctions regarding a heavily worn civilisation divide as regards the 'West and the rest'. In sum, with these multiple figurations of race in mind, we might conclude that, while nation does not, *ipso facto*, need race to engender a comprehensive Othering programme, the particular legacies, determinations and expediencies relevant to Western nation-making projects render race an inevitable and indispensable presence that is continually remade.[102]

Conclusion

This chapter has engaged with the question of nation through a range of openings: an examination of its history, a reckoning with its conceptual specificity, but most importantly, a reading of race's wider place in governing European nation-state politics. The story of nation in western Europe, and certainly Britain, has always been one of race. The two are intricately wedded and that remains the case today – a contemporary situation where Europe has been yet again convulsed by the appeal of nation and the racial demons that such appeals necessarily turn on. To contend anew with the spectre of nationalism without a deep attentiveness to race is to remain tone-deaf to this region's wider political history and memory. It is therefore also to misunderstand the present.

Nationalism can also be many other things. Nationalism includes in many instances an attempt to assert (e.g. national liberation campaigns) or reassert domestic sovereignty. This is partly evident in some of the anti-EU movements in Greece, Spain and perhaps the UK too. It is also partly evident in the secessionist movements of Catalonia and Scotland.

Nationalism might also include, at times, the desperate attempt to stem the unchecked play of global capitalism, through attempts to reintroduce tariffs or checks on capital flight, as seen in Malaysia's prompt action during the 1997 crisis, or simply through attempts to resurrect tax burdens that global corporations have otherwise become so adept at escaping. In this context, an appeal to the nation acts as a fertile sounding board by which to rekindle discontent against the monopoly of market-society norms on what is currently politically effable. Nationalism can also be, as is indeed its more commonplace understanding, a conduit for agitations against shifting cultural mores. Seemingly radical advances in particular social justice causes regarding gender equality and sexuality in particular can orient the nation as the primary means by which suburban conservatives can rail against these advances and the *bien pensant* politics that they are claimed to represent. After all, as has been so systematically unpicked by the voluminous analysis of Spivak and others, conservative renditions of nation are intrinsically invested in the policing of feminine virtue, propriety, chastity and the imperatives of reproduction, unleashing in turn untold violence on its 'own' women in the name of national culture and integrity.[103]

But nationalism, I think, carries a much more likely tendency, particularly when the nation being appealed to already has a strong constitutive affinity to the state. Put simply, when the nation being appealed to already has normative sanction via the state and white majoritarianism alike, its political thrust is of a different racialised political order that outweighs these above possibilities. Its primary definitional orientation, as has been suggested in this chapter ad nauseam, is to move against the Other – as a set of flesh-and-blood peoples against whom state institutions but also the body politic more generally are exhorted to move.

It is this exhortation that western Europe is currently being asked to reckon with. Once again.

2

Notes on two red herrings: progressive nationalism and populism

The previous chapter set out what was an unavoidably dense engagement with the wider body of nation and nationalism theorisation that any book of this sort is obliged to address. Out of gratitude to the reader for having waded through this dense chain of claims, now would be the opportune moment to engage more tangibly with the distinctly contemporary character of Western nationalism, a tangibility that will be parsed in this book through the different ideological registers by which contemporary nationalism is borne.

There are two clarifications that I would first like to address. To those readers eager to move on, this relatively short third chapter can be passed over without it proving costly for their broader understanding of the different arguments that the rest of this book turns on. Should, however, the reader prove tolerant of these tangents, I provide the added solace that these clarifications are by no means extensive, authoritative or even particularly academic.

First, I would like to briefly contest the not infrequently voiced case for *progressive* nationalisms, this being the situation whereby Scotland and Catalonia are often put forth as instances by which an excessively anti-nationalism position ought to be moderated. This argument, which I believe to be misplaced, will only be passingly dealt with, given that these are not empirical contexts particularly germane to the immediate remit of this book. The possibility of more progressive claims to nation, as often ascribed to contemporary Scottish and Catalan politics, is, however, aired sufficiently often for us to address it, if only fleetingly.

The second clarification I have in mind will necessitate a somewhat fuller consideration. This concerns the fashionable intellectual trend to read contemporary political developments not through nationalism *per se*, but through the lens of what is increasingly called populism. Given how prominent this position has become, both academically and publicly, a somewhat more involved discussion is required here. My attention stems from a suspicion that an excessive focus on populism, which is already an analytically dubious concept, risks obscuring the broader politics of racial nationalisms that in fact underlie any such putatively populist moment.

Against progressive nationalism

First, there are many dissenters who cite Catalonia and Scotland as countervailing witnesses to the possibilities of progressive nationalism.[1] For one such emblematic instance, see Tom Nairn and his plaintive question as posed in 1968 about Scotland: 'Is it really impossible that Scotland, which has dwelt so long and so hopelessly on the idea of a nation, should produce a liberated, and revolutionary nationalism worthy of the name and the times?'[2]

My basic claim is that arguments of this sort trade on a partial misrepresentation of nationalism's core character. Put simply, any such reading of a progressive possibility infers too presumptuously from the dream of a nation-state as forged in those circumstances where one does not yet possess any such nation-state. Separatist mobilisation is, after all, only one in a litany of decidedly *germinal* acts vis-à-vis the assertion of nation. To conclude the character of a nation on the basis of its initial resistant moves against a dominant centre located elsewhere is to misunderstand the nature of *nation-state nationalism*. In short, the character of a nation's nationalism cannot be meaningfully read from what it initially resists in the process of claiming a nation-state (e.g. Ireland resisting British supremacy, Greece asserting against the Ottoman Empire a romantic yearning for nationhood, or the assorted postcolonial countries throwing off imperialist domination). In actuality, the nation, *qua* nation, only finds meaningful expression and character once it has the state in its possession. Or rather, the nation only becomes substantive once the state commits its resources, its institutions, its political slogans, its rituals and its symbolism to the *majoritarian* nation in *its* possession. Put bluntly, the litmus test of progressive nationalism is how it acquits itself upon gaining the state that it agitates for. On those terms, it seems premature to suggest that Catalonia and Scotland somehow carry with them a *nationalist* political spirit that can escape the broader sociopolitical and economic winds formative of the North Atlantic. Of course, it might well be that the fuller project intended here is not, as an endgame, nationalist, and is instead fundamentally about a politics of progressive social democracy finding a new lease of sub-national/regional expression. But in that case, it does not bear consideration as part of a debate on what is nationalism and what is not.

However, if some theorists of Scottish and Catalan independence continue to insist that it is in fact a *national* aspiration, but one that will retain or realise a wider political project, cosmopolitan, civic and 'revolutionary' in form, it then seems, as Nasar Meer hints, less credible, less historically feasible.[3] A passing glance at various decolonisation struggles (including the twentieth-century Ireland story) is instructive here. When compared to some of the separatist agitations currently apparent in Europe, these twentieth-century decolonisation contexts boasted a much more fully formed radical political agenda in waging their respective national liberation campaigns. The resulting commitment, however, of these various struggles to the nation in state form nonetheless yielded across the subsequent decades various acts of nationalist violence, directed not against some exogenous force of capital or reaction, but against its constitutive minorities and frontiers, multiple as they often were.

For instance, as many postcolonial theorists have explored in the South Asian context, one of European colonialism's most enduring legacies might in fact be this complex channelling of much Global South politics through the nation-state form.[4] As Goldie Osuri intriguingly comments, 'Contemporary colonialisms and imperialisms may be best diagnosed through the lens of identifying forms of sovereignty [as comprising, in part, nation-state logics] rather than relying on the geopolitical framework of West/non-West recognisable in the conceptual vocabulary of postcolonial theory.'[5] And though Osuri's ultimate call is for a 'theorisation of the postcolonial nation-state as engaging in its [own] expansionary colonial project', her general thesis also has a bold and probing relevance for my own querying of how to read nation and nationalism.[6] In India (and thereby what is now Pakistan and Bangladesh as well), but also, say, Sri Lanka, an independence consciousness was formalised in a manner that became, to some significant degree, wedded to a call for its own sense of nationhood (as a people, history and culture). These national aims were often inextricably joined at the time to broader socialist ideas of liberation and economic autarky but also to radical anti-colonial notions of humanist solidarity and global community – these being pervasive political templates of the era.[7] However, the wider and perhaps superseding sense of liberation as made to cohere around an idea of nation did seem to anticipate the subsequent forms of brutal nation-making exclusion and militarisation that would result in all these countries – for example, Hindutva supremacism in India, the consolidation of decidedly intolerant codifications of Islam in Pakistan, and Sinhala Buddhist chauvinism in Sri Lanka.[8]

These South Asian examples, though only impressionistically addressed, do bear witness to a salutary truth. In short, it is this kind of majoritarian turn to the insular politics of policing the nation that any nationalist campaign often seems fated to realise once it is 'fortunate' enough to have a state in its name.[9] To somehow suggest therefore that recent Scottish and other similar separatist nationalisms from *within* Europe, of all places, would chart a different path seems to hinge on an act of faith that we ought to be cautious about. Important here is the observation that the emergent national spirit, upon having acquired a state and its own numerical majority, struggles to retain the former political centre as its primary negative object, that object being Westminster, Madrid, Moscow, and so forth. The newly minted nation-states can no longer orient their primary nationalist energies against the unit that was previously the potent foil against which the nation cause was asserted. Once this external unit is relinquished / vanquished, the political gaze, if it is to remain a politics of nation, must look elsewhere to locate its sources of negational definition, anxiety, threat and decay. The likely terrain that will prove conducive for any such post-independence national project seems obvious.

Less nationalism, more populism?

The case for such progressive nationalisms via Scotland, Catalonia or otherwise is only of marginal relevance to this book and does not figure much within the wider political moment I wish to address. The above treatment constitutes therefore only a brief note. There is, however, one more theme that requires attention when trying to clarify certain theoretical coordinates relevant to *contemporary* nationalisms. Attempts to grapple with the nationalist politics of today have been greatly mystified in my opinion by the designation of the present as not nationalist, but populist – or, at times, when convenient, nationalist-populist. After all, if there was one word as likely as nationalism to have been attributed to the politics that found its full expression in the *annus horribilis* that 2016 allegedly was, it was populism – the distinguished minds behind the Cambridge Dictionary even decreed it their word of the year,[10] and the *Guardian* ran in 2018 a high-profile series devoted entirely to 'the populist moment'.

It is easy enough to deride this term. The ubiquity of populism as an analytic throwaway can seem, at first glance, to reside entirely in its elastic but pejorative meaninglessness, a meaninglessness that allows it to be bent to serve whatever particular homily the writer might want to issue. To read the popular as being populist does not, after all, seem to serve any viable analytic function beyond denoting some dissatisfaction on the part of the speaker with what purports to be popular at the moment. That various politicians firmly of the establishment persuasion, ranging from Tony Blair to Angela Merkel, have all paraded populism as the primary threat to stability hardly helps the concept's case for analytic credibility.[11]

I do maintain, however, that this term warrants some considered attention. A cottage publishing industry has emerged over the last couple of years that tries to constructively attribute to populism some distinctive properties relevant to understanding the wider appeal of certain political movements at particular conjunctures.[12] The following engagement with this body of writing, where 'the popular is distinguished from the populist', will accordingly help unpick some analytic knots.[13] But a more sustained unpacking of what might be credited as being distinctive to populism will also reveal instructive insights about the nationalist condition more specifically. What will hopefully become apparent here is not that the appellation of 'populism' is an empty signifier wholly without substantive content; rather, I will more prosaically contend that when nationalist politics does garner sway in contemporary times, it is in fact necessarily populist.[14] It will be posited that the charge of populism is in most instances simply superfluous, as nationalism itself, properly understood, exhausts most of the allegedly distinctive principles characteristic of the populist formation.

It is certainly the case that the charge of populism is often merely an empty rhetorical pejorative, a derogatory belittling of a popular *sans culottes* politics that happens to contradict the more rarefied ideological position of the speaker.[15] This wider disregard for explicitly 'populist' politics has a long democratic history, being first prominently deployed by the ruling establishment to disparage the American, generally rural, working-class solidarity politics that emerged in the wake of the Gilded Age's deference to monopoly capital, industrial oligarchs and robber barons.[16] The dismissal of such politics was testament to an elite closure, fortifying an establishment compact between capital and political centrism that scholars sympathetic to populism are rightly suspicious of.

But any such defensive reading of populism is to read it as *only* political theatre and/or elite conceit, as opposed to it denoting anything more properly substantive. In order to sketch out a more robust working of the term, it is worth scanning some other features that are more concretely ascribed to populism. For instance, one working definition of the concept that does seem to have some mileage is the claim that populism necessarily 'simplifies' political discourse to such an 'extreme' extent that it is rendered something distinctive from the ordinary sweep of political debate and contestation.[17] It is suggested here that populism denotes a form of discourse in which political issues and prospective solutions are bludgeoned into impossibly crude dichotomies. Solutions are made to seem eminently painless and straightforward, while culpability for a whole host of economic, security and cultural issues is attributed to a series of minority constituencies or a small remaining league of elites (often foreign, or, better yet, Jewish). Populism engenders in turn a very particular political calculation that hinges on the rapturous identification of a majority free of blemish that is being wronged by a small cabal of elites and/or over-indulged minority populations.

It is this joint tendency towards crude simplification and majority absolution that Yanis Varoufakis identifies as militating against a politics that is substantively left-wing in character:

> A populist promises all things to all people, while preying on their superstitions and fears. In contrast, when I ran for parliament I quoted Winston Churchill in promising 'blood, sweat and tears' as the price of our liberation from debt bondage and from Greece's oligarchy.[18]

A similar recognition of the difficult and complex extrication of self from a prevailing political order is what China Miéville, in his exquisite *October*, places at the heart of the utopian notions of political possibility that intoxicated revolutionary Russia in 1917.[19] This was a revolutionary ecstasy that politicised whole swathes of society without ever simplifying the nature of the political question or future being fought over.

This 'simplification' criterion is, however, insufficient to supply a feasible definition of a populist political position. After all, the distrust regarding what purports to be populist politics does not result from its being a politics that seems exceedingly crude vis-à-vis the complexities of the social problems that it claims to be able to solve. Such distrust does not derive either from the laughable complicity of the champions of such populist politics in the elite social processes that they ostensibly hold in such derision – for example, Berlusconi's and Trump's championing of a vulgar rococo capitalism, Johnson's and Rees-Mogg's unapologetic aristocratism, and Farage's stockbroker-gone-rogue brand of faux-earthiness.

Jan-Werner Müller, increasingly influential on the question of populism, instead observes that populism is unique only insofar as it engineers a political claim in which the conception of *the people* and the posited political position become wholly coterminous.[20] The purported political cause is seen as not merely representative of the people, but as bearing their raw essence – as organic, authentic and proper. Dissenters from the posited cause, on the other hand, obtain a certain kind of constitutional fraudulence – Jewish bankers, elite oligarchs, deracinated liberals, or, and most frequently, particular ethnic minorities who are declared void by their mere existence. Or, if seen through a slightly different inflection, the populist politician claims to represent the only *true* people, whereas those whom it assumes as unlikely to assent to the purported cause are pre-emptively declared artificial – interlopers who have shackled the will of the people.

This populist canard can be distinguished, hinging albeit on a spot of ideal theory hyperbole, from a political position that aspires to have a mass following.[21] All politics can, of course, be seen as attempting to rally a following based on what is believed to be right, just or pragmatically expedient. In the populist formation, however, it is the people, already appointed as such, that is in itself seen as right, just and expedient. The political position thereupon becomes primarily a matter of neutralising the presence or actions of those understood as not *of* the people.

In short, politics, in its ideal incarnation, amounts to a set of principles that 'the people' are invited to consider as being just and/or as remedying injustice. The populist position, on the other hand, amounts simply to the people itself, as already constituted. This critical reading of the populist form is somewhat analogous to what Gilroy has derided elsewhere as 'prepolitical uniformity'[22] – a politics that is only about rehearsing, defending and weaponising the form of particularised normative peoplehood that one has already been ascribed – i.e. the nation. Such a reading of populism as *anti-politics* also marries with what Kierkegaard ridiculed, long ago, as the difference between deep political purpose (*ethics*) and the mere superficial symbolic routine (*aesthetics*) that he equates with the politics of community that polite petit bourgeois society so conscientiously observes.[23] Mocking his fellow Copenhageners (as a proxy for the Hegelian philosophy that so chafed Kierkegaard), who seemed to think that a performance of the prevalent Danish national identity rendered them, by default, Christian in their virtue, Kierkegaard rails against the decorum of community. He sardonically observes how the attachment to community, which often poses as a self-explanatory mark of goodness and right, prevents the lived realisation of any actual ethical project that takes the decidedly radical example of Christ seriously.

Irrespective of what 1840s Denmark might tell us about contemporary challenges, there is in my opinion a salutary note here about the populist condition more broadly. Namely, within the sweep of populist posturing, the political seems only to traffic in notions of the real and authentic people, who are in turn exhorted to take up a war position vis-à-vis the excesses of the outsiders in their midst. Think here of 'the ordinary people of Middle England' so feted by the *Daily Mail* or Nixon's appeal to the 'silent majority', an invocation that is now a staple feature in many a politician's rhetorical repertoire.[24] Populism enacts, in short, a curious sleight of hand, insofar as a particular kind of *qualified* population becomes a metonym for the people in general. As Müller again notes,

> The crucial difference is that populists deny, or wish away, the pluralism of contemporary societies. When they say equality, they mean sameness, which is to say: conforming to some ideal of Middle America, Little England, or whatever a symbolic representation of real peoplehood comes down to for them.[25]

While this postulation might not satisfy all theorists of populism, it remains a workable definition that allows populism to denote something that is not synonymous with just any general definition of the popular.

This definitional base also helps better situate contemporary populism's close affinity to nationalism. Namely, when an appeal to 'the people' is advanced, it almost certainly must source a mediation of peoplehood already available in the common vernacular. The fascination with peoplehood is likely to work through the registers by which recent modernity has already organised our conceptions of the collective. And, as far as the contemporary is concerned, any mobilising of a normative peoplehood does seem obliged to work through its imbrication with the nation. As argued by Müller, when Trump says that 'the only important thing is the unification of the people – because the other people don't mean anything', he can without much difficulty segue such a general principle into his very *particular* barracking of Mexican immigrants, the black inner-city and anti-racism activists, Chinese capitalists and Muslims *tout court*.

This is not entirely dissimilar to Goodhart's claim that the defining political fault-line relevant to Western democracies amounts to a distinction between the 'anywheres' and the 'somewheres' (read: non-people and real people).[26] This is a distinction that marries with a commitment and aversion respectively to the ethos of national community. Such a national community versus rootless cosmopolitanism postulation, though generally associated with today's conservative commentariat, is also echoed in the post-Marxist language of figures such as Wolfgang Streeck.[27] Having won himself a considerable left-wing following, including in Corbynista corners of the Labour Party,[28] Streeck promulgates a state versus market people distinction, what he calls *Staatsvolk* and *Marktvolk*, whereby a common everyday people aligns to the polity (the state), but the others remain hopeless internationalists.[29] This might seem, on its own terms, to be merely a textbook instance of the mobility of elite labour and capital extolled by neoliberals being contrasted to ordinary people's much more wedded reliance on local infrastructures and public provision. But it is to be recalled that the wider traction of Streeck's popularity lies in his rather muscular disparaging of pro-refugee sentiments alongside his calling time on a general politics of pluralism owing to its irreparable elitism.[30] When contextualised within this wider political map, it becomes apparent that a market versus state people postulation bears many resemblances to a more generic populist dalliance with the nation that names certain people as decidedly proper while others become inauthentic.

This potted survey of the nationalist framework that underpins more basic populist claims to peoplehood works us back towards the previous chapter's wider reading of the nation-state's importance to understandings of contemporary communitarian self and politics. This is not to say that other populisms are not possible. The Occupy movement is an exemplary instance. After all, the claim to 99 per cent is as good as claiming the people in its entirety, with just enough spare capacity (1%) to account for the wrong being decried. As Ben Pitcher argues, via a reading of Laclau's radical rehabilitation of the concept, 'populism does not have any necessary characteristics at all – racism is simply an "ontic" content that can be substituted for an infinite variety of other contents, each (theoretically at least) as contingent as the next'.[31] However, it remains necessary also to note – with Pitcher – that populisms have a marked *predisposition* towards nationalist capture – as claims to peoplehood along a register of authenticity, majoritarianism and the general waging of political war against 'constitutive outsides' have all too many family resemblances to the stock motifs characteristic of nationalist assertion. Too much of recent history has heavily couched our vernacular understandings of collectivity within the mythology of nation. Such a historical inheritance entails that any unreflective claim to peoplehood that does not purposefully dissociate itself from a nationalist position cannot but slip into the embrace of all its exclusionary assumptions. Incidentally, this is, as was so expertly spelled out by El-Enany and Keenan, what remains frustrating about the so-called Lexiter position in Britain regarding the EU – it is not that there is no socialist or social democratic case for EU withdrawal, but rather that this position is asserted in such an unreflective and pious, race-blind manner that it is rendered low-hanging fruit, ripe for nationalist picking.[32]

To reiterate the recurring definitional emphasis of the previous chapter, it is my assertion that any consolidation of contemporary populist canards is likely to take shape within a nationalist embrace – likely, in turn, to yield one prevailing political command: to make war on the negative object that is *a priori* the nation's definitional Others, these being the various constitutive Others already within the nation-state's confines or those from outside who threaten to replenish these 'Other' communities.

Conclusion

This chapter has found it necessary to provide some brief commentary on two prominent challenges to how nationalism has been hitherto theorised in this book. These are what I have characterised as being the 'progressive nationalism' and 'populism' challenges. I have suggested that the progressive nationalism case remains too anachronistic and distorted a reading of what contemporary nationalisms, especially those carved from within Europe, are currently capable of. As regards populism, I have suggested that this concept, if even necessary, is best read from *within* nationalism – it enjoys very little substantive content that is sufficiently distinctive to remain meaningfully outside of an understanding of nationalism.

The above has been, however, a decidedly brief engagement, constituting in essence squibs as opposed to more extended and sober analysis. Such debates, as regards both progressive nationalism and populism, are sufficiently alive in today's discourse to merit some attention. But they are not, by my reckoning, sufficiently substantial for them to constitute a lengthier distraction from the more fundamental tramlines of this book.

This book decrees the prevailing nationalist clamour to be its fundamental concern. Having already established what I consider to be nationalism and its wider history as regards western Europe, the overarching focus of this book is how nationalist ways of thinking multiply all around us. The key for me, put differently, is to understand how nationalist sensibilities have managed to land and entrench themselves across a variety of often conflicting and contradictory political languages. It is this multiplicity, this criss-crossing and shrill ideological clamour, that constitutes a vital node of analysis as regards a reckoning with the contemporary political moment, a moment when liberal, neoliberal, conservative and left-wing rationales, idioms and affects are all made to dance to the nationalist song. It is these respective ideological registers, each granted a berth of its own, that will be unpacked in the following chapters.

3

Valuing the nation: liberalism, Muslims and nation-state values

A special brand of not uninviting hubris swept through political theory in the 1990s and early 2000s. Much has already been said elsewhere about the more general 'end of history' thesis and its claims about the triumph of liberal market democracies. But a less noted parallel current was a similarly confident claim about the nature of democratic nationalism. This was the claim regarding a historical shift towards a *civic* nationalism, wherein a liberal value base respectful of difference would set the broader conceptual parameters of what defines the nation and its citizenry. This turn to 'civic nationalism' was tempting insofar as it broke from more ethnically construed conceptions of the polity. This marked a welcome departure from the privileging of ethnic coherence as the precondition for collective citizenship. Ever since nineteenth-century Romanticism gave nationhood its initial contours, an emphasis on ethnic coherence had remained pre-eminent – this being the assorted metaphysical pretences of national belonging as rooted in the 'primordial' and 'culturalist' guises of ethnicism.[1] The mooted turn to the civic was finally putting such pretences under stress. Time was seemingly being called on the conception of the nation that had hitherto traded on a poetics of a 'people that always were, and will forever be'.

This 'civic values' turn was, of course, tempting to anybody wanting to render democratic citizenship more inclusive, a conception of political citizenship that would finally reflect the always diverse populations that the borders of the nation-state contain, as opposed to a conception of nation that traffics only in a majoritarian fantasy where the nation-state acts primarily as an institutional and symbolic expression of the 'authentic' majority's right to priority. The intellectual genealogy of the civic nationalism turn is a broad one. Some even trace it back to Renan's defining commentary in

'What is a Nation?', while also finding a particularly substantive anchoring in Friedrich Meinecke's turn-of-the-century distinction between the state-nation (read political) and the cultural-nation (read ethnic).[2] These early primers aside, the more meaningful reawakening of this distinction is typically attributed to the early 1990s onwards. And although Anthony Smith formally advanced such a civic/ethnic distinction in 1986, its more popular intellectual purchase obtained only in the next decade, finding in time a prominent groove within the political science study of nationalism, some of the better-known examples being Hollinger's call for a 'postethnic nation', Ignatieff's *Blood and Belonging* and Habermas's arguments in *The Postnational Constellation* about 'constitutional patriotism'.[3]

Habermas's position here is not uninteresting. His plea for a European (but also reunified Germany) project that was genuinely radical in democratic spirit drew a strong distinction between the civic and the ethnic, positing the European Union as needing to generate solidarities among its disparate constituents around a set of constitutional principles and procedures. This would result in a new democratic polity that would not simply pool the constitutive nation-states into a Gaullist 'Europe of fatherlands', redundant as that would be, but would instead demarcate a radical rupture in how the politics of community was defined and done.[4] Habermas's advocacy for a European Constitution, in his prominent capacity as a public intellectual, was particularly indicative of the pre-eminent status he accorded to the institutionalisation of a civic political allegiance at a European level: what he described as the prospective manifestation of 'a democratic constitutional state whose integrity is generated through the willing political participation of its citizens'.[5] Habermas traces here the historical transition of European political organisation from 'local and dynastic' to the nation-state form, a transition that helped shape and ground a democratic consciousness.[6] He accordingly posits that it is entirely reasonable to suppose that social contracts will further mature, given that 'the democratic order does not inherently need to be mentally ordered in "the nation"'.[7] Or, as Bauman states in the same context, it is mistaken to take the most recent expression of political consciousness (the nation-state) to be the most elevated form of 'social union/integration'. 'The European Union will not be and cannot be an enlarged copy of a nation-state, just as nation-states were not and could not be bigger versions of estates or parishes.'[8] It must instead reveal a qualitative shift.

To be fair, what Habermas and Bauman were hinting at here is a generally amorphous but still radical hope of simply something else; a future something else that is in part liberal but also exceeds liberalism: for Habermas, a renewed democratic framework that is radically deliberative in form; for Bauman, a rejection of the acquisitive individualism that modern political culture rests upon. It is, however, also clear that such a positioning becomes decidedly more normatively loaded when Western countries were described in some readings as being *already* 'post-ethnic'. This reading into the *present* of such a post-ethnic ideal, as an already tangible reality, in turn did something altogether different to what Habermas and Bauman were pointing to. This claim is much less about a critical political direction for the future, and much more about self-satisfied ethnic triumph as regards the present.[9]

Though now better known for a hapless tenure as leader of Canada's Liberals, Michael Ignatieff suggested in his defining *Blood and Belonging* that France and the United States already demonstrate this civic nationalist ideal: 'A community of equals, rights-bearing citizens, united in a patriotic attachment to a shared set of political practices and values.'[10] Elsewhere, Will Kymlicka suggested that in post-war Western democracies there was an ongoing 'shift towards a post ethnic and thus civic form of nationalism'.[11] Again, if being charitable, we might want to say that such comments are best read as fairly gestural and essentially hopeful statements, warts and all. But these are nevertheless slips that start to make more proximate the 'Eurocentric' terms by which a civic claim to the nation starts to do a decidedly different discursive and ideological work.[12] This is less about an ideal that is more inclusive in its sense of democratic polity, and instead starts to rehearse an already established form of ethnic superiority as appropriate for a decidedly liberal sensibility. It is a form of nationalism that might not pass muster in the trenches of far-right nativism, but enjoys the ostensibly reasonable and polite air that appeals to cabinet offices, the corridors of thinktanks and publishers, and becomes the generic stuff of suburban dinner-table conversation.[13]

We should not forget that it is precisely this ethnically coded distinction that does so much heavy lifting for contemporary new nationalist alarmism, and in particular for contemporary populists and their penchant for liberal pontification vis-à-vis the spectre of Islam. Put frankly, the very act of claiming such a civic mandate for the nation is an important discursive instrument through which an ethnic community is able to confirm for itself a civilisational mastery of liberal objectivity, a mastery that is in turn tied to the political object that they remain most wedded to: the nation. In other words, it engineers a narration of ethnic telos that confers upon the normative citizen an innate quality of neutrality and objective political reason. Or, as is put succinctly by Jason Read, paraphrasing Balibar's unflinching interrogation of civic nationalism: 'the very idea that one's own nation has transcended [ethnic] nationalism is itself a kind of [ethnic] nationalism'.[14]

Liberal nationalism and integration

Let us put this more precisely. Those racialised denizens who fall outside the parameters of a pre-given, automated body politic (i.e. the white ethnic majority seen as constitutive of the nation) are said to encounter liberal democracy from a position of want or lack, a liberal deficit that becomes particularly acute when mobilised vis-à-vis the problem that the contemporary Muslim poses to the civic state. In other words, racialised minorities are intuitively represented as having to learn and adopt these liberal principles that are definitive of the nation. The presupposed white citizen is instilled, by default, with a civic, universalist ethos while the racialised citizen, first-generation *and* otherwise, *acquires* these qualities. This partly explains why and how the concept of integration does so much work in today's nationalist repertoire. Recall here the tonic of 'muscular liberalism' that David Cameron famously touted in Munich when delivering a speech that was, tellingly, about Muslims, terrorism and failed integration.[15] This was allusive of the self-satisfied reading of the nation as a stable, coherent and enlightened entity into which minorities are tasked with the practical and moral burden of integrating.[16] It is a form of nationalist posturing that is often captured in contemporary social theory as being the politics of 'civic integrationism', the underlying assumption being that the relevant ethnic minority is, in its original unreconstructed state, meaningfully inadequate vis-à-vis the values emblematic of the nation.[17]

In the UK context, this increased recourse to the value of integration was again made 'aggressively' apparent in Dame Louise Casey's 2016 report entitled 'A Review into Opportunity and Integration'.[18] This review, commissioned by the government, was preoccupied with charting the many liberal deficits that primarily Muslim communities were putatively suffering from, and for all its affected grandstanding about speaking hard truths, the report was in fact simply another iteration of much of the policy intervention and political hyperventilation that suffused the post-2001, post north-west riots era in British politics.[19] European sociology too, having entertained various detours via both contiguous and oppositional concepts such as cohesion, multi- and inter-culturalism, and cosmopolitanism, has resettled on integration as a substantive ideal vis-à-vis multi-ethnic cohabitation.[20] This rehabilitation is, of course, prompted by broader new nationalist political fashions, of particular prominence being the emphatic pronouncement that multiculturalism 'has failed'.[21] An early primer of this return to an emboldened attachment to integration was the spate of centre-right authorities (e.g. Cameron, Merkel and the Council of Europe) rallying to announce multiculturalism's 'failure' and 'death', reasserting in turn the need for ethnic minorities to 'melt into one national community'.[22] Within this context of multiculturalism's rhetorical repudiation, integration, its alleged antonym, re-entered the political and academic imagination, refurnished with panacean properties as appropriate for an era of renewed ethno-nationalist belligerence.

Needless to say, it is the Muslim who is the primary negative object of these assorted integrationist declamations. Indeed, as was observed when time was initially being called on multiculturalism, this was often less a 'crisis of multiculturalism' but rather a 'Muslim crisis'.[23] To paraphrase Rancière, Muslims are often presented as 'floating' citizens whose status is provisional and indeterminate.[24] They must be thus either denied access (through immigration controls) or reformed (acculturated) in order to realise the civic ethos and principles of liberal equality that render them literate members of the national culture. Some have argued that any such touting of an integrationist ethos might be primarily rhetorical, insofar as governmental hostility to multiculturalism has not necessarily seen the withdrawal of basic faith-based rights regarding worship, education and protection from formal discrimination and 'hate crimes' that Muslim citizens can, in theory, still access.[25] But this integrationist posturing, often in concert with a security doctrine, remains the heavily worn rhetorical framework through which the wider demagoguery against Muslims often finds its fullest and most inextricable discursive footing.[26] This is a demagoguery that renders fraught many Muslim people's experiences in civic and professional life while also upholding the proliferating security-state measures that target Muslim communities. And, as regards the more immediate emphasis of this book, this integrationist lens remains fundamental to generating the wider public impression that the nation is contending with a malignant deluge of an alien, outsider population.

The presumed liberal inadequacy of the Muslim has found many paths of late, ranging from the alleged hollowing out of secularism to the increasingly loud hectoring about the supposed repression of free speech. These are arguments that reach from *Spiked*, to the folksy but outspoken comedian Jonathan Pie, to intellectuals gone public such as Sam Harris, Richard Dawkins and the late Christopher Hitchens. Much of this will recur throughout this chapter. But what might be most straightforward here, in terms of making apparent how the presentation of perceived threats to the national order regularly assumes a series of liberal sensibilities, concerns the theme of Muslims vis-à-vis gender.

The purported 'problem of integration'[27] so central to contemporary European narrations of nation has increasingly utilised the Muslim woman as the 'victim' in whose name it wages liberal warfare.[28] Particularly important here are the news cycles that periodically foreground issues such as the burka and/or hijab, FGM, forced marriages, so-called 'honour killings', gender segregation in schools, handshake etiquette and various other excesses that Muslim men/culture are documented as being perpetrators of. Needless to say, these same critics remain deafeningly silent when the actual well-being of Muslim women is at stake, and particularly so when the struggles of Muslim women are fronted in a manner that does not identify Islam or Muslim men as the culpable agents. The force of the threat that the Muslim man poses becomes all the more foetid when the (imagined) female victim is white. Such a dynamic was particularly apparent in the wake of the 'grooming gangs' revelations in the UK, and also in how the 2015/16 New Year's Eve Cologne incident swept the news waves.[29] And yet again, a marked insincerity manifests here in terms of an actual politics of care vis-à-vis the female victims, even when white. For instance, very few of the frothing commentators seemed at all exercised about the general issues of social care, stigmatisation and destitution that had rendered many of the abused working-class girls so exposed to male exploitation. Similarly, these commentators failed to connect such brutal projections of male violence to other comparable issues: for example, the abuse scandals in the Catholic Church, institutional disregard at the BBC regarding similar abuses, police cover-ups when investigating such accusations, and, at the very least, the more general systemic scourge of sexual violence and sex trafficking.[30]

The decidedly *instrumental* value of gender freedoms in affirming the non-integrated status of the minority ethnic subject has been mapped by a series of critical feminist works – for instance, Bhattacharyya's *Dangerous Brown Men*, Puar's development of the concept of 'homonationalism', Scott's commentary on the gender politics of the veil and French republicanism, Butler's analysis of how torture and war become framed as progressive ventures in the name of sexual freedoms, and Farris's recent working of the concept of 'femonationalism'.[31] All of these speak to the centrality of a putatively liberal feminist symbolism in the determining of renewed European nationalisms, a symbolism that writes itself upon the colonial script that Spivak memorialised as the project of 'white men saving brown women from brown men'.[32]

Seen in these terms, Muslims, as misogynistic by their very disposition, are ascribed a unique cultural property that renders their position in the civic polity subject to scrutiny and disquiet. It is, of course, possible that the white 'native' too might disavow or fail in his commitment to liberal principles of gender equality. However, this position of inadequacy is the Muslim Other's default position. For this reason, they must arrive at the civic, liberal position, while 'the indigenous' is already there. Put differently, the sexism of the Muslim is always by virtue of his being Muslim, while the normative subject, who is spared such interrogation, is either not considered to be sexist in the first place, or is seen as being sexist only in his own individual capacity. As Sara Ahmed put it, 'homophobia [is] viewed as *intrinsic* to Islam, as a cultural attribute, but homophobia in the West would be viewed as *extrinsic*, as an individual attribute'.[33] The integrationist posturing as sourced in a liberal calculus is therefore a complex one. It sets up an evidently exclusionary remit, but does so while fronting a particularly compelling and emotionally rousing defence of freedom and justice: in this particular instance, the freedom of women and sexual minorities.

This liberal integrationist position obtains another level of complexity that merits attention. This concerns the paradoxical simultaneity of expulsion/inclusion as regards the liberal nation. Deepa Kumar's theorisation of liberal Islamophobia grapples well with this particular mechanism, an argument that bears a productive affinity with the wider critical literature on the 'post-race' conceit.[34] Kumar observes how this liberal form of exclusion draws particular normative energy from its ability to extol individual minorities. In a manner analogous to Mamdani's 'good Muslim–bad Muslim' argument,[35] Kumar observes how the complexity of liberal exclusion trades on a particular form of selective accommodation that plays heavily on various intertwining tropes: for example, the model minority, the good immigrant and, of course, the moderate Muslim. Liberal racisms have hereby a particular dexterity as regards how structural exclusion pivots on an individualised inclusion. While conservative visions of the nation posit a more deeply marked and unbridgeable cultural gulf between national subject and minority, immigrant Other, the liberal version remains more nimble and duplicitous. By presenting the liberal repertoire as something that can be ably acquired, many minorities are presented as perfectly credible, indeed commendable denizens of the nation. Importantly, however, such accommodations still fundamentally operate from the core nation–Other pivot (when seen in neo-imperial terms, as Kumar does regarding the US-led war ventures, this is the reheating of the 'White Man's Burden' imperative). It is only as individuals that such subjects become authorised as integrated national subjects, while racialised minorities, *qua* groups, remain collective bodies exogenous to the liberal nation. This individualised accommodation becomes further fraught owing to the various classed resources at the disposal of those minority subjects endowed with a liberal status – resources such as professional and educational attainment, deportment, attire, accent and lifestyle.[36] It is also an individualised accommodation that trades on the identity position (i.e. Muslim) under scrutiny having to serially prove itself to the adjudicating gaze. As was put searchingly by the actor Riz Ahmed in a defining essay, the subject marked as Muslim is always on 'audition';[37] or, to revisit the ever-haunting language of Fanon, the accommodated subject is always 'close to disgrace'.[38]

More than only Muslim

To reiterate, it is the figure of the Muslim who comes to be seen as a particularly ominous and disposable subject within this liberal register of civic nationalism. The Muslim becomes paradigmatic of the 'inassimilable' subject when set against such criteria of civic, liberal nationhood. This has become particularly apparent in how the new far-right draws its popularity in places such as Sweden, the country of my own upbringing.[39] But it is worth bearing in mind, in light of the other concepts of 'cultural' and 'new' racism that suffuse this book, that this liberal framework by which integration acts as a means to police the nation does notionally exceed the Muslim and carries a broader racialised logic as appropriate to the contemporary.

'Cultural racism' is perhaps best summarised as the terms by which subjects racialised as different are assigned particular cultural features and connotations. It is the essentialised 'culture talk' through which racialised outsider communities are ascribed a set of putative characteristics and habits that are seen to constitute some form of cultural pathology and/or incompatibility.[40] At the risk of simplifying a little too breezily, it might be argued here that racism in the contemporary (often theorised as 'post-racial' racism, or 'racism without racists') is rarely presented as discrimination on account of race and ethnicity in itself.[41] Indeed, it is the official narrowing of racism to this particular criterion of explicit hatred and discrimination as premised on skin colour alone that makes it so easy for those propagating racist discourse and practice to dodge such accusations. As opposed to it being a programme of explicit aversion for its own sake, racism aspires to a nobler and inviting mandate. In short, racism is commonly presented as a defensive wager as regards security, stability, productivity; and, of course, as is particularly apparent in this liberal vein through which racisms become 'laundered',[42] racisms are asserted and affirmed in the name of freedom itself – the freedom of the individual, the freedom of the property-owning entrepreneur, the freedom of the low-income wage-labourer, the freedom of speech, the freedom of women, the freedom of sexual minorities, the freedom of conscience, and so forth.[43] The defining *cultural* properties and dispositions ascribed to various racialised outsider groups are in turn asserted as being adversarial to and/or incompatible with these core freedoms, virtues and imperatives.[44] Seen in these terms – where the political object is not perceived as being hatred but rather an affirmation of liberal freedom and culture – racism ably obtains a common-sense rationale. It becomes a 'lay ideology', as Kundnani proposes, that can produce and excuse certain inequalities, oppressions and/or exclusions on account of the supposed cultural tendencies relevant to the group in question. In other words, race is invested with cultural (ethnic) assignations.[45]

Another way of putting this is that, as far as liberal discourse is concerned, it is only the foreigner, racially inscribed, who has ethnicity. Foreigners become the bearers of ethnicity (as a set of cultural properties) while the domestic majority masquerades as the 'neutral' position. The majority is governed by universal values while the racialised outsider is weighed down by the parochialism of a particularised ethnic culture. As Lentin and Titley state, 'Liberals [can purport to] address all human beings, whilst wearing universalism as a badge of transcendent identity, [only] because, to paraphrase Du Bois, they have never been forced to wear any other.'[46] Ethnicity and race are accordingly collapsed here, doing much of the same, mutually reinforcing political work. Or to paraphrase Alexander's comments in a somewhat different context, ethnicity and culture are, within the liberal register, the burden of race.[47] White Europeans are in this context often relieved of an ethnic character, acting only as free individuals. Racialised Others, however, are weighed down by the clutter and paraphernalia of culture – culture that disposes them to particular values and priorities that require redress if the liberal calling of history is to be properly embraced.

Of course, the idea of redress remains in many important aspects disingenuous – if already problematic on its own terms of naturalising the distinction of native host and minority guest while also 'reifying' racialised attributions of culture. There is no real conviction here that this redress can ever be realised in any meaningful sense. Instead, the liberal purposing of integration problematises, *a priori*, the racialised community's inability to disappear, provoking in turn a tautology: the very fact that a minority community is identifiable (as significant) is presented as evidence of the respective minority's inability to integrate, as being 'incurably alien'.[48] This condition of incurable cultural viscosity exercises in the normative national psyche an acute fear about the consequences of this encroachment into the civic body of a permanently Other culture.[49] That the Muslim has been made today into a particularly forceful Other – the exemplar of the proverbial 'allochtoon' to borrow from the Dutch taxonomy[50] – reveals in turn liberalism's particularly decisive role when drawing such culturalised lines of civic belonging to nation. Put differently, and as will be discussed in what follows, the Muslim, through the historically capacious back catalogue of religion and purportedly pre-Enlightenment civilisation that the figure is made to embody, is made to service this liberal brand of cultural racism in a particularly expansive and effective manner.[51]

Revisiting the Orientalist legacy

There are a number of rather obvious but nonetheless important themes through which this process of liberal nationalism can be documented – what Kundnani captured, simply and concisely, as the entrenchment of 'values racism'.[52] These include the aforementioned 'faux-feminist' demonisation of Muslims.[53] It also involves the weaponisation of an entirely imagined endangering of free speech and secularism that the accommodation of Muslim demands engenders. Note for instance that those decrying the putative erosion of free speech are actually decrying the excess of free speech available to critics. Put simply, the free speech warriors are exercised primarily by the fact that others are able to deploy the free speech affordances available to them in order to confront the commentary and platforms that they believe to be demeaning. Equally, a reflection on liberal nationalism would also take note of how a strong defensive assertion of liberalism precipitates a raft of ostensibly illiberal programmes; the extreme version of this being a suite of coerced integration injunctions alongside draconian counter-security programmes whose entire remit rests on Muslims, once rendered a 'suspect community', being stripped of certain liberal protections, not least the right to citizenship.[54]

Much of this will recur in this chapter as it unfolds. I wish, however, to first engage this discussion by revisiting the historical foundations of which this contemporary working of an anti-Muslim pathology is such an obvious iteration. It is clear after all that much of what is being hinted at here belongs to a wider historical tradition of Orientalism (a concept that inevitably lurks throughout this book but is not always made explicitly visible).

An exposition of what we mean by Orientalism would often begin and end with Edward Said.[55] In the interests of avoiding such repetition, I wish to indulge here a different point of departure, namely Alain Grosrichard's somewhat neglected exposition of the eighteenth-century French intelligentsia's *fantastical* representation of Ottoman Sultanate rule, which for me is at once an entertaining but also summarily portentous account of how the denial of the Muslim Other's civic and liberal faculties was central to consolidating a particular European self-presentation of nation and nationhood (what Medevoi has described as being the long history of 'dogmaline racism').[56] Published just a year after Said's landmark *Orientalism*, Grosrichard's *The Sultan's Court* offers us a particularly focused historical lens through which to centre the character and tenor of contemporary Islamophobia vis-à-vis the assertion of national belonging.[57]

Grosrichard shows how the fantastical tropes that figured large in French artistic, literary and philosophical invocations of the Ottoman reached for an interlocking set of emphases on violence, sex and governance. Ottoman administration was, for instance, attributed a beguiling whimsicality and arbitrariness. Coupled to this was a seemingly insatiable proclivity for carnal pleasures. Indeed, navigating an intricate labyrinth of codes and taboos concerning the scores of odalisques adorning every recess of the harem compound is at times presented as the primary 'legal' occupation of the Sultan, viziers and other high-ranking officials. The alleged absence of systematically codified legal parameters (let alone a meaningful conception of secular law) for the administration of the domain at large, alongside the habitual recourse to brutish displays of violence, were presented in French intellectual output as the principal distinguishing features of the Sultan's rule. In short, hedonism and 'Oriental despotism' prevail amid the abject absence of the rule of law, of constitutional checks, of norms of equality, and the absence of an ethos of collective betterment.[58]

A stubbornly unreconstructed Orientalist reader might venture here that Ottoman decision-making structures were in fact so, or something to that effect. Any such facile charge would warrant only an appropriately flippant response. After all, Suleiman is not immortalised in popular history as the 'Lawgiver' for nothing – his carefully administered signature/stamp ('tughra') being widely recognised as symptomatic of a particularly efficient bureaucratic and institutional structure of regulation and law. Nevertheless, as Subrahmanyam alleges in his frustrated take on the fashion for textual inquiry that masquerades as historical analysis – allegedly precipitated by Said and Grosrichard – many exponents of the 'overblown' textual turn seem to forget that there were 'actually societies out there and they were constituted politically even outside the European Imagination'.[59] While accepting the charge, we should note that Said himself is adamant on this very point. As he frequently states, the object of his study was the emergence of an 'idea', the emergence and institutionalisation of a myth about something called the Orient.[60] Or, as far as Grosrichard's take is concerned, it is the French 'fantasy' of the East, and the Seraglio in particular, that he is psychoanalytically interested in. The point is that it is not particularly interesting whether this idea or myth bears a relationship, even an adulterated or bastardised one, to any existing reality. The written and visual text therefore constitutes a valid analytical interface in its own right, as an imagery and 'regime of representation'[61] encoded with certain evaluative frames that shapes a governmental imagination and, in turn, its ethical and political judgements. The fact that a reality exists, independently of this idea, is in itself immaterial.

Grosrichard's work gestures accordingly at the manner in which such taxonomies concerning Ottoman governmental systems are not about 'reality', but are about furthering a hegemonic objective. It is essentially about *self-presentation*, a foil by which to draw the parameters of the collective, the civilisational, the national.[62] After all, many regimes could be described as simultaneously liberal and despotic, and necessarily so: liberal violence is, among other things, the method by which the liberal freedoms of the normative subject can in the first place be obtained, maintained and safeguarded.[63] But by bracketing 'ourselves' (France/Europe) as *only* liberal, as only rational, injustice becomes the preserve of the elsewhere, the way of illiberal Muslims over there. As Mladen Dolar summarises Grosrichard's argument,

> [Eighteenth-century France was the time] of spectacular endeavours proposing a rationally based society, a new concept of state, civil society, democratic liberties, citizenship, division of power, and so on; but in a strange counterpoint, there was the image of Oriental despotism as the very negative of those endeavours, their phantasmic Other.[64]

At the representational level, the Ottoman – unable to envisage a notion of rational universalism and uninterested in inculcating a diffuse civic code of political conduct – is read, quite naturally, as inferior. Indeed, as mentioned before, Montesquieu's concept of Oriental despotism in the *Persian Letters*, which was originally an intricate epistolary device through which to deride Regency France, became in quick time a popular lens by which to characterise 'Asiatic regimes' in a more general sense – a concept that maintains a significant influence upon the intuitive political assessments of today.[65] This has been partly captured in contemporary political theory by Thomas Pogge through his coinage of the concept of 'explanatory nationalism' – a concept that he uses to account for how liberal policymakers in the West intuitively reflect upon the seemingly intractable global inequality divide.[66] (For 'Oriental despotism' see 'banana republics' and 'failed states', the absence of accountability or the 'rule of law', the deference to kleptocratic national elites, and the entrenched 'culture of corruption'.)

The world of ideas that Grosrichard and others described is not, however, to be equated with a total dismissal of the Ottoman mode of power. On the contrary, Orientalism always drew on an arresting paradox, a paradox of desire and repulsion. There was after all much that was alluring for French high society in the Orient. This gaze delights in the male assertion of authoritarian sexual power, in the inviting excess of passively sequestered women, in the abundance of capricious violence and, finally, in the unhurried exotic ease that is absolute power's most alluring property. But alluring is the operative term here. It is seen as a titillating 'fantasy' of power that is, in the final reckoning, contradictory to a society committed to progress, reason and the 'common good'. As Grosrichard takes care to explain, an attraction to such lifestyles was only to ever be indulged momentarily and never to be seen as worthwhile when contrasted to the first-order values of liberal reason readily manifest in 'our' domestic European realm.

This mechanism of titillation by excess, an excess that while arousing and fecund also allows white distinction to be reinforced, comes across particularly well in nineteenth-century art. Somewhat marginal to Said's own commentary, Orientalism was a well-established artistic tradition in its own right and was specifically designated as such. Orientalism, in this specific context, was not a particular technique but denoted a cluster of subject themes. Hence, the expressive Romanticism of Delacroix, the Neoclassicism of Ingres and the saccharine Academicism of Gérôme all fell, on different occasions, under the appellation of Orientalism. Their unity concerns the subject matter portrayed – scenes allegedly sourced from actual 'Oriental' life. In short, the designation was anthropological, as opposed to aesthetic.

The representational standards central to this genre revelled in radiant displays of wanton colour, lounging, docile women, some hint of homoeroticism and pederasty, and a life of languorous ease and enjoyment. However, alongside the much-fetishised harem (within which the regular depictions of enslaved *white* women was testament to the projection of a particularly lascivious European male gaze), there were also a number of paintings that detailed political life, where the Seraglio courts and the norms governing political practice were given thematic prominence.[67]

One such work that overtly centred themes of governance was painted by the now largely forgotten Henri Regnault. The title of the painting – which vividly shows a monumental 'Moor' wielding a sword and standing in stately fashion above a freshly decapitated corpse (the newly shed blood runs in a brilliant dark red) – is itself indicative: *Execution* without *Trial under the Moorish Kings of Granada* (emphasis added). Interesting here is the infatuation with the prevalent practice of extra-judicial summary killing seen as customary to the Orient, whereby nineteenth-century eyes would feast on this intimation of violent melodrama that contrasted so starkly with the civilised ideals of liberal political practice they had arrogated for themselves.

On a less visually kitsch level but equally significant in political terms is Delacroix's 1826 *Greece on the Ruins of Missolonghi*, a visual schema that ties the figurative language of Romantic nationalism to a wider civilisationism that continues to suffuse the 'West and the rest' distinction as active today. The bloody campaign in the early nineteenth century for Greek self-determination – which is allegorically rendered in the painting – had stirred much support among the European left, the struggle being read as one for liberty and being popularly ascribed an incipient republican spirit denied to the Greeks by Ottoman authoritarianism. In the painting, we see the female personification of Greece standing atop the debris resulting from the latest Ottoman massacre, gesturing plaintively as their noble aspiration is yet again thwarted, while a steely dark-skinned Ottoman soldier clutching his standard is glimpsed triumphant in the background. Not incidentally I believe, the female model for Greece is likely the very same as she who embodies the revived spirit of egalitarian republicanism in Delacroix's fabled homage to the failed French revolution of 1830, *Liberty Leading the People*.[68]

Delacroix accordingly projects upon the Greek cause the nascent traces of a universalist political undertaking, while the Ottoman figure represents the grim alternative of tyrannical despotism.[69] This is not to say that his sympathies were misplaced. Indeed, it was in many ways a dignified struggle for national self-determination typical of the Romantic spirit.[70] But the wider

82

political identification with the Greek cause also traded on a representational standard that was indicative of the wider Orientalist ontology that was by then taking a more full-bodied shape. As Febbraro and Schwetje state, 'Europe's intellectuals and artists and patriots, all of them supported the Hellenic cause – considered a people's struggle for freedom – against the Turks, who were equated with cruel and inhuman barbarity.'[71] The sympathisers with the Greek struggle comprised here a combination of Constitutionalists, republicans, nationalists, proto-anarchists and proto-socialists – notable supporters being Lord Byron, Santorre di Santarosa and the Vicomte de Chateaubriand. Byron eventually died in Greece, having journeyed down like many others to assist in the heroic campaign – a death that occasioned a nigh unprecedented round of public mourning back in Britain.

Notwithstanding Greece, what is important for the more immediate purposes of this chapter is that such art was indicative of a wider representational field where the allegedly 'Oriental' political order was denied any conception of justice remotely approximate to the nascent expression of liberal republicanism that was seen as the teleological preserve of Europe. But Orientalism also resonated particularly well because it staged a complex temporal split regarding the European conceptions of nationhood. The broader story in Romantic-era Europe was one of nations discovering their moment of self-determination, vacating in turn a timeless past of illiberal subjugation, a past that was once Europe's own intimate reality – pre-nationhood, pre-liberal republicanism – but was now the preserve of the non-European elsewhere. To again call upon the lessons of art history, it is interesting that Gérôme, at the time the most celebrated of the painters formally designated as Orientalists, alternated his *oeuvre* with dramatically clichéd scenes from a Roman past, these often constituting gory tales featuring sensationalist examples of violence as staged in the Colosseum. This twinning of the Orientalist with the dramatic violence of Rome is interesting. The imaging of a different time – once ours, now only elsewhere – exercised I believe a distinctive claim on the European nineteenth-century gaze, a claim that was able to draw an intimate familiarity with our own historic kin echoing from a lost past, but a past that was declared void and irrational and was now the preserve of Muslims over there. Put more theoretically, the visual scheme active in the Orientalist register exploited a picturing of the irrational brutality of the Muslim East, whose politics of the past affirms the calling of a progressive civic present and future – a civic order around which the European nation coheres.

The circulation of such visual repertoires made it reasonable to consider certain Other figures as inferior 'subject races'.[72] Such depictions served and reproduced in turn a distinct ideological function. They staged a distinctly colonial framework through which the self-described liberal nation could deliver its own requisite exclusionary and extractive violence.[73]

The contemporary

The Ottoman, which I have employed here as a proxy for the wider sense of the Muslim Other (though we should not take the two as being wholly coterminous), was presented as being ill-disposed to cultivate those civic virtues constitutive of an enlightened liberal order. The contemporary exclusion, subjugation, demonisation and/or call to a civilising reconstitution (see 'integration' discourses or the doctrine of humanitarian intervention as targeted against the Middle East/North Africa) rest on a historical replay of this rationale. When the contemporary assertion of nation calls upon the ennobling coordinates of liberalism, it becomes logical to intuitively resent the presence of those figures who are made to appear constitutionally averse to those very values. But, as was customary to the broader Orientalist play, this denigration of Muslim illiberalism is itself coupled to a certain phantasmic and affective regard for Muslim illiberalism. This is a regard that often sublimates into an arresting and shameful sense of sexual frisson and violence, but, elsewhere, sublimates into something more akin to a nostalgic longing – a form of regard that is sourced in the titillating attribution of an exploitative misogyny,[74] in the attribution of a brutal but cunning and disciplined call to religious violence, and perhaps most invitingly, in the attribution of a thickly textured sense of community, faith and cultural cohesiveness. The latter recalls a communal idyll that white modernity has forfeited, in the interests of progress, but has failed to mourn.[75] I do think then that this double play lends liberal nationalism a particularly strong credibility in the mind and body of the relevant agent. Namely, in repressing this form of guilty misidentification, the theatre of steadfastly upholding liberal values takes on an added political heroism. The white European is endowed with a strange impression of being historically obliged to champion the pre-eminence of the liberal project, in spite of the other, more base and tempting callings characteristic of the human condition that the Muslim is made to embody. The commitment to liberal individualism becomes here a heroic, transcendent and stoic form of self-abnegation. In short, the historical project that the liberal purports to bear takes on an ennobling air of civilising sacrifice.

The nation-state is hereby not being fortified in the interest of racist assertion for its own violent sake. It is instead the mobilisation of a liberal common sense rooted in European imperialism that sees the transcendent value order constitutive of the nation being gravely endangered by the excess of typically Muslim outsiders who call the country home but are not of the nation. This then becomes an entirely sanctioned, eminently *reasonable* form of nation-state Othering that exercises a particular strong draw for those often middle-class types who style themselves as polite, moderate and worldly – types who are instinctively averse to the classed vulgarity of far-right activism and similarly unreconstructed claims to the overt logics of racial hierarchy and inferiority.

We have seen a bona fide intellectual industry emerge that is singularly devoted to chronicling the incompatibility of Muslims with what constitutes a liberal future: the Muslim threat to secularism, the Muslim threat to women, the Muslim threat to gay rights, the Muslim threat to young girls, the Muslim threat to free speech and the Muslim threat to even the rights of animals – the allowances made for halal meat production having become of late a particularly disingenuous front through which the illiberalism of Muslims can obtain one more invidious layer. Alma Awad recently noted that 'everyone is a feminist when it comes to Muslims'.[76] We might now add that everyone risks becoming an animal lover as well when it comes to Muslims. As Russell Brand the comedian sarcastically observed: 'If you want to avoid halal meat become a vegetarian not a racist.'[77]

But it is perhaps secularism that has become the most effective and pronounced liberal theme in upholding the 'I am not racist but Muslims are [complete as necessary]' genre of political discourse. A long list of esteemed Anglophone secularists (Sam Harris, Bill Maher, Richard Dawkins and the late Christopher Hitchens) making intellectual war on Islam has become a particularly well-worn and rating-friendly feature of evening panel show debate. Some might think people such as Hitchens and Dawkins undeserving of being bracketed in such a manner. It has, however, long been apparent that the so-called 'new atheism' that Hitchens, Dawkins and friends aggressively championed became, wittingly or unwittingly, simply an attempt to lend further credibility to the wider stereotyping of Muslims and Islam, as was partly evident in Dawkins's juvenile ranking of religions in order of vileness, an endeavour that unsurprisingly saw Islam being crowned the 'world's most evil religion'.[78] This was fully confirmed, I think, in a recent tweet that delighted in the soundscapes of church bells, which Dawkins contrasted to the din caused by the Muslim call to prayer.[79] The muscular home of Laïc anti-Muslim posturing is still perhaps France – the wider Muslim imperilling of the republican spirit formative of the nation having become a particular speciality of French publishing.[80] But this form of political positioning certainly enjoys a wider Western muscle, including a pronounced Anglophone version.

Maher, whose cultural output has a strong transatlantic purchase, is particularly interesting here owing to the ideological foundations that he often lets slip in his more bombastic moments. New atheists of his ilk certainly purport to be against all religion (this being presumably an interesting political position). But what reveals the conceit here is the different logics through which different religions are brought to reproach. The claims about Christianity, Judaism etc., are given a fairly fine specificity (Dawkins calls Christianity a moderating 'bulwark' and 'a relatively benign faith'),[81] while Islam is often singled out as a form of cultural pathology that very quickly ceases to be anything particularly concerned with religion *per se*. It is here that Muslims, in a very wide sense, become the cultural agents of a civilisational pathology. Similarly, what is telling is the form of high-minded liberal alibi that Maher so baldly resorts to, evidenced in his defence in the wake of an attempt by Ben Affleck, as it happens, to claw back against him on an episode of *Real Time*. Maher responded: 'We're liberals! We're liberals! [...] We are not bigoted people. On the contrary! We're trying to stand up for the principles of liberalism!'[82] This is a very naked ideological recourse. As will be discussed in the concluding chapter, it is interesting that much anti-Muslim radicalisation ultimately trades on the very simple interrobang: 'Do they not know what being a "real liberal" is?!'[83]

All this might be familiar, with a long list of distinguished critics making clear the liberal conceit and/or commitment that nourishes contemporary Islamophobia. This form of purported national emasculation found its literary apogee in Michel Houellebecq's novel *Submission*, a strange and allusive novel that describes a set of circumstances that sees an Islamist elected as French president.[84] The novel accordingly binds two key tropes: the gathering forces of an Islamist programme within France alongside the broader impressionable passivity of a white French majority. This surprisingly 'bemusing' literary foray into the 'Eurabia genre' and its key presuppositions had, of course, various intellectual primers that are worth mentioning.[85] One such is certainly the pugnacious Bruce Bawer's *Surrender: Appeasing Islam, Sacrificing Freedom*, the first line of which reads: 'We in the West are living in the midst of a jihad, and most of us don't even realise it.'[86] Another is Christopher Caldwell's *Reflections on the Revolution in Europe: Immigration, Islam and the West*.[87] And then, of course, there is the now ubiquitous Douglas Murray, so feted by the favoured publication outlets of the Tory right, his latest contribution to the genre being *The Strange Death of Europe: Immigration, Identity, Islam*.[88] While some of these harangues belong to a wider nationalist politics discussed elsewhere in this book, what is also decisive is the particular ideological work that the Muslim does for their arguments. Add to this the various weekly screeds of columnists in *The Times*, the *Daily Mail* and the *Telegraph*, or magazines such as *Standpoint* (which once devoted an entire issue to the 'Dark Side of Islam'),[89] and one is left with a comprehensive field of anti-Muslim postulation that calls upon the rationales of a liberal identity under threat, even if the same writers do not consistently associate themselves with a formally liberal tradition or politics. This is in turn a field of discursive prejudice that demonstrably affects the wider British public's views about Muslims and Islam.[90]

Conclusion

What is interesting, when seen along a wider historical sweep, is that this racialised weaponisation of the liberal nation is increasingly all that remains of liberalism in our current political conjuncture. Liberalism – as the staking out of a position that harnesses a commitment to individually anchored rights and freedoms with an acknowledgement of how fellow nationals' exercise of those rights is circumscribed by wider economic imperatives and inequality – is currently without a political programme.[91] Put simply, any overt attempt today at a more principled public defence of liberalism generally amounts to little more than a defence of the centrist position as an end in itself, regardless of what the centrist position actually constitutes at any given moment. This is what Müller has described as being merely a 'self-conscious espousal of moderation', regardless of what one might be moderating between.[92] That liberalism has found itself in this hollow position is not surprising, its meaning having being steadily eroded over an extended period – first, by having gradually conceded its terrain to a more formal doctrine of neoliberal economics, and secondly, by becoming sullied by the ascriptions of lifestyle elitism commonly associated with the self-satisfied professional and/or cultural classes. An orthodox programme of liberalism is therefore rarely appealed to in contemporary western Europe in any substantive sense (one has to see through the rather heavy-handed bluster of 'Macronisme' here).[93] There is little political gain to be had in doing so. To pick from the idioms typical of contemporary politics, the increased use of liberal as a euphemism for elitist, by both left and right alike, begins to hint at some of this vacated authority (though their respective characterisations of the term are, of course, amusingly contradictory). Instead, the claim to a tradition of liberalism seems only to survive, in terms of constituting an assertive programme with vernacular confidence, as a vehicle to repudiate racialised immigrants and Muslims.

It is perhaps the case that liberalism, as a wider political purpose, is fundamentally of the nineteenth century, its late twentieth-century role having been gradually usurped by neoliberalism (see Chapter 5), while its early twentieth-century guise was quelled by the redistributive and collectivist energies of socialism and social democracy. This lengthy hiatus has in turn buried any meaningful memory of the distinct radicalism of its possibilities that characterised various turns during the nineteenth century. It is up to others to determine whether they feel compelled to recover and reanimate this tradition. But what remains important is that when this task is left to self-declared liberals, they seem rather too acquiescent and, sometimes, even actively willing abettors of the concerted weaponisation of liberalism by nationalists – not properly discerning such weaponisation for the racism that it is. Or, to end on a mischievous but urgent remark once issued by *Il Giornale*, 'liberalism is far too serious to be left in the hands of the liberals'.[94]

4

Conservatism and mourning the nation

It will seem odd that a survey of nationalism's ideological presentation has not yet engaged its more formal conservative legacies. After all, contemporary nationalism is commonly reduced in popular analysis to being merely an unreconstructed conservatism, one that is nestled in the crusty recesses of boorish, right-wing politics. As has hopefully been made apparent in the preceding chapters, the reality is very different. Nationalism necessarily sources the entire political spectrum when assembling its ideological language, a spectrum within which conservatism is only one significant strand.

Similarly, it might seem surprising to disentangle neoliberalism from conservatism, given that many of those who champion neoliberal resolutions also seem to hold basic conservative talking points.[1] This too, however, is partly a misnomer. Many politicians of the right do indeed routinely press both platforms, but they do so for political gain and/or to navigate the vagaries of party politics. In actuality, the dominant strains of right politics cleave towards one of the two directions – one flank propagates aggressive neoliberal measures designed to further bolster market-society competitiveness, while the other makes a more impassioned moral defence of traditionalism.[2]

Such a distinction is, of course, too convenient, too neatly bifurcated, to be entirely accurate. However, as a blunt heuristic device, to maintain a conservatism contra neoliberalism distinction does I think move us closer to the working reality of what constitutes the contemporary nationalist right. Put differently, a more variegated feel for nationalist expression is facilitated through analytically edifying conservatism with a berth specific to it.

This becomes all the more necessary given that so many of the core impulses of contemporary conservatism do not flatly acquiesce to the broader competitive market ideals of neoliberalism. This is an important if oft-ignored reality to acknowledge. There remain a multitude of conservative themes via which appeals to cultural meaning and national identity are popularly recalled independently of a neoliberal cost–benefit analysis that is economistic in type. This chapter will accordingly map how these various modalities, through which a distinctively conservative political vision is articulated, culminate in the thickly textured and nostalgically recalled veneration of provincial Englishness, Empire and whiteness more broadly.

A conservatism beyond neoliberalism

To begin, the distinctive character of many conservative attachments is better understood when seen in terms of their partial estrangement from neoliberal orthodoxies. It is helpful to understand how some key conservative attachments act autonomously of a wider neoliberal project, and, at times, in partial hostility to such neoliberal commitments. The first section of this chapter will accordingly scan, as a simple tuning endeavour, some indicative instances of such disjointedness, ranging from NIMBY[3] protectionism to cultural elitism. Importantly, the specific question of nation and nationalism will be postponed during these initial sketches, as it is preferable to first allow conservatism, both culturally and philosophically, its own definitional remit and texture.

Consider, as an opening exercise, the Home Counties conservatives and their deep idealisation of a green and pleasant undulating England. To build further housing in the vicinity, to raise wind farms against its scenic backdrop, to allow new railway lines to cut through its hills, to allow new flight paths to trace some of its suburbs, all meet a nearly blanket opposition. This in itself is perhaps welcome, as there are many reasons to commend this brand of obstinacy, whatever the limitations of NIMBY activism. But important here is also the simple recognition that a commitment to reforms designed to aid, via speed and infrastructure, the competitiveness of British capitalism meets its limits when it threatens some of the other entitlements, privileges and comforts that dispose the rich towards conservatism. Think here of how Zac Goldsmith, as Conservative MP for the affluent Richmond Park, could parade himself as a principled critic of Heathrow's expansion plans.[4] Better yet, simply listen to Simon Jenkins, then chairman of the National Trust, and his excoriation of Cameron and Osborne's 'lack of feel for the countryside'.

I enjoyed *Private Eye*'s spoof of them and their friends travelling to Manchester the other week by train and gazing bemused out of the window. Why were all these hills and fields and trees just lying about doing nothing, when they could be subsidised wind farms, Tesco warehouses and toytown estates?[5]

Importantly, Jenkins's cutting anti-development sentiments were part of a broader lament in the *Spectator* – that bastion of well-heeled conservatism – against wind turbines and their desecration of the nation's 'best views'.

Or, as regards a rather more prosaically conservative aversion to the neoliberal present, take the critique of capitalist individualism and its inability to foster the conceptions of sacrificial and enduring *love* that is commonly attributed to the pre-1968 nuclear family.[6] A contemporary culture of self-regard and materialism is often said to have overwhelmed the virtues of patience, longevity and mutuality that the conservative husbanding of marriage previously prized. Similarly, the advance of neoliberal individualism and its broader ethos of unceasing urbanisation is occasionally perceived as eroding the authority of Christianity as well as gutting rustic England, both of which are popularly evocative of an alluringly slow family life.

Or consider the always cantankerous argumentation of Roger Scruton and his defence of a humanities canon that is being buried by the marketisation of higher education. Scruton's attack on academia is best known for its extraordinarily crude harangues against what he considers to be postmodern leftist waffle.[7] He berates a culture of self-confessed radical cultural theory that desires only to genuflect at the altar of inclusion and tolerance. Scruton's is a brand of conservative muscularity that now operates under the banner of safeguarding pure knowledge from the levelling excesses of 'political correctness' and 'identity politics'. But also apparent in some of the quieter moments of Scruton's sweeping argument is a grievance against contemporary universities' deference to business schools and the general flurry of management mantras that epitomise the 'new spirit of capitalism'.[8]

Much of this general lament turns predictably on reviving a language of civilisation as Western, grandiose and beautifying. This recourse to mythical ideals of European civilisation – as gloried in by Kenneth Clark's iconically conservative 1969 art history series – is riven with simplifications, not to mention the intolerance, contradictions and illusions that it traffics in. We could recall here the still defining quip on the subject offered by Mahatma Gandhi, who, when asked what he thought of 'Western civilisation', drolly noted that 'it would be a good idea'.[9]

But also apparent in its contemporary sense is how a culturally elitist reckoning of tradition and legacy manages to balk at much neoliberal sloganeering. It dismisses it as short-termism, unable to nourish the fundamental cultural goods that make a society whole and worthwhile. It is this tension that partly explains how neoliberal proponents of higher education's marketisation, including their advocacy of a shift away from the arcane (e.g. drama and medieval history) to more avowedly vocational, labour-market oriented degrees, can baldly hector critics for being elitists.[10] Underpinning these exchanges is not simply an opportunistic duplicity (though it is that too), but also the friction that neoliberal evangelism encounters when rubbing up against the lingering formations of paleoconservatism.

We see here in the everyday elitist reckonings with culture the residual influence of somebody like F. R. Leavis raging against the economistic instrumentalisation of a society's cultural endowment.[11] Similarly disreputable to the conservative is the crass commercialism that a capitalist culture industry allows to prevail. The cultural tastes that the market foregrounds allow for a wider degeneracy, leaving only a cultural architecture that is forgettable, simplistic, crude and sensationalist, always satisfying mass appeal while overwhelming all else in its wake. It is a culture that rewards immediacy and quick, mechanistic thrills, harnessing a philistine's disregard for the values of longevity, patience, complexity and form.

The conservative and often maudlin elegy for cricket as a particular marker of rural England is salutary here, a lament that implicitly extols cricket's gentle place in the English id.[12] A regard for cricket is something that the humanist left too will have some sympathy for.[13] But what is telling is the terms by which the conservative defence implicitly centres Matthew Arnold's enduringly conservative definition of culture as being 'the best which has been thought and said'.[14] Cricket is often raised in the conservative imagination as evocative of a country idyll where the virtues of village England are twinned to the edifying influence of elite establishment custodians, a joint governance, one homely, the other grand, that is gradually dissipating amid the assault of a commercial and sensationalist televisual culture.

Such instances of a homely cultural elitism, like the NIMBY rural pastoralism gestured at before, constitute in turn another generative site through which it is possible to isolate a partial disjuncture between what we might describe as conservatism and what will be surveyed in Chapter 5 as neoliberalism. Admittedly, these themes have been hitherto only breezily handled. The aim of this opening section is to give some initial sense of how to treat conservatism as a *distinctive* political culture vis-à-vis the neoliberal commercialism otherwise ascendant as far as right politics is concerned.

However, as noted in Owen Hatherley's *Ministry of Nostalgia* and Arun Kundnani's reading of 'Powellism', it is still certainly the case that conservatism and neoliberalism converge in some important ways, whereby an ideological appeal to conservatism often helps secure the legitimacy of neoliberalism.[15] This uneasy compact is ably theorised in Wendy Brown's 'American Nightmare', though concerning the slightly different context of a Christianist neoconservatism in the United States. Brown notes that while neoliberalism and neoconservatism represent 'two different political rationalities that have few overlapping formal features', there manifests a shared commitment to override the broader 'culture and institutions of constitutional democracy'.[16] Put differently, Brown observes how, under the Bush administration, a seemingly contradictory commitment to both projects was foregrounded, sutured together by a shared affinity for more authoritarian governmental practices: an unaccountable and technocratic state imposing neoliberal reforms on the one hand, and, on the other, the empowerment of the revanchist 'moral-religious' state to dilute the constitutional protections that certain minority constituencies had recently won.[17]

This dual orientation of the political right, in the US but also elsewhere in the West, is not inefficacious. But as Brown also hints, this formation is predicated on an ideological disjointedness that is perhaps becoming increasingly visible in our popular discourse. It is the possibilities of this widening split or cleaving that interest me. As John Gray notes, the habitual claim to tradition while propagating neoliberalism, a move central to Thatcherism's political legitimacy, trades on a fundamental and irreconcilable contradiction. Gray observes that

[Thatcher] fully shared Hayek's view that free markets reinforce 'traditional values', which is an inversion of their actual effect. The conservative country of which she dreamed had more in common with Britain in the 1950s, an artefact of Labour collectivism, than it did with the one that emerged from her free-market policies. A highly mobile labour market enforces a regime of continuous change. The type of personality that thrives in these conditions is the opposite of the stolid, dutiful bourgeois Thatcher envisioned.[18]

This paradox is very well observed. As will be discussed in Chapter 5, it was certainly possible at a certain conjuncture for neoliberalism to manoeuvre itself, as a political rationale, into the cultural slipstream of conservative narrations of petit bourgeois traditionalism. It is, however, increasingly apparent, four decades after Thatcherism's initial forays, that the more avowedly conservative vision of society has been steadily disentangling itself from this co-option. It is accordingly prudent, for the purposes of this chapter, to allow a common conservatism the unique ideological positioning that it often occupies.

Tradition, nation and new racism

Disentangling conservatism from neoliberalism, it becomes possible to realise an analysis of the multiple terms by which an everyday conservative common sense rallies the nation. Conservative idioms remain after all a central anchor for popular nationalist expression. A critical handle on conservatism will also help underscore the unique *emotional* range that it provides nationalism. Namely, while neoliberalism is brash in its advocacy of competitive individualism and its unflinching belief in the efficiency of market reforms, it will become apparent that conservatism provides nationalism with a different, more intimate emotional cipher – unlocking a rich field of loss, mourning, remembrance and melancholy.

That conservatism can do this is centrally connected to the ways in which the popular understanding of what constitutes a British and/or English *tradition* becomes framed. As will be the focus of much of this chapter's analysis, it is the manner in which such notions of lost tradition become suffused by a thick sense of whiteness that constitutes conservatism's distinctive play on the wider nationalist consolidation. This is the putative unity, stability and public morality ascribed to pre-war national whiteness, but also an imperial greatness surrendered, that a popular conservatism routinely mourns.

It is, however, the general place of tradition vis-à-vis conservative politics where closer conceptual clarification is first required. Conservatism does cleave at its simplest to a faith in tradition. A particularly celebrated and ideologically formative commendation of tradition is Edmund Burke's anti-French Revolution treatise – a defining account that valorises the moderating stability of tradition.[19] The Burkean position recoils at radical change, arguing that attempts at the revolutionary and progressive leap result only in a radically anarchic turbulence. Such leaps into the unknown fatally upset the small textures of community life that are hard to quantify but are the very bedrock of a society that is functioning, a society that offers meaning to its inhabitants, a society that safeguards the freedom of its citizens.

The criticisms that might be levelled at such a valorisation of tradition are plenty, not least the many hierarchies, exclusions and unfreedoms intrinsic to the already existing customs and governmental practices at any given time. But perhaps more important here as a critical insight is not the exclusionary structure of tradition itself, but rather the very *mediation* of what comes to be understood as tradition. This is important, as otherwise what is claimed as being tradition in the first place is simply presumed as being a given – ignoring in turn the specific circumstances by which something gets marked out as emblematic of tradition. As many have argued in their canonical deconstruction of national tradition, the recall of a nation's defining customs, rituals and historic events is primarily an exercise in mythmaking epiphenomenal to the political influences and anxieties particular to the present.[20] Put simply, the idea of tradition does not present itself merely of its own irresistible accord. Tradition constitutes instead an attempt by contemporary political actors to frame a preferred notion of historical continuity and inheritance, so as to lend a conservative credibility to their political claim with respect to the present. More specifically, the claim to tradition becomes a way for various conservative political movements to either justify the political projects of the present, as constituting continuity with tradition, or to declare the present deviant and rudderless, as constituting a destructive break with tradition.

Within the latter, which is the more usual strain through which tradition is summoned, radical change does in fact become a viable prospect – on the basis that what is popularly classed as tradition is understood as having been unloved, neglected by a deracinated ruling class, not least 'the cosmopolitan', the 'metropolitan liberal' and the self-loathing, left-wing academic.[21] It is this tension regarding tradition that allows conservatism to break with its more literal sense, insofar as it is about recalling, rescuing and reviving as opposed to preserving or being perennially cautious. Hence, tradition and radical change are not necessarily incongruent, whereby the promise of *lost* tradition is what a nationalist project promises to deliver.

One way in which to unpack this paradox is to employ a slightly irreverent reading of Michael Oakeshott's hallowed analogy regarding the conservative temperament. Oakeshott's oft-circulated postulation recommends that the entire object of politics, navigating the always-stormy circumstances of the present, is to treat tradition as a stabilising lodestar.

> In political activity, men sail a boundless and bottomless sea; there is neither harbour for shelter nor floor for anchorage, neither starting-place nor appointed destination. The enterprise is to keep afloat on an even keel; the sea is both friend and enemy; and the seamanship consists in using the resources of a traditional manner of behaviour in order to make a friend of every hostile occasion.[22]

This might, at first glance, seem straightforwardly consistent with the reading of conservatism as simply the defence of that which already prevails. It is a stay on the temptation to pursue radical transformation based on 'abstract' principles of ideal equality, freedom and culture. As Burke, again, would have it, 'very plausible schemes, with very pleasing commencement, have often shameful and lamentable conclusions'[23] – the sort of condescension that is often used, in contemporary conservative contexts, to deride the allegedly inevitable problems of multiculturalism and immigration, noble yearnings though they might be in the first instance. The unsaid implication, however, of such a disposition is that certain mediations of what is *narrated* as tradition can deem the ship-as-society to have already keeled over. In such a case, the national project, when conservative in form, expends much of its political energies in attempting to restore these lost beacons of national guidance.

It behoves a jobbing sociologist to note in passing that tradition, however remembered, is itself impossible to revive, insofar as it is simply impossible to neatly isolate what in fact preceded us without this narration being heavily distorted and restated in terms determined by concepts and values particular to the present. This point is sometimes forgotten even by those steeped in postcolonial theory, who fail to understand that it is this suspicion of tradition and history, however construed, that was so fundamental to Spivak's era-defining 'Can the Subaltern Speak?'[24] Similarly, it is not possible to transpose tradition, even supposing that a past practice has somehow been remembered with perfect verisimilitude, given that other significant surrounding circumstances of the present have themselves shifted. A bygone value or custom thereby assumes, inevitably, a different resonance when hauled out into the present. For instance, to use a commonplace example, the proscription on sex before marriage becomes particularly absurd and self-frustrating when remade labour market structures and shifts in the life-course more generally have rendered the prospect of marriage less certain and the likely age of marriage considerably later.

Given these practical limits, the political fixation with tradition is more meaningfully accounted for by looking elsewhere. As opposed to a political programme that is substantive in what it asserts, the particular valence of tradition is better seen as stemming from the processes by which certain symbolic markers and ceremonies become identified with a sense of shared national history. Central here is the understanding that the theatre of nation is, to a significant extent, the theatre of tradition – wherein nation-making projects become heavily wedded to the ritualistic rehearsal of a 'tradition' that has in fact been 'invented'.[25] Assertions of nation mobilise in turn an attachment to particular events, customs and symbols and stitch them together to provide a particular iconic sequence of a sovereign history, a history that attempts to identify a coherent conception of a historically bound community, a sense of tradition that becomes ritually performed in everyday culture through what Billig famously conceptualised as the seemingly banal 'flagging' of the nation.[26]

The powerful centrality of gender to this marking out of nation via tradition, particularly the masculinist, martial call to 'protective' action, helps clarify an important temporal feature of this dynamic.[27] Put bluntly, the politicisation of tradition is rarely about a quiet and understated continuity, but is in fact often about the anxiously violent call for *recovery*. It is frequently noted that owing to tradition's emphasis on family, religion and public etiquette, women become the overdetermined and culturally over-policed objects that symbolically carry the nation. Various restrictions regarding national propriety are accordingly vested in the policing of female presentation and sexuality. The male figure obtains for his part the status of martial actor, the one who will actively oversee and protect women from these threats to nation. The recurring conservative paranoia about the lapsing of tradition, though formally configured as an ethnic ontology, does obtain hereby a particularly rousing urgency because of this gendered resonance, whereby the lapsing of tradition comes to represent a status quo where the man has been rendered passive (vis-à-vis a role of valiant action) and the woman has transgressed or has been transgressed.

This brief consideration of a gendered dynamic helps in turn to open up a broader contradiction characteristic of contemporary conservative nationalism, namely, how is it that new nationalist politics can seem so receptive to radical lurches into the seemingly unfamiliar, the seemingly unknown? Trump is, after all, anything but a continuity candidate, promising instead a spectacularly macho and wholesale reversal of all that which currently prevails, a commitment captured most ominously in his serial threat to 'drain the swamp'.[28] This seeming contradiction can be deciphered, however, through the double temporality of the conservative political orientation. It looks into the past for the promise of the future, the intervening present being narrated, in turn, as one of loss, stagnation or degeneracy. Tradition, as temporarily lost – see Caldwell, for instance, on the perils of having replaced 'national tradition' with politically correct 'liberal universalism'[29] – but to be forcefully recovered, plays a particularly important symbolic role in the nationalist repertoire, conferring upon nationalism a validating sense of historical purpose.

But the increased reference to tradition in contemporary political discourse obtains, by my reckoning, an even more robust traction due to its alignment with the broader 'new racism' ideologies that Martin Barker and others started to trace in the 1980s.[30] This was a 'new' racism, elsewhere called 'cultural', that initially informed the emergent far-right parties across Europe, not least the French 'Nouvelle Droite' as spearheaded by Alain de Benoist, but gradually became mainstreamed in centrist political discourse.[31] Key to this new racism was a nominal move away from the biological and geneticist heuristics that had rationalised previous racial hierarchies. The logics of new racism favoured instead a conception of racialised ethnic communities as being permanently sealed by culture, cultures that were fundamentally incompatible with Europe. Equally, these framings of culture were not only premised on notions of mutual exclusivity but also recycled many of the same attributed pathologies commonplace to the more scientifically worded racisms of the nineteenth century, whereby the cultures of racialised ethnic minorities were characterised by various ascriptions of dysfunction, inadequacy and/or unbecoming excess.

This conceptual distinction between new and scientific racism has been rightly criticised in some scholarly circles for overstating the role of geneticism in nineteenth-century and early twentieth-century racism – underplaying in turn the core 'culturalist' distinctions that were hierarchically indexed along categories of nation and race.[32] The analytic sweep of Said's *Orientalism* is after all about systematically theorising the binary *cultural* distinctions that were being operationalised across the nineteenth century by a colonial knowledge, a repertoire of knowledge to which the natural sciences were able to contribute, but about which they were not the only authoritative experts. The entire colonial artifice advanced as much through the attribution of essentialist cultural assignations (barbaric, despotic, misogynistic, mystical, irrational, superstitious, excessively sexual, hysterical, and so forth) as it did through the formal scientific designation of genetic deficiency. Or, to be more analytically precise, genetic coordinates were mapped onto cultural stereotypes, creating the broader epistemes and governances constitutive of colonial raciology.

Nonetheless, in spite of the too simplistic nature of a distinction between scientific and contemporary racisms, a conceptual vocabulary of new and cultural racism has been constructive for understanding the logics of exclusion central to recent political discourses – whereby categories of race and ethnicity are not primarily understood as carrying genetically derived characteristics, but rather, as corresponding with hermetically defined cultures unique to the respective groups. Culture is made permanent here, a repertoire of behavioural and value properties that are indexed along ethnonational taxonomies and their complementary geographies.

The inimitable commentary of Pankaj Mishra is worth quoting at length here:

In [the new racism] vision, cultures rather than biologically defined races were presented as exclusive and unchanging across time and place, with cultural difference treated as a fact of nature – 'rooted' identities, in [David] Goodhart's phrase – that we ignore at our peril. Preferring our own kind, we apparently belong, in defiance of human history, to an immutable community bound by its origins to a specific place, and should have the right to remain distinctive. Hectically naturalising cultural difference, the neo-anthropologists were careful not to preen about their superior origins and heredity as the supremacists of the past had done. They could even claim to be aficionados of racial diversity. 'I love Maghrebins,' Jean-Marie Le Pen declared, 'but their place is in the Maghreb.'[33]

The 'neo-anthropologist' appellation is well observed, capturing pithily the increased 'culture talk' of ethno-racial nativists.[34] But important for this chapter's purposes is the added observation that, within this recoded fold of conservative politics, mediations of tradition obtain a particularly heightened political emphasis, as it is tradition that best flags the core cultural content said to be representative of different ethno-national backgrounds. It is therefore the spectre of tradition – in privileging a particular conception of the past – that takes on an outsized role in organising the yearnings for nation distinctive to the conservative political imagination.

Tradition and homogeneity: blood and soil nationalism

The organising myth central to the entire edifice of a common British past is the presumed continuity of a homogeneous whiteness. Hence, given that the conservative urge is to look backwards in order to mourn the present, whiteness assumes a particularly resonant political charge within the conservative imagination.[35] Put differently, when looking backwards is already mediated as revealing only a sea of edifying and homogeneous whiteness, then an attachment to a notion of injured whiteness is reasserted as holding a particularly resonant key for resolving the troubles of the present.

The entrenched memory of its history as being an unbroken succession of whiteness recently flared up in a particularly unlikely context – a children's cartoon about life in Roman Britain (specifically, daily life in military detachments at Hadrian's Wall). The cartoon happened to include a sketch of a high-ranking Roman soldier's family. The social media furore that ensued hinged on one offending detail – the Roman general was represented as black.[36] Historical evidence unequivocally confirms that Roman generals, soldiers and statesmen were sourced from across the Mediterranean basin, including much of northern Africa, and that some of them were as a result black. Not many, but certainly some. For instance, when Emperor Septimius Severus, himself originally from Libya, was visiting his troops stationed on the northern frontier of the Empire, it was famously noted that a prankster among the soldiers thought it would be entertaining to garland him.[37] That particular prankster was described as 'an Ethiopian'. Or consider the background of Clodius Albinus, the Tunisian Roman governor of Britain towards the end of the second century. And even supposing that this history were not the case, it is fascinating that a BBC cartoon meant to invite curiosity in children about ancient history could have met with such indignation. That it did tells us more about contemporary conservative desiderata than it does about any actual desire to scrutinise history – desiderata that stem from a founding belief in a permanent chain of historical whiteness that has only been undone, rashly, through recent rounds of post-war 'mass migration'.

It would be remiss not to problematise here the conception of homogeneity that colours this historical gaze, even if these critiques are likely to be familiar to many readers. The presence of various non-white peoples in the life of the British Isles offers a corrective to those who remember Britain as permanently white. These non-white peoples included the generals, troops and merchants who arrived via the advance of Roman imperialism; they included the sailors from across the British colonies who gradually settled in various seaports (e.g. Cardiff, Liverpool, London);[38] and they included the various people, via the slave trade and British colonial rule, who found their way to Britain – ranging from the offspring of mixed relationships to members of the colonised nobilities or the emergent Anglophone middle class looking to advance their prospects by coming to Britain.

The arch-conservative's customary riposte in this context would amount to the claim that, while some of the above might be true, it hardly constitutes a *significant* concentration of non-white people. This riposte requires further attention. We must recall that pre-colonial society itself did not rally any workable conception of whiteness. Instead, communal distinctions tracked other conceptions of difference, whether religious, linguistic or proto-racial. These manifest pre-racial differences resulted not only from the various

Roman, Anglo-Saxon, Viking and Norman rounds of settlement but also from the presence of Jewish communities (though subject to an expulsion order by Edward I that was only lifted during the English Commonwealth under Cromwell) as well as various concentrations of Huguenot refugees fleeing the religious wars in France and the Low Countries.[39]

The latter relates indeed to what was a particularly substantial fault-line as regards the British history of community and difference, this being the era-defining distinction during the Reformation between Protestant and Catholic, leading to various non-conformist dissenting communities but also the broader repression of Catholics in Britain across the seventeenth, eighteenth and nineteenth centuries. For instance, it is worth bearing in mind that Locke, in his allegedly magisterial Enlightenment statement on tolerance, steadfastly refused to deem Catholics worthy of the tolerance ideal, the corruptions of the Papist mind being beyond redemption – 'doctrines absolutely destructive to the society wherein they live'.[40] This Catholic malaise (formal 'emancipation' only occurred in 1829) was itself later hitched to the colonial attribution of off-white or 'less than white' status that was conferred upon the Irish slum-dwelling labourers who provided the toil and hardship that carried nineteenth-century industrialism.[41] This potted history of those who peopled the British Isles (disregarding the entire story of colonialism/the colonies themselves) bears revisiting because it provides a salutary caution vis-à-vis the 'island story', and because it casts as myth the claim to whiteness while it also reveals how modern racial tropes have been retrospectively applied to history.

This troubling of the homogeneity thesis is far from original, surfacing fairly regularly in popular commentary, and yet the pervasive understanding of an unblemished British continuity remains largely unmoved. In short, the national myth does not reel in defeat when presented with the corrected historical record. Historical myth is, after all, just that – myth. It is not a claim upon the past that is indifferent to the present, but instead it is a claim upon the present that merely manipulates the past. The conception of a lost homogeneity is thus a crucial device in organising forms of contemporary political reflection. Against the alleged disaffection of the present, a longing glance is directed to the past, a past where the thick textures of community and cultural coherence find alluring definition.

This becomes apparent, for instance, in how the assorted social goods attributed to a common conception of community are frequently contrasted with the fragmentation that ethnic diversity and mass immigration elicit. The 'parallel lives' dystopia circulated by so many merchants of conservative doom, contrary to most existing evidence regarding contemporary residential trends, posits that minority groups opt to live among themselves, resulting in the socially fatal balkanisation of towns and cities.[42] (Perversely, this is also said to produce racial tensions, resulting in an analytic judgement in which racism is identified as an inevitable outcome of diversity.) Similarly, a past homogeneity is regularly contrasted with the many 'insuperable problems of communication' that the multiplication of languages, faiths and taste is said to engender.[43] Multiculturalism, derided as a philosophy that promotes multi-ethnic diversity, is said to rupture the textures of neighbourhood and familiarity that offer meaning beyond the more mechanical drives of individual desire and subsistence.[44] In sum, amid the burgeoning ills of anti-social boorishness, gang crime, sex grooming rings, terrorist cells and, most significantly, the dissipation of neighbourliness as a general form, ethnic diversity becomes a significant causal reference.[45] Against this, a melancholic visualisation of public morality, unity and stability becomes attributed to an era of pre-war white homogeneity.

Importantly, there is a version of this temperament that would not think minority ethnic groups themselves culpable for this social breakdown, the broader malaise being attributed instead to the very condition of ethnic diversity itself. That is the logic of the new right 'xenologies'; a logic that asserts a political cartography of ethnocultural wholes (nation-states, regions, etc.), each thriving on their own terms.[46] For new right xenologies, it is the condition of diversity itself that jeopardises the ability of any society to furnish its inhabitants with meaningful cultural and interpersonal bonds. Such a re-segregated idealism is more bluntly apparent in the hierarchically expressed aspirations of 'neo-reactionism' that furnish the philosophical mooring of the alt-right's self-declared 'hyper-racism'.[47] Here, racism is defended as a basis from which to recover the core cultural foundations of respective ethno-racial clusters.

But it is also a version of this diversity-as-social-corrosion maxim, albeit prettified, that informs most integration discourses, discourses that constitute the centre position of British politics. Integration, whatever its various caveats, amounts to the desired cultivation among the citizenry of a shared communal membership, one that is expressed politically but also culturally and symbolically.[48] The crucial, and ultimately conservative, supposition that prevails here is that ethnic diversity, unless rendered secondary to a shared conception of national membership, undercuts the moral accountability, obligations and shared cultural pleasures that stem from such entrenched bonds of togetherness. The continued vitality of an integration ideal in our wider political imagination, evidenced most recently in the 2016 Casey 'Review on Integration', does considerable work in conceptually holding together the broader nationalist sensibility.[49]

Homeliness and small time

Much of the above commentary regarding the place of tradition and nostalgia in the conservative imagination has perhaps tended too heavily towards conceptual assertion rather than addressing the specific cultural forums that have helped galvanise this political bearing. The remainder of this chapter will therefore synoptically unpack those sites of British life, intellectual and cultural, where politically potent nostalgias for the nation are most prominently mainstreamed.

An obvious point of departure here, in the longing for a shared morality and a homely togetherness, is the role played by a British culture industry committed to the systematic manufacture of conservative nostalgia. Theorised by Patrick Wright as the 'heritage industry', British televisual and publication culture places an outsized emphasis on period drama – the 'costume drama' proper, but also wider motifs redolent of a snug historical provincialism. This thick, and thickening, cultural offering appears in multiple guises.[50]

The pomp of period drama was initially almost entirely Edwardian and interwar in scope, and was somewhat irreverent in tone, P. G. Wodehouse and Agatha Christie being the most bankable adaptations, where mischievous public school humour was never far from view. Consider here the farce and repartee of Jeeves and Wooster or the affected vainglory of Poirot, moustache and shuffling gait on full display. The period touch does, however, now extend more frequently into a slightly more sincere 1950s postwar context. Herein, the period genre, seen as a whole, is characterised by a dashing glamour, a bumbling aesthetic of popinjays and anachronistic aristocrats, but also a 1950s context that, while still eminently twee, does pay some nominal if hollowed-out attention to social issues emblematic of the time. See, for instance, the plotlines of *Call the Midwife* and *Grantchester*, where a sentimental backdrop does episodically give some attention to issues of poverty, sexism and other post-war social themes.

The two standout sensations of recent blockbuster scope – *Harry Potter* and *Game of Thrones* – also fit this narrative, both recycling any number of staples constitutive of a mythologised Britishness. The former assumes the always well-spoken, boarding-school aesthetic of a becoming white adolescence, albeit set in a decontextualised present, while the latter borrows happily from the seemingly more atavistic context of a rugged, pre-modern Britain of monarchy, fable and folklore – an iconography that is permanently buttressed in British television by the fixation with Tudor history.

Stringing together such a list to assert a theme of conservative nostalgia might seem opportunistic, especially given that there is currently a proliferation in televisual content across the board owing to the growth in niche-casting and demand platforms. Such suspicion is warranted. But when seen comparatively, it is not clear that the popular programming of other countries displays anywhere near the same nostalgic attachment.[51] It is, in short, a uniquely British preoccupation.

Part of the burden that Britishness is hampered by here is that it is this very imagery that appeals to a worldwide commercial gaze – one of heritage and timeless gentility. As is sometimes noted by more candid international investors, Britain, notwithstanding its cities' bloated property market, is attractive for only two things – 'heritage tourism' and 'education', both of which are exported though profitable marketing apparatuses. This foreign curating of a British ideal, which also obtains strong purchase via the recent rehabilitation of the monarchy and its cast of personalities, is thereupon replayed into Britain's own conception of its former self.[52] This pastoral visioning of Britain, and perhaps England in particular, supplies the national imagination with its primary vistas. Against the neoliberal rehabilitation of the city and its aesthetics of speed, mobility and the built consumer environment, the conservative idiom of nation returns to the small comforts of landscape and the provincial. This becomes in turn an important node through which ideal whiteness is symbolically spatialised, allowing for the erasure of multi-ethnic multiculture as characteristic of the present. This is a symbolic space where the scruffy urban multiculture of the present is contrasted against a cleaner and smoother white space of the past.[53]

I certainly do not want to suggest that the content of these shows is always serene, though the quaintness quotient is certainly disproportionate to other prominent genres. It is rather that the broader backdrop is nearly always one of a white and genteel community that has been lost. Various tropes evocative of England as it was, could or ought to be find gentle manifestation here, a gentleness that does the work of a nationalist sense of decline far more effectively than those more bawdy and insistent versions of nationalist recall ordinarily deployed by the formal far-right.[54]

Christianism

A minor key within this wider conservative nostalgia is the perceived demise of Christianity's place in organising community life. While formal Christian practice and worship are in actuality likely to have been revived or re-energised through recent migrations to the UK and the various diaspora cultures that have emerged over the last couple of decades, including the Catholicism of some eastern Europeans alongside the various Christian traditions particular to west African communities, there pervades in some circles (the ubiquitous Peter Hitchens being a notable figurehead here)[55] a resentment of the alleged marginality of Church of England Christianity to British life – presumably evidenced in declining attendances at Anglican churches and reduced services in certain areas.

Christians themselves are not necessarily the primary authors of this lament. Indeed, it is not sufficiently noted that, for all the frantic spluttering of certain Christians against advances in the rights of women and sexual minorities, Christianity's more pointed presence in public discourse has been of late a more urgently progressive one. So while Jacob Rees-Mogg, the ostentatiously upper-class Conservative MP doted on by the press, can righteously cite his sacrosanct Catholic conscience as the basis on which he would deny women (including victims of rape) and sexual minorities the most basic of rights (to abortion and marriage, respectively), it is also the case that self-identifying Christians have routinely been at the forefront of campaigns against the neoliberal and conservative politics of the last decade.[56] It was after all the clergy, through its oft-rebuked presence in the House of Lords but also through Church-of-England-commissioned research on welfare cuts and food banks, that sustained some of the most efficient defences of welfare and refugees alike, at a time when both were being maligned in particularly merciless ways.[57]

Incidentally, in the wake of the extraordinary recent political developments in Italy, it was the mayors of Palermo and other prominent southern Italian cities alongside priests such as Fr Gianfranco Formenton of Spoleto who were the boldest in their public defiance, a defiance that provoked the wrath of the gathering fascists.[58] It is evidently the case here that the wider theology of sanctuary, generosity and humility is not always only rhetorical and civilisationist, but also manages to exercise a meaningful claim on the consciences and practices of more than a few Christians.

What remains of interest, in terms of the nationalist play that Christian conservatism energises, is how an appeal to Christianity falls within a wider crisis narrative vis-à-vis ethnic minorities and multiculture. A perceived history of Christianity becomes a reference through which those who consider themselves moral conservatives can ennoble with a wider historical purchase their more base ethnic framings of national decline. Here, the maligning of an excessive racial minority presence is contrasted to the cohesive properties of a shared and morally edifying European Christianity. This reading of a Christian legacy reaches its logical conclusion in the more foetid and violent, 'blood and soil' conservatism of far-right militancy, owing partly to European fascism's increased reliance on anti-Muslim positions. Iconic imagery that traverses the Crusaders, the Cross of Saint George and the gates of Vienna, much fetishised by far-right online culture, allows these entrenched anti-Muslim positions to be written back into a grander historical 'clash of civilisations' thesis. Telling also is the claim to a Judeo-Christian past that is routinely bandied about, despite most of its proponents not being meaningfully Christian, and certainly not Jewish.

It is in turn not the Church but the wider claim to racial conservatism commonly funnelled into an idea of Christianity, in both its everyday and far-right renditions, that furnishes nationalism with another distinctive rationale. The claim to a Christian tradition projects enduring textures of mourning, reaching specifically for a memory of a moral order and/or civilisational anchor that has been prematurely forfeited. This is also a form of lost morality that claims for conservative nationalisms a vital sense of victimhood. Indeed, through contriving a narrative of recent history as one of a multiculturalism that has enjoyed unmitigated state patronage, it is alleged that minority religions, not least Islam, have been favoured at the expense of Christianity, which, on the contrary, has been proactively suppressed. The string of news scandals that offer this narrative can appear comically clichéd, but that does not mitigate their mainstream purchase. Thus there are routine alarms about crosses being banned, about celebrations of Christmas being proscribed, and even about Christian foster children being coerced into the care of burka-wearing, Arabic-speaking, Muslim families, as notoriously (and inaccurately) reported in *The Times* by Andrew Norfolk.[59]

It should be noted that this attachment to Christianity also intermittently derides the excesses of secularisation and its enfeebling of Christianity's institutional presence. It longs in effect for the moral guidance regarding family, sexuality and a general ethos of individual responsibility that Christianity is said to have provided – a lament redolent of the *fin-de-siècle* anxieties that were in fact formative of sociology in its Durkheimian guise. Nonetheless, the public attachment to Christianity in the contemporary does seem to channel much of its intellectual grievance through the excesses of multiculturalism, and, in particular, the excessive accommodation of Muslims.

In keeping with a central technique of nationalist politics, particular invective is reserved here for the ruling class of 'left liberals' presiding over the stigmatisation of Christianity while they happily give favour to the religions of non-white communities. As Salvini, the now ascendant Italian leader of Lega, was alleged to have asserted during a rally, 'Now I understood why on the left they are so angry, they would like to swear on the Quran.' This is a not atypical lament against the liberal merchants of 'white guilt' whom nationalists perceive as having authorised the broader neutering of Western nations. Or, as stated by the religious commentator John Waters, in the course of describing immigration into Europe as the newest phase of colonialism, 'The half-adult descendants of the [former European] colonists have gone into revolt in their home territories, denouncing their own antecedents as war criminals, demanding the demolition of monuments to the colonial adventurers, and speaking darkly of the need for restitution.'[60] Such chastising of the white traitor (read the maligned 'snowflake' for its social media, alt-right equivalent) is not unimportant. The wider critical scholarship on nationalism has consistently identified an intricate irony at its core, where condemnation of the problematic Others in the nation's midst also solicits a denunciatory interrogation of those fellow kinfolk who have been party to the Other's supposed political and economic gain. Put differently, nationalism's affective force and urgency partly lies in its righteous denunciation of the betrayal that fellow nationals have enacted. The truism that nationalism ultimately becomes bound up, counter-intuitively, with the violent policing of its 'own people' lies precisely in this reality. The identification of the canonical Others, upon which the entire nation-state assertion revolves, also precipitates the visceral attack on those compatriots who are said to have facilitated the emasculation of the national self. It is the complicity of one's own in the defeat of the nation that becomes accordingly a key political theme of the nationalist project.

Most readers will find the very notion of a ruling class of white left liberals hell-bent on minority dominance simply a laughable caricature. Rightly so. But I maintain that the very fact that such multiculturalism via immigration was perceived by many to be the ruling culture is what matters here – a perception validated by an array of figures from across the political spectrum, from Slavoj Žižek summarily declaring 'multiculturalism hegemonic' to Lionel Shriver suggesting that the arrival of immigrants is a colonial project comparable to the aspirations of Nazi expansionism.[61] As Mishra comments on Shriver:

> Writing in the *Financial Times* in 2006, Lionel Shriver confessed to feeling pushed out by Guatemalan immigrants who had 'colonised' a recreation area in New York's Riverside Park ('The last few times I practised my forehand, I drew wary looks and felt unwelcome'). Asserting that the 'full-scale invasion of the first world by the third has begun', Shriver anticipated the Brexiteers' comparison of immigration to Nazism. 'Britain,' she wrote, 'memorialises its natives' brave fight against the Nazis in the Second World War. But the arrival of foreign populations can begin to duplicate the experience of military occupation – your nation is no longer your home.'[62]

It would seem difficult to outdo Shriver for bombast and hyperbole. But in my opinion, the most remarkable of recent contributions to this blossoming genre was the above-mentioned piece by Waters – which pulls off the extraordinary feat of reading Fanon, of all people, to claim that immigration to Europe is best read as a form of 'reverse colonialism'.[63] In this context, the more preponderant conservative readings of the multicultural assault (in contrast to the 'multiculturalism gone awry' liberal version) consider Christianity to have been actively coerced into a managed decline. Such a sense of siege provides another register by which the conservative comes to mourn the present. But this manner of mourning, as well as being about the loss of Christianity's gentle guidance as regards provincial community life, also excites a toxic resentment against the eminently 'unfair' patronage offered to the religions of ethnic minorities – religions already dubious in both their moral proclamations and lack of civilisational achievements.

Empire and greatness

It is not, however, only the loss of public morality and homely togetherness that actualises a melancholic condemnation of excessive ethnic diversity. Britishness and/or Englishness, like so many other nationalisms the world over, routinely summons an era of *greatness* against which the present is necessarily found to be wanting. For most Global South countries, needing to delete the period of formal European domination in the course of asserting a national history, this grandeur recalls previous periods of rule, periods when the primordial national culture is alleged to have been promulgated and/or was most resplendent. See, for instance, nationalist claims about the past flourishing of an unsullied and pristine Buddhism, Hinduism and Islam respective to the confessional positions of different South Asian countries (i.e. Sri Lanka, India and Pakistan). In Germanic liberal democracies, the moment of national pride is often yoked to the much more recent period of social democratic corporatism and the joint triumph of liberal norms and socio-economic stability commonly associated with it. In Russia, it is the periods of a Greater Russia pan-Slavism – an orientation that allows for a present hagiography of Peter the Great and Stalin, but not, tellingly, Lenin, as he is perceived as being too overtly committed to an unbecoming internationalism.[64]

In Britain, this anchoring of greatness looks unsurprisingly to a history of Empire as its most fertile source. Such an observation is hardly controversial. The continued inability of our popular culture to work through the corrosive legacies of British imperialism, as domination, extraction and political skullduggery, has become a commonplace theme of critical commentary – the definitive treatise on the subject being Gilroy's *After Empire*, with its poetic unpicking of the 'postcolonial melancholia' that continues to shape so much of this country's political sensibility.[65] While some in the 1990s had sensed that a more sober and reflective reconsideration of Empire was finally taking shape, Gilroy's 2004 statement paid witness to how the 'Rule Britannia' version of Empire continued to assert itself at the centre of our national political culture.[66]

This public regard for Empire is evidenced in two recent attitudinal surveys. A 2016 YouGov poll found that only 19 per cent of the British public considered the Empire to be a 'bad thing' (contrasted to 43 per cent deeming it a 'good thing' and 25 per cent opting for an ambivalent 'neither').[67] The same poll also revealed a majority agreeing that the nation should 'be proud of' Britain's colonial history, with only 21 per cent suggesting that it 'should be regretted' and another noncommittal 23 per cent again opting for 'neither'. In 2015, the same polling agency found that half of Britain believed that former colonies are now 'better off for it' (49%) rather than 'worse off for it' (15%). This poll also revealed that a frankly alarming 34 per cent would 'still like Britain to have an Empire'. While the unpacking of such polls would constitute a departure from this book's preferred analytic temperament, they did find a new lease of Twitter life when the pugnacious historian Niall Ferguson dragged up the results to conclude that he had 'won'.[68] Ferguson, author of the 2003 *Empire: How Britain Made the Modern World*, was of course engaging in a fit of juvenile vainglory; but it was also true that the celebratory account of how Britain both ruled and civilised the colonial world had triumphed and that Ferguson had been a leading figure in steering this vision.

It remains chastening to acknowledge that this warm embrace of Empire still prevails in Britain. Many have rightly argued that European colonialism is yet to be substantially critiqued in a way comparable to other systemic modern oppressions: patriarchy, antisemitism (e.g. the Holocaust), feudal serfdom, or the general absence of workers' rights prior to the twentieth century. European colonialism is still seen, at best, as enjoying a particular kind of ambivalence in the modern imagination, and at worst, with a nostalgic adulation.[69] Considering Aimé Césaire's arresting observation that Hitler only extended into Europe 'procedures which until then had been reserved exclusively for the Arabs of Algeria, the "coolies" of India, and the "niggers" of Africa',[70] it is painful to think that such a vast and systemic programme of oppression and exploitation can still be recalled as a positive feature of Europe's collective history. This is, after all, a political programme that was committed to rampant resource extraction for the benefit solely of western Europe or white settlers. It was a system that engendered processes of labour subjugation (via slavery, indentured labour and peonage) that were necessarily more coercive and denigrating than the many ills of 'wage-slavery' common to capitalist development within Europe. It was a system of capitalist enrichment that actively underdeveloped existing merchant and agricultural networks in the colonial world.[71] And it was a system of governance that resorted to a permanent state of violence, a violence that underpins the seminal 'dominance without hegemony' analysis of Guha and Robinson – wherein the colonised were not, in the main, ably folded into a system of ideological consent, but instead were integrated into the mechanisms of colonial capitalism primarily through force.[72] Most importantly perhaps, this was a system of governance whose multiple aims rested on the racial rationales of white supremacism.

The persistent waves of revolt across the colonies, a proclivity to revolt that necessitated the above recourse of colonial governance to permanent violence, further undermine any suggestion that colonialism was seen by its 'racial subjects' as constituting an agreeable settlement. The historian Richard Gott has done us a great service in pooling this narrative of resistance across the colonial world, while Mishra's *From the Ruins of Empire* chronicles the pained intellectual responses in the colonial world to the humiliation and denigration that Europe had subjected them to.[73] These resistances and intellectual critiques alike – which often laid out strikingly different ambitions, but were united in the basic desire to free their territories of European dominance – make for an unambiguous denunciation of the colonial project and its realities. Priyamvada Gopal similarly documents the long tradition of dissenters from within Britain who attempted to provoke the shame that Empire merited. Gopal relays a litany of internal dissent, including 'English solidarity meetings' that sprang up in the wake of various colonial insurgencies (e.g. the Morant Bay uprising in Jamaica); various philosophical and labour movement objections to the hypocrisy of masking the naked profit motives of colonialism with the edifying alibi of a civilising mission; and an unequivocal denunciation of the violence that the entire imperial project relied upon. As Gopal writes about one such round of critique,

In the 1950s, the writer Keith Waterhouse condemned 'the monocle-flashing warriors of the Empah' who covered up 'the thick catalogue of shameful things that have happened in Kenya in the name of the British empire.' [Or, as stressed by MP Fenner Brockway] critics also criticised unacceptable contrasts: 'African land hunger, European land space, African starvation wages, European comfort.'[74]

These dual projections of resistance – one of actual resistant movements across the colonies, the other a streak of repudiation from within Britain – ought ideally to have provoked a more sober understanding of Empire as a violent and self-serving imposition. The general absence of any notably substantial critical revaluation in popular domestic commentary speaks therefore to a different pressure on the modern British imagination. This is a conservatism that ties narrations of nation to a *glorious* history, a glory that is most firmly rooted in the achievements of Empire. To adjudicate against Empire is therefore to move against the nation itself, to leave it feeble, fallible and, perhaps most fatally, cruel.[75] To revisit an earlier observation, the conservative play on nation is to remember it as great, as triumphant, as aggrandising, and as a force for good that harnesses the authentic spirit of the nation. Empire and the histories of the colonial order intrinsic to it become hereby non-negotiable objects of nationalist recall; it is a recall that must have in its remit the reassuring solace of Empire.

Any such melancholia as framed around British imperial grandeur does, of course, animate the fold of whiteness, as both comforting and productive, in particularly potent ways. A recall of Empire must to some significant degree position whiteness as a unique force of history and attainment. In other words, a celebration of Empire must, to some meaningful extent, readmit the validity of white supremacy's various propositions.

These supremacist positions can certainly tolerate the presence of minority individuals who might successfully assume a congenial presentation of self. Those minorities who are able to engineer a valid presentation of self, often contingent on accessing the cultural and monetary resources appropriate to the relevant interactive space, might be spared negative judgement.[76] But again, this is necessarily an exceptional position. The wider effects of imperial nostalgia are to see many ethnic minorities, *qua* groups, as representatives of an inferior cultural form, an inferior scope of possibilities and achievement. Put differently, the contemporary allowance that the imperial conservative gaze might afford to minorities is always specific to select individuals – and when considered as racialised minority groups, with putative group cultures, the conservative longing for Empire is more prone to seeing the excessive presence of minorities as only hindering greatness.[77]

The Second World War and Churchillism

This above narrative of an Empire warmly recalled is, however, too conveniently linear, if one crucial intervening manoeuvre of British conservative nostalgia goes unaddressed. Namely, it is necessary to unpack here the particular vitality of the Second World War in narratives of British history. Put more specifically, it is instructive to interrogate how a pivot towards the Second World War circumvents the ghosts of colonial brutality that otherwise threaten to haunt Britain's past.

The centrality of the Second World War to contemporary British history becomes constitutive of a broader brand of nationalist politics that Anthony Barnett has identified as Churchillism. Barnett, writing in the heady aftermath of the Falklands War, draws a distinction between the realities of Winston Churchill's consensus government on the one hand, and what is popularly remembered as his legacy on the other. Barnett first notes the reality of messy political alliances alongside the confidence in the virtues of 'state interventionism' that was forged during Churchill's wartime government. Barnett contrasts this reality with the contemporary's much more sentimental and grandiloquent regard for the national wartime spirit synonymous with Churchill's name. As Barnett writes,

> Today Churchillism has degenerated into a chronic deformation, the sad history of contemporary Britain. It was Churchillism that dominated the House of Commons on 3 April 1982 [two days into the Argentinian military operation to land on the island]. All the essential symbols were there: an island people, the cruel seas, a British defeat, Anglo-Saxon democracy challenged by a dictator, and finally the quintessentially Churchillian posture – we were down but we were not out. The parliamentarians of right, left and centre looked through the mists of time to the Falklands and imagined themselves to be the Grand Old Man. They were, after all, his political children and they too would put the 'Great' back into Britain.[78]

Barnett's phrasing is particularly portentous when seen from the vantage point of 2018 – wherein the post-Brexit, post-Trump present has only revealed the increased political potency of a sloganeering that promises a revived greatness – but it also draws attention to the unique workings of British greatness that render the Second World War efforts so attractive. The re-engineering of the Second World War as the defining national event marks out the nation's moral telos in a particularly tidy but thickly textured manner, a story of progress that culminates in an isolated Britain spearheading the fight for good against a historically transcendent evil.

The foregrounding of this conflict in the national consciousness necessarily elides all sorts of inconvenient truths. These include the significant sympathy for fascism within Britain, most baldly declared in the notorious 1938 *Daily Mail* headline, 'Hurrah for the Blackshirts', echoed, it should be remembered, by the *Daily Mirror*'s 'Give the Blackshirts a Helping Hand';[79] the economic as opposed to moral threat to British imperial and political interests that an expansionist Germany represented from the late nineteenth century onwards; and, to reiterate, the processes of British colonial rule and their similarities with the means of German fascism. Eliding in turn these historical inconveniences, the commemoration of Britain's role in the Second World War opts instead for a myth of dignified triumph; a British monumentalisation of self as a moral authority, but also the monumentalising of the might and splendour that obtain from military heroism in the face of a uniquely transcendent killing machine.

As has been noted, the outsized ability of Britain and America to project internationally their preferred narrative of nation partly explains why the Holocaust has gained such a significant profile, in terms of marking out a *singularly* brutal chain of racial violence.[80] The Holocaust becomes here the event against which the West, but Britain and the United States in particular, confirms its national status as a force for good (an ethical mandate that was later laced into the Cold War dichotomy). This foregrounding of an anti-Holocaust status helps the UK and the US displace historical complicity in racist domination, by allowing racism to culminate instead in the Nazi Party and its comic-book caricatures. These simplifications, common to the Second World War narratives that a whole generation of baby boomers were weaned on, effect in sum a particular privileging of British history as not only naturally white and imperially dominant, but also, and crucially, brilliantly righteous.

War and militarism

If 1945 marks out the zenith of this island's modern story, the nation's world-historical moment, the conservative understands the subsequent years to be a period of decay and emasculation. What prevails in the affective bonds of conservative mourning is the righteous greatness of a nation lapsed, a greatness couched in the aforementioned provincial comforts of communal unity and collective valour that mark out pre-war whiteness.

Owen Hatherley's *Ministry of Nostalgia* offers a particularly lucid unravelling of the deeply politicised nostalgia that is attached to the period – a nostalgia that privileges a particular version of that history in order to license various distinctly contemporary political projects. Hatherley's reading places primary emphasis on how the various motifs of wartime resilience and phlegmatic thriftiness lend credibility to the austerity politics of contemporary neoliberalism. But Hatherley also makes apparent how this privileging of the Second World War as the nation's iconic moment carries with it certain pronounced implications in terms of how the nation becomes bound up with a wider militarism – militarism understood here as continued support for military operations but also the increased symbolic visibility of soldiers in quotidian fields of cultural life, including, for instance, the reporting of the two princes', but particularly Harry's, military involvements; the parading of soldiers during half-time pageants at football matches;[81] the advent of the international sporting event the Invictus Games, launched by Prince Harry, whose participants are exclusively armed services personnel who have suffered injuries in the course of service; the survivalist television genre spearheaded by the former SAS trooper Bear Grylls that exalts the elite ability of British soldiers;[82] and the nigh immanent presence of the charity Help for Heroes, and the poppies, organised by the Royal British Legion, worn by the nation across the months of October and November.

This gestural overview of the military's everyday reach reveals two complementary realities. The first, more obvious observation is the routine deployment of British soldiers in line with the war-making agendas of the 'War on Terror'. Hereby, soldiers have become commonplace features of Britain's political reckoning. The second, more ideological observation, however, is the manner in which such a war position reheats conservative nationalism in line with a broader understanding of the nation as a war-state.

Central to that conservative embrace of bellicosity is a well-worn affinity to the figure of the soldier.[83] It is, after all, not incidental that so much of the definitive theoretical work on nationalism has marked out the war condition as an elementary force[84] – from Schmitt, who affirmatively identifies the violent assertion of a friend/enemy distinction as the community's foundational assertion of political sovereignty, to Billig, who speaks of banal everyday flagging as a 'peacetime' precursor or rehearsal of the nation's war-making exigencies.

While all of the aforementioned sites of militaristic commemoration could be meaningfully unpacked here, it is the success of the Royal British Legion's poppy appeal and the charity Help for Heroes that offers a particularly instructive cipher for understanding the militaristic performance of conservative nationalism.[85] First, it is to be noted that the ubiquity of the poppy (generally as a paper or plastic representation of the red flower worn on the lapels of outer garments) is a contemporary form of 'everyday flagging'. We see here a highly casual, seemingly 'banal' symbolic assertion via which a commitment to the nation is publicly displayed. It is a form of 'everyday flagging' that presses the military as a mundane feature of the nation's content while also ably adapting to the techniques key to claiming an effectively hegemonic *contemporary* public presence. As opposed to the ritual raising of the flag, the singing of anthems, or other comparable mid-twentieth-century nation-making practices, public presence is in this instance directed towards the charity drives on high streets and in transport hubs that are such key sites of early twenty-first-century interaction – not to mention the wider circuit of plastic armbands and lapel badges that render vast pools of the public mere semiotic vessels for the nation.[86]

It would be churlish to summarily dismiss such charitable efforts, which are intended to provide support for former soldiers struggling with economic challenges and/or physical and psychological injuries incurred through war. The relevance of the poppy appeal and the Help for Heroes campaigns to a critical reading of conservative nationalism pertains instead to their disproportionate success and pervasive visibility, a success and visibility that has less to do with public sympathy and its material beneficiaries than with the 'flagging' work that the charities do for the nation. The assorted paraphernalia of these charities have become after all a staple feature of public space, with the autumn presence of the poppy in particular obtaining an intensity and scope largely unmatched by any other organisation, enjoying a particularly prominent presence in railway stations and high streets across our cities and towns.[87]

What is indelible about the poppy appeal is its function beyond the terrain of charity. It acts as a shibboleth for a grander nationalist wager about who consents and who dissents, who is and who isn't the nation. It is clear that, during the months of October and November, the professional classes in Britain become subject to something akin to what Marcuse famously described as 'repressive tolerance'.[88] While the red poppy formally simply marks a volitional act of philanthropy, to fail to sport it in public is to fall foul of the unspoken understanding that the poppy invitation is in fact an injunction, is in fact mandatory.[89] The eloquent statements issued by the national newsreaders Charlene White and Jon Snow, feeling increasingly uncomfortable about the public tyranny regarding the poppy, draws momentary attention to this wider truth.[90]

The poppy, having won for itself this broader resonance, ceases to be a charitable gesture but in actuality instantiates a mass ritual of military and soldier worship. The poppy is integrated into an assertion regarding what is, in fact, the defining public culture of the nation. It acts, in the final reckoning, as a proxy for the nation; it is about asserting, claiming or proving membership. To quote the young Muslim woman Tabinda-Kauser Ishaq who designed a poppy-themed hijab, much to the *Sun*'s and *Telegraph*'s delight, the aim of her design was to demonstrate pithy allegiance, an allegiance that is otherwise routinely questioned, denied or deemed impossible. 'I thought it was a really simple and clean way of saying that I'm very proud of being British and Muslim without it being in anyone's face.'[91]

Of interest here is how a nation-making ritual becomes staged via such close affinity with the soldier, an affinity that is rooted in the centrality of Second World War mythology to British nostalgia.[92] Mass sport, famously denounced by Orwell as 'war minus the shooting', can no longer, if it ever did, carry such burdens for the nation.[93] It is too multi-ethnic, too demotic, too commercial and too weighted in favour of the more treacherous allegiances of club and personality that render it such an interesting location for contemporary play, subversion and internationalism. The British soldier's heightened symbolic role reveals in contrast a more tenable conservative modelling of where the nation might be best located – the soldier represents namely a body, purpose and mentality in which the idea of nation can be proudly invested.

What also manifests here is a disturbing ability to silence anti-war critique, insofar as the soldier becomes an object only of virtue and praise.[94] War, via the soldier, is authorised here even if the relevant engagement itself is seen as being foolhardy and without substantial support. The strange penchant for soldiers manning charity stalls to don fancy dress, often as Star Wars characters or lovable cuddly toys evocative of a child's impulsive understanding of play, is particularly arresting here. In short, it seems to execute an erasure of the very thing that the soldier most obviously represents – an agent of violence, destruction and torture, but also a receptacle of pain, trauma and gore.

The juxtaposition of violence (soldier with gun) and childish naivety (soldier as teddy bear) is revealing, however, when the national work being done here is recognised. Namely, this is not about war itself. Instead, as Chamayou and Gregory have pointed out, the normalisation of involvements in war elsewhere relies on stealth, depersonalisation and political obfuscation.[95] Britain's military involvement in assorted conflicts across the Global South is often opaque, shrouded in the interests of neoliberal profit, as well for the opportunity of making war without obtaining popular consent. These are the wars that are not announced, wars in which British private security contractors assume a primary role, wars to which arms deals central to the British armaments industry are pivotal yet are conveniently ignored, wars in which increased automation through drone strikes or 'solely' aerial support render the soldier proper a rather peripheral agent.

It is instead at home, as the arch-national subject of conservative desire, that the soldier remains, his visibility enhanced. The soldier in this guise does the work of war without the pain of war. It is a mediation of Britain as the imperious war-state without its populace having to revisit the brutalities of war itself. What consequently seems to unfold here is the contemporary soldier being paraded as the latest iteration of a longer national history – one that is characterised by the Second World War triumph in particular.

Conclusion

This has been, unsurprisingly, a long chapter. The reach of the conservative fold in the organising of contemporary nationalisms is extensive. That much is generally well understood. But important to this chapter was the concerted attempt to disentangle the conservative temperament from a broader programme of neoliberal capitalism. Doing so allowed us to note the much deeper and more complex foundations upon which conservatism exercises a hold on the political anxieties, logics and horizons relevant to contemporary nationalism – a set of anxieties and horizons that are not simply or even primarily about securing the broader interests of capitalist accumulation and its attendant culture of hyper-individualism and unremitting competition. Indeed, many conservative reflexes often stand in some partial disjuncture vis-à-vis capitalist culture.

The conservative attraction to the ameliorative embrace of nation, and the customary racial demons that this call to nation trades on, operates through a set of themes that prize the textures of a quiet smallness. It is a disposition that recalls the intimate comforts and familiarities of the rustic, the provincial and the orderly. It recalls the gentle but steadying hand of a Christian tradition. It recalls an age of upright and noble masculinity, alongside a suitably rosy but dignified femininity.

But this mystique of 'small time' in the conservative imagination is twinned to its inverse as well. Namely, the conservative also mourns the passing of a time of greatness: a time of absolute sovereignty projected the world over; a time of being the civilising lodestar; a world-historical time. This is a grandeur that lives through a confluence of imperial melancholia, Churchillism and militarism.

This twin disposition lends to the project of nation a deeply resonant and affective key that is not available through nationalism's other ideological repertoires. It is an intimate mourning of both a greatness lapsed and a smallness surrendered. It is also, of course, a logic and affect that is eminently rudderless without a well-defined set of constitutive ethno-racial Others. These Others – the outsider figures who orient the conservative dirge – are, as ever, multiple. They include the spectre of whiteness's weaker normative grip; they include multiculturalism's allegedly hegemonic status; they include Muslims and their role as foil for the war-state; and they include the ostensibly unceasing waves of unsolicited immigration into the sweet fields of England.

In short, the conservative appeal to nation is one of loss, and a sense of loss that is primarily enabled by a diffuse set of racial paranoias.

5

Unholy alliances: the neoliberal embrace of nation

One of the prevailing clichés of contemporary critical commentary is to render everything neoliberal. My proudly old-fashioned colleague who occupies the office opposite me once mischievously fixed to his door, rather Luther-like, a notice decrying this tendency. The notice read (in capitals as it happens, though amended here for reasons of inelegance):

> All visitors welcome except those who use the word neoliberalism in everyday conversation or appeal to neoliberalism as an explanation for any or all of the following – Climate Change; REF; Brexit; Ethnic Cleansing; Decline in Size of Toblerone; Syrian Civil War; Quality of Museum Displays; Result of the Eurovision Song Contest.

I similarly recall the candid remarks of a particularly contemplative group of second-year university students when on a study trip to Amsterdam – the relaxed and sociable context of a study trip being a forum where students feel less inhibited about articulating their more heartfelt frustrations with the curriculum. The students bemoaned the impulse of lecturers to always refer to neoliberalism when offering any causal analysis. They rightly suspected that neoliberalism had become a shorthand that relieved scholars of having to explain precisely what about the chosen object was in fact neoliberal, and crucially, what about it was *not* neoliberal.

It might seem a thankless task to ascertain what neoliberalism specifically is. The term, by its ubiquity, has become a reference that can be bent to meet nearly any political critique an author wishes to advance. Largely deployed as a pejorative, it is generally meant to designate a specific period of capitalism characteristic of the present.[1] However, beyond this basic sense that it applies to capitalist developments over the last three to four decades, there is very little that is precise about its now routine invocation. Nonetheless, this chapter's attempt to account for the distinctive forms of nationalism that neoliberalism facilitates will benefit first from some extended attempt to ground what we might generally mean by neoliberalism.[2]

Put less obliquely, and in more immediate relation to this book's mandate, it is the case that much nationalist politics of today carries a logic and context that is decidedly neoliberal. Such an observation runs counter to the intuitive and often bandied-around notion that neoliberalism is emphatically oriented towards the dissolution of the nation and the nation-state, favouring instead a fully globalised market of borderless freedom. An all-too-unqualified investment in this globalisation thesis has been apparent from across the political spectrum – an investment made apparent in the Fukuyama-esque claims about liberal market democracies' triumph over history, but also in the Marxist-inflected understanding of neoliberalism as finally realising that fundamental mantra that had been long threatened – that under capitalism, 'all that is solid melts into air', including the nation.

This over-reading of globalisation misses in turn the multiple recourses to nation and nationalism that a neoliberal agenda relies upon. It misses how immigration is rendered problematic on explicitly economistic terms; how an invocation of Empire is what allows, implicitly or explicitly, certain pro-business evangelicals to champion Britain as a glorious, all-conquering nation of trade and enterprise; how various racialised minority groups are pathologised as lacking, in their own distinctive ways, a neoliberal spirit; and, perhaps less obviously, how shifts in our economy towards a consumerist, service-sector economy privilege particular racialised aesthetics characteristic of the ideal commercial experience.

These respective and related themes will accordingly be the focal point of this chapter. But to get even a working handle on these requires two preliminary clarifications. First, we need to discern the other decidedly *non-*neoliberal currents that permeate the nationalist platform. This is, of course, the matter of this book's other chapters. Secondly, we need to better streamline what is meant by neoliberalism. This is what I will address below.

There have arisen two complementary traditions through which neoliberalism, as a programme of market supremacy, has been critically addressed: the first, institutional, the second, cultural. In the first, neoliberalism is seen as a phase of capitalism that was steered by an alliance of visionary politicians, cavalier thinktanks and uncompromising supranational institutions committed to unleashing the civilising power of the multinational corporation and deregulated finance capital. This version of the neoliberal triumph privileges a familiar roll call of organisations and characters. Particular attention is reserved here for the role played by the Mont Pèlerin Society, the RAND Corporation, the Institute for Economic Affairs and the Chicago School, where neoliberal mantras were given their most salient intellectual foundations.[3] This style of analysis also foregrounds the broader institutionalisation of this order via the Washington Consensus, yielding particular neoliberal mandates for the International Monetary Fund, the World Bank and the orthodoxies of leading central banks more broadly. As regards particular individuals, Thatcher and Reagan have been commonly identified as the Western figureheads of neoliberal evangelism; but the reformist agendas of those who ushered formerly antagonistic systems and contexts into agreement with the market society have also been identified as playing central roles – for example Augusto Pinochet, Deng Xiaoping and Lee Kuan Yew.[4]

Secondly, there is a well-formed body of writing that has documented the *cultural formation* that neoliberalism represents. So while neoliberalism denotes a direction of governance committed to the marketisation of all social life and provisioning, it is also, as Hall put it, a cultural programme 'deeply lodged in the body-politic'.[5] Hall was one of the most prescient observers of this everyday or 'common-sense' neoliberalism. At a time when the initial warning shots fired by Thatcher were considered by many left critics to be lacking any popular legitimacy, Hall carefully chronicled the 'conjunctural' affinity between a new threshold of capitalist expansion and a whole tranche of deeply entrenched but subtly adapted values and symbolisms emblematic of a petit bourgeois Middle England.

A series of celebrated scholars have subsequently elaborated upon this neoliberal moment, *culturally* construed, and it is accordingly these ideals, desires and moralities that will be the focus of the following section. This body of work tends not, however, to centre on the question of nation and, indeed, at times it presents neoliberalism as being distinctly anti-national in spirit and deed. As such, my consideration of these various insights will draw its own distinctive emphases, emphases that can better allow for a more grounded understanding of how the contemporary political appeal to nation displays, in fact, a distinctly neoliberal aversion for the Other and the outsider.

The responsibilised individual

The most widely commented-upon attribute of neoliberal culture is its valorisation of individual responsibility, or 'responsibilisation' as Foucault would have it – responsibility as the coerced 'obligation to be free'.[6] The individual, modelled as someone who always acts out of self-interest, is understood here as the optimal agent for pursuing those ends best suited to them. The task of governance therefore is to demand of individuals that they exercise that rationally endowed responsibility. This includes the basic postulation that the individual is responsible for resolving or avoiding the various risks and harms that they have encountered or might encounter. Self-care, self-love and rationally pursued self-interest become therein the guiding moral imperatives.

This solipsistic casting of the individual speaks to a frustratingly effective perversion of a particular philosophical history. It is not that the individual was not the primary concern of all moral philosophies significant to the European Enlightenment and onward. It would be disingenuous to deny this wider normative continuity. The neoliberal rendering of this preoccupation is, however, an intentionally naive simplification that understands the individual as abstracted from all other social mores and contingencies, rendering the individual the *sole author* of their own life. The individual is promoted here as one free of external constraints. And even if these constraints are recognised, it is maintained that it is not the proper domain of government to consider any such constraints. It is instead the individual who is tasked with the effort to endure, pre-empt and thereby transcend them. It is indeed presupposed by the ideologues of neoliberalism that for government to intervene in the weighing of these constraints would lead to inverse outcomes – for example a culture of 'welfare dependency' that in fact inhibits the freedom of poor people.

Margaret Thatcher's remark – 'There is no such thing as society, there are individual men and women and there are families' – is widely cited as the definitive assertion of this shift. Note in this notorious claim the emphatic regard for the individual (and the nuclear family as the extension of the responsible individual). This deceptively simple ontological claim is, however, better understood within the wider moral discourse that Thatcher was operationalising such statements and their complementary politics. As Evans and Taylor argue – via a reading of the conservative academic Shirley Robin Letwin – it is Thatcher's dismissal of 'soft' virtues that remains particularly telling about the type of moral society that is being envisaged here. Virtues such as 'kindness, humility, gentleness, sympathy, and cheerfulness, which militate against people taking responsibility for their lives' are traded away in favour of more emboldening, 'vigorous virtues' – independence, rectitude, 'energy, adventurousness and robustness against enemies'.[7] Recognition of this expansive moral presentation as regards character is important. Though neoliberalism is sometimes read as a top-down Establishment imposition uninterested in securing a corresponding public consent,[8] what we see here is in fact the privileging of a very particular moral characterisation – a characterisation that has become central to how we circulate everyday anxieties and aspirations regarding the ideal self.

There is, however, a tendency to speak *only* of this individualised responsibilisation when characterising neoliberalism. As will become more apparent later on in this chapter, mere individualisation is not unique to neoliberalism, given that it is central to the entire project of economic and political liberalism. Complementary therefore to this responsibilisation of the self that sits within the neoliberal psyche is the cult of entrepreneurialism, culminating in the sanctity of the enterprise itself. This is a move that ties the neoliberal individual ('homo economicus') to neoliberalism's preferred organisational unit – enterprise. Under neoliberalism, all entities are re-imaged as enterprises, as accumulating machines. All capital at an individual's disposal shall in turn be rendered profit-oriented – capital as capital but also all aspects of individual capability itself, including our muscular (physical), cognitive (information) and sexual (erotic) fields. The state must also assume a particularly strong role in ensuring that entrepreneurial ideals are introduced to those many domains where they are yet to enjoy access or have failed to embed themselves successfully. The university becomes a company competing for customers (formerly known as students), the neighbourhood doctor becomes a GP clinical commissioning unit, and the student's Instagram profile, no longer simply a peer-to-peer image-broadcasting forum, becomes a platform for product placement and maximised marketisation of the self.[9] The 'greed is good' mantra of yuppiedom incrementally engineers here a reach across all social life, no longer restricted to the already tasteless vulgarity of the corporate boardroom and trading floor. The individual is therefore no longer only an individual, but is converted into the entrepreneurial self.

Put differently, this is the juncture where individuals are asked to become production engines, optimising their ability to transition into the needs and exigencies of existing market demands. The cultural hagiography appropriate for such a conjoining of individualised responsibility and entrepreneurial zest can in turn be fixed in many contrasting dyes: the faux-hippie aesthetic of the new capitalist that Richard Branson, Elon Musk, Gwyneth Paltrow and Steve Jobs solicit; the crass but homespun commercialism of renegade climbers like Donald Trump, Philip Green and Alan Sugar, around whom an entire genre of television was crafted; the avuncular prudence of Warren Buffett and HSBC; or the stylised gangsterism and hustler nous of Pablo Escobar, Jay-Z and 50 Cent.

Within any such sweeping hagiography of meritocratic capitalist success, all other concerns shall ideally be rendered secondary, subsidiary to one's ability to be rendered an enterprise.[10] Seen inversely, all other needs, obligations and desires shall only find expression through the market. For instance, the duty or desire to care for others would ideally rest here on the individual's ability not only to earn the requisite funds, but to thereupon budget appropriately as well as navigate the available market solutions/providers in the optimal manner. Extending this example, it could be noted that care itself is gradually understood as ensuring that those in our intimate environment — partners, children and dependents in a professional capacity (pupils, students, patients) — are inculcated with the proper entrepreneurial drive, whereby their decisions, ambitions and lifestyles are made to accord with a wider ability to optimise their market utility and literacy.[11] This is, for instance, realised through the increasingly punitive moralism directed at working-class parents or in the very mechanisms of state governance itself, through, say, the recasting of welfare as workfare — where the access of the unemployed or underemployed to subsistence resources is tied to their ability to successfully communicate the requisite self-betterment drive.

Any such twin emphasis on responsible selfhood and the sanctity of enterprise cannot, however, be understood without reckoning with the broader ethos of 'competition' that binds the two together. As Will Davies has argued, 'the moral-economic logic of neoliberalism makes competition the basic normative principle of society and *competitiveness* the ultimate individual and collective virtue'.[12] It is, of course, the case that it remains difficult to ably demarcate clear distinctions between the responsibilised individual on the one hand and the injunction to be entrepreneurial on the other. They fold into each other, each reinforcing the rationalisation of the other. But competition might be understood nonetheless as the broader organising principle that binds these two units. The responsible self who aspires to realise a form of enterprise accordingly recognises competition as the baseline principle that produces, organises and provisions goods and deserts in the most *bountiful* but also most *just* form. In short, it is my contention here that competition is the spirit that carries the two relevant units prioritised by the neoliberal – the self-loving individual and the enterprise.

Beyond individualism: neoliberalism and the state

There lingers a recurring confusion here as to why much of the above is not simply understood as capitalist, as opposed to denoting a particular period of the present. Clarification of neoliberalism's socio-historical distinctiveness can be facilitated by briefly distinguishing it from previous regimes of political and economic liberalism. Doing so allows the rejuvenation of the state's role to be acknowledged, lest neoliberalism be mischaracterised as denoting the wholesale retreat of the state.[13] Indeed, a better understanding of the state's reconfigured but intensified role within neoliberalism is decisive in grasping the ways in which the racialised nation figures prominently within neoliberal rationality.

Political liberalism is understood as the framing of individuals as rights-bearing citizens. It is the individual who obtains a variety of inviolable rights – whether negative or positive, whether passive or active.[14] This formal privileging of the individual as the preferred political object signals a nascent affinity with market ideals constitutive of capitalism. But what properly secures the partial imbrication of political liberalism with economic liberalism is the admittance of *property* as a foundational individual right. It is through rendering property individual in type, and sacrosanct in nature, that political liberalism dovetails substantially with the imperatives of economic liberalism.

Economic liberalism, for its part, primarily amounts to the belief that there should be certain areas where only market activity will determine how a good is produced and circulated. This imaging of economic liberalism is often understood to have initially found a particularly expansive expression during the laissez-faire era of the 1830 July Monarchy as presided over by Louis-Philippe I, lionised alternately as the 'citizen' king and the 'bourgeois monarch'; while for Polanyi, 'laissez-faire peaked in England with the introduction in 1834 of the New Poor Law, a punitive welfare system influenced by utilitarian ideas of efficiency and Malthus's theories of population control'.[15]

Importantly, within this framework of economic liberalism, the state should not be present in the direct production of economic goods. The caveat, of course, is that the state will thereupon reserve various domains for itself, as being within its own jurisdiction – for example, healthcare, education, national industries, defence, policing, prisons, public transport and, say, postal services.[16] Neoliberalism dissolves this distinction between private and public goods in a more aggressive fashion. Neoliberalism fundamentally retains and bolsters the state but only to oversee, underwrite or galvanise the ability of capitalist market activity to access *all* fields of social exchange and distribution. Similarly, in idealised economic liberalism, workers taking collective action would be seen as a perfectly legitimate feature of labour freely associating as it sees fit, while in neoliberalism, the state is actively summoned to discourage and even render impossible such actions. As such, the state, by marshalling these roles, becomes bloated in neoliberalism, in authorising but also shielding the market.

Similarly, the state is also vital for the legal-security function it provides neoliberalism.[17] This state – alongside limiting the ability to pursue meaningful union actions – is tasked with managing and 'warehousing' the human debris of neoliberal economics, debris meaning those people who, in being rendered marginal, precarious or superfluous by neoliberalism, threaten to take on a more threatening and hostile attitude to the everyday passing of middle-class civilities and confidence. This is what Wacquant calls 'advanced marginality'. The 'punitive' security state, as an engine of neoliberal statecraft, realises here the necessary forms of everyday policing, incarceration and gatekeeping as regards the excluded, the super-exploited, the disillusioned and the 'idle'. This includes pressing such people into forms of 'prisonfare', wherein incarceration becomes a means to subject people to super-exploitative forms of labour (often within prisons themselves).[18] It ought to be added that the security state is also given a further purpose here in the neo-imperial sense of bludgeoning open new frontier markets that were otherwise not receptive to full-scale commodification or multinational access.[19] The recent war in Iraq is often identified by postcolonial critics as being a particularly iconic instance of this practice.

Immigration and 'low-value people'

The above constitutes only a whistle-stop tour of various motifs and clarifications commonly circulated as being definitive of the neoliberal project. It will, however, have provided the reader with a feel for what constitutes the neoliberal present, at least in terms of its cultural coordinates. Of course, it would be right to wonder consequently what is the story of *nation* here? After all, it is not infrequently suggested that the neoliberal constitutes a departure from the nation-state – often glibly reduced to the concept of globalisation.

As has already been hinted, such an overstated globalisation thesis is highly misleading. It is already erroneous in the simple sense of the above sketch, wherein the state's (as the state in nation-state) role is in fact elevated within neoliberalism. But it is also erroneous in the obvious sense that we do not have anything resembling the free movement of capital, goods and labour. As has been widely documented, the movement of capital and goods is subject to conditions that routinely privilege the more politically powerful states.[20] And as regards labour, it is resoundingly the case that such a principle of free movement does not prevail anywhere. (Even within the EU certain mobility, employment and welfare controls are occasionally implemented: restrictions on how work can be applied for, how welfare can be accessed, and how free movement can be delayed upon a new country's accession to the Union.) Herein, though this is only one synoptic attempt to problematise the generic reading of neoliberalism as being the untethering of capitalism from the nation-state, we already sense a more complex and contrary understanding, one where nationalism is always in play, and where the outsider and the border are as relevant as they have ever been. It is in turn a fuller exploration of this remade attachment to nation as induced by neoliberalism that will be the focus of the following section.

Returning to the core definition that permeates this book, nationalism is the recourse to understanding a society's perceived problems through extensive *negative* reference to the presence of those who do not belong – outsiders who are often construed according to their many ethno-racial guises. Hence, when considering neoliberal nationalism, the objective is to understand how neoliberal rationalities induce particular logics and characterisations by which the outsider is rendered undesirable, ominous and a problem.

There are two principal aspects to this. The first involves already established non-white communities being further 'pathologised' – falling short when appraised against the 'moral-economic' logic unique to a neoliberal temperament. These are the stereotypes that routinely represent certain minority groups as work-shy, prone to welfare dependency, susceptible to nihilistically destructive lifestyles, and/or as groups that remain excessively attached to 'traditional' values that do not accord with the neoliberal call to freedom. It is, however, the second principle, concerning the wider anxieties regarding immigration as a specific political issue, where we ought to start as regards the neoliberal reworking of nationalism.

One might expect champions of neoliberalism to back freedom of movement, with their supposed focus on the 'free exchange' of market goods and labour power in a dynamic, muscular system. But the way in which neoliberal ideologues propose that immigration ought to be handled runs counter to some key intuitive understandings of the neoliberal programme. Neoliberalism is *not*, contrary to popular understandings, pro-immigration. Any permissiveness that it allows for regarding immigration is instead filtered through a moral appraisal respective to its guiding virtues of competition, entrepreneurialism and the responsibilised self: an imperative to filter ideal migrants that was gestured at by Bauman in his inventive 'vagabond' versus 'tourist' heuristic.[21]

The real-world example that best reveals this perhaps abstract assertion is the increased contemporary embrace of the 'Australian' styled 'points system'. The acquiescence to such a technocratic ideal of 'metric-power', by for instance Nigel Farage or in the Tory government's 2018 immigration policy announcements, is of course itself a neoliberal triumph.[22] Questions of obligation or even compassion as might be sourced from other competing ethical repertoires – for instance, a remade legacy of Church teachings regarding refuge and sanctuary – are forfeited in favour of the overriding interests of economic utility. The political right, nationalism and neoliberalism become, in this simple move, one and the same thing.

Davies has offered a typically generative commentary on why the 'work-permit' driven points system appears so attractive to so many merchants of anti-immigration alarmism. Davies notes how a points-system agenda wishes to clarify and simplify the terms by which immigration is realised: 'The points system is to calculate different human capabilities according to the economistic metaphor of human capital.'[23] This is the imperative to appraise the prospective migrant solely in terms of value-added instrumentalism. And inevitably, this appeal to economic technocracy, while formally deferring to the decision-making powers of a market-responsive state bureaucracy, necessarily relies for a more embedded traction on much more everyday discursive ascriptions regarding who is, in fact, the viable/ideal economic migrant. Again, as Bauman developed in his vagabond and tourist distinction, skilled and desirable continue to be principally configured along associations of white, Western provenance.

The first obvious casualty of any such points system is that the very notion of the asylum seeker, and associated protections such as the right to family, are happily reneged upon. Such twentieth-century considerations as located within a more avowedly liberal political tradition were always inadequate, always narrowly selective about who was considered worthy of asylum.[24] But such considerations, whatever their limitations, become decidedly redundant when a points-system rationale begins to monopolise the terms by which immigration is weighed in public political discourse. Simply put, such extra-economistic formalities no longer bear consideration. It is here that we can begin to grasp how neoliberals can mobilise a particularly candid, matter-of-fact dehumanisation when considering refugees, or even immigrants in general. Consider here Iain Duncan Smith's remark, in the context of a 2017 *Newsnight* interview about Brexit and immigration, that 'we [have] had a huge number of very low-value, low-skilled people coming through the EU'.[25] (He went on to explain that exiting the European Union would allow for a more purpose-built filtering of who would be given entry to the United Kingdom.) Or consider how Farage, the stockbroker champion of neoliberal economics, can proudly front a campaign poster that assigns to a line of refugees all the associations of lumpen decay and pestilence.[26] It was, after all, a poster that could just as well be reimaged as insects, as pests, as grotesques.

David Theo Goldberg's recent insistence on recalling a schema of 'animalization' as being central to racism's unique capacity for visceral indifference and violence alike is particularly apposite here.[27] When seen in terms of optimal economic citizenry – those who are able to realise the ideals of independence, enterprise and premium skills – dark-skinned refugees constitute a semiotic antithesis. It is for precisely this reason that migrants' rights groups are reluctant to press an economistic argument about the contribution of immigrants, regarding fiscal gains, surpluses and the like – given that such interventions leave very much intact the longer history of a human/infrahuman distinction that the racialisation of economic utility writes itself upon. (It remains, however, understandable and indeed welcome that the economistic case is still often advanced for pragmatic reasons – the regular debunking offered by Jonathan Portes being particularly effective.)[28]

A closer reading of the prominent intellectual arguments authored by figurehead neoliberals becomes instructive here – the arguments of people such as Douglas Carswell and Daniel Hannan but perhaps also the multi-authored effort by five Conservative MPs, *Britannia Unchained*.[29] These are muscular, action-oriented manifestos that call for the nation to be streamlined, noting how immigration, while itself permissible, must be subject to vital neoliberal checks – who is in fact being given entry, what they do once here, and what the upper limit should be.

For instance, even though the more frenzied right railed against Carswell for being 'pro-immigration',[30] what he was routinely advocating was precisely this surgically neoliberal resolution to the ills of immigration:

> Britain needs a point-based immigration system, similar to that in Australia. An eVisitor visa scheme would make it easy for legitimate visitors and tourists to enter the UK. Parliament would annually agree on a quota of those that would be allowed to permanently settle – and in time acquire citizenship. Places would be allocated on the basis of the skills that those first generation Britons would bring with them.[31]

This is scarcely a pro-immigration position. It is instead a call to manage the world's population against the sole criterion of the alleged human capital gains that the nation-as-enterprise might most require. And even when these and similar arguments are inclined towards a moralising condemnation of the inadequacies of the national population in its entirety, the allegedly lacklustre vetting of immigrants' skills profiles and industriousness remains a key focus.

Similarly, it is to be noted that the global trade utopians who champion Brexit – Liam Fox, Iain Duncan Smith, Michael Gove, Nigel Farage and Boris Johnson – all speak, albeit in somewhat different tones, about the need to render the nation an optimal engine of accumulation. Central to that aspiration, even if mostly implicit, is the management and restructuring of its core stock (i.e. the nation's people). Needless to say, the Eritreans, Pakistanis and Arabs who have braved the unforgiving seas hardly elicit confidence when seen from this particular vantage point of shiny capitalist success.

Of course, this new neoliberal politics of the nation does make certain symbolic exceptions to reflect contemporary shifts in concentrations of global capital – not least a recoding that recognises the rise of China and East Asia more broadly alongside a carefully calibrated reading of, say, India's economic possibilities. These places are no longer homogeneously painted as a hive of menacing foreign perils, but in more complicated terms as also a wellspring of future growth and trade. It is for instance interesting that Carswell, in the course of his anti-EU, pro-points-system vision for immigration, made explicit rhetorical mention of India and Singapore. 'Since 400 million EU citizens have a right to come, lowering immigration numbers means making it harder for non-EU people to enter the UK. Thus do we prioritise a EU citizen with a criminal record over someone with a doctorate from India or Singapore. It makes no sense.'[32]

Such ostensible openness to the world, one that refuses to privilege Europe, has a notionally inviting ring to it. It is also a resounding and pernicious misrepresentation (see, for instance, Theresa May's refusal to relax visa regulations during a 'charm' offensive visit to India).[33] While an Indian doctor, a Ghanaian IT engineer and a Chinese investor might be picked off selectively (via a points system), they represent anomalies in the popular neoliberal gaze – wherein the bulk of those who allegedly threaten to burst through the port patrols at Calais or ask for student visas that might allow them to work do not satisfy even the most basic approximation of an attractive skills portfolio or character matrix. Decades of popular racism and its constitutive stereotypes render these various migrant figures unwanted and disposable. They are, in short, people who can only be found fundamentally wanting when subject to a neoliberal moral appraisal.

East India Company redux

It is also possible to connect the ostensibly neoliberal working of an immigration aversion as regards dark-skinned Others to neoliberalism's broader affinity with the very idea of nation – as construing a particular culture and history into which it writes a neoliberal orientation. Namely, neoliberalism, as a philosophy of enterprise, reclaims the nation as its correct unit. Britain is, of course, unique here.

Britain understands itself as more boldly capitalist in spirit than the European mainstream seemingly allowed for. This partly accounts for the muddled confusions in some left debates about Brexit. While the EU is, of course, a supranational entity formally committed to capitalist ideals, its fondness for market-society reforms lags behind what the neoliberals of Britain have long threatened to do and have long understood Britain as having done in the hallowed past.[34] Similarly, Britain has played a key role in pushing the free-market aspects of the EU, but its resistance to European-level welfare and taxation is revealing about how the neoliberal right perceives its national history, and, in turn, its future. In the post-EU future, those who propagate nationalism imagine the unleashing of a dazzling British appetite for industry. A wholesale recall of the nation is foregrounded – the aforementioned title, *Britannia Unchained*, by Conservative MPs Kwarteng, Patel, Raab, Skidmore and Truss, speaks for itself. Here, all sorts of invigorating market idioms are revisited through the selective narration of national histories: the plucky island nation, the home of the industrial revolution, the capitalist vigour of the Iron Lady, and, not least, Britain as commercial ruler of the world.

What transpires consequently is a neoliberal common sense that summons a particular mapping of the nation's foundational events and history. It is a symbolic terrain that tries to accord to the nation and its body politic an inviolable and enduring capitalist sprit. So while the liberal narrative of British history discussed in Chapter 4 might opt for a particular teleology of liberal constitutionalism – starting with the Magna Carta and culminating, say, in the Glorious Revolution – the neoliberal reaches for industrialisation and, somewhat obliquely, for a memory of Empire.

In some ways therefore, the neoliberal nostalgic is a better student of history than the nationalist who is primarily liberal or left in constitution. The neoliberal nationalist seems to understand that capitalism was itself birthed concomitantly with European colonialism.[35] They were co-articulated ventures, each bolstering the other. The animal spirits of enterprise – as the quest for new materials, new markets and new labour (that could also be subjected to forms of exploitation that prevailing norms and circumstances in Europe would not always allow) – necessarily involved an expansionary violence. Tellingly, it was the nascent form of the company that was so important to the initial charting of European colonialism. The twin operations of the Dutch East India Company (VOC) and British East India Company constituted in some notable ways the first European colonial powers. Here, private investors would buy 'actions' – incidentally still the term for stocks and shares in many Germanic languages – in the resulting profits that would be generated through the company's plundering of the Global South. The sorry stories of the extraordinary violence intrinsic to the respective company operations – the Batavian Massacre or the Great Bengal Famine of 1770, for instance – were portents of the direct colonial rule exercised by European state powers that would find its fullest scope in the nineteenth and early twentieth centuries.

Given this context, the promises made by anti-EU neoliberals about a revived, gloriously British age of enterprise are not unconnected to a nostalgia for Empire. As El-Enany makes apparent in a thrilling excoriation of how Brexit in particular has generated an opening for more emphatic imperial recall:

> Despite the British Empire having been a white supremacist project of conquest, plunder and dispossession requiring the most extreme and brutal forms of violence, since Brexit the nation's appetite for imperial mythology and fantasy has grown. In place of the European market, government officials expected to revitalise long-abandoned trade relationships with the Commonwealth.[36]

Some mischievous civil servants have helpfully retranslated this recurring reference to Commonwealth by Brexit enthusiasts as a campaign for 'Empire 2.0'.[37] While it would be brazen to suggest that an actual replication of Empire is being envisaged here, what the British neoliberals championing Brexit do warmly court is a symbolic economy rooted in an imperial history – a fantasy of the capitalist future that remembers 'the buccaneering spirit of Britain's imperial past'.[38] This affection for a time of Empire was well evidenced in the three Brexiteers' choice of office artwork – a fascinating window into the ideological souls of contemporary politicians. Among other things, Boris Johnson requested a bronze bust of Churchill, Liam Fox a lithograph of Cecil Rhodes alongside depictions of the Great Exhibition, and David Davis, intriguingly, a seventeenth-century engraving called *A New Map of Europe*, depicting a continent carved up along national lines three years after the Nine Years War.[39]

Such nostalgia for imperial time is not, to put it mildly, without consequence. It speaks to a broader inability to reckon with why the world, and its many contemporary injustices, is cast as it is; and, more importantly, it risks reheating particular associations regarding those many non-white peoples who were seen as the rightful subjects of colonial domination. Put differently, any significant form of colonial nostalgia also implicitly recycles notions of colonial hierarchy as regards the natural distribution of talents and roles across a racially indexed economic geography. The prospect of people from the Global South coming to the country and replenishing the concentration of corresponding communities already found in Britain becomes consequently freighted with neoliberal danger – the danger that these people, with their ascribed deficiencies as regards ability, skill and work ethic, threaten to dilute the nation's economic constitution. The selective neoliberal approval of particular migrants through a points system can herein be seen as a corrective political mechanism partially imperial in its mentality, a mentality in which the vast bulk of the world's people are to be seen as inadequate and kept at bay, while the select doctor or high-achieving engineer, recognised as *exceptional*, is quickly ushered into the country, and even construed as a civilising and improving presence.[40]

The crystallisation of neoliberal nationalism is accordingly threefold. First, it engenders a particular set of anxieties regarding immigrants and their less-than-productive economic disposition. Secondly, it rehabilitates Empire and all its unsettling and hubristic associations of a British greatness prematurely surrendered and/or to be forcefully revived. Thirdly, this imperial nostalgia contributes to a hierarchical understanding of ethno-racial place, wherein many of those who are already here or are threatening to arrive induce a racial anxiety about who actually belongs where.

Pathologies of poverty

Much of what has been asserted above might seem presumptuous. It would be right to ask here what exactly are these ascribed meanings and stereotypes that render the non-white outsider so dysfunctional according to a neoliberal metric. It is simply not enough to say that neoliberalism is racially inflected, as this is merely to assert a tautology. Closer substantiation of how certain prevailing representations of various outsider groups obtain an unfavourable neoliberal judgement is therefore required.

As signalled at the beginning of this chapter, neoliberalism is not simply an economic or legislative programme, but is also actively involved in the modelling and realisation of the ideal subject – as self-reliant, responsibilised and entrepreneurial. And while no one is free of the cultural circuits that encourage such dispositions, it is to be understood that various 'regimes of representations'[41] do in fact characterise certain backgrounds as being particularly ill-suited to neoliberal selfhood – or put more abstractly, as unable to realise the freedom that neoliberalism mandates.

As has been common across much of this book's substantive canvas, three subjects become particularly aberrant here: black people, Muslims and immigrants. All three – at times one and the same – become subject to certain presumed shortcomings in the popular imagination, wherein they are condemned to a condition of dependency antithetical to the individual autonomy that neoliberalism extols. It should once again be stressed that a dependency stigma is common to all neoliberal moralising – for instance, the demonisation of the working-class indolence that a far too generous welfarism is alleged to have bred.[42] I contend, however, that these ascriptions are particularly resonant when given certain ethno-racial coordinates.

The young black subject suffers, for instance, from two complementary renditions of neoliberal condemnation. The black male in particular, often conceived as being all body and no mind (all intuition, no culture), is ascribed a condition of wanton nihilism.[43] Seen as the vanguard for an urban decay from which all other dysfunctional street cultures stem, the black male is accordingly seen as lacking the work ethic or betterment agenda that is central to neoliberalism. This ubiquitous representation of the black male, one that also sanctions the routine over-policing of him and his peers, is made available in every new iteration of an urban crime scare.[44] The irony is, of course, that the hip-hop, grime and now drill soundscapes that are routinely submitted as evidence of criminal indolence (see, for instance, David Goodhart's essay, 'The riots, the rappers and the Anglo-Jamaican tragedy')[45] are themselves ambivalently suffused by many of the hustler and graft mythologies held dear by neoliberalism,[46] what Gilroy calls the 'neoliberal thematics of uplift, self-responsibility and self-improvement' married with the 'hustling ethic affirmed in several generations of Hip-hop'.[47] Or as Mark Greif argues, the rich mythology of intense hustle and material pleasure that energises much hip-hop is best read as a phantasmagorical revelation of the very thing that it is not – namely, the sheer destitution and material abjection that characterises the backgrounds of the rappers and the inner-city black spaces that they often hail from.[48]

On a similarly ironic plane, one not insignificant genre of contemporary neoliberal branding relies precisely on the commodification of a certain kind of iconically black, urban male: a trope that trades on a premium coolness that Naomi Klein identified as the turn by many sportswear behemoths in the 1980s to a branding strategy of 'bro-ing'.[49] This was a fetishistic treatment of the black male subject that, while maintaining a safe distance, seductively hints at a rebellious swagger and bodily machismo. There is therefore an ambivalent and cyclical looping here that is important. Namely, the terms by which an ostensibly black presence is won within the wider field of branded consumerist aesthetics are the very terms by which the wider pathologisation of the black, urban subject is upheld/reinforced. Put differently, the basis for most even 'positive' foregrounding of 'Black British culture' as regards the neoliberal ideological present acts in concert with the retrenchment of a wider characterisation of the black subject as suffering a neoliberal character deficit. As popular music and sport still overdetermine black media visibility, this confirms, in the very course of a seemingly affirming symbolic accommodation, the broader understanding of blackness as being outside the domain of a mature economic drive and industry.

Importantly, the neoliberal gaze need not necessarily see this conception of blackness as hampering the economic agility of black people alone. Indeed, as the 2011 riots – an important recent staging event for some of these chronic discursive positions – so ably attested, black culture is in fact occasionally advanced to explain a malaise that scars a whole generation of urban, working-class youth. Here, the 'shock troops' of 'black gang culture' are seen as imperilling urban Britain writ large.[50] As Gilroy so presciently cautioned in 2004,

> Influential pages of publications like *Prospect* and *The Salisbury Review* were groaning under the weight of speculations about the pathological characteristics of black culture, 'black on black' violence, and, worse still, the transmission of antisocial alien mentalities into the urban dregs of wretched white, working class life.[51]

In this context it is worth noting that while some have ascribed to Islamophobia a unique capacity to nurture fear and dread, given that the spectre of the Muslim carries with it a looming threat of *conversion*, it is true that analogous fears regarding contagion have historically been smuggled into the presence of blackness too. Muslims, remembered as a historically formidable power but also in their simple grouping as a *religious* community with a capacity to convert, do perhaps latently provoke in the nationalist psyche the fear of mass proselytisation – invoked most acutely in the still popular 'Eurabia' genre.[52] Blackness too, however, has been periodically marked as contagious. In the 'culturalisation' of what blackness is said to be, it threatens a rabidity that might afflict many others, even those initially characterised as white. It is in this context that we can make sense of David Starkey's now well-flogged line, in the wake of the riots, that 'the whites have become black'. The 'iconic ghetto', the space perceived as being where 'black people live', is in other words likely to claim anybody who might be born within or in intimate proximity to it.[53] Understood in these terms, the threat of blackness does provoke in some quarters a uniquely potent fear regarding neoliberal character, or the absence of it.

These possibilities of a sullied whiteness as engendered through encounters with blackness speak to a wider history about the continued failure of some white working-class people to carry themselves in accordance with a more dignifying decorum.[54] Indeed, the wider play of a derogatory parlance around 'chavs' and 'scallies' in Britain is so arresting precisely because it mediates a pathology of blackness upon a white body. As many have observed, poor black people in urban Britain are rarely understood as 'chavs', primarily because that fundamental condition of an unedifying, disreputable poverty is already written into wider racist understandings of blackness.[55] Whiteness remains, on the other hand, a horizon for success, neoliberal and otherwise. For instance, as Anoop Nayak so carefully documented in his moving ethnography of class and race in Newcastle, the 'real Geordie', who represents a particular regional ideal regarding respectable working-class whiteness, is stunned into a sharp hostility when confronted by the proclivity of some white youth to channel a black American vernacular.[56] The seemingly wilful engagement of blackness provokes all sorts of fears of degeneracy and broader class failure.

But while I have partly framed this pathology as being primarily a characterisation of the young black male, given the heavy associations of street crime and unproductive nihilism ascribed to him, it is clear that the black woman also becomes a uniquely fecund site for neoliberal sanction, in part simply as someone partaking in the alleged decay of black street culture, but also in her role as mother. The mother, as hinted at before, is a more significant character in the neoliberal imagination than generally understood.[57] As neoliberalism is particularly 'hot on the responsibility of the individual',[58] parenting, and a revived version of 'maternal citizenship' in particular, becomes identified as a predictably important site for the mooring of such responsibility. As Angela McRobbie writes,

> This persona of [the middle-class mother who is slim and youthful in appearance], whether in full time work or a 'stay home Mum' is accredited a more substantial professional status [today] than was the case in the era of the 'housewife'. With feminism 'taken into account' she is considered an equal partner in marriage and thus charged with making the right choices and decisions for her family needs. In this neoliberal version of past notions of 'maternal citizenship' a number of sociopolitical processes can be seen at work, [not least] she is compared favourably for her well-planned and healthy life in comparison to her less advantaged, low income, single parent counterparts.[59]

This is a crisp summation of ideal neoliberal motherhood. But, as McRobbie herself intimates, the colour-coding of what Bassel and Emejulu describe as the figure of 'the failed mother' is how such a modelling of ideal motherhood becomes most widely resonant, with the young black mother becoming a particularly potent foil.[60] A cluster of often indignant hostilities coalesce around the young black mother regarding her presumed failure to retain a male presence but also her irresponsible mothering more generally – too young, too many, and unable to inculcate the requisite aspirational values. To briefly borrow from the US rendering of such politics, Brito and Gilman, among others, have shown how the trope of the 'welfare queen', which was so central to the move towards workfarism that the Clinton administration and Gingrich-led House of Representatives co-engineered, was always and necessarily black/non-white.[61] It came, for instance, as no surprise that the infamous cover of the 1996 *New Republic* issue, entitled 'Sign the Welfare Bill Now', featured an image of a young black woman smoking a cigarette with one hand while cradling an infant sucking from a milk bottle with the other. This extension of a Reaganist moral economy as regards racialised condemnation found in the UK its Thatcherite equivalent via the Scarman Report – a much-publicised document, written in the aftermath of the various 1981 urban riots, that integrated into UK policy framings a concern with the pathology of the black family and, therefore, black women.[62]

It is in turn apparent that black pathology assumes many guises here. These aversions, through their masculinised, feminised and familialised registers, all act as interlocking harbingers of neoliberal failure. This is not to say that such hostile mediations are only sourced in a neoliberal morality. Of course not. But it is rather to say that neoliberalism finds such toxic mediations of blackness particularly commanding when weighing the merits and desirability of the population that it seeks to review, extol, punish, reform and/or exclude.

The Muslim denial of freedom

These neoliberal variations on racial inadequacy manifest elsewhere too, the ubiquitous figure of the Muslim becoming particularly telling. So while this book has previously discussed more familiar pathologies regarding Muslim *illiberalism*, a perhaps understated site of Muslim problematisation occurs via their supposed 'traditionalism' – as the undue predilection for custom, family and domesticity.[63] This operates in turn as a contemporary neoliberal inflection of a broader racialised dichotomy of the 1980s and 1990s: while blackness suffers from attributions of *inadequate* family and *inadequate* culture, the South Asian/Muslim suffers from its very excesses.

Lentin and Titley provide particularly sharp witness to this neoliberal unease with the putative privacy of Muslims.[64] They note that, owing to the broader reduction of freedom to the discovery of the self vis-à-vis market activity, much anti-Muslim sentiment draws from many Muslims' apparent prioritisation of non-market life: an unhealthy penchant for familial, religious and traditional life. Recall, for instance, Martin Amis's baffling diagnosis that exposure to Muslim culture and the Asian family is alleged to engender a frustrated male sexuality and unfulfilled freedom.[65] The Muslim man is, in short, saddled by constraints that sublimate in non-productive/destructive forms. Conversely, the Muslim woman constitutes in many such popular representations another extreme altogether. She is not only Muslim but is the entirely passive and dominated object of Muslim life.[66] An inevitable consequence of this subjugation is an inability to exercise the market freedoms and evangelical individualism that a neoliberal sensibility desires.

Some brief asides concerning the place of family in late capitalism must be developed here. Much has been made of how the capacity for sustained intimate relationships and prolonged immersion in extended familial networks is compromised when contending with neoliberal realities. Intimate relationships are always 'under review', always weighed by their convenience to shifting conceptions of one's individuality as well as broader needs regarding professional aspirations – the key operational ideal being mobility.[67] The ideal neoliberal individual is mobile, always responsive to the shifts that new market opportunities might offer. As scholars, conservative and radical alike, have understood, neoliberalism is a gross assault on our abilities to love, care and cohabit because of its compulsion for mobility. That is to say, the individual is made to embrace flux and impermanence, to embrace atomisation – fewer family dinners, more gym time and bespoke dietary regimes.[68]

The popular characterisation of the Muslim, and maybe the South Asian more generally, offends this call to embrace radical individuality.[69] The offence can be seen as twofold. It is on the one hand an inadequacy, a failure that is ultimately vulgar in its outmoded 'conservatism'. However, it is also perhaps a reminder of what could have been and what was before. In other words, everyday assumptions regarding tight-knit communal and familial Muslim society become conspicuous by the void that they reveal at the heart of much middle-class, white life. A uniquely split capacity for exaggerated irritation at a Muslim presence consequently materialises via this particular rendition of a neoliberal reality. It at once condemns just as it envies a lost national idyll – a texture of familial and communal life that the Other (the Muslim) allegedly possesses.

If, however, seen solely through an uncompromising and strictly neoliberal sensibility, this split desire for the Muslim becomes ably defused, leaving only the underlying condemnation of the Muslim's inability to embrace the market freedoms and cult of individualised competition that Western modernity proffers. It is the Muslim's penchant for yearnings extraneous to neoliberalism that is found wanting here, a deficit that is not only obscene, by its very inability to prioritise appropriately, but that also threatens to undo the wider economic health of the neoliberal nation.

The wrong migrant

The final iconic subject regarding the ability of neoliberalism to rally a deeply nationalist anxiety is the figure that this chapter first addressed: the immigrant writ large, but the racialised, non-white migrant in particular. One theme that is key to anti-immigration belligerence is the supposed work-shy opportunism of the migrant. (A parallel fear is the migrant's *excessive* propensity to work, but the mediation of such a fear belongs to a different ideological repertoire, and is, from within neoliberalism, anything but problematic.)[70] To state the obvious, our tabloid press and chattering classes alike bristle with indignation at the rampant scheming of migrants. They rail against migrants' exploitation of the European welfare state's largesse and are indignant at migrants' unashamed capacity to live on the fruit of industrious, taxpaying Europeans. This is a motif that runs across twentieth-century European modernity, from Bhownagree's leafleting in 1885 about 'foreign paper aliens' straining the coffers and rents of Bethnal Green, to the iconography of Powellism about the postcolonial migrant's ill-merited claims on the welfare state, to the more familiar jargon of benefit tourism.[71]

A wider culture of welfare shaming has been pervasive across the last two decades, and was central to the electoral triumph of David Cameron in 2010 – see the campaign motifs of 'Broken Britain' and Cameron's reliance on a striver and skiver distinction.[72] But a politics of welfare shaming becomes particularly foetid with regard to an everyday suspicion of migrants' desire to live in the West, a situation where the alleged proclivity for accessing welfare while not belonging carries with it a particular scope for causing offence and resentment: that is, being perceived as an outsider helping oneself to another's purse.

It was telling therefore that when Cameron tried, in vain, to appease two different wings of the Conservative Party regarding the European Union, his emphasis was on restructuring the rights of EU migrants to access certain welfare benefits.[73] Some background about Cameron's own journey is required here. He had himself previously sought to earn political capital for the Conservatives through sustained anti-EU posturing. Concomitantly, he was also front and centre in moralising about the poor in general – and immigrants in particular – having recourse to welfare provisions. As a self-styled arch-neoliberal, Cameron could then only revert to one possible ploy when trying to square these two positions in favour of an anti-Brexit/pro-Europe politics. Namely, his much-anticipated promise to secure a renegotiated relationship with the EU placed almost all its emphasis on scaling back the welfare rights that EU migrants supposedly enjoyed. Great energy was expended on celebrating the concessions that the EU subsequently granted, concessions that would neutralise the migrant's ability to 'game' the welfare state. Little did Cameron realise that the public no longer had any faith in such bureaucratic manoeuvres, as entrenched deep in the national psyche was the understanding that immigrants would *always* manipulate the welfare state, and that, by equal reckoning, the state, whatever its nominal rhetoric, would always give them, *qua* immigrants, *preference*.

There is a particularly potent angle here that is rarely raised in critical analysis. In short, a formative moment might have been the sudden visibility of Roma people on British streets, headlines and television. The Roma, and the permanent condition of absolute exclusion that they have been subjected to, speak to a particularly deep groove of racialised oppression in Europe that is poorly understood and conveniently ignored. This disregard is particularly strong in northern Europe, whose governmental and civic reckonings have been largely restricted to certain 'gypsy and Traveller communities' but not the Roma themselves.[74] The flurry of public attention subsequently obtained by Roma people in the UK was an unedifying spectacle, reaching one of its many nadirs in Rod Liddle's typically unoriginal rant ('They out-crim even the Jamaicans and the Somalians, which is an incredible achievement, really') as well as their prominence in the much-discussed TV programme *Benefits Street*, a show already noted for perfecting the 'poverty porn' form.[75] The show prompted Fraser Nelson, one of the country's most vaunted Tory intellectuals, to applaud 'the incredibly positive light' in which it portrayed an otherwise maligned community – 'It's probably the most positive portrayal you will see this year.'[76] Such an insight into the right-wing psyche hardly invites confidence. If Nelson found this to be compassion, it raises particularly unsettling fears about what indifference or, worse yet, antipathy actually look like.

Important here is what Fox et al. described as the 'Roma frame' with regard to the recent demonisation of eastern European EU migrants. While this frame was already taking shape in the late 1990s – a frame that was both new but also 'stepped right into home-grown narratives about Gypsies and Travellers' – it gradually became a master frame of sorts in the aftermath of A2 (the EU accession of Bulgaria and Romania) migration.[77] This is a scenario in which tabloid mediations of eastern European migrants in the A2 era were increasingly funnelled through this overarching 'Roma frame'. Importantly, and this is vital to appreciate, many 'Eastern Europeans who would not necessarily identify themselves as Roma' were also 'liberally' subjected to this frame – 'In particular, Romanians (especially those supposedly involved in shadowy or criminal activities such as begging, trafficking, thievery, or prostitution) have been frequently described in tabloid accounts as simply Roma.' What consequently manifests here is what Fox et al. describe as a broader 'Romacizing of [the] migrant "hordes" flowing in from Eastern Europe'.[78]

This frame is characterised by its emphasis on the criminal, work-shy and welfare-dependent culture attributed to the Roma: a culture of crime and welfare dependency that only a wilfully toothless 'liberal' ruling class would readily admit into the country. It might consequently be suggested that it was the incorporation of Roma into the nationalist charge sheet that constituted a racial tipping point regarding the national mood, whereby the general nationalist alarm regarding outsiders' raiding of welfare resources became irreversibly foetid once the Roma, a community with a particularly unique racial strain, was added to the list of culprits. Put differently, the Roma (and by extension, the A2 2007 expansion) became in part a bridging constituency that tied conventional neoliberal vexations against non-European 'bogus asylum seekers' to the general sweep of EU migrant flows itself. In sum, I am tentatively suggesting here that the Roma were a watershed for that decisive moment when neoliberal nationalism's general aversion to mass migration from a civilisational elsewhere became much more concretely rooted against the interior of the European Union itself.

Neoliberalism and the consumer city

This chapter has tried to offer an account of the layered demonisation of the racialised national outsider as occasioned by evaluations conceptually unique to a neoliberal sensibility. As David Theo Goldberg has laid out in multiple works, the neoliberal project is not possible without race. Race sits deeply wedded in its institutional and state mentality, and as Bassel and Emejulu have discussed, it is minorities, and minority women in particular, who bear the brunt of neoliberalism's redistributive violence.[79] The primary emphasis of this book is not, however, government, institutions, policy or even lived material effects. It is instead about political mentalities, cultural logics and evaluative rationales. This chapter has therefore attempted to contribute to the wider marking out of race within the neoliberal form by drawing particular connections to how it comes to agitate a specifically contemporary and specifically *nationalist* political mentality.

The final stretch of this chapter will engage a much more oblique, ill-defined line of inquiry regarding the neoliberal moment, a line that is far less familiar but nonetheless illuminating, I believe, once given due attention. Neoliberalism is not, even when restricted to this cultural register, merely a cognitive exercise. It is not merely a set of concepts and representations that prioritises certain values and concerns. It is important therefore to reckon with its more affective and temporal qualities, allowing for consideration of how neoliberal principles govern everyday rhythms and regimentations of space and how such influences might also contribute to certain ethno-racial evaluations. One accordingly instructive way of anchoring neoliberalism here is to consider its shaping of everyday *urban* life. In short, in what significant ways does neoliberalism restructure the ways in which denizens inhabit and engage shared urban space?

One theme that has captured the critical imagination regarding neoliberalism's uncompromising remaking of the city is gentrification. While an issue that might be considered relevant to all urban change, it is said that neoliberalism has galvanised a particularly aggressive but still surgical ability to displace people from areas previously understood as mixed-income or poor. Various neoliberal policies around housing play a central role in actualising such gentrification trends. These multiple policies include the forfeiture of existing social housing stock to the market through 'regeneration' policies and what is called in Britain 'right to buy'. It includes the political refusal to build new public housing targeted at low-income households. It includes the deregulation, or the inability to sufficiently regulate, rental and 'buy-to-let' markets. It includes the preference given to the commercial development of office and consumer spaces. And it includes, inevitably, the preferential extension of mortgage credit lines to those with more secure earning capacities. A body of writing has consequently arisen charting the vanguard neoliberal front that housing policy and gentrification represent.[80] Some of the most hitting yet invitingly snappy public essayistic work of the contemporary has in fact been fashioned by geographers and urbanists – a distinction previously reserved for art, theatre and film criticism – critically building in some ways on and against the tradition pioneered in Jane Jacobs' *The Death and Life of Great American Cities*.[81]

Quite rightly, much has been made here of the underlying but also epiphenomenal racial effects of gentrification, whereby often multi-ethnic inner-city populations are shunted out by mostly white, middle-class, young professionals and corporate property developers. (Though in certain areas this is also understood as being spearheaded by absentee property owners and speculators who traverse the West/Global South oligarchic spread.) And while it is not possible to rehearse here every inflection and casualty of this process, I do want to explore the particular *cultural* regard for the inner city engendered by neoliberalism that gentrification is, in part, a symptom of.

There is one outstanding question that requires asking: why has the city become so culturally attractive to the aspirational professional? Inversely, why has the suburb and its contained circuit of shopping malls and leafy but immaculately planned spacious lanes lost its allure in certain quarters as being the primary horizon of aspirational middle-class life? Many answers might be mooted here: for instance, the proximity of inner-city locations to contemporary tertiary work opportunities and the perhaps inadequate nature of public transport links and rising motoring costs. Similarly relevant might be the willingness of university graduates to trial improvised stints in relatively youthful districts of the city, given that a permanent career position is now only likely to materialise later in the life-course – facilitating in turn a broader habituation of the city as their preferred location even once they are more formally settled into career and family obligations. But much of the explanatory case also probably lies in the gradual triumph of *consumerism* as our primary expressive structure. And, as will be suggested below, this capture by consumerism of our everyday urban engagements does carry with it certain ethno-racial aesthetic properties that produce a not insignificant set of frustrations regarding minority and new migrant presences.

Consumerism refers here to the increased frequency with which expendable objects and transient experiences are purchased in the marketplace. That is to say, at its simplest, consumerism is about encouraging the citizen to regularly purchase non-essential discretionary goods – ranging from another pair of trainers, to a battery-operated candle, to a hand-selected hybrid bag of superfood grains and pulses, to new wall paint from Farrow & Ball, to a personalised card for one's niece.[82] Contrary to popular critique, consumer capitalism is not about prioritising purchases from large multinational corporations (though for various reasons, the multinational corporation does tend to enjoy pre-eminence). Late capitalism's operational baseline is far more prosaic. It is simply about ensuring that purchases always transpire and that as little friction materialises in the process of converting desire or routine into an active acquisition. Consumer capitalism is about guaranteeing that an individual always structures their routines and realises their needs through some significant engagement with a consumer market, whether it be a New Balance item or a craft ale from a local micro-brewery.

All this might be familiar. But it should be noted that the radical departure constitutive of the consumer age is *not* an increased partiality to the commodified *object*. It is instead the proliferation of the commodified *experience* that is the proper emphasis of consumer capitalism. The shift of most Western countries towards a service-sector economy is premised on a cornucopia of experiences, most of which require monetary exchange. These experiences can be as mundane as a visit to a cinema preceded by dinner at a franchised Italian restaurant; or they can appear far more tailored and niche – such as a 'go ape' excursion, a rock-climbing stint in the nave of a converted church, a members-only late-night opening at Tate Modern, or a weekend visit to a deluxe spa hotel. Either way, experience, doing something as opposed to possessing something, becomes the most bankable commodity of contemporary sellers. The inverse implication is that *doing* is no longer absent of the market – doing requires purchasing. As put succinctly by Hari Kunzru, 'Instead of citizens, we are now to be customers, and our right to the city is contingent on the agreement of the private owners of those spaces.'[83]

The *reductio ad absurdum* of this scenario is the much-maligned hipster. The hipster, if stripped of all the paraphernalia that renders him an all-too-easy object of derision, is in fact the exemplary consumer citizen. He takes the purchase to be the correct domain of individual expression, and in so doing, subjects the consumer purchase, including of an experience, to a heightened discrimination and level of 'micro-connoisseurship' that is surprising to a previous generation – hence the incessant mockery. Put differently, if expression of self happens via the purchase, then the purchase should be the reflection of hyper-distinction, of considered education and literacy in the relevant commodity genre.

The ideal consequence of this subject orientation as far as neoliberalism is concerned is that the commodity purchase is gradually rendered inevitable – given that what the individual is actually doing via the purchase is accessing an appropriate field of experience that allows them to be – allowing them to communicate selfhood as well as to socialise.[84] Put more directly, what is interesting here is the ways in which a field of consumer experience becomes part of our urban background and routine, whereby the purchase is itself merely an incidental necessity for realising contemporary sociability and social expression. This normalisation engenders accordingly a distinctive relationship with the city. Consumer capitalism requires the city, whereby the grounding of experience requires spatial coordinates. Consumer capitalism guts in turn the city's centre and its contiguous districts of anything that rejects the commodification of experience. It is no good for the consumer capitalist to be restricted to the suburb or the provincial town, as the sphere of bankable experiences that might be sold there is always too limited. It is the city's centre and surrounding areas that becomes here the ideal location, concentrating a vast pool of footfall in order to create a dizzying sequence of consumer experience.

This might seem a rather circuitous way of talking about nationalism and its attendant racial anxieties. How after all does this exegesis of the city as commodified experience relate to a way of problematising the presence of non-belonging, of migrants, of ethnic minorities? The answer, in my mind, is an aesthetic one.

As Sharon Zukin has argued, if the city is experience, and if experience is an immaculately curated and monetised social environment, the city gaze develops a particularly low tolerance towards those who appear commercially aimless, those people who display an unprepossessing, un-ironic ugliness or what Bauman describes as 'flawed consumers' lacking the resources to exercise their 'consumer citizenship'.[85] In short, when the urban location becomes idealised as a site of discerning consumption and suave commercial perfection, the exclusion of poorer migrants and minorities from cities becomes an inevitable feature of this space being reclaimed.[86] Visualisations of the ideal consumer space, now strongly staked at the heart of the city, bring with them projections of the accompanying ideal subject: a subject position that is summarily ill at ease with the residual presence of unruly, multi-ethnic youths and off-colour migrants who had previously laid more effective claim to the relevant city space in its pre-consumerist guise.

An interesting contrast transpires here. While the conservative modelling of ideal space takes us *further away* into the rural idyll of English arcadia, as a site of antediluvian refuge when contending with the migrant, multicultural deluge, the neoliberal *returns us* to a newly whitened city. Revisiting the treasure-trove that is *Against Everything*, Greif's observations about the aforementioned 'hipster' are particularly apposite here.

> [Embryonic hipster culture] recalled the seventies culture of white flight to the suburbs, and the most uncanny thing [therefore] about the turn-of-the-millennium hipsters is that symbolically, in their styles and attitudes, they seemed to announce that whiteness and capital were flowing back into the formerly impoverished city.[87]

This is eminently well observed. Millennial hipsters and their middle-aged imitators, almost always white, do indeed rush back into the city, newly armed with a purchasing power portfolio that is thirsting to be quenched. Racialised minorities, for their part, sully the carefully beautified consumer street that the city now promises. The surrounding urban architecture (including the people populating it) that frames the experience must seem effortless, non-intrusive, never jolting. The racial minority, suffering from so many ascriptions of poor taste, is out of keeping with this mediation of the inner city.

Some readers might sense a certain awkwardness in the above argument, given that considerable stress is given by certain urbanists, often Marxist, to the distinctly *cosmopolitan* idioms that lend the consumer city its enduring lustre. Attention is given here to how different parts of the city are often branded through certain 'ethnic' exoticisms and how it is the wider appetite for a worldly omnivorism, an affected cosmopolitanism so to speak, that makes the confident professional classes most keen to spend their way through the city. There is certainly some truth in this wider reading. But this particular conceptualisation of urban consumer experience is by my reckoning also grossly overstated. 'Exotic' restaurants yes, new migrants less so; black music yes, black women less so.[88] (I might add that such a pronounced appetite for cosmopolitan affect is only found in certain select parts of a few iconic global cities, for example London, Singapore, Berlin, New York, San Francisco, etc.)

Zukin et al.'s study of social media reviews of restaurants in New York makes fascinatingly apparent the racialised meanings that govern consumer cartographies of the ideal urban habitat.[89] The researchers found that restaurants that operate against a backdrop of whiteness were decreed comfortable and 'cosy', routinely receiving favourable customer reviews. The reviews contributed therefore to a form of 'discursive investment' whereby online commentary helps to publicly authorise the relevant gentrifying space as worthwhile and credentialled consumer terrain.[90] Those restaurants, however, that were situated in areas whose gentrification was incomplete or 'black-led' were viewed with suspicion, their seeming rough edges receiving coded rebukes through associations of 'dirt and danger'. This insight into the seemingly banal world of Yelp as regards New York is not exceptional and nods at a wider truth about how consumer space is ideally experienced by the middle-class white subject across the metropolitan West writ large. The cosmopolitan ideal is revealed in turn as being nothing but a euphemism for an upbeat consumer shine denoting an eclecticism regarding the consumer experiences available, and has accordingly little to do with the spatial accommodation of non-white subjects.

For instance, at its most blunt, it could be said that the Roma are rendered eyesores. Groups of inner-city black youth spoil the sonic and visual field.

Gatherings of Somali women reveal the artifice. This might have already been the case, but I think it obtains a particular purchase when the urban ideal against which the minority presence is implicitly judged has itself been remade so significantly in particular commercial directions. If the city's streets are no longer a site where people primarily loiter, mill about, work and cohabit, but are instead where people engage carefully calibrated commercial experiences, then the city is more sensitive to the seemingly disruptive presence of those who are not coded into the relevant experience. As Kunzru captures again very well,

> The typical [...] streetscape of pound shops and groceries may be unaesthetic, but it represents interwoven circuits of production and consumption that are local and targeted at the people who are already here, instead of those developers would like to see coming, people with more disposable income and fewer social problems. [The] poorest will be shunted out.[91]

My own navigation of suburban and new town mundanity[92] has made this distinction particularly apparent. The multi-ethnic suburb (Harrow, Milton Keynes, Cheetham Hill, Ilford, Croydon) seems to elicit an intuitive aesthetic condemnation, from conservatives and progressives alike, partly because it is always incorporating new iterations of migrant settlement, what Michael Keith calls an 'accelerated urban temporality' and all the 'unruly' human flux amid conditions of restricted purchasing power that this instantiates.[93] When seen in the context of the neoliberal appraisal of the city, there is something eminently mediocre about the multicultural suburb. This mediocrity is about people inhabiting places where their primary emphasis is merely to make do with the existing leisure infrastructure and to uncover ways of interaction that have little to do with discerning consumption. This mediocrity transplanted to the city centre or areas close to it is, however, a problem when the city centre is recoded as spectacular, stylish, smooth.

Aesthetic judgement is, of course, always an artefact of prevailing social priorities and hierarchies. The Ottoman coastal city, the nineteenth-century Victorian docks and the teeming South Asian megalopolis seem therefore less likely to induce this level of dismissal regarding everyday multiculture. It is instead a neoliberal conception of the city as suffused by ideals of the consumer experience that actualises a unique set of affective intuitions that render the migrant and minority presence less than desirable. Faltering command of the preferred language and/or accent and an inability to assume the proper sartorial code and gait converge to produce a particularly viscous mass ill-suited to signifying the correct urban ambience.

Again, as is customary, much of what is said here could be understood through a class lens, but this would only explain half of what is unfolding. Yes, as argued by Bauman and followers, a general inability to adopt the appropriate consumer script is often a reflection of class penalties, and overt, un-ironic working-class signifiers are unlikely ever to resonate well. The layering of various racial and ethnic cues does, however, intensify any such impression. Similarly, it is not necessarily the case that those ethnic minorities who people inner-city environs are summarily working class. Indeed, many of them might be instantiating some relevant aspirational indices of consumerist urban life, but their inscribed racial visibility − provided that it constitutes more than just the odd dark-skinned man or hijabed woman here and there − is unlikely to allow for straightforward incorporation into any such circuit.

More importantly, as regards the broader nationalist appetite, the manner in which many minorities, but new migrants in particular, are increasingly rendered conspicuous by their being out of step with the preferred urban aesthetic *amplifies* their perceived presence.[94] This 'matter out of place' scenario creates an accrued impression that there are simply too many of them. And that, after all, is the anxiety fundamental to a nationalist moment. Not that there are Others, but that there are too many.

Conclusion

The anxiety is that there are too many being given entry to the country without possessing the correct skills portfolio to ring the approving 'points-system' bell. That there are too many disposed to the cultures of nihilist dependency characteristic of the pathologies of blackness. That there are too many who seem to labour under anachronistic attachments to matters of Muslim culture and Asian community, attachments averse to the neoliberal call to freedom. And, as has been discussed just now, that there are too many sullying the urban environment, encumbering the city's capacity to stage an inviting culture of commercial experience.

Neoliberalism is, as seen here, a very distinct reckoning with nation and Othering. And by giving it such distinctiveness, by dislodging it from the conservative and/or liberal bedfellows it is wrongly conflated with, a much sharper sense of the nation's embrace of neoliberalism becomes apparent. It is a type of nationalism that disavows the motifs of blood and soil in favour of enterprise and productivity. It is a type of nationalism that disavows the gentility of lost idylls in favour of consumer metropolitan shine. It is a type of nationalism that is anti-migrant while managing to seem receptive to qualified immigration. In sum, it is a nationalism that is uniquely its own.

6

Left problems: the left and welfare state nationalism

Crises abound. Crises that might be productively seized, or crises that threaten to usher in a new threshold of capitalist governance no longer tempered by the nominal equality of juridical liberalism or the egalitarian reflexes of redistributive social democracy. Whatever else Brexit, Trump, Farage, Le Pen, Sanders, Corbyn and Five Star are, they seem to indicate crisis – a moment of rupture, a proliferation of new horizons and a centre that cannot hold. On the left, the 'full automation now' and 'universal basic income' neo-Keynesianism of the bright young things finds affinity in the avuncular socialism of Sanders and Corbyn.[1] Elsewhere, a popular authoritarianism, committed among other things to overseeing the full ravages of climate change, butts up against alt-right 'neoreaction'.[2]

Many of these positions found some degree of articulation in the run-up to the 2017 UK General Election – an election initially intended to clear the path for Theresa May's 'Home Office' patented authoritarianism.[3] Thankfully, Jeremy Corbyn's Labour Party won an unexpected number of seats, forcing a shift in parliamentary discourse. This shift moderated right-wing populist vehemence and, following the tragedy of Grenfell, contributed towards a renewed consideration of social welfare. However, a revanchist nationalism had already firmly consolidated itself at the centre of English politics, and, in spite of the renewed optimism of the Corbyn moment, that formation has only marginally dissipated.

Much of the past decade had after all seen nationalism become the most reliable broker of electoral power. It had informed the rise of far-right populisms while also fortifying centre-right rule across the West. This nationalist revival manifested along multiple registers. At times, the emphasis is economic protectionism. Elsewhere, it rails, not without justification, against the neoliberal dictates and administrative opacity of various supranational institutions, not least the European Union. Sometimes, it amounts primarily to a rustic nostalgia for something primordial. Common, however, is a consistent compulsion to place the bulk of a society's problems at the door of racialised ethnic communities, domestic and foreign.

As Western capitalism reneges on some of the key promises of the *trente glorieuses* (1946–75), creating a new political vacuum, it is painfully frustrating that nationalism is rehabilitated as the most efficient custodian of political discourse.[4] It is doubly frustrating that some who advocate a left alternative also seem wedded to the nation – in asserting control over migration, over defence, over security and over how we imagine our everyday sense of community. As these frustrations multiply, it becomes timely to sketch out a more historically attuned reckoning with the relationship between the current crisis and xeno-racist nationalism, including an engagement with how taxonomies of the working class have been remediated through a fascination with whiteness. At its simplest, it is only the importance of recognising the central role of racial nationalism in recent governance that requires attention here. The overarching contention, however, of this chapter is that a realisation of alternative left visions for governance must as a minimum start with the repudiation of nationalism's hold on contemporary politics, and the left's routine submission to its lustre.

That reckoning is, in a small way, necessary to appreciate the initial electoral success delivered by a Corbyn-led Labour Party. Any alternative model for mutual care and sociability will ultimately be sustained by energies outside the Labour Party, not within it. But it is nonetheless vital to note that Corbyn not only insisted on a substantial social democratic programme – rare to recent centre-left agendas; he also declined the call to rally nationalist shibboleths – although he did not advocate for migrants' rights either. His partial success is then accounted for by not having bartered with key nationalist agitations. Instead of capitulating to these, he presented an anti-establishment social democracy with popular appeal.

But to say this is also to note that nationalist agitations remain intact. Contrary to Paul Mason's delight when claiming that Corbyn 'has publicly destroyed the logic of neoliberalism and forced the ideology of xenophobic nationalist economics into retreat', it is apparent that nothing approximating the latter retreat from a nationalist politics has even remotely transpired.[5] As the dust settled on the election, nationalism returned to left politics, parliamentary and otherwise, because it never went away.[6]

In parliamentary Labour, we have seen Corbyn's initial quietism on migrants' rights accumulating at times a more recognisable anti-immigration tone (observed, for instance, in his ham-fisted comments about the 'wholesale importation' of workers which 'destroys conditions'); we see it in the pronouncements of MPs Sarah Champion, Gloria de Piero and Graham Jones on the white working class;[7] we see it in the continued interventions of Blue Labour, the wing of Labour that insists on a communitarian solution to the excesses of market individualism; and we see it in the formation of John Denham's English Labour Network. We also see it more formally in the continued inability of Labour to assume on Brexit the type of spirited and critical cogency that has coloured its other political interventions. Even at the height of the brief respite supplied by the Windrush blowback against the blanket licence otherwise given to May's 'hostile environment', Labour stalwarts faltered. Labour veterans such as Abbott and Lammy, so eloquent and clinical in their defence of the many black Britons being summarily stripped of their dignity and security, were reluctant to confront wider anti-immigration sentiment. They instead continued to rehearse, implicitly and explicitly, a self-defeating distinction between deserving, noble migrants contra illegal, criminal migrants. As such, aside from a limited defeat of right-wing authoritarianism, it seems little else has changed since the 2017 election. Optimism has certainly returned, even the word 'socialism', but the crisis that forged the nationalist demand, that props up its contradictions, that keeps Philip May's investments in tax-avoiding multinationals healthy, is still very much a reality.[8]

That the left has struggled to steer clear of the nationalist project, or at least some of its key tropes and temptations, will be documented at length throughout this chapter. It is, however, with the recurring inability of many on the left to resolutely read how nationalism relates to recent modalities of capitalist governance – both Thatcherite and Blairite – that we need to start.

Thatcherism, Blairism and the many uses of nation

Stuart Hall, unsurprisingly, is a generative point of departure here. Until recently a less-remarked dimension of his thought, Hall's commentary on the 'crisis' has been recalled.[9] The parallels between now and then are clear enough. Hall's crisis of 1970s and 1980s social democracy is after all the direct antecedent of our own, wherein the *popular* gradually yielded to the *populist*.[10]

Hall observed how under Callaghan (but more prominently under Thatcher), the formal ideals of social democracy became eroded, accruing a more authoritarian guise.[11] As market-society programmes were enforced, the broader conditions necessary for labour security, social mobility, comprehensive public provision and affordable networks of community-based leisure dissipated. Confidence in the democratic contract was accordingly threatened. What supplanted the resulting democratic void was an intensified emphasis on belonging to the nation, a belonging premised on certain fundamental exclusions. That is to say, there was a renewed and affirming cult of 'Little Englander' belonging based on identifying the threats posed by generally racial, frequently classed, and sometimes unionised outsiders. Here, a familiar cast of pathological presences threatening the nation begin to obtain their fuller political definition – the nihilistic black male, the degeneracy of the multi-ethnic inner city and, not least, the migrants 'swamping' the realm.[12] These appeared alongside the periodic assertion of remembered imperial glory via select military campaigns – the Northern Ireland Troubles and the Falklands being particularly significant.

The slide towards nationalist authoritarianism could then be narrated (employing a degree of hyperbole) along the following lines. The democratic project no longer hinged on the conception of a collective good; no longer aspired to deliver a shared social arrangement; no longer envisioned a society that could deliver a socio-economic stake for all of its denizens. Instead, the democratic moved its operational centre towards identifying populist objects of threat, disruption, decay and dependency both within the nation and at its borders. For Hall, this was not the same as saying that racialised alarmism and policing offered cover for market reforms, though it is partly that. It was to note the more fundamental shift in the locus of democratic governance and desire itself – a pivot towards authoritarian populism, understood elsewhere as 'parliamentary dictatorship', collected and 'sutured' by nationalism.[13]

Of course, the advent of 'Third Way' Blairism seemed initially to constitute a departure from this doubling of capital and nation. While Blairism certainly represented the consolidation of neoliberal common sense, tying the cult of enterprise[14] and the animal spirits of competition[15] to an edifice of urban chic, it also momentarily muted the Little Englander defensiveness characteristic of Thatcherite neoliberalism.

This popular reading is, however, somewhat misjudged. First, the initial (if piecemeal) commitments to race equality legislation and multicultural Britain were in actuality awkwardly embedded within a resurgent core of white popular cool, as embodied by the rehashing of an indie music scene and its upbeat, white nostalgia.[16] Secondly, the move away from heavily worn assertions of Britishness, minority threat and xeno-racism was largely reversed through the return to a 'community cohesion' thesis borne out of the 2001 northern disturbances and increased inveighing against asylum seekers,[17] a reversion to intolerance that was ably aided by the palace sociologist of Blairism, Anthony Giddens.[18] As was witheringly stated at the time by Gilroy regarding the Third Way's descent into a less equivocating anti-migrant politics:

> Giddens seems to be playing Piglet to Blunkett's [Home Secretary at the time] dozy Pooh Bear. Two timid creatures tramping round and round the national spinney finding but not recognising their own footprints, and then freaking out about the prospect of assault by BNP [British National Party] woozles. The fascistic resonance of the term third way always raised an eyebrow, but perhaps it was a clue to the deeper alignments buried in New Labour's corporate populism.[19]

This recourse of Third Way Blairism to what we might call integrationism[20] was then also indirectly hitched to the already available imperial nostalgia that was being rekindled in the post-9/11 aftermath, an imperial nostalgia that was lived through and repackaged in a manner suitable for early twenty-first-century sensibilities via the militarism of 2001 onwards, but already primed in the seeming successes of Kosovo and Sierra Leone.

It was, of course, not only the Labour Party that rehearsed the return of nationalism. After a confident first three years, New Labour became reactive, easily pressed into a political agenda compelled by the opposition Conservatives and their own well-worn nationalist impulses. Failing to redistribute wealth and lacking anything substantive to champion beyond a scramble for a fetishised 'centre' as an end in itself, Labour in the 2000s was apologetic and defensive, dancing uneasily to the tune of an emboldened right-wing press.[21]

Owing to these various processes, it was during New Labour's reign that a popular consensus around immigration as unequivocally problematic, Muslims as unequivocally ominous, and multiculturalism as unequivocally bust was secured. In short, the 'soft racism of the hard centre' became firmly entrenched.[22] All that subsequently remained was for its more virulent spokespersons to promise nationalism's more spectacular palliative potential.

The resulting nationalist consolidation occurred, however, under conditions distinct from those discussed by Hall. In Hall's analysis, the ideal subject lionised by Thatcherism was the self-determined, meritocratic individual – personified in the petit bourgeois shopkeeper (and therefore in Thatcher herself). The threading of free-market capitalist ideology through the mundane fabric of the new town and suburban high street permitted the dismantling of the welfare state and the incremental application of market logics to all human relations. It was consequently the petit bourgeois Poujadist who became the ideal nationalist subject, characterised by a deep private innocence and smallness under siege, but also an innocence largely at home with capitalist mantras.[23]

Today the mythopoesis of the shopkeeper, the 'self-made man' and the striver scarcely delivers in material terms. It is not even a consistent emphasis in Tory dogma. Rather, 'the market' gradually displaces the myth of the shopkeeper as the ideal neoliberal subject. The market is, of course, a pseudonym for the triumph of global finance capital. On Home Counties' high streets, we see this operationalised in the Conservatives' house-price-indexed business rate hikes.[24] Bases of traditional Conservative power, such as the fabled entrepreneur, are sacrificed to the exigencies of the corporate multinational, to Tesco and Costa, and to the rationales of the market. However, this shift from local to global is certainly not a rejection of the nation. Indeed, the Brexit-themed neoliberalism of global trade utopians Liam Fox, Nigel Farage, Boris Johnson and David Davis engineers its own potent version of nationalist assertion. Neoliberalism is first and foremost an ideology of enterprise and all objects come under its purview, including the nation. Construed as a competitive, cost-effective engine of pure accumulation, the nation too is then reimagined as enterprise – a visualisation with overtly colonial overtones. It is the ghost of the East India Company that haunts Liam Fox's desire for an 'Empire 2.0'.[25]

This remains, however, a particular rendering of the national project that reneges on a formal affinity with Little England. It is a neoliberal nationalism that is uninterested in petit bourgeois conservatism. But this is not to say that neoliberalism does not continue to inform the quotidian fabrics of local life. The ideology of the free market is still found in street-level anxiety about the failure to self-actualise the myth of merit, but these fixations with the optimising self sit alongside the reality of job precarity, income stagnation, widening inequality, diminished public services, the advent of disciplinary welfare ('workfarism'), rising costs of living, accelerated urban restructuring, the formal end to the promise of social mobility and increased social atomisation. As such, while our dominant 'structure of feeling' may still be petit bourgeois capitalism, the truth is that its conceits of mobility and meritocracy run up too frequently against social and economic realities. The cultural investment in ideals of competition and the sanctity of enterprise does not even remotely align with the wider realities of socioeconomic stagnation, austerity regimes, rising living costs, and the resultant individual struggles and hardships. Contemporary neoliberalism is global hegemonic, and as such, any promise of freedom it does contain is, for the majority, too far away.

It is because of these increasingly undeniable realities that we are said to be currently witnessing the partial crumbling of the neoliberal consensus.[26] Across Europe, more confident challenges to the austerity conceit are materialising. It causes concern, however, that the potential diminution of neoliberal logics still leaves intact the emboldened chauvinistic attachments to nation and whiteness that characterised the other side of that same governmental coin. Put differently, nationalism is all that remains of the established ruling culture when, or if, the consensus around neoliberalism and its austerity politics starts to slip. As I have briefly summarised above, the appeal of nation has been made to figure in substantial ways through both the Thatcherite and Blairite shepherding of neoliberal capitalism. This was not simply a recent history of a neoliberalism unto itself, but represented two expressions of populist neoliberalism as twinned to two respective conditionings of nation and nationalism. The task of a renewed left should therefore be to subject all calls to nationalist myopia and defensiveness to the same hard-won rebuke that leftists otherwise reserve for neoliberal capitalism. To soft pedal on this task, or worse yet, to accept some core nationalist nostrums would be to succumb to the shape of governance already rehearsed over recent history – only now, its partial untethering from former capitalist bedfellows allows for xeno- and anti-Muslim racisms to obtain a greater and more pernicious autonomy.

Nation and the Marxist canon

To extend further the polemical style I have hitherto deployed is tempting. There is after all plenty that could be subject to withering scrutiny; the ability of the left to map the transformations by which governance over recent decades has steadily courted nationalist attachments has been at times woeful. Indeed, some otherwise very intelligent and morally sensitive corners of the left are fond of citing the nationalisms of Trump, Brexit and Le Pen as the result of straightforward anti-capitalist impulses.[27] This version of political analysis, endorsed occasionally by Corbyn court scribe Paul Mason,[28] and often put forward by merchants of progressive contrarianism and/or self-styled spokespersons of working-class authenticity, then accepts retrenchment to the nation as an anti-neoliberal move.[29] The fact that some middle-class people oppose nationalism further compounds their mistaken notion that the new nationalist cry must be anti-capitalist, or at the very least, a recognisable act of anti-elite, working-class assertion. This is bad Marxism done worse. It takes the metaphor of oppositional class interests and writes it into every streak, corner and recess of culture and ideology. And while I cannot address every rendition of how nationalism obtains a leftist inflection, the remainder of this chapter will address a select few angles that have become particularly misleading – with an emphasis on the 'frantic circulation of a pseudo-class discourse' that lends to nationalism a left validity that it cannot obtain elsewhere.[30]

However, prior to any such scan of how contemporary nationalist politics recycles ideals that are putatively left-wing in character, it is worth restating in fuller terms some of the core theorisations of nation as proffered through a critical Marxist sensibility. A basic reckoning with Marxist analysis not only orients us towards many premises key to a proper theoretical account of the nation form, but it also reveals how easily a Marxist intuition can be corrupted, knowingly and unknowingly, to the service of more explicitly nationalist commands.

Most familiar here is the foundational argument that the consolidation of nation and nationalism within modernity is a simple ploy to 'buy in' the proletariat's commitment to a broader capitalist order. If class struggle is the fundamental fracture definitive of modernity, nation is then the fundamental reconciliation of that fracture. It is nation that bridges this antagonism. It is nation that balms the war position that class otherwise invites, carving out of an irreconcilable class hierarchy a 'deep, horizontal comradeship'.[31] This is, in short, the language of false consciousness.[32] The clarity with which the realities of class conflict and exploitation would otherwise be apprehended is said to become obscured by the diversionary investments in the false unity of nation – a unity that ties the corporate director to Joe the plumber, the cut-throat employer to the wage slave, the landlord to the squeezed middle, and the self-made business tycoon to the legion of young, underemployed professionals contending with the realities of the social mobility crisis.

While the words of people such as Eric Hobsbawm and E. P. Thompson helped secure the core British Marxist pivots through which to situate the nation formation, it is in fact a range of stock continental cultural Marxist concepts that helped clarify this sensibility with a more expansive ideological intricacy – a clarification regarding the decisive place of a nation mythology within twentieth-century capitalist *culture*. This includes, inevitably, Gramscian notions of hegemony and Althusserian elaborations of the 'ideological state apparatus'; but perhaps most pertinently, it also includes the Frankfurt School's culture industry thesis. Of interest here is the prevailing emphasis of Adorno, Horkheimer and Marcuse on how twentieth-century culture fully consolidates the broader project of capitalism, a project that asserts moral, aesthetic and affective claims on the modern subject. This operates through the inculcation of key values – for example, profit is good, the individual is sacrosanct; it operates through the ritualisation of certain mythologies – for example, the 'self-made man' and the American Dream; and it operates through the standardisation of certain temporalities – the latter comprising, according to Adorno and Horkheimer, a popular culture that presses narrative structures that are numbing, repetitive and interchangeable ('das immergleiche')[33] and thereby conducive to the mechanised capitalist division of labour. These multiple domains press in turn an ideological programme, both cognitive and embodied, that is eminently receptive to the ethos and imperatives distinct to twentieth-century capitalism.[34]

Much of this might be so familiar by now as to have become cliché, even among many 'anti-system' teenagers. But it should be recalled that there is also in the Frankfurt School thesis the accompanying emphasis on capitalist culture as being distraction (instantly satisfying spectacle) and illusory ('pseudo-individualisation').[35] The nation in particular becomes therefore a particularly resonant political cipher for generating these multiple aims: diversionary, spectacular, illusory and, ultimately, a satisfying and invigorating sense of collective and transcendent unity that is sutured together by the comforting 'slice of eternity' that the nation promises.[36]

In terms of engendering a slightly broader historical Marxist analysis, this hegemonically fashioned unity as engendered via the nation form also partly accounts for some other key twentieth-century processes. For instance, as regards the formalisation of the welfare state, the sedimentation of the nation idea helps explain how the domestic proletariat became 'deserving' of certain redistributive allowances – in the form of welfare state protections, graduated taxation, workers' rights and public-spending programmes. The very real consolidation of the nation idea does, after all, have effects that do not simply dovetail at every turn with the profit motives of the bourgeoisie. The mobilisation of a collective principle at the heart of the political contract that the nation generates allows the immiserated working class, but also the vulnerable petit bourgeoisie, who are exposed to the 'naked' cruelties of corporate capitalism, to campaign more effectively for their demands.[37] Their cry for amelioration obtains here a more credible pathos; and even their more belligerent acts of collective political disruption still obtain an intelligible moral authority and symbolism.

As regards the specifics of Great Britain, Alastair Bonnett's 'How the British Working Class Became White' captures this gradual shift particularly well. Bonnett addresses here the precise ways in which it was the formalisation of British national unity vis-à-vis a wider imperial project that helped yield a more interventionist governmental attitude when contending with the ravages of laissez-faire capitalism; a nineteenth-century situation where the domestic British sphere was initially characterised by largely chaotic and experimental free-market commitments was incrementally supplanted by the further ideological embedding of a commitment to national peoplehood – a multi-class peoplehood to whose interests imperialist capitalism must be actively bent. Put differently, Bonnett argues that imperialism, in generating extraordinary revenues for the metropole but also through establishing in the wider imagination a globally indexed, ethno-racial hierarchy, helped further a profound sense of societal obligation to safeguard as well as enable the wider flourishing of the British working class.

> Imperialism introduced significant non-market, state interventionist and social consensus (most importantly, popularist nationalism) tendencies into British society [...] Imperialism signalled a shift within capitalism, a move away from laissez-faireism and the exclusion of the 'British', 'white' working class from key national-racial symbols and towards an interventionist, social consensus oriented form of capitalism. In such a society symbols of social status and images of the national ideal could begin to be adopted and adapted for popular usage.[38]

This important historical analysis runs counter to the argument most recently put forward by the ever-truculent Vivek Chibber.[39] Chibber suggests, in his celebrated anti-postcolonial theory polemic, that the nineteenth- and twentieth-century gains of working-class struggle in the West are exemplary witness to the virtues of bloc political will. And it is certainly true that these cultural and political efforts to politicise and coordinate collective working-class action cannot be understated; so many of the welfare state's accomplishments are indeed the hard-won fruits of concerted political and cultural struggle. It is, however, also essential to acknowledge that the fuller sedimentation of the nation idea is what allowed the domestic working class to more effectively rally a sense of entitlement that obtained a political traction to which the imperial bourgeoisie, in their respective national guises, had to buckle, even if only in part.

This is a form of working-class consolidation, routed through the semiotics of nation, that *preserves* a class hierarchy while ameliorating its coarser, more brutalising effects. As the young Stuart Hall observed long ago,

> The Welfare State – with its three main planks, social security, income redistribution and nationalization – had valid but *limited* objectives. It sought to redistribute wealth towards the middle, and buttress the structure of 'opportunity' from below. It tried to redress the balance of social forces in the community – but not to alter the relationship of one group to another, within the still hierarchical structure of British society.[40]

Hall's insight is instructive. But at the risk of reaching for perhaps too strong a historical analogy, I believe there is also an instructive insight to be drawn here from classical theorisations of fascism. It is worth remembering that fascism – which, among other things, is nationalism reaching for its logical extreme[41] – is ultimately involved in precisely this complex but emphatic privileging of nation over class. Fascism apprehends the classed divisions characteristic of capitalism as being necessary and non-negotiable. But fascism also acknowledges these class hierarchies as being chronically destabilising. It maintains accordingly that such class cleavages should be violently and resolutely subsumed into the emolliating, ordering and empowering embrace of the nation. As was seen in Chapter 1's discussion of Arendt, fascism simply further enables the nation's gradual 'conquest' of the centralised state, a broader tendency towards conquest that long precedes any formal decree of the fascist resolution.[42] If incorporating, however, the decidedly more Marxist lens largely rejected by Arendt, this constitutes in essence national identity's conquest of the state in a manner that, through its muscular and unremitting emphasis on nationalist causes, throws otherwise insuperable class divisions into a manageable abeyance.

Or, as Badiou recalled amid the more recent resurgence of authoritarian nationalisms the world over, the fascist mentality firmly maintains that democratic law exists only for the assertion of the nation.[43] While fascist politics is willing to smuggle its way in through democratic legal instruments, should it be frustrated through these channels it does not hesitate to pursue other means. In short, fascism, by definition, is perfectly willing to pursue the extra-democratic in the course of reasserting the political primacy of the nation solution. This becomes in turn a form of democratic selectiveness that renders fascism a particularly efficient arbiter of class crisis – whereby its forceful summoning of the nation is not encumbered by the relative autonomy of existing legal instruments or democratic organs. Put differently, when read through these extremes characteristic of fascism, it becomes possible to bring into better analytic relief the *nation's* role as the exemplary reconciler of capitalist crisis. To recall the haunting phraseology of Walter Benjamin, 'behind every fascism lies a failed revolution'. The nation, in both concealing class and deflecting class conflict, becomes here the great alternative to the socialist threat, the socialist *raison d'être* being, in essence, the full inversion of fascism – to actively foreground and intensify class conflict.

The Marxist temperament in caricature

Much of the above, ranging from the nation as the deflection of class struggle to the nation as the mollifier of class struggle (i.e. the welfare state), is typical of orthodox Marxist analysis. And while it might be tempting to dismiss this analysis as too crudely deterministic, too neatly bending nation to the exigencies of capital, there is not all that much to quibble with here. As regards, for instance, the historical thrust of the Marxist argument, it remains largely undeniable that the consolidation of the nation idea as a political unit does certainly correspond to what Balibar describes as the 'development of the market structures and class relations' specific to modern capitalism – '[i]n particular, the proletarianization of the labour force, a process which gradually extracts its members from feudal and corporatist relations' and ties them instead to a territorially specific, localised national bourgeoisie.[44] And as Neil Davidson explains elsewhere, it is evident that nascent formulations of national consciousness were very much co-emergent with the advent of a capitalist mode of production across the various formative centres of the capitalist sprit (England, the United Provinces and the colonial United States). This is in partial contrast to the Gellnerian reading of national identification being harnessed only by early nineteenth-century *industrial* capitalism.

Similarly, as Davidson repeats, it is to some significant extent undeniable that nationalism is intrinsic to the capitalist project, as without identification with the nation, there is the much more profound and irreversible risk that the labouring masses begin to identify with their class interests. 'The danger [for capitalism] is always that workers will identify, not with the "national" interest of the state in which they happen to be situated, but that of the class to which they are condemned to belong, regardless of the accident of geographical location.'[45] This is again a perfectly interesting observation that must remain important in any attempt to come to terms with the nation-form's political viscosity. Nonetheless, it remains the case that much of what passes for Marxist analysis relies on caricatured expression, allowing for simplifications that are of a decidedly more dangerous political order, a genre of bad Marxism that allows vernacular nationalisms to absorb only hazily remembered and heavily dismembered popular socialisms.[46]

Alberto Toscano's recent 'Notes on Late Fascism' sets up some of the problems characteristic of crude Marxist reckonings with the contemporary hard nationalist moment – wherein, he identifies a litany of important slips and misdirections characteristic of much commentary that purports to do materialist analysis but only ends up doing nationalist apologia. He argues that it remains fundamentally misplaced to reduce nationalist politics to being *only* or even *primarily* concerned with resolving the contradictions of class and/or uncovering new horizons of capital accumulation when at a conjunctural impasse. As he notes, only the better of Marxist analyses were willing to recognise 'the contradictions between the autonomy or primacy of the political brutality asserted by fascist movements and the possibility of a reproduction of the capitalist mode of production'.[47] In identifying this gap, this absence of absolute convergence between intensely nationalist politics on the one hand and capitalist imperatives on the other, Toscano re-identifies the need to think beyond reduction at every turn, a reduction where nation only does the bidding of capital.

Toscano proceeds to suggest that our contemporary circumstances draw out this capital–nation gap in particularly pronounced ways, arguing that 'the intensely superstructural character of our present's fascistic traits seems instead to warrant looking elsewhere'.[48] The 'elsewhere' denotes here a need to look beyond an interpretation of the contemporary as being a crisis in capitalist accumulation – whereby the consolidation of a discrepant nationalism is not primarily about the attempt by capital to establish or recover zones of profit when confronted by, among other things, a large-scale labour movement (the latter being, of course, entirely chimerical as far as the present is concerned). This base–superstructure tension that Toscano wedges open offers in turn a generative way of phrasing the inadequacy of many pseudo-Marxist readings of the new right's electoral triumph across so much of Europe.

As Toscano importantly adds, it is in fact the case that the fascist desire incubates as well as draws upon certain latent *anti*-capitalist spirits, but these remain spirits that are not easily married to a contemporaneous socialist programme. These are the various deep histories – the multiple psychosocial 'desires', myths and 'fears' that belong to various non-synchronic periods of popular history – that the strong claim to the nation re-energises.[49] This is a point that Anson Rabinbach, via his reading of Bloch, puts forth particularly well: 'For Marxism the problem is that fascist ideology is not simply an instrument of deception but [for instance] "a fragment of an old and romantic antagonism to capitalism", derived from deprivations in contemporary life.'[50]

Nationalism's discrepant relationship to capitalism, one made apparent in much of the Brexit and Trump campaigning, raises therefore two significant problems for popular analyses as contoured by Marxism. It first raises the problem of nationalism not being simply a bourgeois ruse; never simply a tool of bourgeois deception employed to placate and absorb the frustrated proletariat. But secondly, and perhaps more importantly, this very acknowledgement also raises the possibility of the popular left actively misidentifying with certain variants of nationalist politics, a misidentification that results from misdiagnosing the anti-capitalist temporalities that a popular nationalism often commandeers.

This observation regarding the anti-capitalist urges within nationalist politics, though not central to Toscano's own argument, does help prise open a different and decidedly more problematic tendency of popular Marxist analysis that is of more immediate interest to this book's wider argument. In short, while the preceding précis of Marxist analysis has emphasised its perhaps over-zealous impulse to read nationalism as only, or primarily, a bourgeois conceit, this remains a fairly benign form of reductionist analysis. The rather more problematic tendency is in fact the inverse of this heavily worn historical determinism. The real trouble lies in those instances where nationalist politics is read as a misdirected anti-capitalist politics ripe for socialist capture. This is, in short, the widely disseminated notion that there is an anti-capitalist energy coursing through vernacular nationalist politics that is not only meritorious but also available for left-wing conversion.

A working-class insurrection?

Put bluntly, what I have in mind here are the concrete left-wing tropes and attachments that have embedded themselves deep into the contemporary nationalist logic, lending nationalism an integral, indeed indispensable sense of struggle, injury and revolutionary affect. One such prominent left-nationalist move regarding the contemporary crisis is the 'working class has spoken' ploy. Here, the multiple dimensions of nationalism are reduced to a working-class politics, an insurrection via the ballot box. Anti-immigration becomes a normalised sentiment of working-class populations (denying the petit bourgeois triumph that the nation actually is) at the same time as it is read as anti-capitalist politics (as opposed to the anti-minority xeno-racism that it so belligerently affirms).[51]

Needless to say, readings of this sort distort the demographic reality of the anti-immigrant nationalism that proved decisive to Brexit and Trump's election, the two events considered exemplary in such analysis. Drawing on Danny Dorling's correctives to the common orthodoxies of political punditry, Virdee and McGeever comment that the 'proportion of Leave voters who were of the lowest two social classes was just 24%'.[52] This is a sobering reminder that the much-discussed 'left behind' were not even remotely central to delivering these political ructions.[53] And yet the 'left behind' thesis still looms large in our wider political conversation – a new nationalist politics that is seen as coterminous with a working-class rebellion; a cry of defiance from an otherwise downtrodden and heroic mass; or, in the more emphatic phrasing of McKenzie, a great, anti-establishment, 'two-fingered salute from the working class'.[54]

One trope particularly key to this reading is a supposed 'cosmopolitanism' versus 'working-class culture' distinction.[55] Consider May's inaugural party conference statement that 'citizens of the world are citizens of nowhere', a statement, heavily steered by the 'Erdington Conservatism'[56] that informed May's inner circle, which sought to shore up her politically hollow but nonetheless rhetorically insistent claim that she would 'put the power of government squarely at the service of ordinary working class people'.[57]

This working class versus cosmopolitanism assertion is also the basic premise that informs the communitarian position of the Blue Labour school – a school of thought whose titular champion, Lord Glasman, wishes to revitalise a 'deeply conservative socialism that places family, faith and work at the heart of a new politics of reciprocity, mutuality and solidarity'.[58] This Blue Labour position channels a solidaristic leftism that extols the 'thick affective' virtues of community as necessary for the defence of a welfare state principle, in contrast to the 'thin, abstract altruism' that is attributed to the allegedly noble but entirely impracticable ideal of cosmopolitanism.[59]

This working class/cosmopolitanism distinction has accordingly two dimensions that merit closer scrutiny. First, it is said that the working class lacks the resources to cultivate attitudes more receptive to immigration and its resultant ethnic diversity; and secondly, cosmopolitanism (read multiculture and anti-racism) is characterised as merely an exercise in middle-class metropolitan self-aggrandisement that is ultimately superfluous to any genuinely progressive project. By channelling what might best be described as a post-Marxist brand of political economy analysis, there is a heavy investment here in an anti-cosmopolitan spirit that is insistently ascribed to working-class life by various prominent commentators such as Wolfgang Streeck and Joan Williams;[60] what Rob Ford and the ubiquitous Matthew Goodwin dub the latte-drinking cosmopolitanism of the metropolitan elites versus the good old provincial 'left behind'; what Paul Collier, through resorting to a tortured neologism, calls the *'sans cool'*, described as 'toiling provincials' who rail against a liberal class that has 'embraced a globalized identity' and 'espouse multiculturalism';[61] or what Goodhart sets up as the 'Anywheres' (metropolitan liberals) versus the 'Somewheres' (provincial nativists).[62] This distinction primed Goodhart's more wholesale descent into a strange brand of parody racism – recall here his headline claim that 'White self-interest is not the same as racism', a title that managed to prove even more exculpatory of racism than his first claim to incendiary fame, his essay for *Prospect*, 'Too Diverse?' – the question mark here being entirely notional.[63] And while Goodhart's pugnacious crudeness does render him a rather obvious target, it is worth noting that this line of neglected working class versus effete cosmopolitanism argumentation has even seen well-recognised academics lend the English Defence League (EDL) a measure of political dignity that would just a few years ago have been considered *verboten* – a group that is, as far as contemporary Britain is concerned, the epitome of far-right street politics.[64]

Whence and whither working-class multiculture?

These various arguments, symptomatic of a wider political common sense, allege that a resource deficit is said to explain resentment towards migration and ethnic diversity among the working class. And, by the same token, it is argued that cosmopolitan resources are the preserve of the middle classes. Ignorance of this resource deficit is then put down to the smug arrogance of metropolitan elites.

Some important truths need to be restated here. First, this conceit ignores many apparent dynamics of British cities. The unspectacular commitment to multiculture occasioned by the quotidian textures of much urban life – that is to say, a city habitus common to many black, brown and white working-class people – is well documented.[65] As Jeremy Gilbert puts it,

> The problem with [the Cruddas-led Blue Labour] approach, as interesting as it is, is that it tends to argue as if neoliberal cosmopolitanism were the only form of cosmopolitanism that had ever existed or could ever be imagined […] Critics of contemporary cosmopolitanism seem to struggle with taking seriously the fact that for many inhabitants of cities like London and Glasgow – including many poor and working class people – cosmopolitanism is just as real and authentic a characteristic of our identities, our histories and our communities as localism and nativism might be for others.[66]

This indelible multicultural energy, though hardly sufficient to constitute a political programme in its own right, will be extensively profiled in the concluding chapter as giving vital momentum to those organised movements trying to challenge the nationalist political present. It suffices, however, to note for now that it is hard to seriously justify the suggestion that an alleged liberal middle class has the resource monopoly on cosmopolitanism.

The fact remains that while many middle-class people might nominally share the rhetorical commitment to multiculturalism, they are scarcely its only or even its primary agents or symbols. Indeed, much, though not all, of what is narrated as being a middle-class embrace of cosmopolitanism might instead be seen as the rather thin marketplace consumption of ethnic diversity – which is nowhere as well put as in bell hooks's defining coinage, 'eating the Other'.[67] It is often a form of cosy realisation of self via consumer discernment – rather than an extension of sociability, care and concern – that is sometimes forgotten when Polish off-licences outnumber bespoke coffee shops, when multicultural neighbours become noisy nuisances, and when these personal discomforts are weaponised through the police, spending power and property prices.

To reiterate, the reality of many urban working-class areas discredits the thesis that a resource deficit between middle-class and working-class populations explains the wariness of migration and ethnic diversity. The suspicion of what is called cosmopolitanism here, when it does indeed materialise, is therefore best accounted for elsewhere. Namely, the presence of ethnic minorities becomes a basis for resentment only when it runs up against thickly textured defensive narratives of the nation.

This assertion about 'working-class cosmopolitanism' should not be read as suggesting that all historically working-class areas are somehow the same.[68] It is evidently the case that different histories of recent industrial employment, and accompanying decline, alongside different patterns of migrant settlement and incorporation as specific to different areas of a country will yield sufficiently different class dispositions to the question of nation, immigration and discontent. After all, the study of less fabled locations might reveal different and more fragile multicultures when compared to the Londons and Manchesters that are ordinarily the focus of research into multi-ethnic cohabitation. The work of Daniel Burdsey on the British seaside, Julius Baker's doctoral work on Epsom, and Ben Rogaly on Peterborough, alongside writings on the ill-defined contours of multi-ethnic suburbia, all ably contribute to this complex reading of what multiculture is when staged in contexts that are reflective of the British population's more likely geographic surroundings – not 'global cities' but the small-time 'mediocrities' of the suburban and provincial alike.[69] But any such assertion of working-class multiculture also helps refute the more maximalist argument that working-class people, by virtue of a fundamental financial or cultural deficit, remain hostile to a cosmopolitan politics.

Who is the nationalist subject?

Similarly, it ought to be recalled that those susceptible to strong anti-minority and anti-immigration views, at least in electoral terms, are not actually more likely to live in areas with large ethnic minority and migrant populations. See, for instance, Derek Sayer's extended deconstruction of this myth as regards the Brexit vote:

> We need to be wary of what we infer from Lincolnshire[70] and similar areas. The great majority of the 102 districts in England and Wales where 60% or more voted Leave are among the most ethnically homogeneous – which is to say, the least exposed to immigration, from the EU or anywhere else – in the country. Seven had a white British population of over 95%, 62 of 90–94%, 29 of 80–89%, and only four of below 80%. More than fourth-fifths (85) had a white British population above the England and Wales average of 83.35%.[71]

Sayer accordingly summarises that, 'far from the presence of immigrants inclining people to vote Leave, the more ethnically diverse the area, the more likely it was to vote Remain'.[72] The argument of Rydgren and Ruth on the 'halo-effect' and the politics of the radical right in Sweden provides here another complementary conceptual detail. The 'halo-effect' is the term the authors deploy to capture the 'propensity' of far-right voting to be higher among those 'native' voters living *close to* 'immigrant-dense areas' but, importantly, not actually *in* those pathologised areas.[73] Or, as regards a more internationally iconic political scene, consider the fact that it is the 'rural heartlands' that form the core support of the French Front National (now trading as National Rally).[74]

These various details, regarding Brexit, the Swedish far-right and the rehabilitation of France's Front National, are not insignificant observations, given how emphatically they run counter to the otherwise commonplace assumption that hostile attitudes to immigration and multiculturalism are driven by grounded, working-class experiences of living amid these processes. The ubiquity of this intimation that hostile sentiments are most intense in areas that have indeed been heavily affected by immigration therefore needs to be placed under even further analytic stress.

It is in this context that the aforementioned Jeremy Gilbert, who otherwise qualifies his cosmopolitanism versus working-class thesis with characteristically learned nuance, issues his most awkward analysis. Gilbert, a figure who remains one of the most constructive voices in shaping a meaningfully popular Labour movement, is ordinarily alert to the ways in which popular discourses are mediated through the alarmist perils of race meaning. And it is this deep literacy that makes his own susceptibility to the 'white-working-class-has-spoken' myth so telling – revealing the deep reach of nationalist maxims into various corners of today's political psyche.

In his paper for the Stuart Hall Foundation, Gilbert rallies the metaphor of a hypothetical 'housing co-op' not welcoming newcomers unless previously vetted, which is in turn rendered comparable to the political classes' failure to 'consult ordinary local communities' (read the white working class) about immigrant arrivals.[75] What Gilbert takes for granted here is telling. First, there is the assumption that 'ordinary local communities' (say in Stoke or Swindon) have indeed had immigration *imposed* upon their specific locales; and secondly, there is the assumption that these experiences of immigration have been, on the whole, destabilising. The metaphor becomes in turn particularly indicative of how nationalism is able to press any number of sleights of hand, whereby ordinary xenophobic racisms obtain an ennobling and defensive *innocence*.[76] Such a metaphor is also surprisingly unreflective about its acquiescence to Romanticism's formative invocation of nation as 'home' – whereupon outsiders are pictured as encroachers, raiders, pollutants, occupiers or, at best, guests who must perform the correct degree of gratitude.[77] This psychosocial working of the national home, a characterisation of deep homeliness through which yearnings for care and fortification alike are threaded, has been ably picked up in the recent theorisations of what is called 'domopolitics'.[78]

Gilbert also intimates in the course of his argumentation a *cultural* thesis on community that seems to be indexed to ethnicity, a particularly odd tenet to press when exalting the work of Stuart Hall – a celebration of Hall being the wider context in which Gilbert is speaking here.

> [Their] grievance is simply this: nobody asked them. Nobody asked these people if they wanted a significant cultural recomposition of their communities and nobody talked to them about why it might be happening and why it might be beneficial or necessary and on what terms it might be managed so as to make it feel like less of an immediate threat.[79]

It is, of course, unclear why culpability for cultural 'recomposition' is being primarily attributed to alleged migrant arrivals. Similarly, it ought to be asked what kind of cultural coherence is actually meant to have predated this migrant-driven 'recomposition'. If something approximating a contained cultural network and shared structure of feeling were indeed available, it is likely to have been just as much a result of other, largely non-ethnic circumstances, not least the particular availability and character of permanent local employment, the particular spatialisation of complementary residential provisions, and the intervening infrastructural circuits of shared leisure and political engagement. Significant shifts in these respective domains would seem to have more bearing on the altered cultural content of an area than the ethnic constitution of its population. Ethnicity, as Alexander, Brah, Gilroy and Hall have revealed with so much acuity, remains a highly unreliable and fallible witness to culture.[80]

The bundling of immigration as representing a lived and cultural threat to local working-class populations remains therefore particularly unhelpful; and, in spite of his own analytic care and wider political commitment to anti-racist futures, Gilbert does briefly succumb to an anxiety axiomatic of the very populist nationalisms across Europe of which he is such an impassioned critic. Seen more broadly, as in Žižek's recent spluttering about acknowledging hard 'realities',[81] any such reading of a cultural assault on working-class familiarities is one in a broader sequence of propositions central to a contemporary anti-migrant alarmism that appropriates a language of class injustice: one, working-class areas hostile to immigration have first-hand negative experiences of contending with immigration; two, these working-class areas have been denied by the 'liberal establishment' a democratic structure through which they might have been consulted about this remaking of their locales;[82] and, three, this remaking of working-class areas is in many crucial ways *cultural* in form.

Whitening the working class

That this analysis exercises such popular traction is perhaps on account of the melancholic visualisation of the working class as white, and only white. Conversely, non-white working-class people are denied a class status, their entire constitution and experience being read exclusively through the lens of racialised identification. Put aphoristically, class becomes to a significant extent white, and race becomes to a significant extent black/non-white. It becomes particularly important therefore to deconstruct this invocation of a white nativist monopoly on working-class experience because of the sense of victimhood and injury it offers nationalism. In this assessment, the working class is invested with whiteness, and this whiteness is presented as being under threat from migration, political correctness, equalities politics and the very idea of a multi-ethnic society itself. Left punditry has become troublingly good at recycling this canard, where either class exclusion is used to explain all other features of modernity, and/or white interviewees' testimonies on the dangers of migration are presented as unmediated social truths. Anti-immigration sentiment is read here as a transparent grievance *authentically authored* by the forgotten (read: white) working class. In both cases, proper analyses of culture and race go missing. These articulations occur in a wider left discursive environment that too often presumes the historic entitlement of 'indigenous' white working-class people. Weaned on soap operas, the memory of the Blitz spirit, the golden era of the welfare state and football as it used to be, many left vanguardists indulge this position by distinguishing the entitlements of the white working class against the illegitimate claims made by 'new migrants'.

This heavily whitened reading of class has become perhaps the most deafening feature of contemporary left nationalism, a nationalism in which defensive working-class positions are asserted against the spectre of immigration. As such, by way of concluding this chapter, a closer historical interrogation of how the notion of a national working class became suffused by whiteness is instructive, this being a historical insight that makes apparent the difficulties that the non-nationalist left must prepare for when trying to reclaim more inclusive ideas of working-class identity. It is accordingly Robbie Shilliam's *Race and the Undeserving Poor* that proves particularly timely here, a book that carefully unpacks the colonial raciology that incrementally allowed the working class in Britain to be re-envisaged as subjects deserving of dignity and state provision.[83] Shilliam traces the broader histories of how the emergence of the British welfare state was contingent on broader colonial conceptions of a *deserving* white poor vis-à-vis the undesirability of the racialised, non-white colonial poor. He offers in turn a genealogy of how contemporary mobilisations of the 'white working class' as a political category speak to this long and deeply entrenched colonial lineage.

It is difficult to do justice either to the breadth or the empirical precision of Shilliam's historical gaze here. In eliding, however, his more intricate attentiveness to various legislative proceedings, it is possible to sketch his general argument. Shilliam first observes that ever since the sixteenth-century Elizabethan Poor Laws, a governmental distinction between the deserving ('lame, impotent, old or blind') and undeserving ('idle and vagrant') poor has been ably pressed into popular circulation, the former receiving respite and 'relief', the latter a moralising punishment.[84] But crucially, as Shilliam rightly stresses, this emergent distinction was only initially restricted to the class parameters of Britain itself, gradually coming to enjoy far more expansive colonial insinuations. As imperial capitalism further developed and so too its complementary programmes of poverty-relief provisioning, this broader governing frame of deserving and undeserving took on more explicitly colonial and racial associations. This was reconsolidated, according to Shilliam, with the twentieth-century founding of the welfare state and its notion of a 'national compact' that traded on a conception of the white working class's natural entitlements – this being a conception that was necessarily connected to the active denial of a 'universal welfare' to the racialised, non-white citizens of Empire.[85]

Shilliam argues that this more explicit working of a racialised conception of working-class entitlement first hinged on eugenicist fears that the stock of white English workers, unless shielded in terms of the 'health, sanitation, habitation and food' deficiencies so endemic to industrial capitalist life, was at risk of 'degenerating' into a condition unbecoming to their national calling; a condition more natural to the various armies of colonial, non-white workers.[86] This hygienist degeneration thesis is well noted. Recall, for instance, the thoroughly unflattering Renan passage dug out by Césaire when he excoriates the brutal labour hierarchies that colonial registers of racialisation were able to conjure, conceptions that Césaire rightly insisted were as likely to be subscribed to by scholarly 'humanists' like Renan as by more militant merchants of imperial civilisationism. Indeed, as Césaire asks when sardonically pondering the provenance of the following passage: 'Hitler? Rosenberg? No, Renan.'

> The regeneration of the inferior or degenerate races by the superior races is part of the providential order of things for humanity. With us, the common man is nearly always a déclassé nobleman, his heavy hand is better suited to handling the sword than the menial tool. Rather than work, he chooses to fight, that is, he returns to, his first estate. *Regere imperio populos*, that is our vocation. Pour forth this all-consuming activity onto countries which, like China, are crying aloud for foreign conquest. Turn the adventurers who disturb European society into a *ver sacrum*, a horde like those of the Franks, the Lombards, or the Normans, and every man will be in his right role. Nature has made a race of workers, the Chinese race, who have wonderful manual dexterity and almost no sense of honor; govern them with justice, levying from them, in return for the blessing of such a government, an ample allowance for the conquering race, and they will be satisfied; a race of tillers of the soil, the Negro; treat him with kindness and humanity, and all will be as it should; a race of masters and soldiers, the European race. Reduce this

noble race to working in the *ergastulum* like Negroes and Chinese, and they rebel. In Europe, every rebel is, more or less, a soldier who has missed his calling, a creature made for the heroic life, before whom you are setting *a task that is contrary to his race* –, a poor worker, too good a soldier. But the life at which our workers rebel would make a Chinese or a fellah happy, as they are not military creatures in the least. *Let each one do what he is made for, and all will be well.*[87]

While there is certainly a lot jostling for prominence in this extract, the base European perception of a racial propriety as regards the differentiated protections that the labouring classes ought to enjoy is what is most starkly evident. And it is precisely these broader racial coordinates that Shilliam argues helped cement in Britain, as elsewhere in Europe, a fuller public commitment to a domestic working class that was now envisaged as white. As the specifically British regard for a domestic working class steadily accrued further conceptual definition alongside commitments from across the political spectrum, it yielded, in time, the now immortalised 1942 Beveridge Report. This was ostensibly a political moment that conclusively 'dissolved' any internal discrepancies among the English between deserving and undeserving.[88] But importantly, any such dissolution, whether complete or partial, was never one of dissipation. It was instead the case, often naively missed, that this distinction had only been more forcefully and comprehensively redirected.

The governing distinction of deserving and undeserving was now reconstituted in a racialised form through both the 'informal colour bars' that were being implemented by some union, labour and housing sectors, but also via the wider entanglement of welfare and colonial policy.[89] Shilliam meticulously observes here how different restrictions were placed on the briefly mooted application of this newly minted welfare provisioning to the colonies. These formal restrictions were then complemented by the parallel and subsequent wave of parliamentary Acts that disinherited many colonial subjects of their British citizenship.[90] This joint legislative programme allowed in turn for the white British working class to be decreed, institutionally and imaginatively, the only true subject of welfare. Or, as put stridently in the words of Bonnett, 'Welfare came wrapped in a Union Jack'.[91]

Some of this historical complexity might be familiar to certain circles – circles less susceptible to the naive belief that capitalism is committed to a telos of gradual progress best embodied by the accomplishments of the welfare state, important as those accomplishments are. But any such awareness of the welfare state's more complicated provenance is not in itself without hazard. If the founding sin of the welfare state is indeed understood to be its broader colonial context (other non-'reformist' Marxists might also add that the welfare state retards the possibility of a revolutionary working-class consciousness), then the lapsing of formal colonialism might risk being read as conclusively expiating this sin.

It is therefore necessary to note that this investment of the welfare project in the symbolic order of nativist whiteness becomes in actuality just as well articulated in the wake of colonialism's retreat. For instance, regarding Miles's canonical thesis on the 'migrant labour model', the 'racialization' of migrant workers allows them to become 'a substratum of the proletariat', a substratum for whom welfare state obligations are less forthcoming and to whom workers' rights and security do not obtain as easily.[92] Moreover, as regards the vicissitudes of British history, once the *spectre* of immigration incrementally became, from Thatcherism onwards, such an outsized issue in British political discourse, the semiotics of welfare state entitlement took on an ever deeper racialised logic of 'bordering',[93] a discourse that Sivanandan harnessed particularly well through his concept of 'xeno-racism'.[94] This is a framework that centres migrants, in their multiple, often racialised guises (asylum seeker, labour tourist or rapacious foreign capitalist), as the primary object of political alarm and securitised exclusion. In turn, other residual political anxieties, including those that belong to a wider tradition of twentieth-century social democracy – whether the welfare state, visions of local community and leisure, the NHS, or the quality of local schools – become more assertively pressed into this overarching fault-line that immigration comes to represent. Within this framework, one that partially traces the initial colonial/native working class taxonomy that Shilliam attributes to the promulgation of these welfare, nationality and immigration Acts, 'there is no politics of class that is not already racialized. Class is race.'[95]

This overview of Shilliam's argument, one which ably complements recent publications by Gargi Bhattacharyya and Satnam Virdee, allows us in turn to better rebuff the re-centring of specifically 'white' working-class suffering in recent political deliberation.[96] When left thinkers intimate that the white working class have unique grievances against capitalism, coterminously understood as legitimate grievances against the pressures placed on them by immigration, they are not sufficiently interrogating the historical relation between whiteness and the nation.[97] What is more, revisiting an earlier phase of this chapter, they are also conveniently constructing a lived defensive reality of whiteness that is not easily borne out in many working-class, multi-ethnic neighbourhoods, although the discursive operationalisation of a uniquely white working-class grievance certainly threatens to remake the embryonically radical cultural realities of these areas.

Such a position also refuses to acknowledge the contingent porosity of whiteness, and how the 'wages of whiteness' are often claimed by populations who a generation or two ago might not have been white enough.[98] It is worth remembering here the various symbolic illegitimacies that Irish, Italian and Jewish working classes had to contend with throughout much of the last two centuries, with accommodation into the figurations of whiteness being often only partial and, at times, simply non-existent. It becomes similarly necessary to observe how a safer claim on the nation and/or escaping one's own Othered status often involves an incremental chain of claiming the proprieties of respectable, middle-class whiteness and/or mimicking the demonisation of the new migrant Others that the national assertion at any given moment might be trafficking in.[99] It is accordingly through this historic lens, which acknowledges the strategic and often uneven passing into national whiteness, that it becomes possible to get a better grasp on the ways in which whiteness and anti-immigration sentiments coexist, and the ways in which they become a repertoire through which some working-class people are encouraged to make sense of their social and economic marginalisation.

But, as argued by Malcolm James, it is also from here that the complexities of xeno-racism that might characterise multi-ethnic parts of our cities can also be accounted for: where hostility to 'newcomers' can be easily mobilised by those who claim whiteness, 'but related exclusions can also be adopted by some ethnic minority residents who reject white supremacy yet favour exclusionary territorial claims – "I was here first."' This 'internally discrepant but nonetheless majoritarian discourse of exclusion' that invests heavily in the politics of anti-immigration is where analytic attention should be directed.[100]

In sum, the left-nationalist argument hinges on a conflation of essentialised and fetishised whiteness with working-class struggle and anti-capitalism. The defence of class then becomes a defence of whiteness, and by extension of the nation, a defence of anti-immigration politics. This reading of working-class politics is in short an argument for nationalism, and for racism, and inevitably harms working people.

Another left, another politics?

Much of the above might risk indulging in a far too sobering, cynical and even defeatist understanding of the British left and how its attempts to politicise class consciousness become wedded to a nationalist horizon. A more constructive reading would first observe that contemporary nationalist discourse is certainly not a speciality of the working class but has historically developed across a number of prominent platforms, each of which has been important to the recent political history of western Europe. As charted across much of this book, these multiple discursive heritages include but are not limited to the *liberal* – nation in relation to Eurocentric interpretations of tolerance, free speech, secularism, the rule of law and civility; the *neoliberal* – nation as mediator of economic enterprise and 'homo economicus'; and the *conservative* – nation in nostalgic relation to the provincial, imperial, Christianist or rustic white. And, inevitably, the *communitarian left* too – nation in relation to the welfare state and broader anti-market, anti-globalisation sentiments. The ideological contouring of nationalism at the present moment calls upon all these various repertoires.

This observation constitutes an important reminder to those with left or left-of-centre leanings. Just because contemporary nationalism might carry with it certain leftist registers, it does not then mean that this iteration of nationalism is somehow more manageable, redeemable or convertible. Put differently, nationalism is itself the populist play. All else is simply marshalled in its service. Of course, to realise a winning politics that avoids the temptations of anti-immigrant populism might presently seem a thankless task. But it is a task that must be contended with, as otherwise one merely gives succour to the nationalist call. Nationalism is never simply a means to other political ends, not least left collectivism. Nationalism is always, in the final instance, about its own exclusionary racisms – anything else is a convenient bedfellow rallied to make its appeal more likely.

Or, to end with the challenging words of Richard Seymour, who remains one of the sharpest and most uncompromisingly constructive friends of the Corbyn left:

> We on the Left are having a good campaign about class and economic issues right now, but to an extent we seem to want to have anti-fascist conversations without seriously addressing the centrality of race, nation, war and the colonial legacy. The national question, which in Britain is always a racial question, has become more and not less central. We would not be facing a Tory electoral behemoth now, had Brexit not completely transformed the terrain. Too much of the Left, including some of the Corbynite Left, would rather not have that conversation for reasons of electoral expediency. It would simply cost too much to have that conversation in the short run. What they don't realise is what it will cost them in the long run not to have that conversation.[101]

Seymour's cold clarity is timely. The organised left, newly emboldened and exhilaratingly so for many, still seems, at best, to tend towards quietism and, at worst, to wilfully partake in the demonisation of the migrant. Any such susceptibility of the left to this politically expedient, anti-migrant race-baiting remains an eminently misplaced and self-destructive undertaking. The mimicry of nationalist tropes is not only an anti-working-class politics (a working class that supersedes the mediations of whiteness), constituting in turn a fundamental betrayal of a left politics worth its historical mandate; it is also a politics that will always run free of the left's attempt to harness it, a politics that will always be better owned by the far-right and its more mainstream imitators. As such, all that the left does in the long run, when parlaying with nationalist anxieties, is to lend the broader nationalist thesis an added validity that is (then) straightforwardly co-opted by the nationalist right proper, who remain far more credible and affirmative custodians of the nationalist call.

It is, accordingly, the alternative non- and anti-nationalist energies so central to the possibility of another left emerging out of the current debris that will be more aggressively profiled in the following, concluding chapter. A future politics that is more meaningfully inclusive is what is at stake if nationalism's current resurgence is going to prove merely a desperate final hurrah prior to its conclusive burial, as opposed to nationalism announcing itself as the political thesis that will be definitive of the coming and extended post-neoliberal era.

Conclusion: absences and futures

This book risks having drawn a decidedly sublime vision of contemporary nationalism. As the nationalist clamour multiplies through each ideological fold, the sheer reach of its cognitive, emotional and symbolic grip can seem suffocating. Neoliberal immigration controls here; conservative mourning for the Empire there. Liberal reproach of Muslims one day; pseudo-socialist expressions of white working-class grievances the next. These ideological rationales 'intertwine' with time into 'one snarling vine',[1] creating a nationalist *sense-making* system that is expansive and a nationalist *affective* register that is deep and resonant. Nationalism becomes, in short, sublime. To meet this sublime, from a position of anti-nationalism, is to be repulsed, to be rendered dizzy, to be overawed. But invariably, to meet the sublime is also ultimately to submit to it – its power, reach and spirit appearing too comprehensive to be reversed.

This won't do. These final few pages advance therefore a corrective on how *resistance* to the new nationalist wave might best be profiled. First, on a practical level, I observe that much of this resistance is already available, though censure and intimidation are ever-present. Secondly, on a more overtly ideational level, I note that any such attempt to destabilise the nationalist project would comprise picking apart the ideological contradictions as they sit within the nationalist return.

Having established these openings, I revisit the hope for an anti-nationalist energy that some see in the project being currently charted by the Labour Party. This hope is not without merits but equally, as discussed in Chapter 6, an anti-nationalist left politics risks being denied, undone or frustrated by the competing and ultimately irreconcilable interests, visions

CONCLUSION

and strategies that the current Labour movement finds itself navigating. In trying therefore to better fortify a popular left's anti-nationalist appetite, I end this book on a more vernacular note. If nationalism's political success lies partly in its ability to reach deep into the ideological common sense, then it is fitting to more forcefully gesture at the other everyday alternatives that also compete for a claim on this same common sense. This chapter ends therefore with a reflection on the various, often innocuous cultural features of everyday British life and popular culture that readily lend themselves to husbanding an alternative to the nationalist political wager. Particular emphasis will be placed on what is commonly called 'multiculture'. I contend that this everyday multiculture, in its very banality, remains a widespread but underutilised cultural energy ripe for political conversion by a movement sufficiently alive to its possibilities. Importantly, this is not simply a passing attempt to acknowledge such possibilities; instead, it is my modest hope here to give proper political weight and appreciation to the urgent power and necessity of these alternative tendencies, tendencies that will prove vital to steering a different course for the political future that awaits us.

The current party-political picture in Britain is exceptionally volatile and fast-moving, whereby a confident assessment of who will be in government and who will be in opposition is difficult to foresee. Such parliamentary vicissitudes regarding the near future are not, however, of immediate concern to the broader argument of this book. As has hopefully become apparent, this book is an interrogation of contemporary nationalism's ideological assertions and their complementary racialised registers. These registers will continue to define much of the politics that Europe reckons with over the next decades. This diffuse reality accordingly lends this book a purchase that escapes, I believe, the particular profile and composition of the politicians who might or might not be in power at any given moment; whether, for example, the British premiership is held, should circumstances be particularly unkind, by Boris Johnson, or, if circumstances prove rather more daring, Jeremy Corbyn or some suitable successor. Put differently, the challenge of the nationalist moment will have to be surmounted, with gusto, irrespective of whatever immediate turns the politics of the coming years bring.

Gaps

Before proceeding, I am wary that readers might have become frustrated by the yawning thematic gaps in this book's account of nationalism. By involving itself so heavily in the specifically *ideological* content of contemporary nationalism, and with such an emphasis on the multiple ethno-racial demons that nation politics is wedded to, the book is inevitably limited. There is, after all, so much more that must be accounted for.

Some of these seeming gaps are more a matter of degree, as opposed to constituting wholesale omissions. There has been, for instance, an emphasis throughout the preceding chapters on various economistic themes regarding class, capitalist culture and explicitly materialist readings of the nation-state's history. For instance, Chapter 5's discussion of the wider play of neoliberal *morality*, the mooted merits of a 'points-system' solution to the ills of immigration, and also the consumerist remaking of the urban experience; and Chapter 6's profiling of capitalist crisis, class subjectivity and certain totemic Marxist/post-Marxist sentiments that characterise left-inflected nationalisms.

There are, however, some still significant themes that have been more systematically neglected and that require attention here. These themes include, as far as the particulars of the contemporary nationalist project are concerned: the role of social media and, contingently, the more febrile politics of what is now called the 'alt-right'; the twinning of such alt-right reflexes with an explicitly chauvinistic politics of male resentment; and perhaps most importantly, the much wider *global* dimensions of how strongman authoritarian nationalism has been rehabilitated as the political force of our times. This notion of nationalism constituting a decidedly global contemporary phenomenon poses particularly thorny questions for my own analysis, insofar as my focus on Britain, and western Europe more generally, has prevented me from gesturing at the more world-historical sweep of contemporary nationalism.

Social media

A dose of analytic caution first. There exists today a growing stream of commentary decrying social media's remaking of everything we held sacred, even implying via its 'post-truth' and 'fake-news' neologisms that what prevailed before was a glorious era of truth.[2] Many would agree that there is a great deal of mystification in this intimation, a mystification that lends establishment politics in its late twentieth-century guise a political credibility that it does not deserve – a type of media disavowal that risks being merely a reheated version of various anti-mass/anti-mob elitist reflexes once so prominent among the intelligentsia of the mid-twentieth century.[3] After all, is it not telling that the champions of the recently dethroned centrist political class are the ones who seem to rail most insistently against the political effects of social media? It can, for these and similarly intuitive reasons, be ventured that social media has not done everything that is being ascribed to it.

Nevertheless, it would be intellectually dishonest to deny that social media has released a toxic political nativism. The work of Mike Wendling and Angela Nagle is salutary here, both having authored popular works that map the social media dynamics underpinning the new right. Alongside Shuja Haider's 'Darkness at the End of the Tunnel', they have done me the favour of rooting out the darkest corners of alt-right online life so that I have myself been spared the horror of extended first-hand encounter.[4] And though Wendling's *Alt-Right* is less confident about promoting a broader intellectual thesis regarding what is currently afoot, it does avoid being drawn into the moments of equivalency that have rendered Nagle's intervention polarising, the latter having been accused of suggesting in her *Kill All Normies* a certain equivalency between the hard nativism of the newly emboldened right and the allegedly righteous identitarianism of the university-educated left – a purported equivalency that not only elides the differences in scale and influence but also collapses the important difference between normative normativity and counter-normative normativity.[5]

These broader debates aside, an important emphasis in the above is the proverbial 'echo chamber' or 'filter-bubble'.[6] This refers to the ability of social media platforms to generate a dense whirlwind of information that simply confirms the shared political or identity claims that the relevant echo chamber is already defined by. It is the looping of self-declared cause/identity with the information that the relevant user encounters, with little intervening friction. It also involves a selective rejigging of how mass media (the much-maligned 'MSM') is accessed – whereby an online commentariat, as already algorithmically endorsed by a user, effectively 'captions' or 're-captions' how the relevant mass media item is to be received. A body of increasingly streamlined information accordingly takes concrete shape, a body of information that dovetails with and reinforces a select political world-view and its constitutive 'culture wars' as defined along communitarian fault-lines.[7] In summarily dispensing with any dissent, or more moderate opinion when inconvenient, a self-sustaining and relatively well-sealed informational sphere gradually emerges.

As far as this book's key themes are concerned, the sustained effect of such social media 'sealing' is not that it creates nationalist ideological enclosures – 'twas likely ever thus. Rather, the effect of sealing in the social media era carries a perhaps historically unique capacity to stir the urgency with which the perceived demise of the nation is experienced. The hegemonic domain of the mass media era was the ability to delineate the 'mainstream' – an ability to restrict and determine the frame of debate.[8] The social media effect, however, often renders the very idea of debate itself moot. A notion of debate is instead supplanted by already designated political positions around which relevant individuals are encouraged to assume a figurative war position, provided to them by a supply of corroborative stories and commentary.[9] What transpires is an intensification of new nationalist talking points, which, absent of any mitigating mechanisms, acquire a certain frenzied immediacy and, at times, even apocalyptic character. This form of masochistic intensification marries with what Jodi Dean called the 'circuits of drive', a concept that pithily captures the affective and psychoanalytic dimensions of the digital.[10] We can think here of the histrionic shrieks about demographic crises as tied to immigration and 'Eurabia', or see the manic online circulation of racial 'data' about crime, welfare, economic productivity and even the quackery of IQ race claims. Social media portals are also good at bridging the different ideological repertoires outlined in this book. To suggest one such possibility, an online story about the imperilling of working-class dignity by migrant wage-cutting can be made to flow seamlessly from a preceding anecdote about the illiberal misogyny of Muslim culture. Put in more theoretical terms, social media circulations act as a particularly efficient conduit through which such nationalist alarmism, as expressed through contradictory ideological rationales, can be funnelled into one ostensibly coherent space or sequence.

CONCLUSION

The contemporary nationalist purchase of these social media effects – as discursive 'sealing' and ideological 'bridging' – needs, however, to be situated within some of the wider contexts through which they operate. First and foremost, the formalisation of an online field of media consumption has generated a *transnational field* of nationalist politics – whereby frantic nationalist arguments stitch together globally distributed sequences of hysteria concerning domestically relevant national Others. For instance, the trope of the Muslim terrorist does not function within a territorially demarcated symbolic landscape; instead, it absorbs incidents, anecdotes and scandals from *wherever* they might be available. As I have argued elsewhere, a rapidly thickening anti-Muslim sentiment in the UK rests on a regional and/or international parade of events (each renewing the previous): Paris after Paris, Copenhagen after Toulouse, Cologne after Birmingham, Manchester after Barcelona, Brussels after Raqqa.[11] This transnationalisation of national dissolution is also visible vis-à-vis the general spectre of immigration: swarms of black and brown youths overwhelming French and Swedish cities; uncouth refugees running amok in Italy and Greece; and 'no-go zones' where white people dare no longer venture proliferating across European cities, cities such as Malmö that are often pictured as former bastions of tranquil cohesion. A dizzying map of diffuse crisis accordingly takes shape, regardless of the specific geographic location of the concerned observer. Indeed, the anti-immigration strain in Finland hinged significantly on the projection of such a European malaise into the *future* of Finland, given that no such immigrant or Muslim population was particularly prominent there yet.[12] But there is also an extra-European dimension to this transnational scan. This is made starkly apparent in Trump's recent nod to the far-right's increased profiling of the alleged plight of white South African farmers.[13] But it is also apparent in the disingenuous but still symbolically charged show of solidarity with the plight of certain Christian communities in assorted Muslim-majority countries.[14] This diffuse sense of global crisis is galvanising. It furnishes the nationalist psyche with an unceasing supply of globally dispersed battlefronts that are then written into the vicissitudes of the local – what Gavan Titley concisely named, during one round of such transnational nationalism, as 'Swedens of the mind'.[15]

Connected to this, the other important feature of the echo chamber effect is the powerful impression that the anointed group is waging a war on the ruling establishment and the *bien pensant* values that it allegedly propagates – these being the proverbial 'normies' that Nagle documents as being the formal target of online alt-right confrontationalism. The operational claim here is that the state is currently under capture by an elite class of self-satisfied liberals beholden to a shallow and hypocritical set of social equality mantras. The purported values of equality and tolerance are seen to be hypocritical because they constitute a culture of elite lifestyle distinction and because they are actively aimed at promoting only minority rights/interests – a minority fetishism that comes at the expense of more timeless notions of nature, justice and general ideals of liberal and/or libertarian equality. Hence the collective task for the alt-right's online brigades is not to reason but to simply 'transgress', to mock, ironise and scandalously jolt the entire liberal class, allegedly prone as it is to shallow performances of sensitive indignation.[16] There is obviously a particularly strong masculine demonstrativeness in this practice, which marries well with the alt-right's other great white whale – the restoration of male dominance. These potent corners of social media provide thus a frantic whirlpool of strong guttural urges, twinning the historically powerful impulses of communitarian violence and defiant male assertion with a wider intimation of nobly rebellious struggle against the wider establishment. Put differently, new nationalist politics obtains here a distinctive and particularly seductive psychoanalytic charge – one that ties the frisson of 'insubordinate' rebellion with the muscular masculinity of apprehending oneself as superior and unique, swimming against a tide of preciously sensitive conformists.[17]

Seen in these terms, Sara Ahmed's observation that hegemonies often pretend that they are anti-hegemonic is given a unique inflection. As she argued, 'One suspects that hegemonies are often presented as minority positions, as defences against what are perceived to be hegemonic, which is how they can be presented as matters of life and death.'[18] This is an instructive observation as regards the contemporary. The nationalist cause is animated today by a perversely thrilling sense of being under siege – railing not only against impending civilisational crisis as spearheaded by the excessive presence of various ethno-racial Others, but also purporting to resist the all-powerful Liberal establishment against whom the new nationalist opposition speaks truth.[19]

CONCLUSION

But there is more to this than is commonly imagined. There is also the creep of such distinctly online controversialism, even conspiratorialism, into seemingly unrelated social media channels, channels that have a more mass profile. Particularly interesting, I believe, are performers such as PewDiePie and Joe Rogan. The alt-right and its foetid online world might indeed be drawn to its stable of 'darkweb philosophers' such as Nick Land and Curtis Yarvin/Moldbug, and the 'neoreactionist' brand of 'hyperracism' that they so baldly husband via 4chan, obscure subreddits, gab.ai, and elsewhere.[20] But our understanding of online media's alt-right work should not end here.

As Titley argues in his recent *Racism and Media*, what makes YouTube in particular far more interesting than 4chan and the like is the scale of production and reach available to it.[21] A decisive factor is the 'recommender systems' that underpin YouTube's (or rather, Google's, as the parent company) advertising strategy – a strategy that trades on the logic of 'recommending' ever-more-radical content. This is an algorithm that is primed to intensify engagement, an objective that is in turn understood as being coterminous with providing more radical material specific to the topic accessed.[22] Hereby, the sheer fact of platform reach, the bias towards more radical entrenchment and the reality of tangible commercial revenue all interact to yield a media ecosystem where major YouTube figures act as formidable nodes linking multiple 'recommender systems/networks' sympathetic to new nationalist politics.[23]

Put in more direct terms, it is simply the case that these figures reach enormous audiences and that they operate on a broader commercial platform that rewards certain sensationalist strategies. So, as opposed to dwelling too much on the far-right radicalisation that transpires on Reddit and 4chan, it is the translation and amplification work that takes place on YouTube that gives such politics a wider but also more homespun and indirect force – a force all the more effective precisely because it is so indirect. For example, Rogan, in the course of expounding his command of the UFC and boxing world, alongside a complementary regard for mass sports and 1990s hip-hop, frequently smuggles in a particular brand of rather boyish pondering of Trump and other such 'anti-establishment' politics. This boyishness becomes rather less innocent when lending credibility to leading figures such as Milo Yiannopoulos, Sam Harris, Steven Crowder and even Alex Jones, or when impugning the 'MeToo' movement. PewDiePie (Felix Kjellberg) for his part has gained a notorious reputation, while carrying on with his prankish gaming and meme commentary, for deliberate offensiveness that operates under a voguish alibi of irony. As the journalist Paul MacInnes observes,

> Kjellberg's ironic tone means he rarely says anything explicitly offensive. But the themes and memes that recur in his videos are consistent: images of famous African-Americans (Neil deGrasse Tyson, Barack Obama) captioned with the wrong names; a meme to which the punchline is 'respecting women'; African voices sampled and replayed in incongruous situations; recitations of English language posts on Indian Facebook. Pepe the Frog will also make appearances. As for Book Review, the final item on last month's edition was Jordan B Peterson's *12 Rules for Life*. Kjellberg gave it a rave review. 'I really enjoyed this book,' he said, 'it made me understand people around me better.'[24]

This tendency, in his capacity as YouTube's most popular performer by a comfortable margin,[25] is indicative of a wider trend in which gatekeepers such as Kjellberg become efficient, if seemingly innocuous, launderers of alt-right discourse. As MacInnes concludes, 'to call Kjellberg an alt-right agitator would perhaps be unfair as he has never publicly identified with the proto-fascist movement. But he shares much of their culture and amplifies it across the world.'[26]

This is important. In trying to account for the contemporary crisis in democratic deliberation, too much has been made of the conspiratorial information cycles that seem to be gaining force.[27] First, it is not self-evident that this conspiratorial streak is much more pronounced than before. Secondly, there exists at the moment a wide array of conspiratorial gambits that vie for prominence. The question therefore is not *why* conspiracy, but why only some of these gain a wider traction. This inverts in turn how we read social-media-led conspiracy. It is not the tail that wags the dog, but is simply the tail; conspiracies and self-styled controversialists gain prominence when they chime with a wider political current coursing through a polity, the only distinctiveness of the agitator and/or conspiratorialist being their projection of a more histrionic and autodidactic quality. The role of popular online commentators becomes therefore ever more significant here. It is not that they are card-carrying, right-wing contrarians, but they do lend some of its tropes an undemonstratively vernacular and casual legitimacy.

We should also not neglect the role of well-moneyed backers in trying to harness the political influence of the alt-right-inflected social-media movements in order to sway key political campaigns.[28] When we speak only of ideology, it is easy to forget the serious money involved. We have seen, for instance, Peter Thiel of PayPal fame play a particularly prominent public role in endorsing and funding Trump and Trumpist campaigns in the US.[29] Relatedly, Robert Mercer's very deep pockets were decisive in backing the hard right's strategies to become surgical manipulators of social media feeds during both the Trump campaign and the EU referendum[30] – for instance, efforts to better exploit emergent 'psychographic profiling' techniques, which have finally received some critical scrutiny in the wake of the Cambridge Analytica allegations (of which Mercer and Steve Bannon were key backers).[31] There have been allegations about the use of mass data harvesting from social media accounts;[32] allegations about the conversion of psychographic profiling into micro-targeted political adverts – which some have likened to both voter manipulation and causing strategically targeted voter disengagement;[33] and allegations about the potential contravention of electoral laws.[34] These are also allegations that have been connected to the activities of Arron Banks, one of the key financers of UKIP and the Leave campaign, as well as being a major backer of affiliated online politics (see his launch of 'Westmonster', an attempt to create a Breitbart equivalent in the UK).[35]

We sense accordingly that social media's shepherding of political discourse still works through forces not untypical of the twentieth century: on the one hand, the role of certain public intellectuals alongside prominent online cultural figures, such as Joe Rogan and company, who do the work in a much more incidental manner of popularising more rabid versions of new nationalist postulations; and, on the other hand, the background role of big-money bankrollers such as the 'Mercer family',[36] Thiel, Banks and others such as Robert Shillman, who either by conviction or opportunism become drawn to causes that might once have seemed hopelessly fringe.[37] So while it is right to acknowledge the 'social media factor', some caution is I believe healthy when considering its causal pre-eminence or distinctiveness.

And as regards the particulars of this book's wider argument, the nationalist radicalisms articulated via social and digital media still rely upon the disparate intellectual and symbolic vocabularies charted in the previous chapters. It is, for instance, telling, as this testimony of an unassuming man's alt-right radicalisation makes apparent, that much of the Muslim-baiting that takes place trades on a fairly conventional conception of liberal values vis-à-vis the misogynistic and inassimilable Muslim. This account describes a YouTube-led vortex that commenced with the gateway drug that is a Sam Harris video and ended in a dark pit of putrid anti-Muslim venom.

> Moving on from Harris, I unlocked the Pandora's box of 'It's not racist to criticise Islam!' content [...] Eventually I was introduced, by YouTube algorithms, to Milos Yiannopoulos and various 'anti-SJW' videos [...] They were shocking at first, but always presented as innocuous criticism from people claiming to be liberals themselves, or centrists, or sometimes 'just a regular conservative' – but never, ever identifying as the dreaded 'alt-right'. Fear-mongering content was presented in a compelling way by charismatic people who would distance themselves from the very movement of which of they were a part. [As time passed and the more I 'passively consumed'] I started to roll my eyes when my friends talk about liberal, progressive things. What was wrong with them? Did they not understand what being a *real* liberal was?[38]

The 'real liberal' motif is an instructive coda here – gesturing at how more rabidly right-wing social media politicisation still calls upon well-established ideological contestations. While digital media has no doubt transformed the manner in which political information is circulated, the ideological contouring prevalent here is still the stuff of the conceptual, value and symbolic spectrums as overseen in this book.

Nation here, there, everywhere

The second thematic gap that requires attention is, for me, a much more difficult conundrum. In short, what is it about nationalism that can excite in so many different *global* contexts? The story of the nation's resurgence that has been surveyed in this book is hardly unique to Europe. Iconic cases of nationalism's resurgence abound across the world: Putin and his programme of Greater Russia jingoism; Hindutva's political gains in India; China's aggrandising belligerence that trades on a very pronounced sense of unitary national identity; Hungary and Croatia's increasingly confident version of fascist apologia-cum-denialism; Myanmar and Sri Lanka's respective renditions of clerically sponsored Buddhist chauvinism; the notorious Bolsonaro's presidential victory in Brazil; Japan's Abe who maintains longstanding political and symbolic ties to the country's imperialist factions; and the different forms of religiously framed ethno-nationalism affecting various Muslim-majority democracies such as Pakistan, Bangladesh, Indonesia and, not least, Turkey. Seen in this broad light, nationalism is revealed as being truly transnational, upholding across the world various right-wing governments and the majoritarian communal politics that they give emphatic priority to. That the world's most populous countries are all represented in the above list further confirms, albeit incidentally, the sheer scale and force of contemporary nationalism.

It remains in this context an oft-remarked conundrum that the nation-state has been restored at a time when the political challenges that it contends with are so qualitatively *global* in scope and scale.[39] The most defining of these challenges, when apprehended from a left-wing perspective, is the prospect of ecological collapse, as engendered by the 'anthropocene'/'capitalocene', that is already well under way.[40] But also to be reckoned with here, as far as a left perspective is concerned, is finance capital's twinkle-toed global mobility. From the inverse right-wing perspective, the most animating issues are, of course, very different: the relentless global march of mass migration, the transnational nature of Islamist violence, and the sustained rise of China's distinctly global influence, picking off roads and farmlands the world over, as well as owning the lion's share of global container port operations.[41] What binds these two contrasting political points of departure is the global scale of the respective problems that they seek to act against. That it is nevertheless the nation-state that is being rehabilitated as the preferred political unit can hence seem perplexing.

Žižek once gestured at this through his wider notion of 'parallax'.[42] And while Žižek's more recent brand of tedious contrarianism has diminished his reputation, there lurks here a credible psychoanalytic thesis as regards the contemporary nation-state complex. As the world's winds blow all the more violently, the certainties and stability of the local political unit are what is most desired. A myopian drive for home becomes the most psychoanalytically resonant political reflex against the indistinct but also overwhelming scale of the global. If the general threatens only danger and excess, then the particular becomes the comforting antithesis – the antithesis that returns to the political subject a satisfying sense of proportion, familiarity, continuity and, also, a deeply embalming notion of authentic, primordial origins.

Any such thesis requires, however, a broader socio-historical contextualisation of why it is specifically the nation-state that is restored as the contemporary's pre-eminent political reference. First, as discussed in Chapter 1, the nation-state is not an idle motif of *modernity*. As far as modern political expression is concerned, the nation-state is the territorial unit and cultural logic alike that was, in time, rendered primary. It was the nation-state that gradually managed to obtain a near monopoly on the terms by which a conception of political peoplehood in whom sovereignty was to be vested could be articulated – even if, as we know, the forces of capitalism and allied supranational bodies tightly circumscribed the practical exercise of that sovereignty, particularly in the Global South. That the nation-state therefore extends its hold into the present is not unexpected.

It is also not surprising that the nation-state also obtains a particularly momentous renewal at a time when capitalism seems more formally at ease with authoritarian state command, known in some circles as 'state capitalism', than it does with some of the inconveniences of liberal democratic procedure – however inadequate liberal democracy undoubtedly is when seen from its margins. Put differently, any appetite for authoritarian state command is likely to reach for the nationalist pose as being its most legitimating sociocultural ally – the state's claim to assertive existence being so intimately wedded to the appeals and demarcations of nation.

These reflections constitute only cursory gestures at factors that might be informing nationalism's global re-entrenchment. And while an attentiveness to the conflicting and contradictory ideological vocabularies as mapped in this book does allow for an insight into how nationalism can claim so many disparate constituencies in western Europe, the particular constellation and constitutive symbolic emphases as regards any such ideological cacophony will, of course, be very different as we escape this analytic provincialism. Chatterjee once noted that it is one thing to say that it was a European colonial modernity that first gave expression to the nation as being the pre-given political unit; it is altogether different to suggest that this approach to nation was simply mimicked by the postcolonial countries. And as Anne McClintock decried, one of Hobsbawm's less analytically shrewd moments was his extremely coarse dismissal of postcolonial renditions of nation-state politics as being simply derivative, or worse.

> Nationalisms are invented, performed and consumed in ways that do not follow a universal blueprint. At the very least, the breathtaking Eurocentricism of Hobsbawm's dismissal of Third World nationalisms warrants sustained criticism. In a gesture of sweeping condescension, Hobsbawm nominates Europe as nationalism's 'original home', whilst 'all the anti-imperial movements of any significance' are unceremoniously dumped into three categories: mimicry of Europe, anti-Western xenophobia, and the 'natural high spirits of martial tribes'.[43]

Recalling this exchange is important when restating, with due contrition, the definite limitations of my own book's argument that derive from the particularities of its Western location. And though any such location is always relational, the specific anchoring of this book's empirical field needs to be carefully noted whenever any wider global or comparative inferences are made.

With this important caveat duly noted, a different set of more constructive intellectual possibilities occur that I will address in the remainder of this chapter. As opposed to trying in vain to offer a globally definitive take on the shared factors that might be driving these multiple nationalist advances, it is more practicable to look further at the immediate British context for emergent challenges to the nationalist ascendancy. And in so doing, openings for a politics that is anti- and/or post-national in character are glimpsed in a manner that might also hint at *analogous* movements and energies as they surface in other international contexts.

While I do not presume any such international comparisons, Britain does constitute a reasonably thrilling point of departure, insofar as the country has just witnessed the rise of a genuinely popular and genuinely progressive parliamentary movement. This is, of course, a seldom seen distinction for Britain — what Seymour has fittingly entitled *The Strange Rebirth of Radical Politics*.[44] But the fact that it exists, and the fact that it remains formidable, does allow a commentary on Britain to carry a more generative political salience than would ordinarily be the case.

Corbyn?

Recent developments in the UK electoral sphere, where a confident Labour Party is again visible, allow us to tentatively ask what kind of rebuke to nationalist populism is possible where socialist and social democratic programmes are again a possibility in political discourse. And despite the extensive analysis in Chapter 6 of the left's pronounced nationalist tendencies, including continued investment in the allure and entitlements of national whiteness, this revitalised left current in Britain evinces a number of unique and productive openings that might qualitatively distinguish it from previous iterations.

We see, for instance, a peppy urban enthusiasm for Corbyn's Labour, an urban context that is importantly also where the lived realities of multiculture and migration are most readily rooted. This urban orientation makes for a natural bulwark against this revived left reverting to a nationalist closure without it proving very costly. In what might be a wider portent of electoral things to come across Europe, a high-profile splinter faction of Germany's Die Linke is currently attempting to distinguish itself by taking a more hard-line stance on immigration and borders. This is a political pivot, spearheaded by the popular Sahra Wagenknecht, that is being carefully watched no doubt by the European left.[45] It is in this worrying context that the prominence of Corbyn's urban support seems to me crucial, representing a strong check on comparable attempts to fully formalise more nationalist left-wing politics within the UK.

Not unrelatedly, the public has seen a broad range of high-profile minority voices – Diane Abbott, Clive Lewis, Rupa Huq, Dawn Butler, Faiza Shaheen, Marsha de Cordova and, occasionally, even David Lammy – front the Labour Party, though their support is certainly not unqualified nor uncomplicated. Importantly, these figures are not incidental presences shunted to the margins, but have become crucial players in popularising the party's programme, if also, at times, weathering the disproportionate brunt of the often vicious blowback.[46] Such a frontline guard is also allied with the wider emergence of a non-white commentariat who, while dedicated to the Labour renaissance, are also intent on interrogating the nationalist tendencies within the party. An illustrative instance is the stratospheric rise of Ash Sarkar; but consider here also the continued veteran guidance of somebody like Gary Younge. Such a vocal race-conscious backing also bolsters, and is bolstered by, the proliferation of online political platforms as well as the multiple activist networks of migrants' rights and anti-racism groups. The latter comprise more established anti-fascist organisations, but also new groups contending with the very particular challenges of the present, not least Islamophobia. Seen as a whole, all this represents an exhilarating vector cutting through the new political moment. It is a form of avowedly race-conscious participation in a mainstream left politics that was implausible during the apogee of Blairism but was also rendered marginal during previous twentieth-century renditions of trade union labourism.

The chances of a radically pluralistic Labour left politics acquiring long-term durability are also aided by the counter-intuitive argument that the current hardening of political nativism might be understood as its misdirected death rattle – one final lung-bursting surge prior to nationalism's impending historical banishment. A few factors figure in this reading.

One is the dry sociological fact of demographic shifts. European countries are becoming less white and certainly less mono-ethnic – this impression is particularly vivid when contemporary *youth* demographics are considered. Taxonomies of race and national belonging are certainly never stable, and a minority today need not remain a minority tomorrow; or at the very least, it might remain a minority but still enjoy some accommodation within the symbolism and the wider institutions of national belonging. Yet the formal rupture in western Europe of the white population's automatic status as numerical majority is certainly not uninteresting. Any such weakening of white majoritarianism would certainly open up possibilities for a more productive political discourse, one less beholden to the strains of *ethno-national* belonging and entitlement.

The second factor influencing the long-term viability of a Labour left is an extension of the above trend: emerging youth generations are said to be more receptive to non-nationalist social democratic politics. A recent flurry of agonised introspection by conservative scholars speaks to the generational problems that the political right might have to contend with over the coming years.[47] This youth wave is alleged not only to harbour a more pronounced hostility to neoliberalism, but is also seen as being more sincere in its sympathy for and/or identification with various liberation causes, be they anti-racist, feminist, LGBTQ+ or environmentalist.

Importantly, the emergence of such a wave is not easily dismissed as constituting simply a body of effete 'metropolitan liberals' – a disingenuous construction convenient to the 'authentic working class versus deracinated liberal elites' dichotomy discussed in Chapter 6. On the contrary, it has very significant consequences for the putative manifestation of a new set of working-class political constituencies. As Virdee put it, 'if one fraction of the working class has shifted towards the racist right as part of a long-term process of technical and political class decomposition, what has been striking is how another [equally significant] element has remained largely unmoved by such politics'. Virdee summarises this alternatively configured working class in the following manner:

> These working classes are to be found disproportionately in large urban centres as well as university towns; they tend to be younger (by which I mean under the age of 45) and significantly, they are both a multinational and multi-ethnic working class comprising: i. recent migrants from Europe and elsewhere; ii. black and brown Britons; and of course, iii. the white British who reject such an identification being tied to racist projects.[48]

This clearly put summation does ably point to an important site of hope regarding a future class-based but race-conscious politics. The promise of any such demographic shift is therefore not to be taken lightly.

Fade to cynicism

However, one of the better-founded laws of the social sciences is the fallibility of presumed generational continuity. The dispositions of youth politics should always be understood as a relational artefact unique to the contemporary – that is, as indicative of a particular relationship between an age-sensitive social location on the one hand, and a wider set of economic circumstances as well as exposure to particular youth cultures on the other. While some might claim that we are witnessing a 'cohort effect', this is still by no means a reliable indicator of how the same cohort is likely to orient itself in the future, owing to their own progression through the life-course but also other wider shifts in the prevailing socio-economic and sociocultural context that awaits them.

I also note that, for all the above optimism, the left still lives in abject defeat. Every meaningful political event of the last two decades has been a defeat – the Iraq War, the Blairite normalisation of a neoliberal centrism, the capitalisation of the right on the Great Recession of 2008, the decade-long round of austerity doctrine, and then, of course, Brexit. And for all the spectacular advances of a newly invigorated Labour left during 2016 and 2017, the party remains in opposition. A glimmer here and there, but, ultimately, only glimmers.

And when considering the other intervening European contexts since Corbyn's quasi-success on 8 June 2017, events in Poland, Denmark, Austria, Norway and, in particular, Italy all signalled the further consolidation of new xenologies as the pre-eminent governmental/political force of the times.[49] It is, for instance, remarkable that a crank separatist party that was staring existential oblivion in the face as recently as the mid-2000s is now home to Italy's most influential politician, a politician whose many alarming ambitions can be concisely captured in the simple observation that he wilfully courts an association with Il Duce (see Salvini's celebratory use of the phrase, 'Molti nemici, molto onore').[50] This is, however, very tangibly the present case in Italy – the 2018 elections resulted in the far-right Lega[51] becoming the country's most politically visible and most emboldened party.[52] If Salvini and his ilk are therefore emblematic of trends currently prevailing in Europe, some healthy caution is warranted regarding the Labour left's political hopes. This is a sobering reality that is further compounded by the fact that a European movement comparable to Corbynism has failed to register any formal success over the interim period.

It is also no minor detail that this Labour movement is contending with a Conservative regime that has enjoyed nine years of political zealotry, overseeing some of the most swingeing neoliberal (austerity) and anti-immigration ('hostile environment'/immigration cap) programmes that a right-wing government could ever hope to institute. It is worth remembering that the ideological conviction of the Cameron government was so very deep that some began to think, understandably, that a second electoral victory was less important to the Conservatives than their commitment to overseeing a drastic material move to the right. The Cameron government of 2010 comprised after all a stable of Thatcher acolytes who were not going to let a good crisis go to waste. A recall of how emphatically doctrinaire this period of Tory rule has been should temper in turn any triumphalism about the current revival of Labour under Corbyn. To appreciate that nearly a decade of the Conservatives' shock and awe rule could still return a hard right party to government constitutes a bitter reminder of where Britain's political compass continues to point.

Multiculture and vernacular post-nationalism

What can nonetheless be posited is that a left alternative does exist, an alternative that has caught a particularly popular groove in contemporary Britain. This is to be celebrated, harnessed and elaborated upon. As just discussed, this constitutes first the promise of a different future, anti-capitalist in temperament. (Whether such a critical appetite is ultimately affirmative of a social democratic or socialist bent is largely immaterial as far as the present is concerned, a present that can otherwise seem so truculently neoliberal.) But, as I will now discuss, it is also a future alternative well placed to disrupt questions of nation and belonging as currently construed.

I argue that equally important to charting the contradictions and gaps within the contemporary nationalist conjuncture is a more determined attentiveness to the well-worn, deeply lived-in ethnic and racial diversity that characterises so many British people's everyday realities – a habituation that is not simply about living with and amid difference, but that also generates an anti-nationalist literacy hungering to be given wider political articulation. Put more frankly, it is the realities of *everyday multiculture* that constitute for me a ready-made counterpoint to the nationalist capture. It is in the recesses of this multiculture that anti-nationalism might find the initial solace but also the relevant political and symbolic resources to stake a wider claim on the future.

By multiculture, I mean specifically the humdrum, multi-ethnic cultural textures and interactive circuits that have become so commonplace to many low- and middle-income urban areas, of which white people themselves are of course a substantial constitutive presence. Such multiculture certainly does *not* characterise all of Britain's cities or towns. It doesn't even characterise most of them. But it is a more fluent feel for these everyday interactive formations when and where they do emerge that remains vitally important. While this might not be the basis of any grander revolutionary politics or the like, any such attentiveness to the multicultures that dot so many urban and semi-urban areas does help furnish the broader polity with important anti-nationalist political tools, both conceptual and attritional. Put differently, the interactive and expressive circuits available in some of these areas over any meaningful duration signal to me a highly productive disengagement from the politics of communitarian demagoguery. Such multicultural circuits take the presence of difference alongside flows of migration into and out of a locale as being a pre-given, non-negotiable feature of urban life. The normalisation of such ground rules creates in turn a pre-figurative base for other, more far-reaching political coalitions and affinities. In other words, to bundle two somewhat different coinages of Paul Gilroy, the 'ludic cosmopolitan energies' and the 'feral beauty of the postcolonial metropolis' are where social alternatives to nationalist closure might best be had.[53]

A few further clarifications are necessary here, lest all this be misunderstood as haplessly naive romanticism. 'Everyday multiculture' does, as a minimal point of departure, refer to the highly casual, nigh banal interactive practices that emerge in spaces characterised by ethnic diversities – practices that undemonstratively cultivate dispositions less prone to nationalisms and other derivative forms of overtly communitarian claim-making on space, culture and politics. It is *not*, however, the case that the people living in such areas, generally working or lower middle class, are any less likely to assert their identifications as premised along frameworks of ethnic and racial difference. It is only that such myriad identifications – alongside the complementary iterations of unceasing migration in and out of a particular space – become normalised as being a pre-given, natural feature of social life.[54] In the habituation of such features of shared space and interaction, many people, including the many white people who call such places home, increasingly find the political appeal to nation to be summarily anachronistic, uninteresting and, frankly, wrong. The cultural and political energies that flow accordingly from such everyday practices offer a very useful and underappreciated indication of how an alternative, postnational popular politics might be envisaged as well as pursued. This is in contrast to what is generally meant by the political possibilities of multiculturalism

— which is best read as being a governmental and/or rhetorical aspiration that is primarily about group cultural rights and formal institutional inclusion and/ or recognition, as opposed to it politically purposing in a more direct manner the lived-in textures of residential, civic and leisure-derived multi-ethnic cohabitation, and remaining unable to harness the more lofty notions of a postcommunitarian sensibility that is still fluent in claims to ethnic and racial difference.

A wealth of empirical sociology has helpfully emerged of late that documents the robust ordinariness of this multiculture.[55] And importantly, these more recent works have gone against the initial research that only located this multiculture in the global cities, a selectiveness to which I too have been party when conducting previous research in London and Stockholm. Much emergent research has instead successfully relocated its focus towards those semi-urban and provincial settings that are much more representative of where most of the British population is likely to be living.

The breadth of this research is substantial. It includes the work of Huq, Saha and Watson, and Jones et al. on *suburbia* proper,[56] moving beyond the over-studied and perhaps even fetishised fixation with the inner city – a fetishism that runs unsettlingly close to the consumerist frisson for all things inner-city. As put in the punchy prose of Rhys-Taylor,

> As part of the city's post-industrial invasion [by an middle-class consumer class], something important is [happening] to its erstwhile suburban spaces. Thereon, amidst the landscapes of cul-de-sacs, secondary shopping malls and franchise cafes, a number of recent studies have found convivial multiculture alive and well. Apparently, under the cloak of mirrors, tiles and fordist sensations, cultural differences and individual auras are not entirely stultified [...] Thus, in contrast to the new open-air markets of the bourgeois inner-city, it is the 'blandscapes' typically associated with suburbia, retail parks and identikit high streets that nurture the city's convivial multiculture.[57]

This important reworking of convivial multiculture that Rhys-Taylor refers to becomes particularly apparent in the related research attempt to profile more 'middling' towns such as Milton Keynes,[58] suburban Leicester,[59] Epsom (the subject of Julius Baker's ongoing doctoral research), as well as Burdsey's highly textured and original commentary on the 'English seaside'.[60] Both the suburb and the provincial town become hereby vital sites through which multiculture is ascribed by contemporary sociology a wider political berth. But in terms of its most acute political purchase, this burgeoning research field has also moved its focus to those areas now considered politically emblematic of economic distress and working-class nativism, as seen for instance in recent studies of Peterborough[61] and also Nayak's multisited work involving various north-east locations,[62] all of which try to bring through a carefully observed notion of 'working-class cosmopolitanism'.[63] These are all efforts that prove particularly adept at balancing an appreciation for the everyday breaching of ethnic divides with a close attentiveness to the continued re-entrenchment of white nationalist nativism, nativist pressures that risk becoming further emboldened when contending with grinding austerity and a complementary sense of political disaffection.

Seen as a whole, this general ability to root multiculture in such disparate contexts has given this research field a robust complexity that was initially lacking – tending as it was towards a certain 'descriptive naivete'.[64] This was a research situation where the utterly mundane truism that multi-ethnic life exists seemed to constitute a valid conclusion in its own right, analogous to what Wise and Noble have described as the risk of advancing an unduly 'romantic', 'happy-clappy' view of 'togetherness'.[65]

The fresh injection of vitality into the field accordingly prevents any such exaggeration of multiculture's presence as well as foregrounding the eminently fragile nature of any such multiculture when and where it does in fact manifest. After all, the original conceptualisation of multiculture was only ever interesting precisely because it was understood as trying to wage an everyday battle against the wider forces of nativist racism (and the essentialising view of minority communities that is a partial extension of such racism). It is often forgotten that this was the fraught tension that Gilroy focused on in *After Empire*. This book was not about convivial multiculture on the one hand and melancholic nationalism on the other. It was instead very much about how both projections are *simultaneously* competing for validity in the lives of modern Britons. Or as Karner and Parker articulated it when discussing an oft-derided area of already unloved Birmingham: conviviality becomes empirically distinctive only because it is always existing contiguously to the multiple divisions that are routinely framed by race and ethnicity.[66] In short, it is conviviality *in spite of* racialised nationalism that gives it a unique political and conceptual vitality. The point therefore, as I see it, is not that multiculture triumphs regardless, but that it endures and gets remade, releasing energies waiting to be harnessed by a less apologetic, less integrationist political programme that might command mass purchase.[67]

This everyday multicultural sensibility has certainly found its political voice independently of the Labour Party. But this is also a political voice that has been proactively eager to lend its buoyant and youthful immediacy to Corbyn. There is an abundance of indicative people, cultural artefacts and campaigns that could be fronted to make this affinity evident. I have, however, certain personal favourites. Consider here the ever-charming David Vujanic, primarily known as the co-host of a general 'youth culture chat meets football' YouTube channel, sporting a Corbyn 'swoosh' shirt while eloquently chastising the political class's complicity in the Grenfell tragedy.[68] Or consider Big Narstie's impassioned excoriation, during an extended Radio 1Xtra interview, of those who fail to recognise that the broader experience of acute poverty constitutes grime's baseline iconography:

> Hear what I am trying to say. Sitting in the passenger seat of the car and seeing things happen and being first-hand, knowing that it's your life that is going to be real, cuz, is a different thing [...] Man who is doing stuff out here for fancy trainers to buy Balenciagas and that, cuz, is different from the man who is tearing man down road to go Iceland and make sure his mum's okay [...] So man don't come with their Vaseline lips talking about nice stuff over here. About Grime.[69]

A more resonant and unaffected imagery vis-à-vis a social realism purpose-built for the present would be hard to come by, partly evidencing, as recently witnessed in Britain and expertly summarised by Monique Charles, the fluent synchronisation of grime with a popular left politics.[70] This popular affinity is free of the cheapening, unconvincing and often exclusionary righteousness that is otherwise customary for those forms of popular culture that knowingly press a progressive political narrative. This gives in turn some important context for understanding the special role of 'Grime for Corbyn' in injecting the Labour campaign with an easy working-class and multicultural credibility, a form of cultural advocacy that remains exemplary of how an anti-racist multiculture-cum-popular-left-pivot is likely to look.

But this goes well beyond popular culture, important as that is,[71] with the aforementioned Grenfell tragedy being a particularly bracing example here.[72] The politics released by this haunting moment seamlessly alternated between, on the one hand, an uncompromisingly vocal forcefulness, and, on the other, a dignified silence that is deafening in its pathos – I mean by this the silent marches that are held on a monthly basis. But this is also a moment that has firmly but also creatively insisted on its victims being understood as multi-ethnic *and* 'multi-status'.[73] Grenfell was a particularly resonant microcosm of a broader working-class community – neglected and overexploited – that is deeply marked by a vertiginous array of not only ethnic backgrounds but also citizenship statuses. The political aftermath of Grenfell certainly foregrounded this reality in particularly powerful ways, tacitly reminding the social democratic left that it must always recognise poverty's multi-ethnic, 'migrant city' realities.[74] As the cultural output and interventions of someone such as Akala have made powerfully evident, this is a reminder that a politics of class worth its name must always remain attentive to the migrant subject as key to its programme, as opposed to setting up a shameless and ultimately counter-productive working class versus immigration false dichotomy.[75]

The future

In this battle lies the future fate of the left in Britain. Its cautiousness hitherto in challenging the various nationalist fault-lines governing contemporary politics is certainly understandable – given that the Labour left is still struggling to find its footing amid sustained attempts at de-legitimation from many factions and forces, both external and internal. But as this book has argued, this question of nation is not like other issues where one might be able to bide one's time. It is instead the case that, as we witness a partial unravelling of the neoliberal consensus, it is the race-baiting nationalist right that is rapidly positioning itself as the most likely heir to formal governmental power. To remain silent on its suite of racialised demons and complementary policies is therefore to allow the quickening march of nationalism the free path it is now eyeing, a free path to consolidate itself as the politics of the future – no longer merely a deeply resonant echo of high modernity, but instead a nation politics that is staking a uniquely powerful claim for managing the twenty-first century and its assorted anxieties, imperatives and even visions of utopia.

Notes

Notes to the Introduction

1. R. Eatwell and M. Goodwin, *National Populism and the Revolt against Liberal Democracy* (London: Pelican, 2018); E. Kaufmann, *Whiteshift: Populism, Immigration and the Future of White Majorities* (London: Allen Lane, 2018); J. Lanchester, 'Brexit blues', *London Review of Books* 48:15 (2016), 3–6, www.lrb.co.uk/v38/n15/john-lanchester/brexit-blues (accessed 26 February 2019); G. Younge, 'Don't pity May. Her immigration obsession helped get us into this mess', *Guardian*, 13 December 2018, www.theguardian.com/commentisfree/2018/dec/13/dont-pity-theresa-may-immigration-mess (accessed 26 February 2019).
2. N. Malik, 'Hillary Clinton's chilling pragmatism gives the far right a free pass', *Guardian*, 23 November 2018, www.theguardian.com/commentisfree/2018/nov/23/hillary-clinton-populism-europe-immigration (accessed 26 February 2019).
3. J.-W. Müller, 'What Cold War liberalism can teach us', *New York Review of Books*, 16 November 2018, www.nybooks.com/daily/2018/11/26/what-cold-war-liberalism-can-teach-us-today/ (accessed 26 February 2019).
4. This being the much-commented-upon incident when Hillary Clinton described Donald Trump's supporters as 'deplorables'. This was perhaps comparable, in the UK context, to Gordon Brown's infamous 'bigot-gate' incident, when he was caught on-mic making an unflattering remark about a Labour supporter who had just challenged him about being too lax on immigration.
5. A. Abrahamian, 'There is no left case for nationalism', *Nation*, 28 November 2018, www.thenation.com/article/open-borders-nationalism-angela-nagle/ (accessed 26 February 2019).
6. R. Merrick, 'Nigel Farage says Theresa May is winning because she has stolen all his policies', *Independent*, 7 May 2017, www.independent.co.uk/

NOTES

news/uk/politics/election-latest-nigel-farage-theresa-may-stolen-ukip-pol icies-brussels-bashing-immigration-a7722346.html (accessed 26 February 2019).

7 R. Ford and M. Goodwin, *Revolt on the Right: Explaining Support for the Radical Right in Britain* (London: Routledge, 2014).

8 C. Taylor, *Sources of the Self* (Cambridge, MA: Harvard University Press, 1992).

9 M. Rapport, *1848: Year of Revolution* (London: Abacus, 2009).

10 A. Hoogvelt, *Globalization and the Postcolonial World: The New Political Economy of Development* (London: Macmillan Educational, 2001).

11 R. Dasgupta, 'The demise of the nation state', *Guardian*, 5 April 2018, www.theguardian.com/news/2018/apr/05/demise-of-the-nation-state-rana-dasgupta (accessed 26 February 2019); M. Hamid, 'The rise of nationalism: "In the land of the pure, no one is pure enough"', *Guardian*, 27 January 2018, www.theguardian.com/books/2018/jan/27/mohsin-hamid--exit-west-pen-pakistan (accessed 26 February 2019).

12 F. Fukuyama, *The End of History and the Last Man* (London: Penguin, 2012 [1992]).

13 L. Menand, 'Francis Fukuyama postpones the end of history', *New Yorker*, 3 September 2018, www.newyorker.com/magazine/2018/09/03/francis-fukuyama-postpones-the-end-of-history (accessed 26 February 2019).

14 T. Mills, *The BBC: The Myth of a Public Service* (London: Verso, 2016).

15 A. Lentin and G. Titley, *The Crises of Multiculturalism: Racism in a Neoliberal Age* (London: Zed Books, 2011).

16 R. Seymour, 'The Brexit debacle: an interview with Richard Seymour', *Jacobin*, 4 December 2018, www.jacobinmag.com/2018/12/richard-seymour-interview-brexit-theresa-may (accessed 26 February 2019).

17 J. Bourne, 'Grievance as identity', *Institute of Race Relations*, 3 April 2017, www.irr.org.uk/news/grievance-as-identity/ (accessed 26 February 2019); R. Seymour, 'The phony martyrdom of Tommy Robinson', *Jacobin*, 8 August 2018, www.jacobinmag.com/2018/08/tommy-robinson-fascist-bbc-prison-sentence (accessed 26 February 2019).

18 J. Surowiecki, 'Trump's other tax ploy', *New Yorker*, 17 October 2016, www.newyorker.com/magazine/2016/10/17/trumps-other-tax-ploy (accessed 26 February 2019).

19 T. Frank, 'Donald Trump is moving to the White House, and liberals put him there', *Guardian*, 9 November 2016, www.theguardian.com/commentisfree/2016/nov/09/donald-trump-white-house-hillary-clinton-liberals (accessed 26 February 2019).

20 A. Shatz, 'The nightmare begins', *London Review of Books* blog, 10 November 2016, www.lrb.co.uk/blog/2016/11/10/adam-shatz/the-nightmare-begins/ (accessed 26 February 2019).

21 L. Bassel and A. Emejulu, *Minority Women and Austerity: Survival and Resistance in France and Britain* (Bristol: Policy Press, 2017); F. Shaheen, '"White working class": the label that seeks to divide and rule', *Guardian*, 22 March 2017, www.theguardian.com/commentisfree/2017/mar/22/white-working-class-label-minority-ethnic-inequality (accessed 26 February 2019); F. Shaheen and O. Khan (eds), *Minority Report: Race and Class in Post-Brexit Britain* (London: Runnymede, 2017); Z. Williams, 'Forget angry, Brexity stereotypes – the "white working class" does not exist', *Guardian*, 1 August 2018, www.theguardian.com/commentisfree/2018/aug/01/white-working-class-stereotypes (accessed 26 February 2019).

22 D. Sayer, 'White riot: Brexit, Trump, and post-factual politics', *Journal of Historical Sociology* 30 (2017), 92–106.

23 S. Bangstad, *Anders Breivik and the Rise of Islamophobia* (London: Zed Books, 2014).

24 J. B. Judis, *The Populist Explosion* (New York: Columbia Global Reports, 2016).

25 T. May, 'Theresa May's conference speech in full', *Telegraph*, 5 October 2016, www.telegraph.co.uk/news/2016/10/05/theresa-mays-conference-speech-in-full/ (accessed 26 February 2019).

26 A. Asthana, 'Tories would even surprise Enoch Powell, says Kenneth Clarke', *Guardian*, 31 January 2017, www.theguardian.com/politics/2017/jan/31/article-50-mps-must-honour-british-peoples-leave-vote-david-davis-brexit (accessed 26 February 2019).

27 E. Hobsbawm and T. Ranger (eds), *The Invention of Tradition* (Cambridge: Cambridge University Press, 1983); B. Anderson, *Imagined Communities: Reflections on the Origin and Spread of Nationalism* (London: Verso, 1983).

28 Hobsbawm and Ranger (eds), *The Invention of Tradition*, p. 134.

29 Z. Bauman, *Postmodern Ethics* (Oxford: Blackwell, 1993).

30 T. Parsons, 'Full citizenship for the Negro American? A sociological problem', *Daedalus* 94:4 (1965), 1009–54.

31 For a thorough scrutiny of the statement's perhaps apocryphal origins, see S. M. Hom, 'On the origins of making Italy – Massimo d'Azeglio and "Fatta l'Italia, bisogna fare gli Italini"', *Italian Culture* 31:1 (2013), 1–16.

32 H. K. Bhabha, *Nation and Narration* (London: Routledge, 1990); N. Yuval-Davis and F. Anthias (eds), *Woman, Nation and State* (Basingstoke: Macmillan, 1989).

NOTES

33 E. Balibar, 'The nation form: history and ideology', *Review (Fernand Braudel Center)* 13:3 (1990), 349.
34 S. Hall, 'The West and the rest: discourse and power', in S. Hall and B. Gieben (eds), *Formations of Modernity* (Cambridge: Polity Press, 1992), pp. 276–331.
35 P. Gilroy, *There Ain't No Black in the Union Jack: The Cultural Politics of Race and Nation* (Abingdon: Routledge, 2002 [1987]); D. T. Goldberg, *The Racial State* (Oxford: Blackwell, 2002).
36 J. Solomos and L. Back, *Racism and Society* (Basingstoke: Palgrave Macmillan, 1996), pp. 18–19.
37 M. Goodfellow, 'What should Jeremy Corbyn's brand of leftwing populism look like?', *Guardian*, 19 December 2016, www.theguardian.com/commentisfree/2016/dec/19/panel-jeremy-corbyn-brand-+leftwing-populism-yanis-varoufakis (accessed 26 February 2019).
38 https://twitter.com/AyoCaesar/status/818768092209774592 (accessed 26 February 2019).
39 Malik, 'Hillary Clinton's chilling pragmatism gives the far right a free pass'.
40 P. Norris and R. Inglehart, *The Cultural Backlash* (Cambridge: Cambridge University Press, 2019).
41 W. Brown, 'American nightmare: neoliberalism, neoconservatism, and de-democratization', *Political Theory* 34 (2006), 690–714.
42 S. Hall, 'The problem of ideology: Marxism without guarantees', *Journal of Communication Inquiry* 10 (1986), 29.
43 Brown, 'American nightmare', 690.
44 A. Kundnani, 'Multiculturalism and its discontents: left, right and liberal', *European Journal of Cultural Studies* 15:2 (2012), 155–66.
45 G. Bhattacharyya, *Dangerous Brown Men* (London: Zed Books, 2008).
46 S. Farris, *In the Name of Women's Rights: The Rise of Femonationalism* (Durham, NC: Duke University Press, 2017).
47 N. Rashid, 'Veiled concerns: the faux-feminism of far right populism', *Sociological Review*, 9 September 2018, www.thesociologicalreview.com/blog/veiled-concerns-the-faux-feminism-of-far-right-populism.html (accessed 22 March 2019).
48 G. Titley, D. Freedman, G. Khiabany and A. Mondon, *After Charlie Hebdo* (London: Zed Books, 2017).
49 P. Gilroy, *After Empire: Melancholia or Convivial Culture?* (Abingdon: Routledge, 2004).
50 J. Rhodes, 'Remaking whiteness in the "postracial" UK', in N. Kapoor, V. Kalra and J. Rhodes (eds), *The State of Race* (London: Palgrave, 2013), pp.

49–71; S. Valluvan, N. Kapoor and V. Kalra, 'Critical consumers run riot in Manchester', *Journal for Cultural Research* 17:2 (2013), 164–82.
51 O. Hatherley, *A New Kind of Bleak: Journeys through Urban Britain* (London: Verso, 2012).
52 Z. Bauman, *Collateral Damage: Social Inequalities in a Global Age* (Cambridge: Polity Press, 2011).
53 G. Prakash, 'Whose cosmopolitanism? Multiple, globally enmeshed and subaltern', in N. Glick Schiller and A. Irving (eds), *Whose Cosmopolitanism?* (New York: Berghahn Books, 2015), p. 28.
54 D. Janjevic, 'New "Aufstehen" movement of Sahra Wagenknecht is shaking up leftists', *Deutsche Welle*, 11 August 2018, www.dw.com/en/germany-new-aufstehen-movement-of-sahra-wagenknecht-is-shaking-up-leftists/a-4504 7762 (accessed 26 February 2019).
55 M. Goodwin and O. Heath, 'The 2016 referendum, Brexit and the left behind', *Political Quarterly* 87:3 (2016), 323–32.

Notes to Chapter 1

1 S. Garner, *Racisms: An Introduction* (London: Sage, 2010), p. 49; A. Wimmer, *Nationalist Exclusion and Ethnic Conflict* (Cambridge: Cambridge University Press, 2008).
2 D. McCrone, *The Sociology of Nationalism: Tomorrow's Ancestors* (London: Routledge, 2002), p. vii.
3 *The Economist*, 'Whither nationalism?', 19 December 2017, www.econom ist.com/christmas-specials/2017/12/19/whither-nationalism (accessed 26 February 2019).
4 K. Tharoor, 'Epic fails: "Outlaw King" and Netflix's nationalism problem', *The Nation*, 29 November 2018, www.thenation.com/article/historical-epi cs-outlaw-king-nationalism/ (accessed 26 February 2019).
5 This was the German-language artistic and literary movement of the late eighteenth century that foregrounded the wild spirits and emotion of life and nature against the strict and cold restraint of Enlightenment-based rationalism. The movement is particularly associated with the young Goethe and Schiller.
6 C. Pinney, 'Things happen: or, from which moment does that object come?', in D. Miller (ed.), *Materiality* (Durham, NC: Duke University Press, 2005), p. 262; R. J. Schmidt, 'Cultural nationalism in Herder', *Journal of the History of Ideas* 17:3 (1956), 407–17.
7 H. K. Bhabha, *The Location of Culture* (Abingdon: Routledge, 2004 [1994]), pp. 199–244; J. W. Goethe, *Italian Journey* (1816–17) (London:

Penguin, 1970); N. Smith, 'Blood and soil: nature, native and nation in the Australian imaginary', *Journal of Australian Studies* 35:1 (2011), 1–18; B. Pitcher, 'Belonging to a different landscape: repurposing nationalist affects', *Sociological Research Online* 21 (2016), www.socresonline.org.uk/21/1/8.html (accessed 22 March 2019).

8 V. H. Miesel, 'Philipp Otto Runge, Caspar David Friedrich and romantic nationalism', *Yale University Art Gallery Bulletin* 33:2 (1972), 37–51.

9 S. Grosby, 'The verdict of history: the inexpungeable tie of primordiality', *Ethnic and Racial Studies* 17:1 (1994), 164–71.

10 A. Smith, *Ethno-Symbolism and Nationalism: A Cultural Approach* (London: Routledge, 2009).

11 A. G. Rabinbach, 'Toward a Marxist theory of fascism and National Socialism', *New German Critique* 3 (1974), 127–53.

12 B. Anderson, *Imagined Communities: Reflections on the Origin and Spread of Nationalism* (London: Verso, 1983), p. 7.

13 J. R. Llobera, *God of Modernity* (Oxford: Berg, 1996); J. R. Llobera, *Foundations of National Identity: From Catalonia to Europe* (New York: Berghahn Books, 2005).

14 A. Smith, *Nationalism: Theory, Ideology, History* (Cambridge: Polity Press, 2010 [2001]), pp. 38–9.

15 H. K. Bhabha, *Nation and Narration* (London: Routledge, 1990); R. Brubaker, *Ethnicity without Groups* (Cambridge, MA: Harvard University Press, 2004), pp. 31–2; C. Calhoun, *Nationalism* (Minneapolis, MN: University of Minnesota Press, 1997); R. Wodak, R. de Cillia, M. Reisigl and K. Liebhart, *The Discursive Construction of National Identity* (Edinburgh: Edinburgh University Press, 2009 [1999]).

16 R. Brubaker, *Nationalism Reframed: Nationhood and the National Question in the New Europe* (Cambridge: Cambridge University Press, 1996).

17 E. Renan, 'Qu'est-ce qu'une nation?' (1882), in J. Hutchinson and A. Smith (eds), *Nationalism* (Oxford: Oxford University Press, 1994), p. 17.

18 Ibid., p. 18.

19 Anderson, *Imagined Communities*.

20 M. Weber, *Economy and Society* (New York: Bedminster Press, 1968 [1922]). Durkheim lists the nation as the primary 'political' unit into which one is ideally 'integrated'; the other forms of integration being the 'domestic' via the family and the 'religious' via the Church. E. Durkheim, *Suicide* (Abingdon: Routledge, 2002 [1897]).

21 D. Chernilo, *A Social Theory of the Nation-State: The Political Forms of Modernity Beyond Methodological Nationalism* (Abingdon: Routledge, 2007); C. Wight, 'Book review: *A Social Theory of the Nation-State: the political forms*

of modernity beyond methodological nationalism', *Journal of Critical Realism* 9:1 (2010), 112–18; A. Wimmer and N. Glick Schiller, 'Methodological nationalism and beyond', *Global Networks* 2:4 (2002), 301–34.

22   P. Gilroy, *Between Camps: Nations, Cultures and the Allure of Race* (Abingdon: Routledge, 2004 [2000]), pp. 57–8.

23   A. Nayak, 'After race: ethnography, race and post-race theory', *Ethnic and Racial Studies* 29:3 (2006), 411.

24   It is for this reason that popular attempts to unsettle the origin myths of a 'pure' nation are in all likelihood quixotic, entertaining as they are as scholarly efforts (see R. Winder, *Bloody Foreigners* [New York: Little, Brown, 2004]). To document the multiple waves of human movement that furnished a nation's population (Britain as Huguenot, Jewish, Irish, Windrush, etc.), in order to disrupt the toxic but commonplace contemporary appeal to a history of homogeneity, misunderstands where the emphasis of nationalism is drawn. The nature of its politics is such that 'the [actual] ethnographic history of a people is often of little pertinence to the study of nation-formation'; W. Connor, 'When is a nation?', *Ethnic and Racial Studies* 13:1 (1990), 92. Nationalism is, after all, not primarily about the past as pure, but rather the present as impure. When the various 'outsiders' characteristic of the present are seen as posing insoluble problems, a stress on the past's unruly and decidedly diverse content ceases to be the complication to nationalism that one would hope. In fact, the exclusionary nationalism of the present can sometimes rally this past history of ostensible pluralism for its own opportunistic gain: documenting a history of inclusion that is said to be embedded in the nation's character but is now under duress, contending as it is with a variety of ungrateful, inassimilable ethnic Others – ethnic Others who represent a uniquely unbridgeable civilisational gulf when contrasted to the previous waves of migrants who are retrospectively seen as having gradually settled without complication. Indeed, even some of the recently hard-won sympathy for the Windrush-era migrants and their brutal treatment by the Home Office does trade on a certain kind of good migrant/bad migrant dichotomy that can be written across this temporality: e.g. previous migrants as decent and respectable, current migrants as criminal and disruptive. Two important pieces on the 2018 Windrush scandal are L. de Noronha, 'The Windrush deportations were wrong – and so are all the others', *Guardian*, 7 June 2018, www.theguardian.com/commentisfree/2018/jun/07/windrush-legal-illegal-migrants-caribbean-deportation-uk (accessed 26 February 2019), and N. Kapoor, 'On Windrush, citizenship and its others', 1 May 2018, www.versobooks.com/blogs/3774-on-windrush-citizenship-and-its-others (accessed 26 February 2019).

NOTES

25 R. V. Mongia, 'Race, nationality, mobility: a history of the passport', *Public Culture* 11:3 (1999), 527–55.
26 R. Shilliam, *Race and the Undeserving Poor* (Newcastle upon Tyne: Agenda Publishing, 2018).
27 C. Schmitt, *The Concept of the Political* (Chicago: University of Chicago Press, 2007 [1932]); G. Balakrishnan, *The Enemy: An Intellectual Portrait of Carl Schmitt* (London: Verso, 2000).
28 'Targeted' is the best of way of typifying this because, for Schmitt, the assertion of outsider status does not actually trade on anything 'substantive'. The assertion of enmity traffics instead in a decidedly arbitrary principle of distinction – as opposed to it requiring any actual cultural differences, any actual religious conflict, or any actual contestation over competing moral compasses.
29 A. Triandafyllidou, 'National identity and the "other"', *Ethnic and Racial Studies* 21:4 (1998), 593–612.
30 Note that the national government recently approved the change to the country's hotly contested official name, which will now be North Macedonia.
31 Triandafyllidou, 'National identity and the "other"', 605–7.
32 F. Anthias and N. Yuval-Davis, in association with H. Cain, *Racialized Boundaries: Race, Nation, Gender, Colour and Class and the Anti-Racist Struggle* (Abingdon: Routledge, 1993), p. 2.
33 Such a reading of nationalism becomes particularly pertinent to those countries that are to some significant extent avowedly multi-ethnic in their constitution and narration – i.e. lacking an obvious nativist claim to homogeneity – or when the country is characterised by frameworks of political devolution as well as acknowledged waves of past immigration.
34 M. James, 'Whiteness and loss in outer East London', *Ethnic and Racial Studies* 37:4 (2014), 652–67.
35 N. Fadil, 'Performing the *salat* [Islamic prayers] at work: secular and pious Muslims negotiating the contours of the public in Belgium', *Ethnicities* 13:6 (2013), 729–50.
36 V. Ware, 'Towards a sociology of resentment: a debate on class and whiteness', *Sociological Research Online* 13:5 (2008), 9, www.socresonline. org.uk/13/5/9.html (accessed 22 March 2019).
37 S. Farris, *In the Name of Women's Rights: The Rise of Femonationalism* (Durham, NC: Duke University Press, 2017).
38 J. K. Puar, *Terrorist Assemblages: Homonationalism in Queer Times* (Durham, NC: Duke University Press, 2007).
39 R. Ehsan, 'Inside the British Asian Brexit vote – and why it contains a few surprises', *The Conversation*, 16 February 2017, https://theconversation.

NOTES

com/inside-the-british-asian-brexit-vote-and-why-it-contains-a-few-surprises-72931 (accessed 26 February 2019).

40 See, for instance, Anderson's distinguishing of nationalism from racism: 'The fact of the matter is that nationalism thinks in terms of historical destinies, while racism dreams of eternal contaminations, transmitted from the origins of time through an endless sequence of loathsome copulations: outside history [...] The dreams of racism actually have their origin in ideologies of class, rather than in those of nation: above all in claims to divinity among rulers and to "blue" or "white" blood and "breeding" among aristocracies.' Anderson, *Imagined Communities*, p. 149.

41 P. Gilroy, *There Ain't No Black in the Union Jack: The Cultural Politics of Race and Nation* (Abingdon: Routledge, 2002 [1987]), p. xx.

42 Ibid., pp. 50–2.

43 Ibid., p. 56.

44 M. Flemmen and M. Savage, 'The politics of nationalism and white racism in the UK', *British Journal of Sociology* 68:1 (2017), 233–64; N. Gidron, 'The Left shouldn't fear nationalism. It should embrace it', *Vox*, 8 February 2018, www.vox.com/the-big-idea/2018/2/8/16982036/nationalism-patriotism-left-right-trump-democrats-solidarity (accessed 26 February 2019); T. Hunt, 'Labour must embrace Englishness – and be proud of it', *Guardian*, 5 February 2016, www.theguardian.com/commentisfree/2016/feb/05/labour-embrace-englishness-proud-patriotism (accessed 26 February 2019).

45 Gilroy, *There Ain't No Black in the Union Jack*, pp. 55–8.

46 E. Balibar, 'The nation form: history and ideology', *Review (Fernand Braudel Center)* 13:3 (1990), 329–61.

47 Chernilo, *A Social Theory of the Nation-State*, p. 92.

48 Balibar, 'The nation form', 340.

49 H. Arendt, *The Origins of Totalitarianism* (London: Harvest Books, 1973 [1951]), p. 275.

50 R. Guha, *Dominance without Hegemony: History and Power in Colonial India* (Cambridge, MA: Harvard University Press, 1997); G. Bhambra, *Rethinking Modernity: Postcolonialism and the Sociological Imagination* (Basingstoke: Palgrave Macmillan, 2007), pp. 106–23.

51 C. J. Robinson, *Black Marxism: The Making of the Black Radical Tradition* (Chapel Hill, NC: University of North Carolina Press, 2000 [1983]), p. 164.

52 Bhabha, *The Location of Culture*, pp. 212–30.

53 Balibar, 'The nation form', 344. As Balibar again comments, paraphrasing the work of the historian Eugen Weber and his landmark *Peasants into Frenchmen*, it is only this retrospective claim on the state by a nationalist political project that facilitates a more concerted and total 'nationalization'

of the state population within its remit: 'This is what I shall call the delayed nationalization of society, which first of all concerns the old nations themselves and is so delayed that it ultimately appears as an endless task. An historian like Eugen Weber has shown (as have other subsequent studies) that in the case of France, universal schooling and the unification of customs and beliefs by interregional labour migration and military service and the subordination of political and religious conflicts [and regional dialects it might be added] to patriotic ideology did not come about until the early years of the twentieth century. His demonstration suggests that the French peasantry was only finally "nationalized" at the point when it was about to disappear as the majority class (though this disappearance, as we know, was itself retarded by the protectionism that is an essential characteristic of national politics).' This nationalising struggle over language is still residually apparent in certain parts of France (the Basque Country and Corsica, for instance), where regional languages have proven stubbornly resilient. These difficulties are particularly apparent in those nation-states where language differences proved permanently indelible (e.g. Belgium or Quebec in Canada), or, of course, in most postcolonial Global South nation-state contexts. Sri Lanka and the civil war that it became so associated with, though not reducible by any reckoning to language, did find its more seminal moment of rupture in the attempt by the nascent state to nationalise the majority language (Sinhala). Another potent context is the politics that informed the newly formed Pakistan's attempt to institutionalise Urdu, leading, among other things, to the violent falling out with East Pakistan (now Bangladesh).

54 N. Doharty, '"Is it because I'm black?" Personal reflections on Stuart Hall's memoir *Familiar Stranger*', *Identities* 25:1 (2018), 14–21.
55 B. Byrne, *Making Citizens: Public Rituals and Personal Journeys to Citizenship* (Basingstoke: Palgrave Macmillan, 2014); M. Billig, *Banal Nationalism* (London: Sage, 1995), p. 8.
56 J. Appleby, *The Relentless Revolution: A History of Capitalism* (New York: W.W. Norton, 2010); E. M. Wood, *The Origin of Capitalism* (London: Verso, 2002).
57 Anderson, *Imagined Communities*; K. Kumar, *The Making of English National Identity* (Cambridge: Cambridge University Press, 2003); E. P. Thompson, *The Making of the English Working Class* (London: Penguin, 2013 [1963]).
58 Balibar, 'The nation form', 340.
59 E. Gellner, *Nations and Nationalism* (Oxford: Blackwell, 2006 [1983]), pp. 1, 54.
60 S. Garner, *Racisms: An Introduction* (London: Sage, 2010), p. 49.

61 G. Simmel, 'The metropolis and mental life' (1903), in G. Bridge and S. Watson (eds), *The Blackwell City Reader* (Oxford: Wiley-Blackwell, 2002), pp. 11–19.
62 M. Mamdani, 'Making sense of political violence in post-colonial Africa', *Socialist Register* 39 (2003), 139–40.
63 Arendt remains a controversial figure in anti-racist and anti-imperialist circles, owing both to her often naive and contrarian writing on 'race relations' in the United States, but also to her flatly dismissive writings on the question of radical violence. The former misdiagnosis of the politics of civil rights and integration in the US remains particularly irredeemable. Another key postcolonial critique of Arendt is that she does seem occasionally to intimate that the fundamental issue with colonial modernity is that the technologies of racial governance as rehearsed in the colonies are then repatriated to the metropole/Europe itself. This strain in her argument is troubling insofar as the violence and injustices that take place in the colonies (her understanding of which can itself be rather clumsy), and which non-Europeans are subject to, seem at times to be only of secondary concern.
64 Arendt, *The Origins of Totalitarianism*, p. 299.
65 As Césaire wrote: 'Yes, it would be worthwhile to study clinically, in detail, the steps taken by Hitler and Hitlerism and to reveal to the very distinguished, very humanistic, very Christian bourgeois of the twentieth century that without his being aware of it, he has a Hitler inside him, that Hitler *inhabits* him, that Hitler is his *demon*, that if he rails against him, he is being inconsistent and that, at bottom, what he cannot forgive Hitler for is not *crime* in itself, *the crime against man*, it is not *the humiliation of man as such*, it is the crime against the white man, the humiliation of the white man, and the fact that he applied to Europe colonialist procedures which until then had been reserved exclusively for the Arabs of Algeria, the "coolies" of India, and the "niggers" of Africa.' A. Césaire, *Discourse on Colonialism* (New York: Monthly Review Press, 2000 [1955]), p. 36.
66 Arendt, *The Origins of Totalitarianism*, p. 275.
67 U. Freitag, '"Cosmopolitanism" and "conviviality"? Some conceptual considerations concerning the late Ottoman Empire', *European Journal of Cultural Studies* 17:4 (2014), 375–91.
68 Said's immediate context here is rather different, regarding how racialised non-Europeans might come to perceive themselves and their neighbours; but this general sense of an Orientalist structure through which life and self are perceived also applies to how people might pursue nation-state projects, as a course of ostensible resistance that still upholds Orientalist taxonomies of ethnic formation, distinction and culture. His objective, namely, was 'to

illustrate the formidable structure of cultural domination [that is Orientalism] and, specifically for formerly colonized peoples, [to illustrate] the dangers and temptations of employing this structure upon themselves or upon others'. This is somewhat contiguous to Fanon's impossibly moving passage where he is tempted by an affirming Négritude philosophy of reclaiming the beauty of blackness, only to fear that much of this reclaiming is fated to end up rehearsing the very stereotypes and classifications that only colonial raciology had itself birthed: 'But I was haunted by a galaxy of erosive stereotypes: the Negro's *sui generis* odor ... the Negro's *sui generis* good nature ... the Negro's *sui generis* gullibility'. E. Said, *Orientalism* (London: Penguin, 2003 [1978]), p. 33; F. Fanon, *Black Skins, White Masks* (London: Pluto Press, 2008 [1952]), p. 99.
69 Arendt, *The Origins of Totalitarianism*, p. 272.
70 Said, *Orientalism*, p. xvi.
71 S. Makdisi, 'The architecture of erasure', *Critical Inquiry* 36:3 (2010), 519–59.
72 P. Beaumont, 'EU leads criticism after Israel passes Jewish "nation state" law', *Guardian*, 19 July 2018, www.theguardian.com/world/2018/jul/19/israel-adopts-controversial-jewish-nation-state-law (accessed 26 February 2019).
73 A. Mbembe, *Critique of Black Reason* (Durham, NC: Duke University Press, 2017), p. 183.
74 Ibid.
75 A. Chua, *Political Tribes: Group Instinct and the Fate of Nations* (London: Bloomsbury, 2018); G. Fraser, 'Diversity can distract us from economic inequality', *Guardian*, 17 November 2016, www.theguardian.com/commentisfree/belief/2016/nov/17/diversity-can-distract-us-from-econom ic-inequality (accessed 26 February 2019); M. Lilla, 'The end of identity liberalism', *New York Times*, 18 November 2016, www.nytimes.com/2016/11/20/opinion/sunday/the-end-of-identity-liberalism.html (accessed 26 February 2019); S. Jenkins, 'Blame the identity apostles – they led us down this path to populism', *Guardian*, 1 December 2016, www.theguardian.com/commentisfree/2016/dec/01/blame-trump-brexit-identity-liberalism (accessed 26 February 2019); J. D. Vance, *Hillbilly Elegy: A Memoir of Family and Culture* (New York: Harper Collins, 2016).
76 A. Haider, *Mistaken Identity: Race and Class in the Age of Trump* (London: Verso, 2018); A. Olaloku-Teriba, 'Afro-pessimism and the (un)logic of anti-Blackness', *Historical Materialism* 26:2 (2018), 96–122.
77 Arendt, *The Origins of Totalitarianism*, p. 292.
78 R. Brubaker, 'Between nationalism and civilizationism: the European populist moment in comparative perspective', *Ethnic and Racial Studies* 40:8 (2017), 1192.

79 Ibid., 1193.
80 Ibid., 1211.
81 Ibid., 1191.
82 N. Fadil, 'Are we all secular/ized yet?', *Ethnic and Racial Studies* 39:13 (2016), 2261–8.
83 N. Kapoor, *Deport, Deprive, Extradite: 21st Century State Extremism* (London: Verso, 2018); L. de Noronha, 'Deportation, racism and multi-status Britain: immigration control and the production of race in the present', *Ethnic and Racial Studies* (forthcoming).
84 S. Hall, 'The West and the rest: discourse and power', in S. Hall and B. Gieben (eds), *Formations of Modernity* (Cambridge: Polity Press, 1992), pp. 276–331.
85 C. Hall, *Civilising Subjects – Metropole and Colony in the English Imagination: 1830–1867* (Cambridge: Blackwell, 2002).
86 A. Grosrichard, *The Sultan's Court: European Fantasies of the East* (London: Verso, 1998 [1979]).
87 A. McClintock, *Imperial Leather: Race, Gender and Sexuality in the Colonial Contest* (London: Routledge, 1995).
88 P. Mishra, 'How colonial violence came home: the ugly truth of the first world war', *Guardian*, 10 November 2017, www.theguardian.com/news/2017/nov/10/how-colonial-violence-came-home-the-ugly-truth-of-the-first-world-war (accessed 26 February 2019).
89 Brubaker, 'Between nationalism and civilizationism', 1211.
90 B. McGeever and S. Virdee, 'Antisemitism and socialist strategy in Europe, 1880–1917', *Patterns of Prejudice* 51:3–4 (2017), 221–34; J. Renton and B. Gidley (eds), *Antisemitism and Islamophobia in Europe: A Shared Story?* (London: Palgrave Macmillan, 2017); S. Virdee, 'Socialist antisemitism and its discontents in England, 1884–98', *Patterns of Prejudice* 51:3–4 (2017), 356–73; G.L. Mosse, *Toward the Final Solution: A History of the Final Solution* (New York: Howard Fertig, 1978).
91 D. T. Goldberg, *Are We All Postracial Yet?* (Cambridge: Polity Press, 2015).
92 Needless to say, as much as any such culture-clash framework homogenises a sense of outsider culture while already rendering ethnicity the primary marker of culture, it also presumes, in turn, a shared *internal* culture. Any such notion of a national culture is, of course, preposterous. The nation, contrary to its cultural pretences to ethnic exclusivity, is in fact without a shared cultural bond. At the risk of seeming flippant, it remains frankly absurd to suggest that the England of Wayne Rooney's Liverpool and the England of Zara Phillips' equestrian shires has anything that constitutes a shared cultural script or inheritance. Similarly, the Friday night punch-up

outside the 'working man's' Bolton pub or Manchester's Printworks shares as much with the organised male violence of Eton's rugby fields as it does with the merry tumult of an Istanbul street market. Or consider the lack of any meaningful resemblance between evangelical church practice as imported from the United States and the High Church Anglicanism of English elites. Or simply consider Hobsbawm and Kertzer's rather more wry, if somewhat exaggerated, observation that all talk of 'our way of life' is not only illusory, but, if anything, that the only 'our way' in new times is simply a massified American popular culture: *'Culturally*, the most militant gangs who beat up immigrants in the name of the nation belong to the international youth culture and reflect its modes and fashions, jeans, punk-rock, junk food and all. Indeed, for most of the inhabitants of the countries in which xenophobia is now epidemic, the old ways of life have changed so drastically since the 1950s that there is very little of them left to defend. It actually takes someone who has lived through the past 40 years as an adult to appreciate quite how extraordinarily the England of even the 1970s differed from the England of the 1940s, and the France, Italy or Spain of the 1980s from those countries in the early 1950s.' E. J. Hobsbawm and D. J. Kertzer, 'Ethnicity and nationalism in Europe today', *Anthropology Today* 8:1 (1992), 7.

93 E. Bergmann, *Nordic Nationalism and Right-Wing Populist Politics: Imperial Relationships and National Sentiments* (London: Palgrave Macmillan, 2017), p. 49.

94 J. Meek, 'Why are you still here?', *London Review of Books* 37:8 (2015), 3–14, www.lrb.co.uk/v37/n08/james-meek/why-are-you-still-here (accessed 22 March 2019).

95 J. Allouche, 'Water Nationalism: An Explanation of the Past and Present Conflicts in Central Asia, the Middle East and the Indian Subcontinent?', PhD thesis, Institut universitaire de hautes études internationales, Université de Genève, 2005.

96 Hobsbawm and Kertzer, 'Ethnicity and nationalism in Europe today', 7.

97 J. Mikanowski, 'Behemoth, bully, thief: how the English language is taking over the planet', *Guardian*, 27 July 2018, www.theguardian.com/news/2018/jul/27/english-language-global-dominance (accessed 26 February 2019); P. Roger, *The American Enemy: The History of French Anti-Americanism* (Chicago: University of Chicago Press, 2005).

98 A. Lentin, 'Europe and the silence about race', *European Journal of Social Theory* 11:4 (2008), 487–503.

99 Gilroy, *There Ain't No Black in the Union Jack*, p. xxxiii.

100 B. St Louis, 'Can race be eradicated? The post-racial problematic', in K. Murji and J. Solomos (eds), *Theories of Race and Ethnicity* (Cambridge: Cambridge

University Press, 2015), pp. 114–38; S. Upstone, *Rethinking Race and Identity in Contemporary British Fiction* (New York: Routledge, 2017), p. 48.
101 S. Valluvan, 'What is "post-race" and what does it reveal about contemporary racisms?', *Ethnic and Racial Studies* 39:13 (2016), 2241–51.
102 Or to quote from Mitchell: 'Contrary to [the] claim that "there is nothing in the world that can do all we ask 'race' to do for us", the truth is that there is nothing else in the world, or in language, that can do all that we ask race to do for us.' W. J. T. Mitchell, *Seeing Through Race* (Cambridge, MA: Harvard University Press, 2012), p. 14.
103 McClintock, *Imperial Leather*; G. C. Spivak, 'Nationalism and the imagination', *Lectora* 15 (2009), 75–98; N. Yuval-Davis and F. Anthias (eds), *Woman, Nation and State* (Basingstoke: Macmillan, 1989).

Notes to Chapter 2

1 J. R. Llobera, *Foundations of National Identity: From Catalonia to Europe* (New York: Berghahn Books, 2005). See also Tom Nairn's collection of articles for *openDemocracy*: www.opendemocracy.net/author/tom-nairn (accessed 26 February 2019).
2 Nairn, quoted in N. Davidson, *Holding Fast to an Image of the Past* (Chicago: Haymarket, 2014), p. 6.
3 N. Meer, '"We're a' Jock Tamson's bairns!" Race equality, migration and citizenship in Scotland and the UK', *Discover Society*, 30 September 2014, https://discoversociety.org/2014/09/30/were-a-jock-tamsons-bairns-race-equality-migration-and-citizenship-in-scotland-and-the-uk/ (accessed 26 February 2019).
4 D. Anand, 'China and India: postcolonial informal empires in the emerging global order', *Rethinking Marxism* 24:1 (2012), 68–146; P. Chatterjee, *Nationalist Thought and the Colonial World: A Derivative Discourse* (London: Zed Books, 1993 [1986]); K. Jayawardena, *Feminism and Nationalism in the Third World* (London: Verso, 2016 [1986]); E. Said, *Orientalism* (London: Penguin, 2003 [1978]).
5 G. Osuri, 'Imperialism, colonialism and sovereignty in the (post)colony: India and Kashmir', *Third World Quarterly* 38:11 (2017), 2428.
6 Ibid., 2432.
7 P. Mishra, *From the Ruins of Empire: The Intellectuals Who Remade Asia* (New York: Farrar, Straus and Giroux, 2012).
8 H. Rambukwella, *The Politics and Poetics of Authenticity: A Cultural Genealogy of Sinhala Nationalism* (London: UCL Press, 2018).

9 Though writing within a different debate, see also Yasmeen Narayan's recent 'Intersectionality, nationalisms, biocoloniality', an article that carefully restates the need for a transgressive commitment to undoing the communitarian inheritance of colonial modernity (not least fixed figurations of race and nation). Y. Narayan, 'Intersectionality, nationalisms biocoloniality', *Ethnic and Racial Studies* (2018), www.tandfonline.com/doi/full/10.1080/01419870.2018.1518536 (accessed 22 March 2019).

10 C. Mudde, 'Why nativism, not populism, should be declared word of the year', *Guardian*, 7 December 2017, www.theguardian.com/commentisfree/2017/dec/07/cambridge-dictionary-nativism-populism-word-year (accessed 26 February 2019).

11 G. Gordon, 'Rise in populism threatens democracy, warns Tony Blair think tank', *Independent*, 29 December 2017, www.independent.co.uk/news/world/europe/populism-tony-blair-think-tank-european-democracy-global-change-p-a8132681.html (accessed 26 February 2019); DW, 'Germany's Angela Merkel decries right-wing populism as "poison" at Davos summit', *Deutsche Welle*, 24 January 2018, www.dw.com/en/germanys-angela-merkel-decries-right-wing-populism-as-poison-at-davos-summit/a-42292865 (accessed 26 February 2019).

12 B. Bonikowski, 'Three lessons of contemporary populism in Europe and the United States', *Brown Journal of World Affairs* 23:1 (2016), 9–24; M. Canovan, 'Trust the people! Populism and the two faces of democracy', *Political Studies* 47:1 (1999), 2–16; J. B. Judis, *The Populist Explosion* (New York: Columbia Global Reports, 2016); Y. Mounk, *The People vs. Democracy: Why Our Freedom is in Danger and How to Save it* (Cambridge, MA: Harvard University Press, 2018); C. Mudde and C. R. Kaltwasser, *Populism: A Very Short Introduction* (Oxford: Oxford University Press, 2017); T. Pauwels, *Populism in Western Europe: Comparing Belgium, Germany and the Netherlands* (Abingdon: Routledge, 2014).

13 M. James, 'Authoritarian populism/populist authoritarianism', in A. Duman, D. Hancox, M. James and A. Minton (eds), *Regeneration Songs: Sounds of Investment and Loss in East London* (London: Repeater, 2018), pp. 291–306.

14 E. Fassin, M. Tazzioli, P. Hallward and C. Aradau, 'Left-wing populism: interview with Éric Fassin', *Radical Philosophy* 2:2 (2018), www.radicalphilosophy.com/article/left-wing-populism (accessed 26 February 2019).

15 M. d'Eramo, 'They, the people', *New Left Review* 103 (January–February 2017), 129–38.

16 A. Jäger, 'The myth of "populism"', *Jacobin*, 1 March 2018, www.jacobinmag.com/2018/01/populism-douglas-hofstadter-donald-trump-democracy (accessed 26 February 2019).

17 S. Farris, *In the Name of Women's Rights: The Rise of Femonationalism* (Durham, NC: Duke University Press, 2017), p. 133.
18 Y. Varoufakis, 'What should Jeremy Corbyn's brand of leftwing populism look like?', *Guardian*, 19 December 2016, www.theguardian.com/comme ntisfree/2016/dec/19/panel-jeremy-corbyn-brand-leftwing-populism-yanis-varoufakis (accessed 26 February 2019).
19 C. Miéville, *October: The Story of the Russian Revolution* (London: Verso, 2017).
20 J.-W. Müller, *What is Populism?* (London: Penguin, 2016).
21 J. T. Levy, 'There is no such thing as ideal theory', *Social Philosophy and Policy* 33:12 (2016), 312–33.
22 P. Gilroy, *Between Camps: Nations, Cultures and the Allure of Race* (Abingdon: Routledge, 2004 [2000]), p. 8.
23 S. Kierkegaard, *Concluding Unscientific Postscript* (Cambridge: Cambridge University Press, 2009 [1846]).
24 D. Critchlow, 'Politicians have long used the "forgotten man" to win elections', *The Conversation*, 1 October 2018, https://theconversation.com/ politicians-have-long-used-the-forgotten-man-to-win-elections-103570 (accessed 26 February 2019); P. Harris, 'Ding dong! Meet the quiet, decent majority: the ordinary people of Middle England who turned out for Margaret Thatcher's funeral', *Daily Mail*, 17 April 2013, www.daily mail.co.uk/news/article-2310745/Margaret-Thatcher-The-ordinary-people-Middle-England-turned-Prime-Ministers-funeral.html (accessed 26 February 2019).
25 J.-W. Müller, 'Trump, Erdoğan, Farage: the attractions of populism for politicians, the dangers for democracy', *Guardian*, 2 September 2016, www. theguardian.com/books/2016/sep/02/trump-erdogan-farage-the-attract ions-of-populism-for-politicians-the-dangers-for-democracy (accessed 26 February 2019).
26 D. Goodhart, *The Road to Somewhere: The Populist Revolt and the Future of Politics* (London: C. Hurst and Co., 2017).
27 W. Streeck, 'Trump and the Trumpists', *Inference Review* 3:1 (2017), https:// inference-review.com/article/trump-and-the-trumpists (accessed 22 March 2019); W. Streeck, *How Will Capitalism End?* (London: Verso, 2016).
28 A. Chakrabortty, 'Wolfgang Streeck: the German economist calling time on capitalism', *Guardian*, 9 December 2016, www.theguardian.com/books /2016/dec/09/wolfgang-streeck-the-german-economist-calling-time-on-capitalism (accessed 26 February 2019).
29 A. Lentin, 'On class and identity politics', *Inference Review* 3:2 (2017), https:// inference-review.com/letter/on-class-and-identity-politics (accessed 26

February 2019); A. Tooze, 'A general logic of crisis', *London Review of Books* 39:1 (2017), 3–8, www.lrb.co.uk/v39/n01/adam-tooze/a-general-logic-of-crisis (accessed 22 March 2019).
30 W. Streeck, 'Scenario for a wonderful tomorrow', *London Review of Books* 38.7 (2016), 7–10, www.lrb.co.uk/v38/n07/wolfgang-streeck/scenario-for-a-wonderful-tomorrow (accessed 22 March 2019); W. Streeck, 'Exploding Europe: Germany, the refugees and the British vote to leave', *Sheffield Political Economy Research Institute Paper* 31 (2016), 1–7.
31 B. Pitcher, 'Racism and Brexit: notes towards an antiracist populism', *Ethnic and Racial Studies* (forthcoming).
32 N. El-Enany and S. Keenan, 'Beware the ivory dwellings of the Left: political purity in the face of fascism', *Critical Legal Thinking*, 2 December 2016, http://criticallegalthinking.com/2016/12/02/beware-ivory-dwellings-left-political-purity-face-fascism/ (accessed 26 February 2019).

Notes to Chapter 3

1 P. Kelly, 'Liberalism and nationalism', in S. Wall (ed.), *The Cambridge Companion to Liberalism* (Cambridge: Cambridge University Press, 2015), pp. 329–52.
2 E. Renan, 'Qu'est-ce qu'une nation?' (1882), in J. Hutchinson and A. Smith (eds), *Nationalism* (Oxford: Oxford University Press, 1994), pp. 17–18; R. Brubaker, 'The manichean myth: rethinking the distinction between "civic" and "ethnic" nationalism', in H. Kriesi, K. Armingeon, H. Siegrist and A. Wimmer (eds), *Nation and National Identity* (Zurich: Ruegger, 1999), pp. 55–6.
3 D. A. Hollinger, *Postethnic America: Beyond Multiculturalism* (New York: Basic Books, 2000 [1995]); M. Ignatieff, *Blood and Belonging: Journeys into the New Nationalism* (London: Vintage, 1993); J. Habermas, *The Postnational Constellation* (Cambridge: Polity Press, 2001), pp. vii, 74–6.
4 Habermas, *The Postnational Constellation*, pp. 64–73.
5 J. Habermas, 'Why Europe needs a constitution', *New Left Review*, September–October 2001, www.newleftreview.org/II/11/jurgen-habermas-why-europe-needs-a-constitution (accessed 26 February 2019).
6 Habermas, *The Postnational Constellation*, p. 102.
7 Ibid., p. 76.
8 Z. Bauman, *Europe: An Unfinished Adventure* (Cambridge: Polity Press, 2004), p. 135.
9 P. Pathak, *The Future of Multicultural Britain: Confronting the Progressive Dilemma* (Edinburgh: Edinburgh University Press, 2008).

10 Ignatieff, *Blood and Belonging*, p. 6.
11 W. Kymlicka, *Politics in the Vernacular: Nationalism, Multiculturalism and Citizenship* (Oxford: Oxford University Press, 2001), pp. 282–3.
12 D. Matic, 'Is nationalism really that bad? The case of Croatia', in S. Ramet and D. Matic (eds), *Democratic Transition in Croatia* (College Station, TX: Texas A&M University Press, 2007), p. 328.
13 C. Allen, 'Passing the dinner table test: retrospective and prospective approaches to tackling Islamophobia in Britain', *SAGE Open* 3:2 (2013), 1–10.
14 J. Read, 'Writing in the conjuncture', *Borderlands* 3:1 (2004), 6. See also N. de Genova, 'Inclusion by exclusion: implosion or explosion?', *Amsterdam Law Forum* 1:1 (2008), 43–52; E. Balibar, *We, the People of Europe?* (Princeton, NJ: Princeton University Press, 2004).
15 BBC, 'State multiculturalism has failed, says David Cameron', *BBC News*, 5 February 2011, www.bbc.co.uk/news/uk-politics-12371994 (accessed 26 February 2019).
16 S. Castles, M. Korac, E. Vasta and S. Vertovec, 'Integration: mapping the field', *Home Office Online Report* 28:3 (2002), 11.
17 C. Joppke, 'Beyond national models: civic integration policies for immigrants in western Europe', *West European Politics* 30:1 (2007), 1–22.
18 A. Travis, 'Louise Casey's integration plan is behind the times', *Guardian*, 5 December 2016, www.theguardian.com/uk-news/2016/dec/05/louise-caseys-integration-plan-is-behind-the-times (accessed 26 February 2019).
19 V. Kalra and J. Rhodes, 'Local events, national implications: riots in Oldham and Burnley 2001', in D. Waddington, F. Jobard and M. King (eds), *Rioting in the UK and France* (Abingdon: Routledge, 2009), pp. 41–54.
20 A. Amin, *Land of Strangers* (Cambridge: Polity Press, 2012); L. Back, M. Keith, A. Khan, K. Shukra and J. Solomos, 'New Labour's white heart: politics, multiculturalism and the return of assimilation', *The Political Quarterly* 73:4 (2002), 45–54.
21 A. Lentin and G. Titley, *The Crises of Multiculturalism: Racism in a Neoliberal Age* (London: Zed Books, 2011).
22 N. Sarkozy, quoted in P. Hollinger, 'Council of Europe warns on multiculturalism', *Financial Times*, 16 February 2011, www.ft.com/content/72c02d9a-39c6-11e0-8dba-00144feabdc0 (accessed 15 January 2019).
23 Lentin and Titley, *The Crises of Multiculturalism*, pp. 27–35.
24 J. Rancière, 'Racism: a passion from above', *Monthly Review*, 23 September 2010, https://mronline.org/2010/09/23/racism-a-passion-from-above/ (accessed 26 February 2019).

25 V. Uberoi and T. Modood, 'Has multiculturalism in Britain retreated?', *Soundings* 53 (2013), 133–4.
26 S. Miah, *Muslims, Schooling and Security: Trojan Horse, Prevent and Racial Politics* (Basingstoke: Palgrave Macmillan, 2017); T. G. Patel, 'It's not about security, it's about racism: counter-terror strategies, civilizing processes and the post-race fiction', *Palgrave Communications* 3 (2017), 1–8; K. Sian, 'Born radicals? Prevent, positivism and "race-thinking"', *Palgrave Communications* 3 (2017), 1–8.
27 Lentin and Titley, *The Crises of Multiculturalism*, p. 166.
28 H. Mirza, 'Muslim women and gender stereotypes in "new times": from multiculturalism to Islamophobia', in N. Kapoor, V. Kalra and J. Rhodes (eds), *The State of Race* (Basingstoke: Palgrave Macmillan, 2013), pp. 86–119; N. Rashid, *Veiled Threats: Representing the Muslim Woman in Public Policy Discourses* (Bristol: Policy Press, 2016).
29 W. Tufail, 'Rotherham, Rochdale, and the racialised threat of the "Muslim grooming gang"', *International Journal for Crime, Justice and Social Democracy* 4:3 (2015), 30–43; S. C. Boulila and C. Carri, 'On Cologne: gender, migration and unacknowledged racisms in Germany', *European Journal of Women's Studies* 24:3 (2017), 286–93.
30 Such as Trevor Phillips and his 2015 documentary, 'Things We Won't Say About Race'. See also Adam Elliott-Cooper's BBC news interview, though addressing a slightly different context, for a surgical deconstruction of this discursive strategy as propagated by Phillips, formerly the chairman of the Equality and Human Rights Commission. www.youtube.com/watch?v=Tzq6jF94b34 (accessed 26 February 2019).
31 G. Bhattacharyya, *Dangerous Brown Men* (London: Zed Books, 2008); J. Butler, 'Sexual politics, torture, and secular time', *British Journal of Sociology* 59:1 (2008), 1–23; S. Farris, *In the Name of Women's Rights: The Rise of Femonationalism* (Durham, NC: Duke University Press, 2017); J. K. Puar, *Terrorist Assemblages: Homonationalism in Queer Times* (Durham, NC: Duke University Press, 2007); J. Scott, *The Politics of the Veil* (Princeton, NJ: Princeton University Press, 2007).
32 G. C. Spivak, 'Can the subaltern speak?', in P. Williams and L. Chrisman (eds), *Colonial Discourse and Post-colonial Theory: A Reader* (New York: Columbia University Press, 1994), pp. 92–3.
33 S. Ahmed, 'You are oppressing me!', *Feminist Killjoys*, 17 February 2016, www.feministkilljoys.com/2016/02/17/you-are-oppressing-me/ (accessed 26 February 2019).
34 D. Kumar, *Islamophobia and the Politics of Empire* (Chicago: Haymarket, 2012), p. 133.

35 M. Mamdani, *Good Muslim, Bad Muslim: America, the Cold War and the Roots of Terror* (New York: Penguin Random House, 2005).
36 S. Valluvan, 'Racial entanglements and sociological confusions: repudiating the rehabilitation of integration', *British Journal of Sociology* 69:2 (2018), 452.
37 R. Ahmed, 'Typecast as a terrorist', *Guardian*, 15 September 2016, www.theguardian.com/world/2016/sep/15/riz-ahmed-typecast-as-a-terrorist (accessed 26 February 2019).
38 F. Fanon, *Black Skins, White Masks* (London: Pluto Press, 2008 [1952]), p. 89.
39 D. Mulinari and A. Neergaard, 'We are Sweden Democrats because we care for others: exploring racisms in the Swedish extreme right', *European Journal of Women's Studies* 21:1 (2014), 48–9.
40 M. Mamdani, 'Good Muslim, bad Muslim: a political perspective on culture and terrorism', *American Anthropologist* 104:3 (2002), 766–75.
41 E. Bonilla-Silva, *Racism without Racists: Color-blind Racism and the Persistence of Racial Inequality in the United States* (Lanham, MD: Rowman and Littlefield, 2010).
42 Lentin and Titley, *The Crises of Multiculturalism*, p. 8.
43 D. Losurdo, *Liberalism: A Counter-history* (London: Verso, 2011).
44 A. Kundnani, 'Multiculturalism and its discontents: left, right and liberal', *European Journal of Cultural Studies* 15:2 (2012), 163.
45 A. Kundnani, 'Draft paper on Islamophobia as lay ideology of US-led empire', 13 January 2016, www.kundnani.org/draft-paper-on-islamophobia-as-lay-ideology-of-us-led-empire/ (accessed 26 February 2019).
46 Lentin and Titley, *The Crises of Multiculturalism*, p. 105.
47 C. Alexander, 'The culture question: a view from the UK', *Ethnic and Racial Studies* 39:8 (2016), 1426–35.
48 Z. Bauman, *Postmodern Ethics* (Oxford: Blackwell, 1993), p. 101.
49 G. Hage, *Is Racism an Environmental Threat?* (London: Polity Press, 2017).
50 P. Essed and S. Trienekens, '"Who wants to feel white?" Race, Dutch culture and contested identities', *Ethnic and Racial Studies* 31:1 (2008), 62–3.
51 L. Medovoi, 'Dogma-line racism', *Social Text* 30:2 (2012), 43–74; S. Sayyid, *A Fundamental Fear: Eurocentrism and the Emergence of Islamism* (London: Zed Books, 2003).
52 Kundnani, 'Multiculturalism and its discontents', 160.
53 N. Rashid, 'Veiled concerns: the faux-feminism of far right populism', *Sociological Review*, 9 September 2018, www.thesociologicalreview.com/blog/veiled-concerns-the-faux-feminism-of-far-right-populism.html (accessed 22 March 2019).
54 N. Kapoor, *Deport, Deprive, Extradite: 21st Century State Extremism* (London: Verso, 2018).

55 There are, of course, voluminous exegeses about what precisely constitutes Orientalism by Said's reckoning and what does not. There are also exegeses about how other European systems of knowledge helped to uphold and administer the colonial project. See Hallaq for a recent restaging of this discussion; such debates are, however, not within the purview of my own argument. W. B. Hallaq, *Restating Orientalism: A Critique of Modern Knowledge* (New York: Columbia University Press, 2018).
56 Medovoi, 'Dogma-line racism'.
57 A. Grosrichard, *The Sultan's Court: European Fantasies of the East* (London: Verso, 1998 [1979]).
58 Ibid., p. 92.
59 S. Subrahmanyam, 'Frank submissions: the Company and the Mughals between Sir Thomas Roe and Sir William Norris', in H. V. Bowen, M. Lincoln and N. Rigby (eds), *The Worlds of the East India Tea Company* (Woodbridge: Boydell Press, 2002), p. 70.
60 E. Said, *Orientalism* (London: Penguin, 2003 [1978]), pp. 5–6.
61 S. Hall, 'The West and the rest: discourse and power', in S. Hall and B. Gieben (eds), *Formations of Modernity* (Cambridge: Polity Press, 1992), pp. 276–331.
62 Grosrichard, *The Sultan's Court*, pp. 135–9.
63 Losurdo, *Liberalism: A Counter-history*; C. W. Mills, *The Racial Contract* (Ithaca, NY: Cornell University Press, 1999).
64 M. Dolar, 'Introduction', in Grosrichard, *The Sultan's Court*, p. xi.
65 Grosrichard, *The Sultan's Court*, pp. 26–35.
66 T. Pogge, *World Poverty and Human Rights* (Cambridge: Polity Press, 2008).
67 C. Peltre, *Orientalism* (Paris: Terrail, 2004).
68 F. Febbraro and B. Schwetje, *How to Read World History in Art* (New York: Abrams, 2010), pp. 254–62.
69 Delacroix's perhaps more famous painting in the same thematic sequence is his 1824 *Massacres at Chios*.
70 Kelly, 'Liberalism and nationalism', p. 336.
71 Febbraro and Schwetje, *How to Read World History in Art*, p. 256.
72 Said, *Orientalism*, p. xvi.
73 Losurdo, *Liberalism: A Counter-history*; Mills, *The Racial Contract*.
74 Bhattacharyya, *Dangerous Brown Men*; A. McClintock, *Imperial Leather: Race, Gender and Sexuality in the Colonial Contest* (London: Routledge, 1995); C. Ueno, 'In the feminine guise: a trap of reverse Orientalism', *U.S.-Japan Women's Journal* 13 (1997), 3–25.
75 M. James, *Urban Multiculture* (Basingstoke: Palgrave Macmillan, 2015), pp. 30–45.

76 A. Awad, 'It is women who have most tried to oppress me', *SBS*, 2 May 2018, www.sbs.com.au/topics/life/culture/article/2018/05/01/it-women-who-have-most-tried-oppress-me (accessed 26 February 2019).
77 https://twitter.com/rustyrockets/status/464184830318882816?lang=en (accessed 26 February 2019).
78 S. Knapton, 'Richard Dawkins: religious education is crucial for British schoolchildren', *Telegraph*, 11 June 2018, www.telegraph.co.uk/science/20 17/06/11/richard-dawkins-religious-education-crucial-british-schoolchi ldren (accessed 26 February 2019); R. Seymour, *Unhitched: The Trial of Christopher Hitchens* (London: Verso, 2012).
79 S. Osborne, 'Richard Dawkins accused of Islamophobia after comparing "lovely church bells" to "aggressive-sounding Allahu Akhbar"', *Independent*, 17 July 2018, www.independent.co.uk/news/uk/home-news/richard-dawkins-allahu-akhbar-church-bells-criticism-religion-a8451141.html (accessed 26 February 2019).
80 G. Titley, D. Freedman, G. Khiabany and A. Mondon, *After Charlie Hebdo* (London: Zed Books, 2017); Scott, *The Politics of the Veil*; O. Roy, *Secularism Confronts Islam* (New York: Columbia University Press, 2009).
81 D. Hurd, '"The most evil religion in the world has to be Islam": atheist warns about decline of Christianity', *CBN News*, 26 March 2018, www1.cbn.com/cbnnews/world/2018/march/leading-atheist-dont-celebrate-decline-of-christianity-in-europe (accessed 26 February 2019).
82 R. Jalabi, 'A history of Bill Maher's "not bigoted" remarks on Islam', *Guardian*, 7 October 2014, www.theguardian.com/tv-and-radio/tvandradioblog/2014/oct/06/bill-maher-islam-ben-affleck (accessed 26 February 2019).
83 Anonymous, '"Alt-right" online poison nearly turned me into a racist', *Guardian*, 28 November 2016, www.theguardian.com/commentisfree/2016/nov/28/alt-right-online-poison-racist-bigot-sam-harris-milo-yiannopoulos-islamophobia (accessed 26 February 2019).
84 M. Houellebecq, *Submission* (London: William Heinemann, 2015).
85 A. Shatz, 'Colombey-les-deux-Mosquées', *London Review of Books* 37:7 (2015), 15, www.lrb.co.uk/v37/n07/adam-shatz/colombey-les-deux-mosq uees (accessed 22 March 2019).
86 B. Bawer, *Surrender: Appeasing Islam, Sacrificing Freedom* (New York: Anchor Books, 2009).
87 C. Caldwell, *Reflections on the Revolution in Europe: Immigration, Islam and the West* (London: Penguin, 2010).
88 D. Murray, *The Strange Death of Europe: Immigration, Identity, Islam* (London: Bloomsbury, 2017).

89 This issue of *Standpoint* included a contribution by Michael Gove and John Ware. Ware later wrote for the same magazine a cover feature entitled, 'The battle for British Muslims' integration'.
90 S. H. Jones, R. Catto, T. Kaden and F. Elsdon-Baker, '"That's how Muslims are required to view the world": race, culture and belief in non-Muslims' descriptions of Islam and science', *Sociological Review* 67:1 (2019), 161–77; A. Saeed, 'Media, racism and Islamophobia: representation of Islam and Muslims in the media', *Sociology Compass* 1:2 (2007), 443–62.
91 Kelly, 'Liberalism and nationalism', 329–52.
92 J.-W. Müller, 'What Cold War liberalism can teach us', *New York Review of Books*, 16 November 2018, www.nybooks.com/daily/2018/11/26/what-co ld-war-liberalism-can-teach-us-today/ (accessed 26 February 2019).
93 E. Fassin, 'The neo-fascist moment of neoliberalism', *openDemocracy*, 10 August 2018, www.opendemocracy.net/can-europe-make-it/ric-fassin/neo -fascist-moment-of-neoliberalism (accessed 26 February 2019); R. Seymour, 'The undead centre. Or, what is a Macron?', *Patreon*, 27 June 2017, www. patreon.com/posts/undead-centre-or-12162326 (accessed 26 February 2019).
94 I came across this line in a very particular context – it is one of the 'praise' quotes for Domenico Losurdo's intimidatingly well-read *Liberalism: A Counter-history*. It is, however, too good a line to not smuggle into my own chapter.

Notes to Chapter 4

1 See Kundnani for a recent argument about Powellism's reconciliation of neoliberalism with conservatism. Virdee and McGeever, however, distinguish Powellism from neoliberalism, what they describe as 'insular' provincialism versus a 'globalizing' capitalist confidence as sourced in colonial nostalgia and hubris. A. Kundnani, 'Disembowel Enoch Powell', 18 April 2018, www.kundnani.org/disembowel-enoch-powell/ (accessed 26 February 2019); S. Virdee and B. McGeever, 'Racism, crisis, Brexit', *Ethnic and Racial Studies* 41:10 (2018), 1802–19. See also S. Hirsch, *In the Shadow of Enoch Powell* (Manchester: Manchester University Press, 2018); C. Schofield, *Enoch Powell and the Making of Postcolonial Britain* (Cambridge: Cambridge University Press, 2013).
2 A. E. Ansell (ed.), *Unravelling the Right: The New Conservatism in American Thought and Politics* (London: Routledge, 2001 [1998]); A. E. Ansell, *New Right, New Racism: Race and Reaction in the United States and Britain* (Basingstoke: Macmillan, 1997); A. Winter, 'The "new" right: definition, identification, differentiation', *Sociological Research Online* 5:1 (2000), 1–6,

https://journals.sagepub.com/doi/abs/10.5153/sro.451 (accessed 22 March 2019).
3 'Not In My Backyard', this being a form of generally middle-class defensiveness about one's own locality/property.
4 B. Kentish, 'Zac Goldsmith accused of "staggering hypocrisy" for standing as Conservative candidate again', *Independent*, 27 April 2017, www.independent.co.uk/news/uk/politics/zac-goldsmith-conservative-candidate-area-staggering-hypocrisy-general-election-london-mayor-a7705396.html (accessed 26 February 2019).
5 S. Jenkins, 'Why a wind farm will never be as beautiful as a railway viaduct', *Spectator*, 12 October 2013, www.spectator.co.uk/2013/10/simon-jenkinss-country-notebook-why-wind-turbines-will-never-be-as-beautiful-as-railway-viaducts/ (accessed 26 February 2019); see also S. Jenkins, 'In the wind turbine debate, who dares utter the B-word?', *Guardian*, 1 November 2012, www.theguardian.com/commentisfree/2012/nov/01/wind-turbine-debate (accessed 26 February 2019).
6 P. Bruckner, *The Paradox of Love* (Princeton, NJ: Princeton University Press, 2012).
7 R. Scruton, *Fools, Frauds and Firebrands: Thinkers of the New Left* (London: Bloomsbury, 2015 [1985]).
8 See this conversation between Terry Eagleton and Roger Scruton, hosted by Intelligence Squared, for an instructive instance of this theme (the relevant reflection by Scruton on universities as the humane 'imparting of culture' commences at the 24.10 mark). www.youtube.com/watch?v=qOdMBDOj4ec (accessed 26 February 2019). L. Boltanski and E. Chiapello, *The New Spirit of Capitalism* (London: Verso, 2005).
9 V. Lal, 'Gandhi's West, the West's Gandhi', *New Literary History* 40:2 (2009), 281.
10 Jo Johnson, minister for higher education at the time, presented this as being the need to look at higher education as the platform 'to reskill, retrain and adapt to a changing economy' and for universities to strongly reconsider their degree provisioning within a 'value for money' context. H. Pavey, 'Two thirds of students dropping out of some courses at UK's biggest universities', *Evening Standard*, 21 September 2017, www.standard.co.uk/news/two-thirds-of-students-dropping-out-of-some-courses-at-uks-biggest-universities-a3640286.html (accessed 26 February 2019); M. Savage, 'Universities win permission to charge £2,000 premium for two-year degrees', *Guardian*, 10 December 2017, www.theguardian.com/education/2017/dec/10/universities-can-charge-two-thousand-pounds-more-for-fast-track-degrees (accessed 26 February 2019).

11 C. P. Snow, *The Two Cultures* (Cambridge: Cambridge University Press, 1998 [1964]).
12 R. Scruton, *England: An Elegy* (London: Continuum, 2000), pp. 14–15. See also J. Major, *More Than a Game: A Story of Cricket's Early Years* (London: HarperCollins, 2007).
13 M. Marqusee, 'Why do we play cricket?', *Guardian*, 10 December 2014, www.theguardian.com/sport/blog/2014/dec/10/why-do-we-play-cricket (accessed 26 February 2019).
14 M. Arnold, *Culture and Anarchy* (Oxford: Oxford University Press, 2006 [1869]), p. 5.
15 O. Hatherley, *The Ministry of Nostalgia: Consuming Austerity* (London: Verso, 2016); Kundnani, 'Disembowel Enoch Powell'.
16 W. Brown, 'American nightmare: neoliberalism, neoconservatism, and de-democratization', *Political Theory* 34 (2006), 691.
17 Ibid., 697.
18 J. Gray, 'Thatcher, Thatcher, Thatcher', *London Review of Books* 32:8 (2010), 19, www.lrb.co.uk/v32/n08/john-gray/thatcher-thatcher-thatcher (accessed 22 March 2019).
19 E. Burke, *Reflections on the Revolution in France* (Oxford: Oxford University Press, 2009 [1790]).
20 P. Chatterjee, *Nationalist Thought and the Colonial World: A Derivative Discourse* (London: Zed Books, 1993 [1986]); E. Gellner, *Nations and Nationalism* (Oxford: Blackwell, 2006 [1983]); E. Hobsbawm, and T. Ranger (eds), *The Invention of Tradition* (Cambridge: Cambridge University Press, 1983).
21 As Pascal Bruckner put it in *The Tyranny of Guilt*, 'Nothing is more Western than hatred of the West', an argument rehearsed multiple times by Bruce Bawer, perhaps the most influential intellectual of this movement. P. Bruckner, *The Tyranny of Guilt: An Essay on Western Masochism* (Princeton, NJ: Princeton University Press, 2010), p. 33; B. Bawer, *Surrender: Appeasing Islam, Sacrificing Freedom* (New York: Anchor Books, 2010).
22 M. Oakeshott, *Rationalism in Politics and Other Essays* (London: Methuen, 1962), p. 127.
23 Burke, *Reflections on the Revolution in France*, p. 61.
24 G. C. Spivak, 'Can the subaltern speak?', in P. Williams and L. Chrisman (eds), *Colonial Discourse and Post-colonial Theory: A Reader* (New York: Columbia University Press, 1994), pp. 66–111.
25 Hobsbawm and Ranger (eds), *The Invention of Tradition*.
26 M. Billig, *Banal Nationalism* (London: Sage, 1995), p. 8.

27 P. Chatterjee, 'Colonialism, nationalism, and colonized women: the contest in India', *American Ethnologist* 16:4 (1989), 622–33; J. Nagel, 'Masculinity and nationalism: gender and sexuality in the making of nations', *Ethnic and Racial Studies* 21:2 (1998), 242–69.
28 B. Samuels, 'Trump: "It may not look like it, but we are draining the swamp"', *The Hill*, 12 April 2018, https://thehill.com/homenews/administration/382883-trump-it-may-not-look-like-it-but-we-are-draining-the-swamp (accessed 26 February 2019).
29 C. Caldwell, *Reflections on the Revolution in Europe: Can Europe be the Same with Different People in It?* (London: Penguin, 2010).
30 M. Barker, *The New Racism: Conservatives and the Ideology of the Tribe* (Frederick, MD: Aletheia Books, 1981).
31 C. Bhatt, 'The new xenologies of Europe: civil tensions and mythic pasts', *Journal of Civil Society* 8:3 (2012), 307–26.
32 A. Lentin and G. Titley, *The Crises of Multiculturalism: Racism in a Neoliberal Age* (London: Zed Books, 2011).
33 P. Mishra, 'What is great about ourselves', *London Review of Books* 39:18 (2017), 4, www.lrb.co.uk/v39/n18/pankaj-mishra/what-is-great-about-ourselves (accessed 22 March 2019).
34 M. Mamdani, 'Good Muslim, bad Muslim: a political perspective on culture and terrorism', *American Anthropologist* 104:3 (2002), 766–75.
35 D. L. Phillips, *Looking Backward: A Critical Appraisal of Communitarian Thought* (Princeton, NJ: Princeton University Press, 1993).
36 S. Boseley, 'Mary Beard abused on Twitter over Roman Britain's ethnic diversity', *Guardian*, 6 August 2017, www.theguardian.com/uk-news/2017/aug/06/mary-beard-twitter-abuse-roman-britain-ethnic-diversity (accessed 26 February 2019).
37 M. Nicholls, 'How diverse was Roman Britain', *University of Reading: Connecting Research*, 28 July 2017, http://blogs.reading.ac.uk/the-forum/2017/07/28/how-diverse-was-roman-britain/ (accessed 26 February 2019).
38 N. Myers, 'The black poor of London: initiatives of Eastern seamen in the eighteenth and nineteenth centuries', *Immigration and Minorities* 13:2–3 (1994), 7–21; M. Sherwood, 'Race, nationality and employment among Lascar seamen, 1660 to 1945', *Journal of Ethnic and Migration Studies* 17:2 (1991), 229–44.
39 R. Winder, *Bloody Foreigners* (New York: Little, Brown, 2004).
40 In the same year as the publication of his 'Letter Concerning Toleration', 1689, Locke had decreed much of the non-European world, via his 'labour theory of property', ripe for conquest. See also Simmons for more historical

context regarding Locke's aversion to Catholicism. J. A. Simmons, *On the Edge of Anarchy: Locke, Consent and the Limits of Society* (Princeton, NJ: Princeton University Press, 1993), pp. 125–8.

41 S. Virdee, 'Racialized capitalism: an account of its contested origins and consolidation', *Sociological Review* 67:1 (2019), 3–27.

42 N. Finney and L. Simpson, *'Sleepwalking to Segregation'? Challenging Myths about Race and Migration* (Bristol: Policy Press, 2009); D. Phillips, 'Parallel lives? Challenging discourses of British Muslim self-segregation', *Environment and Planning D: Society and Space* 24:1 (2006), 25–40.

43 P. Gilroy, 'Multiculture in times of war: an inaugural lecture', *Critical Quarterly* 48:4 (2006), 40.

44 Take, for instance, the following fairly generic David Brooks statement: 'These white identitarians have taken the multicultural worldview taught in schools, universities and the culture and, rightly or wrongly, have applied it to themselves. As Marxism saw history through the lens of class conflict, multiculturalism sees history through the lens of racial conflict and group oppression.' D. Brooks, 'How Trump kills the GOP', *New York Times*, 29 August 2017, www.nytimes.com/2017/08/29/opinion/trump-identity-politics.html (accessed 26 February 2019). In blaming multiculturalism for white nationalism (i.e. it is allegedly the fault of liberals for trying to assist minorities), what Brooks summarily fails to understand is that white identitarianism is qualitatively unique, in that it has always masqueraded as being the universal. So the putative threat to whiteness is, in fact, to its mourners, a double loss at once. It is a *particularity* threatened but it is also the dilution of the *universality* principle. This is why identity politics is still a slur that in popular usage is only attached to minority campaigns.

45 In Denmark, for instance, the 'cosiness' that neighbourliness is said to engender is often evoked in political discussion, as a specific and worthwhile ideal, through the ubiquitous term 'hygge'.

46 C. Bhatt, 'The new xenologies of Europe: civil tensions and mythic pasts', *Journal of Civil Society* 8:3 (2012), 307–26.

47 S. Haider, 'The darkness at the end of the tunnel: Artificial Intelligence and neoreaction', *Viewpoint Magazine*, 28 March 2017, www.viewpointmag.com /2017/03/28/the-darkness-at-the-end-of-the-tunnel-artificial-intellige nce-and-neoreaction/ (accessed 26 February 2019).

48 M. Gordon, *Assimilation in American Life: The Role of Race, Religion, and National Origins* (New York: Oxford University Press, 1964).

49 M. Taylor, 'Casey report criticised for focus on UK Muslim communities', *Guardian*, 5 December 2016, www.theguardian.com/society/2016/dec/05/

casey-report-criticised-for-focus-on-uk-muslim-communities (accessed 26 February 2019).
50 P. Wright, *On Living in an Old Country* (Oxford: Oxford University Press, 2009 [1985]).
51 B. Graham, G. J. Ashworth and J. E. Tunbridge (eds), *A Geography of Heritage: Power, Culture and Economy* (Abingdon: Routledge, 2016 [2000]).
52 The restoration of the monarchy's public appeal in the post-Diana era represents a particularly powerful bastion of nation-making nostalgia as complementary to the conservative temperament and its various strands: Elizabeth II as the majestic but becalming and sensible matriarch, William and Kate as the stately couple, Harry and his laddish militarism, Meghan Markle as the post-racial alibi for a monarchy purporting to be 'traditionally modern', and Charles's yearning, albeit polarising, for a rustic architecture. For more, see Laura Clancy's ongoing doctoral work at Lancaster University, 'The (Family) Firm: Representation and Power in the British Monarchy'.
53 Incidentally, there has recently been a spate of self-absorbed, blog-driven testimony declaring the city to be no longer inhabitable. It is interesting that this lament ostensibly assumes a left-wing orientation, bemoaning the rise in living costs and the merciless imperative of speed imposed upon the urban professional. Unmentioned, however, is that delight in the rural as an alternative horizon also necessarily involves the absence of ethnic difference, its unruliness, and its unpretty, matter-of-fact banality.
54 These tropes include a well-spoken eloquence, a phlegmatically upright and noble masculinity, a tastefully understated and invitingly rosy feminine beauty and comportment, and a well-defined moral order that, while periodically threatened, is either restored or gently remade. Common throughout these forays is a staging of place, both ideal and prosaic, as white and provincial.
55 In an interview, Hitchens claims, among many other things, that 'Christianity has been defeated in this country'; 'I think it is quite likely that this could be a Islamic country in a century' (to which his interviewer responds, 'That is quite optimistic'); he also states that 'one of the things he admires about [Muslims] is that they are completely single-minded about it and loyal to their faith'. www.youtube.com/watch?v=mv3cZ7qdajs (accessed 26 February 2019).
56 J. Elgot, 'Jacob Rees-Mogg opposed to gay marriage and abortion – even after rape', *Guardian*, 6 September 2017, www.theguardian.com/politics/2017/sep/06/jacob-rees-mogg-opposed-to-gay-marriage-and-abortion-even-after (accessed 26 February 2019).

57 A. Brown, 'This welfare bill has united bishops like never before', *Guardian*, 23 January 2015, www.theguardian.com/commentisfree/andrewbrown/2012/jan/23/welfare-bill-bishops-lords (accessed 26 February 2019); 'Letter: Refugee Reform Bill', *The Times*, 15 December 2017, https://churchinparliament.org/2017/12/15/bishops-show-support-for-refugees-family-reunion-bill/ (accessed 26 February 2019).
58 A. Giuffrida and L. Tondo, 'Italian Catholic priests go to war with Salvini over immigration', *Guardian*, 9 July 2018, www.theguardian.com/world/2018/jul/09/italian-catholic-priests-go-to-war-with-salvini-over-immigration (accessed 26 February 2019).
59 A. Norfolk, 'Christian child forced into Muslim foster care', *The Times*, 28 August 2017, www.thetimes.co.uk/article/christian-child-forced-into-muslim-foster-care-by-tower-hamlets-council-3gcp6l8cs (accessed 26 February 2019). Norfolk's reports were widely discredited in subsequent inquiries by Tower Hamlets council and the Independent Press Standards Organisation: J. Grierson, 'Inquiry rejects press claims about "Christian" girl fostered by Muslims', *Guardian*, 1 November 2017, www.theguardian.com/society/2017/nov/01/inquiry-rejects-press-claims-about-christian-girl-fostered-by-muslims (accessed 26 February 2019); J. Grierson, 'Complaint upheld over Times story about girl fostered by Muslims', *Guardian*, 25 April 2018, www.theguardian.com/media/2018/apr/24/complaint-upheld-over-times-story-about-london-girl-fostered-with-muslim-family (accessed 26 February 2019).
60 J. Waters, 'Fanon's warning', *First Things*, August 2018, www.firstthings.com/article/2018/08/fanons-warning (accessed 26 February 2019).
61 S. Žižek, 'Appendix: multiculturalism, the reality of an illusion', *lacan.com*, 2013, www.lacan.com/essays/?page_id=454 (accessed 26 February 2019).
62 Mishra, 'What is great about ourselves', 6.
63 Waters, 'Fanon's warning'. The relevant quote reads thus: 'Since Fanon's death, a great change has taken place in the postimperial picture. It is doubtful that Fanon in 1961 anticipated that the final collision and conflagration he was announcing might play out at the heart of the West. Yet this is now unfolding, in two unexpected ways. In the first, the pattern of colonialism has been unleashed in reverse through the waves of immigrants that have flooded Europe since the removal of the Gaddafi regime in Libya.'
64 C. Miéville, 'Why does the Russian revolution matter', *Guardian*, 6 May 2017, www.theguardian.com/books/2017/may/06/russian-revolution-matter-china-mieville (accessed 26 February 2019).
65 P. Gilroy, *After Empire: Melancholia or Convivial Culture?* (Abingdon: Routledge, 2004).

66 See this BBC Timewatch episode from 2017, 'British Empire: Heroes and Villains', for a measured overview of how different, more critical narratives slipped into popular view during the 1990s. www.bbc.co.uk/programmes/b08cwrf2 (accessed 26 February 2019).
67 J. Stone, 'British people are proud of colonialism and the British Empire, poll finds', *Independent*, 19 January 2016, www.independent.co.uk/news/uk/politics/british-people-are-proud-of-colonialism-and-the-british-empire-poll-finds-a6821206.html (accessed 26 February 2019).
68 https://twitter.com/nfergus/status/888086778732728320?lang=en (accessed 26 February 2019).
69 N. El-Enany, 'The next British Empire', *Progressive Review* 25:1 (2018), 30–8.
70 A. Césaire, *Discourse on Colonialism* (New York: Monthly Review Press, 2000 [1955]), p. 36.
71 W. Rodney, *How Europe Underdeveloped Africa* (Cape Town: Pambazuka Press, 2012 [1972]).
72 R. Guha, *Dominance without Hegemony: History and Power in Colonial India* (Cambridge, MA: Harvard University Press, 1997); C. J. Robinson, *Black Marxism: The Making of the Black Radical Tradition* (Chapel Hill, NC: University of North Carolina Press, 2000 [1983]), p. 164.
73 R. Gott, *Britain's Empire: Resistance, Repression and Revolt* (London: Verso, 2011); P. Mishra, *From the Ruins of Empire: The Intellectuals Who Remade Asia* (New York: Farrar, Straus and Giroux, 2012).
74 P. Gopal, 'The British empire's hidden history is one of resistance, not pride', *Guardian*, 28 July 2017, www.theguardian.com/commentisfree/2017/jul/28/british-empire-hidden-history-solidarity-truth-resistance (accessed 26 February 2019).
75 It is interesting here that all European nations actualise a remembrance of their imperial greatness in ways that also distinguish them from other imperial formations, through the most contrived of denials and the narcissism of small differences – the French claim that they were successfully assimilationist and post-racially republican, the British that they were moderate and non-violent, the Belgian and Dutch assert that they were only briefly imperial forces, while others deny that they had an empire in the first place. This is what Gloria Wekker theorises as the historical projection of 'white innocence'. G. Wekker, *White Innocence: Paradoxes of Colonialism and Race* (Durham, NC: Duke University Press, 2016).
76 S. Valluvan, 'Racial entanglements and sociological confusions', *British Journal of Sociology* 69:2 (2018), 436–58.

77 Similarly, an unreconstructed view of Empire prevents a more meaningful conversation on some of the core political realities of today, realities that otherwise loom large in contemporary political discourse. These issues include the rise of violent Islamisms, the wider disintegration of states in the Middle East and the Horn of Africa, the continued amassing of refugees across the Mediterranean basin, alongside the wider imperial role in engendering a variety of structural economic disparities that neoliberal global governance only helps to exacerbate. Continued imperial nostalgia and/or the denial of Empire when surveying these contemporary phenomena reinforces what Thomas Pogge has usefully called 'explanatory nationalism'. This is the tendency of political punditry to emphasise allegedly dysfunctional national *cultures* and the self-engendered ineptitude of the governing classes of the affected regions as being the primary causes of their continued struggles. T. W. Pogge, *World Poverty and Human Rights: Cosmopolitan Responsibilities and Reforms* (Cambridge: Polity Press, 2008).
78 A. Barnett, *Iron Britannia: Time to Take the Great out of Britain* (London: Faber and Faber, 2012 [1982]).
79 R. Greenslade, 'Don't damn the *Daily Mail* for its fascist flirtation 80 years ago', *Guardian*, 6 December 2011, www.theguardian.com/media/greenslade/2011/dec/06/dailymail-oswald-mosley (accessed 26 February 2019).
80 A. Lentin, 'Not your Holocaust, Michael Pezzullo', *alana.lentin.net*, 9 March 2016, www.alanalentin.net/2016/03/09/not-your-holocaust-michael-pezzullo/ (accessed 26 February 2019).
81 J. Kelly, 'Popular culture, sport and the "hero"-ification of British militarism', *Sociology* 47:4 (2012), 722–38.
82 A. Kokoli and A. Winter, 'What Bear Grylls can't do: survivalist mediascapes in austerity Britain', *IMR Slides*, 30 November 2015, www.slideshare.net/etussey14/winter-kokoli-what-bear-grylls-cant-do-final (accessed 26 February 2019).
83 V. Ware, *Military Migrants: Fighting for YOUR Country* (Basingstoke: Palgrave Macmillan, 2012).
84 J. Nagel, 'Masculinity and nationalism: gender and sexuality in the making of nations', *Ethnic and Racial Studies* 21:2 (1998), 242–69.
85 V. M. Basham, 'Gender, race, militarism and remembrance: the everyday geopolitics of the poppy', *Gender, Place and Culture* 23:6 (2016), 883–96.
86 This reading of the poppy as command, not invitation, was made further apparent when FIFA (the international federation of national football associations) ruled that the poppy could not be embossed on to the England football jersey for international fixtures as it constituted too avowed a political statement. The poppy was seen as contravening FIFA's injunction

on making political statements. The media furore that ensued in Britain traded on the elemental confusion about how a national symbol, immanent as it now was, could ever be considered political. The resulting punditry made plain the poppy conceit – it was no longer considered a choice that represented a statement of support for a particular cause, but instead had become fundamental to the demonstration of commitment to the nation-state in its most elemental sense. Another related scandal is the annual chastising of the Irish footballer James McClean, who boldly and eloquently opts out of the poppy, an act that renders him, every autumn, a national pariah. As he observes, 'If the poppy was simply about World War One and Two victims alone, I'd wear it without a problem ... I would wear it every day of the year if that was the thing but it doesn't, it stands for all the conflicts that Britain has been involved in. Because of the history where I come from in Derry, I cannot wear something that represents that.' P. Hayward, 'Fifa finally sees sense by taking politics out of poppies', *Telegraph*, 25 September 2017, www.telegraph.co.uk/football/2017/09/24/ending-ban-fifa-have-finally-de-politicised-poppy/ (accessed 26 February 2019); N. Stromberg, 'Why doesn't James McClean wear a poppy on Remembrance weekend?', *Independent*, 5 November 2017, www.independent.co.uk/sport/football/premier-league/why-james-mcclean-doesnt-wear-poppy-west-brom-remembrance-poppy-appeal-a8037391.html (accessed 26 February 2019).

87 M. Andrews, 'Poppies, Tommies and remembrance: commemoration is always contested', *Soundings* 58 (2014), 104–15.

88 H. Marcuse, 'Repressive tolerance', in R. P. Wolff, B. Moore Jr and H. Marcuse (eds), *A Critique of Pure Tolerance* (Boston, MA: Beacon Press, 1965), pp. 81–123.

89 An interesting development, in the wake of the red poppy's ubiquity, is the increased campaigning around the alternative that the white poppy might constitute. The white poppy, while recognising the suffering and death of soldiers, steadfastly upholds an explicitly pacifist ideal. A. Rigby, 'A peace symbol's origins', *Peace Review* 10:3 (1998), 475–9.

90 L. Okolosie, 'The message to a poppy-less Charlene White: black women should be seen but not heard', *Guardian*, 14 November 2013, www.theguardian.com/commentisfree/2013/nov/14/charlene-white-poppy-black-women (accessed 26 February 2019); S. Usborne, 'The great "poppy war": how did we get here?', *Guardian*, 4 November 2016, www.theguardian.com/uk-news/2016/nov/04/the-great-poppy-war-how-did-we-get-here (accessed 26 February 2019).

91 R. Sanghani, 'Why British Muslims need a "poppy hijab" to remember World War One', *Telegraph*, 10 November 2015, www.telegraph.co.uk/

women/womens-life/11985648/World-War-One-Remembrance-Day-British-Muslims-must-wear-poppy-hijab.html (accessed 26 February 2019).

92 The mythologisation of the First and Second World War campaigns also, and perhaps necessarily, often writes out the presence of soldiers from the nonwhite colonies who were fighting for the British and French. One glaring and recent instance of this erasure was the highly anticipated Christopher Nolan film, *Dunkirk*. Sunny Singh excoriated this portrayal as 'fantasy disguised as history': 'The stories that we share among ourselves give us the vision of our individual and collective identities. When those stories consistently – and in a big budget, well-researched production like *Dunkirk*, one must assume, purposely – erase the presence of those who are still considered "other" and less-than-equal, these narratives also decide who is seen as "us" as opposed to "them". Does this removal of those deemed "foreign" and "other" from narratives of the past express a discomfort with the same people in the present? More chillingly, does it also contain a wish to excise the same people from a utopian, national future?' S. Singh, 'Why the lack of Indian and African faces in *Dunkirk* matters', *Guardian*, 1 August 2017, www.theguardian.com/commentisfree/2017/aug/01/indian-african-dunkirk-history-whitewash-attitudes (accessed 26 February 2019). See also Ware, *Military Migrants*; P. Mishra, 'How colonial violence came home: the ugly truth of the first world war', *Guardian*, 10 November 2017, www.theguardian.com/news/2017/nov/10/how-colonial-violence-came-home-the-ugly-truth-of-the-first-world-war (accessed 26 February 2019).

93 P. J. Beck, '"War minus the shooting": George Orwell on international sport and the Olympics', *Sport in History* 33:1 (2013), 72–94.

94 Kelly, 'Popular culture, sport and the "hero"-ification of British militarism'.

95 G. Chamayou, *Drone Theory* (London: Penguin, 2015); D. Gregory, 'From a view to a kill: drones and late modern war', *Theory, Culture and Society* 28:7 (2015), 188–215.

Notes to Chapter 5

1 J. Ferguson, 'The uses of neoliberalism', *Antipode* 41:1 (2010), 166–84.

2 J. Peck, *Constructions of Neoliberal Reason* (Oxford: Oxford University Press, 2010).

3 P. Mirowski and D. Plehwe (eds), *The Road from Mont Pèlerin; The Making of the Neoliberal Thought Collective* (Cambridge, MA: Harvard University Press, 2009). See also Desai, who sardonically identifies the Mont Pèlerin Society as being the *fons et origo* for this neoliberalism-as-thinktank genre that sprang up in the 1980s and 1990s: R. Desai, 'Neoliberalism and cultural

NOTES

nationalism: a *danse macabre*', in D. Plehwe, B. Walpen and G. Neunhöffer (eds), *Neoliberal Hegemony: A Global Critique* (London: Routledge, 2006), p. 223; S. M. Amadae, *Rationalizing Capitalist Democracy: The Cold War Origins of Rational Choice Liberalism* (Chicago: University of Chicago Press, 2003).

4 J. Cassidy, 'Can authoritarian capitalism outlive Lee Kuan Yew?', *New Yorker*, 24 March 2015, www.newyorker.com/news/john-cassidy/can-autho ritarian-capitalism-outlive-lee-kuan-yew (accessed 26 February 2019); S. Žižek, 'Berlusconi in Tehran', *London Review of Books* 31:14 (2009), 3–7, www.lrb.co.uk/v31/n14/slavoj-zizek/berlusconi-in-tehran (accessed 22 March 2019).

5 Hall was, of course, penning this argument in 1979, on the very cusp of Margaret Thatcher winning her first election. The broader successes and longevity of Thatcherism (the concept that he coined) could therefore only be speculated about. As such, Hall's enduring essay, though now vindicated as singularly prophetic, is suffused with a mature cautiousness about what it was that we were in fact witnessing in 1979. The longer version of the above quote, for instance, reads thus: 'There is still some debate as to whether [Thatcherism] is likely to be short-lived or long-term, a movement of the surface or something more deeply lodged in the body politic.' S. Hall, 'The great moving right show', *Marxism Today*, January 1979, 14.

6 N. Rose, *Governing the Soul: The Shaping of the Private Self* (Florence, KY: Routledge, 1999 [1990]).

7 B. Evans and A. Taylor, *Salisbury and Major: Continuity and Change in Conservative Politics* (Manchester: Manchester University Press, 1996), p. 226.

8 O. Jones, *The Establishment* (London: Penguin, 2014).

9 S. Brown, 'Fake it till you make it: meet the wolves of Instagram', *Guardian*, 19 April 2018, www.theguardian.com/news/2018/apr/19/wolves-of-ins tagram-jordan-belmont-social-media-traders (accessed 26 February 2019).

10 J. Littler, 'Meritocracy as plutocracy: marketising equality under neoliberalism', *New Formations* 80/81 (2013), 52–72.

11 C. Kulz, *Factories for Learning: Making Race, Class and Inequality in the Neoliberal Academy* (Manchester: Manchester University Press, 2017); K. Morrin, 'Tensions in teaching character: how the "entrepreneurial character" is reproduced, "refused", and negotiated in an English academy school', *Sociological Research Online* 23:2 (2018), 459–76.

12 W. Davies, 'Populism and the limits of neoliberalism', *Democratic Audit*, 23 April 2017, www.democraticaudit.com/2017/04/23/essay-william-davies -on-populism-and-the-limits-of-neoliberalism/ (accessed 26 February 2019).

13 D. T. Goldberg, *The Threat of Race: Reflections on Racial Neoliberalism* (Malden, MA: Blackwell, 2009); M. Tucker-Abramson, 'Chile–Seattle–Cairo 1973–2017? Or, globalisation and neoliberalism', in I. Szeman, S. Blacker and J. Sully (eds), *A Companion to Critical and Cultural Theory* (Oxford: Wiley, 2017), pp. 146–65.
14 P. Kelly, *Liberalism* (London: Polity Press, 2005); D. Losurdo, *Liberalism: A Counter-history* (London: Verso, 2011).
15 K. Navickas, 'What's missing?', *London Review of Books* 40:19 (2018), 35, www.lrb.co.uk/v40/n19/katrina-navickas/whats-missing (accessed 22 March 2019).
16 M. Walzer, *Spheres of Justice: A Defense of Pluralism and Equality* (New York: Basic Books, 1983).
17 R. Knox, 'Against law-sterity', *Salvage*, 13 December 2018, www.salvage.zone/in-print/against-law-sterity/ (accessed 26 February 2019).
18 L. Wacquant, *Urban Outcasts: A Comparative Sociology of Advanced Marginality* (Cambridge: Polity Press, 2008); L. Wacquant, *Punishing the Poor: The Neoliberal Government of Social Insecurity* (Durham, NC: Duke University Press, 2009 [2004]). See also G. Bhattacharyya, *Rethinking Racial Capitalism: Questions of Reproduction and Survival* (London: Rowman and Littlefield, 2018); R. W. Gilmore, *Golden Gulag: Prisons, Surplus, Crisis, and Opposition in Globalizing California* (Berkeley, CA: University of California Press, 2007).
19 D. Harvey, *A Brief History of Neoliberalism* (Oxford: Oxford University Press, 2007), pp. 6–7.
20 H. Chang, *23 Things They Don't Tell You About Capitalism* (London: Penguin, 2011).
21 Z. Bauman, 'Tourists and vagabonds: victims and heroes of postmodernity', *SSOAR* 30 (1996), www.ssoar.info/ssoar/handle/document/26687# (accessed 26 February 2019).
22 D. Beer, *Metric Power* (Basingstoke: Palgrave Macmillan, 2016); BBC, 'UKIP's Nigel Farage calls for immigration visa points system', *BBC News*, 4 March 2015, www.bbc.co.uk/news/av/uk-politics-31724979/ukip-s-nigel-farage-calls-for-immigration-visa-points-system (accessed 26 February 2019).
23 W. Davies, 'What is "neo" about neoliberalism?', *New Republic*, 13 July 2017, www.newrepublic.com/article/143849/neo-neoliberalism (accessed 26 February 2019).
24 H. Arendt, *The Origins of Totalitarianism* (London: Harvest Books, 1973 [1951]); N. Kapoor, *Deport, Deprive, Extradite: 21st Century State Extremism* (London: Verso, 2018).

25 C. Brinkhurst-Cuff, 'Meeting Britain's "low value immigrants"', *Vice*, 28 May 2017, www.vice.com/en_au/article/bjg494/meeting-britains-low-value-immigrants (accessed 26 February 2019).
26 O. Wright, 'Nigel Farage accused of deploying Nazi-style propaganda as Remain crash poster unveiling with rival vans', *Independent*, 16 June 2016, www.independent.co.uk/news/uk/politics/nigel-farage-brexit-poster-vans-eu-referendum-london-remain-breaking-point-a7085396.html (accessed 26 February 2019).
27 D. T. Goldberg, *Are We All Postracial Yet?* (Cambridge: Polity Press, 2015).
28 J. Portes, 'Brexit Britain, beware: the supply of Europeans is drying up', *Guardian*, 27 March 2018, www.theguardian.com/commentisfree/2018/mar/27/brexit-britain-beware-europeans-migration-report-uk (accessed 26 February 2019).
29 D. Carswell and D. Hannan, *The Plan: 12 Months to Renew Britain* (London: Douglas Carswell and Daniel Hannan, 2008).
30 N. Farage, 'Douglas Carswell has brought constant division and is actively working against Ukip. He has to go', *Telegraph*, 28 February 2017, www.telegraph.co.uk/opinion/2017/02/27/nigel-farage-tells-paul-nuttall-time-throw-ukips-mp-douglas/ (accessed 26 February 2019); T. Young, 'Douglas Carswell is on manoeuvres. But will his pro-immigration rhetoric sink Ukip?', *Telegraph*, 24 February 2015, www.telegraph.co.uk/news/politics/ukip/11432380/Douglas-Carswell-is-manoeuvres.-But-will-his-pro-immigration-rhetoric-sink-Ukip.html (accessed 26 February 2019).
31 D. Carswell, 'Speech by Douglas Carswell MP: "Why Powell was wrong about immigration"', *British Future*, 24 February 2015, www.britishfuture.org/articles/news/douglas-carswell-mp-positive-immigration/ (accessed 26 February 2019).
32 Ibid.
33 S. Ley, 'India: Theresa May's charm offensive leaves many unmoved', *BBC News*, 13 November 2016, www.bbc.co.uk/news/uk-politics-37950198 (accessed 26 February 2019).
34 G. Peretz, 'Four reasons Jeremy Corbyn is dead wrong about EU state aid', *Guardian*, 27 December 2018, www.theguardian.com/commentisfree/2018/dec/27/four-reasons-jeremy-corbyn-wrong-eu-state-aid (accessed 26 February 2019).
35 E. Williams, *Capitalism and Slavery* (Chapel Hill, NC: University of North Carolina Press, 1994 [1944]).
36 N. El-Enany, 'The next British Empire', *Progressive Review* 25:1 (2018), 31–2.

37 D. Olusoga, 'Empire 2.0 is dangerous nostalgia for something that never existed', *Guardian*, 19 March 2017, www.theguardian.com/commentisfree/2017/mar/19/empire-20-is-dangerous-nostalgia-for-something-that-never-existed (accessed 26 February 2019).
38 B. Quinn, '"Three Brexiteers" chase buccaneering spirit of empire in choice of art', *Guardian*, 2 July 2017, www.theguardian.com/politics/2017/jul/01/three-brexiteers-chase-buccaneering-spirit-of-empire (accessed 26 February 2019).
39 The Nine Years' War is a somewhat forgotten late seventeenth-century conflict that is considered, in some noteworthy ways, to be the first global imperial war of 'the European era'. It involved, in essence, a series of European powers, including Britain, aligning to fight against the France of Louis XIV: the conflicts played out mostly in Europe, but also across the emergent colonial map – including North America and India.
40 F. Fanon, *Black Skins, White Masks* (London: Pluto Press, 1986 [1952]), p. 51.
41 S. Hall, *Representation: Cultural Representations and Signifying Practices* (London: Sage, 1997). Importantly, it is not to be assumed that these representations have universal purchase all of the time. It is not the case that all or even most people familiar with these stereotypes actually do subscribe to them uncritically. As Stuart Hall and others make clear, all representations of difference remain contradictory, never neatly reduced to one given characterisation. It is, however, to be assumed that representations of certain groups do have certain dominant tendencies, and these tendencies can become pronounced at certain political moments. And though the stereotypical caricatures sketched in this chapter can seem somewhat crude, it should be noted that some variations of such stereotypical ascriptions, even if often milder or caveated, do circulate regularly in our current news, commentary and cultural spheres.
42 I. Tyler, 'The riots of the underclass: stigmatisation, mediation and the government of poverty and disadvantage in neoliberal Britain', *Sociological Research Online* 18:4 (2013), www.socresonline.org.uk/18/4/6.html (accessed 22 March 2019).
43 C. Alexander, 'The culture question: a view from the UK', *Ethnic and Racial Studies* 39:8 (2016), 1426–35; S. Benson, 'Asians have culture, West Indians have problems', in T. Ranger, Y. Samad and O. Stuart (eds), *Culture, Identity and Politics* (Aldershot: Avebury Press, 1996), pp. 47–56.
44 T. Chowdhury, 'Policing the "black party" – racialised drugs policing at festivals in the UK', in K. Karam (ed.), *The War on Drugs and the Global Colour Line* (London: Pluto Press, 2019), pp. 48–65; L. Fatsis, 'Grime: criminal subculture or public counterculture? A critical investigation into

the criminalization of Black musical subcultures in the UK', *Crime, Media, Culture* (2018), https://doi.org/10.1177/1741659018784111 (accessed 22 March 2019); J. White, 'Making music videos is not a criminal activity – no matter what genre', *The Conversation*, 22 June 2018, https://theconversation.com/making-music-videos-is-not-a-criminal-activity-no-matter-what-genre-97472 (accessed 26 February 2019).

45 The subtitle to Goodhart's essay asks: 'Did hip-hop culture play a part in last week's riots?' D. Goodhart, 'The riots, the rappers and the Anglo-Jamaican tragedy', *Prospect*, 17 August 2011, www.prospectmagazine.co.uk/magazine/riots-goodhart (accessed 26 February 2019).

46 See also White for an original reading of how involvement in urban music needs to be read as enterprising participation in an 'informal creative economy'. J. White, *Urban Music and Entrepreneurship: Beats, Rhymes and Young People's Enterprise* (London: Routledge, 2016).

47 P. Gilroy, '"We got to get over before we go under...": fragments for a history of black vernacular neoliberalism', *New Formations* 80/81 (2013), 23.

48 M. Greif, *Against Everything* (London: Verso, 2016).

49 N. Klein, *No Logo* (New York: Picador, 2009 [2000]), p. 75.

50 T. Parsons, 'UK Riots: Why did the riots happen? Who are the rioters? What can we do to end this madness?', *Daily Mirror*, 13 August 2011, www.mirror.co.uk/news/uk-news/uk-riots-why-did-the-riots-happen-who-147237 (accessed 26 February 2019).

51 P. Gilroy, *After Empire: Melancholia or Convivial Culture?* (Abingdon: Routledge, 2004), p. 134.

52 J. Vaisse, 'Eurabian follies', *Foreign Policy*, 4 January 2010, https://foreignpolicy.com/2010/01/04/eurabian-follies/ (accessed 26 February 2019).

53 E. Anderson, 'The iconic ghetto', *The Annals of the American Academy of Political and Social Science* 642 (2012), 8.

54 S. Lawler, 'White like them: whiteness and anachronistic space in representations of the English white working class', *Ethnicities* 12:4 (2012), 409–26; M. Wray, *Not Quite White: White Trash and the Boundaries of Whiteness* (Durham, NC: Duke University Press, 2006).

55 I. Tyler, '"Chav mum chav scum": class disgust in contemporary Britain', *Feminist Media Studies* 8:1 (2008), 17–34.

56 A. Nayak, *Race, Place and Globalisation: Youth Cultures in a Changing World* (London: Berg, 2003).

57 K. Allen and Y. Taylor, 'Placed parenting, locating unrest: failed femininities, troubled mothers and rioting subjects', *Studies in the Maternal* 4:2 (2012), 1–25; U. Erel, *Migrant Women Transforming Citizenship* (London: Routledge, 2009).

NOTES

58 Hall, quoted in D. Featherstone, 'Stuart Hall and our current conjuncture', *Progressive Review* 24:1 (2017), 41.
59 A. McRobbie, 'Feminism, the family, and the new "mediated" maternalism', *New Formations* 80/81 (2013), 119.
60 L. Bassel and A. Emejulu, *Minority Women and Austerity: Survival and Resistance in France and Britain* (Bristol: Policy Press, 2017), p. 94.
61 T. L. Brito, 'From madonna to proletariat: constructing a new ideology of motherhood in welfare discourse', *Villanova Law Review* 44:3 (1999), 415–44; M. E. Gilman, 'The return of the welfare queen', *Journal of Gender, Social Policy and the Law* 22:2 (2014), 247–79.
62 In the interests of more nuanced context, the full quote by Gilroy is I believe worth reproducing. 'In 1981, a framing narrative had emerged across government, state, and media to explain but never to excuse the crimes of the rioters. It centred on the idea of the black communities' familial pathology and related identity conflicts. The mob's public crimes were the result of cultural difference visible along generational lines: primarily between the Victorian attitudes of immigrant parents and the more modern outlook of their disobedient, locally born children whose vulnerability was compounded by their psychological and cultural disorientation. Drawing heavily on US discourse of the Kerner/Moynihan variety, this approach was given the official imprimatur in the report into the riots that was written for the government by Lord Justice Scarman. He identified the pattern of female-headed households and the intergenerational tensions but held firmly to an explanation that strove to present the actions of the rioters within a coherent sociological framework. At that time, acceptable political speech was not so narrowly focused on ritual acts of denunciation that serve as points of entry into the possibility of being taken seriously. In other words, a gap was still audible between explanations of the riots and sympathy with the rioters. In that sense, Scarman's approach did not deviate far from the demotic attempt at contextualization presented at the time by Jerry Dammers' 2 Tone group, the Specials, whose classic commentary "Ghost Town" held the number one chart position while the flames scraped skyward.' P. Gilroy, '1981 and 2011: from social democratic to neoliberal rioting', *Libcom.org*, 8 August 2013, https://libcom.org/library/1981-2011-social-democratic-neoliberal-rioting-paul-gilroy (accessed 22 March 2019).
63 G. Bhattacharyya, *Dangerous Brown Men* (London: Zed Books, 2008), p. 51.
64 A. Lentin and G. Titley, *The Crises of Multiculturalism: Racism in a Neoliberal Age* (London: Zed Books, 2011).

NOTES

65 M. Amis, 'The age of horrorism: part one', *Guardian*, 10 September 2006, www.theguardian.com/world/2006/sep/10/september11.politicsphiloso phyandsociety (accessed 26 February 2019).
66 N. Rashid, *Veiled Threats: Representing the Muslim Woman in Public Policy Discourses* (Bristol: Policy Press, 2016).
67 Z. Bauman, *Liquid Love* (Cambridge: Polity Press, 2003).
68 I. Lorey, *State of Insecurity: Government of the Precarious* (London: Verso, 2015).
69 Lentin and Titley, *The Crises of Multiculturalism*.
70 S. Habib, *Learning and Teaching British Values: Policies and Perspectives on British Identities* (Basingstoke: Palgrave Macmillan, 2017), p. 131.
71 D. Casciani, 'Is there benefit tourism in the UK?', *BBC News*, 27 November 2013, www.bbc.co.uk/news/uk-25127344 (accessed 26 February 2019).
72 Z. Williams, 'Skivers v strivers: the argument that pollutes people's minds', *Guardian*, 9 January 2013, www.theguardian.com/politics/2013/jan/09/ skivers-v-strivers-argument-pollutes (accessed 26 February 2019).
73 BBC, 'Cameron's EU changes: will they work in practice?', *BBC News*, 4 February 2016, www.bbc.co.uk/news/uk-politics-35486520 (accessed 26 February 2019); N. Watt, 'David Cameron to make final push on EU migrant benefit restrictions', *Guardian*, 7 December 2015, www.theguardian.com/ politics/2015/dec/07/cameron-summit-eu-migrant-benefit-changes-fo ur-year-ban (accessed 26 February 2019).
74 J. E. Fox, L. Moroşanu and E. Szilassy, 'The racialization of the new European migration to the UK', *Sociology* 46:4 (2012), 688.
75 R. Liddle, 'I'd rather have a German next door too – and I have the figures to show why', *Spectator*, 24 May 2014, www.spectator.co.uk/2014/05/id-rath er-have-a-geman-next-door-too-and-i-have-the-figures-to-show-why/ (accessed 26 February 2019); T. Jensen, 'Welfare commonsense, poverty porn and doxosophy', *Sociological Research Online* 19:3 (2014), 1–7.
76 J. Plunkett, '*Benefits Street*: Immigration episode likely to spark fresh Twitter outrage', *Guardian*, 13 January 2014, www.theguardian.com/media/2014/ jan/13/benefits-street-immigration-channel-4-twitter (accessed 22 March 2019); see also F. Nelson, 'In defence of Channel 4's *Benefits Street*', *Spectator*, 10 January 2014, https://blogs.spectator.co.uk/2014/01/in-defence-of-cha nnel-4s-benefits-street/ (accessed 22 March 2019).
77 Fox, Moroşanu and Szilassy, 'The racialization of the new European migration', 688.
78 Ibid.
79 Bassel and Emejulu, *Minority Women and Austerity*.

80 M. Desmond, *Evicted: Poverty and Profit in the American City* (New York: Crown Publishing Group, 2016); A. Duman, D. Hancox, M. James and A. Minton (eds), *Regeneration Songs: Sounds of Investments and Loss in East London* (London: Repeater, 2018); L. Lees, T. Slater and E. Wyly, *Gentrification* (London: Routledge, 2007); P. Marcuse and D. Madden, *In Defence of Housing: The Politics of Crisis* (London: Verso, 2016); N. Thoburn, 'Concrete and council housing: the class architecture of Brutalism "as found" at Robin Hood Gardens', *City* (2018), DOI: 10.1080/13604813.2018.1549203 (accessed 26 February 2019); S. Zukin, 'Gentrification: culture and capital in the urban core', *Annual Review of Sociology* 13 (1987), 129–47.

81 O. Hatherley, 'Where are all the people?', *London Review of Books* 39:15 (2017), 13–18, www.lrb.co.uk/v39/n15/owen-hatherley/where-are-all-the-people (accessed 22 March 2019).

82 Z. Bauman, *Work, Consumerism and the New Poor* (Maidenhead: Open University Press, 2005); Z. Bauman, *Collateral Damage* (Cambridge: Polity Press, 2011).

83 H. Kunzru, 'East End', *Intelligent Life* (July/Aug 2012), 82.

84 A. Mbembe, 'Aesthetics of superfluity', *Public Culture* 16:3 (2004), 373–405.

85 S. Zukin, 'Consuming authenticity', *Cultural Studies* 22:5 (2008), 724–48; Z. Bauman, 'Collateral causalities of consumerism', *Journal of Consumer Culture* 7:1 (2008), 25.

86 G. Millington, *Urbanization and the Migrant in British Cinema: Spectres of the City* (London: Palgrave Macmillan, 2016).

87 Greif, *Against Everything*.

88 A. Hirsch, 'London clubs and racism: "the West End is a hostile environment"', *Guardian*, 4 July 2018, www.theguardian.com/world/2018/jul/04/london-clubs-and-racism-the-west-end-is-a-hostile-environment (accessed 26 February 2019).

89 S. Zukin, S. Lindeman and L. Hurson, 'The omnivore's neighborhood? Online restaurant reviews, race, and gentrification', *Journal of Consumer Culture* 17:3 (2017), 459–79.

90 Ibid., 459.

91 Kunzru, 'East End', 87.

92 R. Huq, *On the Edge: The Contested Cultures of English Suburbia* (London: Lawrence and Wishart, 2013); A. Saha and S. Watson, 'Suburban drifts: mundane multiculturalism in Outer London', *Ethnic and Racial Studies* 36:12 (2013), 2016–34.

93 M. Keith, *After the Cosmopolitan? Multicultural Cities and the Future of Racism* (Abingdon: Routledge, 2005), pp. 3, 150–1.

94 N. Puwar, *Space Invaders: Race, Gender and Bodies Out of Place* (Oxford: Berg, 2004).

Notes to Chapter 6

1 R. Bregman, *Utopia for Realists* (London: Bloomsbury, 2014); N. Srnicek and A. Williams, *Inventing the Future: Postcapitalism and a World Without Work* (London: Verso, 2015); G. Standing, *Basic Income* (London: Pelican, 2017).
2 S. Haider, 'The darkness at the end of the tunnel: Artificial Intelligence and neoreaction', *Viewpoint Magazine*, 28 March 2017, www.viewpointmag.com /2017/03/28/the-darkness-at-the-end-of-the-tunnel-artificial-intellige nce-and-neoreaction/ (accessed 26 February 2019).
3 W. Davies, 'Home Office rules', *London Review of Books* 38:21 (2016), 3–6, www.lrb.co.uk/v38/n21/william-davies/home-office-rules (accessed 22 March 2019).
4 J. Fourastié, *Les Trente Glorieuses: ou la révolution invisible* (Paris: Fayard, 1979).
5 Mason, quoted in C. Green, 'Poor Gramsci', *New Socialist*, 8 July 2018, https://newsocialist.org.uk/poor-gramsci/ (accessed 26 February 2019).
6 For sharp, real-time accounts of this partial return, see C. Lucas, 'Corbyn is wrong to indulge migration myths – free movement must be defended', *Novara Media*, 26 July 2017, http://novaramedia.com/2017/07/26/corbyn-is-wrong-to-indulge-migration-myths-free-movement-must-be-defended/ (accessed 26 February 2019); M. Goodfellow, 'Labour isn't flip-flopping on Brexit – this is practical politics', *Guardian*, 12 December 2017, www.theguardian.com/ commentisfree/2017/dec/12/brexit-jeremy-corbyn-keir-starmer-labour (accessed 26 February 2019); A. Sarkar, 'With a year to go until Brexit day, the left needs to promote a progressive migration strategy', *Independent*, 28 March 2018, www.independent.co.uk/voices/brexit-one-year-left-wing-migration-strategy-detention-centers-a8278386.html (accessed 26 February 2019); R. Shabi, 'How Brexit Britain can reset the immigration debate', *The New York Times*, 1 August 2017, www.nytimes.com/2017/08/01/opinion/brexit-cor byn-labour-immigration.html (accessed 26 February 2019); D. Wearing, 'Labour has slipped rightwards on immigration. That needs to change', *Guardian*, 25 July 2017, www.theguardian.com/commentisfree/2017/jul/25 /labour-immigration-jeremy-corbyn-attitudes (accessed 26 February 2019).
7 R. Syal, 'Senior Labour figures clash over concerns of working-class votes', *Guardian*, 4 July 2017, www.theguardian.com/politics/2017/jul/04/seni or-labour-figures-clash-over-concerns-of-working-class-voters (accessed 26 February 2019); Press Association, 'Sarah Champion: Labour's "floppy left" falls silent when issues touch on race', *Guardian*, 2 September 2017, www.theguardian.com/politics/2017/sep/02/sarah-champion-labours-floppy-left-falls-silent-when-issues-touch-on-race (accessed 26 February 2019).

8   T. Jeory and J. Stone, 'Theresa May's husband is a senior executive at a $1.4tn investment fund that profits from tax avoiding', *Independent*, 12 July 2016, www.independent.co.uk/news/uk/politics/theresa-may-philip-may-amazon-starbucks-google-capital-group-philip-morris-a7133231.html (accessed 26 February 2019).
9   D. Featherstone, 'Stuart Hall and our current conjuncture', *Progressive Review* 24:1 (2017), 36–44.
10 M. James, 'Authoritarian populism/populist authoritarianism', in A. Duman, D. Hancox, M. James and A. Minton (eds), *Regeneration Songs: Sounds of Investment and Loss in East London* (London: Repeater, 2018), pp. 291–306.
11 S. Hall, 'The great moving right show', *Marxism Today* (January 1979), 14–20; S. Hall and M. Jacques (eds), *The Politics of Thatcherism* (London: Lawrence and Wishart, 1983); S. Hall, *Thatcherism and the Crisis of the Left: The Hard Road to Renewal* (London: Verso, 1988).
12 S. Jeffries, '"Swamped" and "riddled": the toxic words that wreck public discourse', *Guardian*, 27 October 2014, www.theguardian.com/uk-news/20 14/oct/27/swamped-and-riddled-toxic-phrases-wreck-politics-immigr ation-michael-fallon (accessed 26 February 2019).
13 S. Hall, 'Who needs "identity?"', in S. Hall and P. Du Gay (eds), *Questions of Cultural Identity* (London: Sage, 1996), pp. 1–17.
14 R. Seymour, *Against Austerity* (London: Pluto Press, 2014).
15 W. Davies, *The Limits of Neoliberalism: Authority, Sovereignty and the Logic of Competition* (London: Sage, 2014).
16 R. P. Sayeed, *1997: The Future that Never Happened* (London: Zed Books, 2007); N. Zuberi, *Sounds English: Transnational Popular Music* (Urbana, IL: University of Illinois Press, 2001).
17 L. Back, M. Keith, A. Khan, K. Shukra and J. Solomos, 'The return of assimilationism: race, multiculturalism and New Labour', *Sociological Research Online* 7:2 (2002), 1–10; V. Kalra and N. Kapoor, 'Interrogating segregation, integration and the community cohesion agenda', *Journal of Ethnic and Migration Studies* 35:9 (2009), 1397–415; A. Kundnani, *The End of Tolerance* (London: Pluto Press, 2007).
18 A. Giddens, 'The third way can beat the far right', *Guardian*, 3 May 2002, www.theguardian.com/politics/2002/may/03/eu.thefarright (accessed 26 February 2019).
19 P. Gilroy, 'Letters: populism and Le Pen', *Guardian*, 4 May 2002, www. theguardian.com/world/2002/may/04/france.guardianletters (accessed 26 February 2019).
20 D. McGhee, *The End of Multiculturalism?* (Maidenhead: Open University Press, 2008).

21 R. Seymour, 'The undead centre. Or, what is a Macron?', *Patreon*, 27 June 2017, www.patreon.com/posts/undead-centre-or-12162326 (accessed 26 February 2019).
22 R. Seymour, 'Where we go from here', *Novara Media*, 11 June 2017, https://novaramedia.com/2017/06/11/where-we-go-from-here/ (accessed 26 February 2019).
23 Gordon Brown, in a previous guise that allowed him to occasionally pen searching commentaries for, among other publications, the *London Review of Books*, once drew attention to this specific form of Poujadism which anchored Thatcher's political mystique. 'Margaret Roberts moved from her Anglo-Poujadist origins via Oxford, the lab and the bar to eventual leadership and Gaullist ambitions, more honoured in rhetoric than in achievement [...] The roots of the [Thatcher] experiment are [, however, still] broadly Poujadist: petty-bourgeois resentment of big government and organised labour; sado-sentimental attachment to the concept of the strong state; a naive yearning for the simplicities of an Arcadian marketplace unspoiled even by the sinister insights of the historical Adam Smith. The appeal is broad but superficial: Thatcherism is designed for an older, simpler world that never actually existed.' G. Brown, 'Thatcherism', *London Review of Books* 11:3 (1988), 3, www.lrb.co.uk/v11/n03/gordon-brown/thatcherism (accessed 22 March 2019).
24 G. Ruddick, 'Business rates rise is biggest issue for small firms in London', *Guardian*, 17 February 2017, www.theguardian.com/business/2017/feb/17/business-rates-rise-biggest-issue-small-firms-london (accessed 26 February 2019).
25 S. Coates, 'Ministers aim to build "empire 2.0" with African Commonwealth', *The Times*, 6 March 2017, www.thetimes.co.uk/article/ministers-aim-to-build-empire-2-0-with-african-commonwealth-after-brexit-v9bs6f6z9 (accessed 26 February 2019).
26 A. Beckett, 'How Britain fell out of love with the free market', *Guardian*, 4 August 2017, www.theguardian.com/news/2017/aug/04/how-britain-fell-out-of-love-with-the-free-market (accessed 26 February 2019).
27 G. Fraser, 'How strange that capitalism's noisiest enemies are now on the right', *Guardian*, 4 May 2017, www.theguardian.com/commentisfree/belief/2017/may/04/how-strange-that-capitalisms-noisiest-enemies-are-now-on-the-right (accessed 26 February 2019); J. Harris, 'Britain is in the midst of a working-class revolt', *Guardian*, 17 June 2016, www.theguardian.com/commentisfree/2016/jun/17/britain-working-class-revolt-eu-referendum (accessed 26 February 2019).
28 P. Mason, 'How we can escape Brexit doom with one small tweak to free movement', *Guardian*, 16 January 2017, www.theguardian.com/commentisf

ree/2017/jan/16/we-can-escape-brexit-doom-with-one-small-tweak-to-free-movement (accessed 26 February 2019).
29 See here the incendiary and much-publicised essay by A. Nagle, 'The Left case against open borders', *American Affairs* 2:4 (2018), https://americanaffairsjournal.org/2018/11/the-left-case-against-open-borders/ (accessed 26 February 2019).
30 A. Toscano, 'Notes on late fascism', *Historical Materialism*, 2 April 2017, www.historicalmaterialism.org/blog/notes-late-fascism (accessed 26 February 2019).
31 B. Anderson, *Imagined Communities: Reflections on the Origin and Spread of Nationalism* (London: Verso, 1983), p. 7.
32 For a restating of the nationalism–false consciousness pivot, see A. L. Allahar, 'False consciousness, class consciousness and nationalism', *Social and Economic Studies* 53:1 (2004), 95–123.
33 A concept that essentially translates as 'always-the-same'.
34 M. Horkheimer and T. W. Adorno, *Dialectic of Enlightenment* (Palo Alto, CA: Stanford University Press, 2002 [1944]); H. Marcuse, *One-Dimensional Man* (Abingdon: Routledge, 1991 [1964]).
35 T. W. Adorno, *The Culture Industry* (London: Routledge, 2001 [1972]), p. 14.
36 G. L. Mosse, *Nationalism and Sexuality: Respectability and Abnormal Sexuality in Modern Europe* (New York: Howard Fertig, 1985), p. 9.
37 K. Marx and F. Engels, *The Communist Manifesto* (New Haven, CT: Yale University Press, 2012 [1848]), p. 76.
38 A. Bonnett, 'How the British working class became white: the symbolic (re)formation of racialized capitalism', *Journal of Historical Sociology* 11:3 (1998), 329.
39 V. Chibber, *Postcolonial Theory and the Spectre of Capital* (London: Verso, 2013).
40 S. Hall, 'The new Conservatism and the old', *Universities and Left Review* 1:1 (1957), 21.
41 Fascism is also often considered a particularly efficient expression of certain organisational imperatives central to modernity: authoritarian assertions of a centralised state power; a mastery of bureaucratic technologies that harness industrial levels of state administration; as well as historically particular compromises with capital as it contends with the mass labour movements also dialectically characteristic of capitalism.
42 H. Arendt, *The Origins of Totalitarianism* (London: Harvest Books, 1973 [1951]), p. 275.
43 A. Badiou, 'Reflections on the recent election', 15 November 2016, www.versobooks.com/blogs/2940-alain-badiou-reflections-on-the-recent-election (accessed 26 February 2019).

44 E. Balibar, 'The nation form: history and ideology', *Review (Fernand Braudel Center)* 13:3 (1990), 343.
45 N. Davidson, 'The national question, class and the European Union: an interview with Neil Davidson', *Salvage*, 22 July 2017, http://salvage.zone/online-exclusive/the-national-question-class-and-the-european-union-neil-davidson/ (accessed 26 February 2019).
46 S. Virdee, 'Racialized capitalism: an account of its contested origins and consolidation', *Sociological Review* 67:1 (2019), 3–27.
47 Toscano, 'Notes on late fascism'.
48 Ibid.
49 Bloch's wider reading of this historical multiplicity is something the reader might find to be of particular interest. As Toscano argues, Bloch's claim is that the political psyche of any present is in fact figured by 'plural temporalities' – that is to say, various versions of popular political expression are in fact not easily synced with the class structures and accumulative strategies most characteristic of that present. There is, in short, a temporal disjuncture between political discourse and the material facts, or what Toscano calls 'this lived experience of uneven development'. As Bloch observed in this vertiginous reading of the 'temporal multiplicity' that German fascism called upon: 'The infringement of "interest slavery" (*Zinsknechtschaft*) is believed in, as if this were the economy of 1500; superstructures that seemed long overturned right themselves again and stand still in today's world as whole medieval city scenes. Here is the Tavern of the Nordic Blood, there the castle of the Hitler duke, yonder the Church of the German Reich, an earth church, in which even the city people can feel themselves to be fruits of the German earth and honor the earth as something holy, as the confession of German heroes and German history [...] Peasants sometimes still believe in witches and exorcists, but not nearly as frequently and as strongly as a large class of urbanites believe in ghostly Jews and the new Baldur. The peasants sometimes still read the so-called Sixth and Seventh Books of Moses, a sensational tract about diseases of animals and the forces and secrets of nature; but half the middle class believes in the Elders of Zion, in Jewish snares and the omnipresence of Freemason symbols and in the galvanic powers of German blood and the German land.' Bloch, quoted in Toscano, 'Notes on late fascism'.
50 Rabinbach, quoted in Toscano, 'Notes on late fascism'.
51 A more complex version of this line of reasoning does acknowledge that the politics that is finding present expression is indeed deeply belligerent and xenophobic, what Glenn Greenwald terms 'tribalistic scapegoating', but this is pitched as being a direct consequence of people 'suffering economically'.

Greenwald, quoted in D. Sayer, 'White riot – Brexit, Trump, and postfactual politics', *Journal of Historical Sociology* 30:1 (2017), 95.
52   S. Virdee and B. McGeever, 'Racism, class, Brexit', *Ethnic and Racial Studies* 41:10 (2018), 1803.
53   Unless the squeezed middle and the other middling constituencies weathering perceived stagnation are also being bracketed into this wider 'left behind' thesis.
54   L. McKenzie, 'Brexit: a two-fingered salute from the working class', *Red Pepper*, 22 August 2016, www.redpepper.org.uk/brexit-a-two-fingered-salute-from-the-working-class/ (accessed 26 February 2019).
55   J. Coman, 'How the Nordic far-right has stolen the left's ground on welfare', *Guardian*, 26 July 2015, www.theguardian.com/world/2015/jul/26/scandinavia-far-right-stolen-left-ground-welfare (accessed 26 February 2019).
56   M. Wallace, 'Can Theresa May's secret weapon save her faltering campaign?', *Guardian*, 29 May 2017, www.theguardian.com/commentisfree/2017/may/29/theresa-may-labour-voter-base-erdington-brexit-corbyn (accessed 26 February 2019).
57   T. May, 'Theresa May's conference speech in full', *Telegraph*, 5 October 2016, www.telegraph.co.uk/news/2016/10/05/theresa-mays-conference-speech-in-full/ (accessed 26 February 2019).
58   M. Glasman, quoted in C. H. Tuohy, 'Small is big: red Toryism and the political debate in Britain', *Policy Options*, 1 May 2011, http://policyoptions.irpp.org/magazines/provincial-deficits-and-debt/small-is-big-red-toryism-and-the-political-debate-in-britain/ (accessed 26 February 2019).
59   G. Prakash, 'Whose cosmopolitanism? Multiple, globally enmeshed and subaltern', in N. Glick Schiller and A. Irving (eds), *Whose Cosmopolitanism?* (New York: Berghahn Books, 2015), p. 28.
60   W. Streeck, 'Trump and the Trumpists', *Inference Review* 3:1 (2017), https://inference-review.com/article/trump-and-the-trumpists (accessed 22 March 2019); J. C. Williams, *White Working Class: Overcoming Class Cluelessness in America* (Boston, MA: Harvard Business Review Press, 2017).
61   P. Collier, 'How to save capitalism from itself', *The Times Literary Supplement*, 25 January 2017, www.the-tls.co.uk/articles/public/how-to-save-capitalism/ (accessed 26 February 2019). Collier is worth quoting from more fully, as his colourful prose gives many of these core post-Marxist nationalist themes a full-throttled and entertaining rhetorical bluster: 'The ill-educated, toiling provincial has replaced the working class as the revolutionary force in society: not the *sans culottes* so much as the *sans cool*. So what are these people angry about? Partly their gripes are economic. The fortunes of the new elite have risen, often undeservedly,

whilst those of the *sans cool* have deteriorated. Anger is tinged with fear: for the *sans cool* economic security is collapsing. But anger and fear go beyond the economic: people see that the members of the educated southern/coastal elite are intermarrying ("assortative mating") and embracing a globalized identity, whilst asserting their moral superiority by encouraging their favoured priority groups to elevate characteristics such as ethnicity and sexual orientation into exclusive "community" identities. The *sans cool* understand that both the withdrawal by the elite and the emergence of new favoured groups apparently creaming off benefits weaken their claim to help, just as their need for support is increasing. In liberal circles, shared identity has been replaced by an ostensible espousal of diversity. But acceptable diversity is confined to the favoured groups: it does not extend, for example, to most readers of the *Daily Mail*, or indeed to any of the *sans cool*. Shared identity based on nationalism has been so universally condemned as to have become unacceptable. Liberal disdain has been driven by fears that nationalism would incite a return to majority violence against minorities, and by the hope that nation-based governance can be superseded by multiculturalism and global citizenship. Neither the fears nor the hopes are well founded.'

62 D. Goodhart, *The Road to Somewhere: The Populist Revolt and the Future of Politics* (London: C. Hurst and Co., 2017).

63 D. Goodhart, 'White self-interest is not the same thing as racism', *Financial Times*, 2 March 2017, www.ft.com/content/220090e0-efc1-11e6-ba01-119a44939bb6 (accessed 26 February 2019); D. Goodhart, 'Too diverse?', *Prospect*, 20 February 2004, www.prospectmagazine.co.uk/magazine/too-diverse-david-goodhart-multiculturalism-britain-immigration-globalisation (accessed 26 February 2019).

64 S. Hall, 'When the Left abandons workers, they are easy prey for the Right', *The Full Brexit* (2018), www.thefullbrexit.com/edl (accessed 26 February 2019); H. Pilkington, *Loud and Proud: Passion and Politics in the English Defence League* (Manchester: Manchester University Press, 2016); S. Winlow, S. Hall and J. Treadwell, *The Rise of the Right: English Nationalism and the Transformation of Working-class Politics* (Bristol: Policy Press, 2017).

65 P. Gilroy, *Between Camps: Nations, Cultures and the Allure of Race* (Abingdon: Routledge, 2004 [2000]).

66 J. Gilbert 'The crisis of cosmopolitanism', *Stuart Hall Foundation* (2017), http://stuarthallfoundation.org/library/the-crisis-of-cosmopolitanism/ (accessed 22 March 2019).

67 b. hooks, *Black Looks: Race and Representation* (Abingdon: Routledge, 2015 [1992]), pp. 21–40.

68 B. Rogaly, *Stories from a Migrant City: Non-elite Cosmopolitanism and Provincial Urban Citizenship* (Manchester: Manchester University Press, forthcoming).
69 D. Burdsey, *Race, Place and the Seaside* (London: Palgrave Macmillan, 2016); Rogaly, *Stories from a Migrant City*; R. Huq, *On the Edge: The Contested Cultures of English Suburbia* (London: Lawrence and Wishart, 2013); A. Saha and S. Watson, 'Suburban drifts: mundane multiculturalism in Outer London', *Ethnic and Racial Studies* 36:12 (2013), 2016–34.
70 Sayer is alluding here to the journalistic process by which counties/regions that were erstwhile seemingly marginal to the national political conversation have suddenly been re-centred as the engine of Brexit-themed anxieties. For the best of this, see James Meek for a careful discussion of Grimsby's recent history – a town that is exemplary of a Lincolnshire in decline – and how the town hosts many of the tensions regarding the disavowal of the Labour Party alongside a complementary reassertion of a political nationalism. J. Meek, 'Why are you still here?', *London Review of Books* 37:8 (2015), 3–14, www.lrb.co.uk/v37/n08/james-meek/why-are-you-still-here (accessed 22 March 2019).
71 Sayer, 'White riot', 99.
72 Ibid.
73 J. Rydgren and P. Ruth, 'Contextual explanation of radical right-wing support in Sweden: socioeconomic marginalization, group threat, and the halo effect', *Ethnic and Racial Studies* 36:4 (2013), 711–28.
74 K. Willsher, 'Rural heartland offers Le Pen her last chance to take on Parisian elite', *The Observer*, 6 May 2017, www.theguardian.com/world/2017/may/06/marine-le-pen-rural-france-message-division-front-national (accessed 26 February 2019).
75 Gilbert, 'The crisis of cosmopolitanism'.
76 G. Wekker, *White Innocence: Paradoxes of Colonialism and Race* (Durham, NC: Duke University Press, 2016).
77 W. Brown, *Regulating Aversion: Tolerance in the Age of Identity and Empire* (Princeton, NJ: Princeton University Press, 2006); J. Derrida, 'A dialogue with Jacques Derrida', in G. Borradori (ed.), *Philosophy in a Time of Terror: Dialogues with Jürgen Habermas and Jacques Derrida* (Chicago: University of Chicago Press, 2003), pp. 124–7.
78 G. Lonergan, 'Reproducing the "national home": gendering domopolitics', *Citizenship Studies* 22:1 (2018), 1–18; G. Titley, 'Getting integration right? Media transnationalism and domopolitics in Ireland', *Ethnic and Racial Studies* 35:5 (2012), 817–33; W. Walters, 'Secure borders, safe haven, domopolitics', *Citizenship Studies* 8:3 (2004), 237–60.

NOTES

79   Gilbert, 'The crisis of cosmopolitanism'.
80   C. Alexander, *The Art of Being Black: The Creation of Black British Youth Identities* (Oxford: Oxford University Press, 1996); A. Brah, *Cartographies of Diaspora: Contesting Identities* (London: Routledge, 1996); P. Gilroy, *Black Atlantic: Modernity and Double Consciousness* (London: Verso, 1993); S. Hall, 'Cultural identity and diaspora', in P. Williams and L. Chrisman (eds), *Colonial Discourse and Post-Colonial Theory* (New York: Harvester Wheatsheaf, 1993), pp. 392–403.
81   S. Žižek, *Against the Double Blackmail: Refugees, Terror and Other Troubles with the Neighbours* (London: Penguin, 2016). See also A. Merelli, 'Marxist philosopher Slavoj Zizek explains why we shouldn't pity or romanticize refugees', *Quartz*, 9 September 2016, https://qz.com/767751/marxist-philosopher-slavoj-zizek-on-europes-refugee-crisis-the-left-is-wrong-to-pity-and-romanticize-migrants/ (accessed 26 February 2019).
82   L. McKenzie, 'The refugee crisis will hit the UK's working class areas hardest', *Guardian*, 16 September 2015, www.theguardian.com/society/2015/sep/16/refugee-crisis-hit-uk-working-class-powerless (accessed 26 February 2019).
83   R. Shilliam, *Race and the Undeserving Poor* (Newcastle upon Tyne: Agenda Publishing, 2018).
84   Ibid., p. 9.
85   Ibid., p. 83.
86   Ibid., p. 49. There is an interesting, often overlooked, chapter in British history that Shilliam does well to recover. A significant moment in his historical analysis turns on the agonised governmental soul-searching that was provoked by the Boer War experience – increased Establishment concern about the indigence and moral decrepitude of the English working class that had allegedly been made starkly apparent in their inability to resist the Boer campaigns. It was in the midst of this political crisis, one that married with a broader dystopian poetics characteristic of *fin-de-siècle* writing, that a need to better inoculate the native working classes from the ravages of capitalism is said to have found greater political traction. Shilliam's point here is that it was this specific political pivot that properly embedded an Establishment will to keep the British working class in good order: cultivating Edwardian virtues of responsibility, industry and good health that in turn were important not only to the profit-seeking imperatives of business but also to the imperial ambitions of the state. Industrial capitalism's cycles of unemployment and deskilling were, as a result, seen as being contrary to these goals – breeding degeneracy and idleness.

87 Renan, quoted in A. Césaire, *Discourse on Colonialism* (New York: Monthly Review Press, 2000 [1955]), p. 38.
88 Shilliam, *Race and the Undeserving Poor*, p. 84.
89 Ibid., p. 92.
90 G. Bhambra, 'Brexit, the Commonwealth, and exclusionary citizenship', *openDemocracy*, 8 December 2016, www.opendemocracy.net/gurminder-k-bhambra/brexit-commonwealth-and-exclusionary-citizenship (accessed 26 February 2019); N. El-Enany, 'Things fall apart: from Empire to Brexit Britain', *Bath Institute for Policy Research*, 2 May 2017, http://blogs.bath.ac.uk/iprblog/2017/05/02/things-fall-apart-from-empire-to-brexit-britain/ (accessed 26 February 2019).
91 Bonnett, 'How the British working class became white', 329.
92 S. Ashe and B. McGeever, 'Marxism, racism and the construction of "race" as a social and political relation: an interview with Robert Miles', *Ethnic and Racial Studies* 34:12 (2011), 2009–26.
93 I. Tyler, 'The hieroglyphics of the border: racial stigma in neoliberal Europe', *Ethnic and Racial Studies* 41:10 (2018), 1783–801.
94 L. Fekete, 'The emergence of xeno-racism', *Race and Class* 43:2 (2001), 23–4.
95 Shilliam, *Race and the Undeserving Poor*, p. 180.
96 G. Bhattacharyya, *Rethinking Racial Capitalism: Questions of Reproduction and Survival* (London: Rowman and Littlefield, 2018); S. Virdee, 'Racialized capitalism: an account of its contested origins and consolidation', *Sociological Review* 67:1 (2019), 3–27.
97 G. Bhambra, 'Brexit, Trump, and "methodological whiteness": on the misrecognition of race and class', *British Journal of Sociology* 68:1 (2017), 214–32; A. Lentin, 'On class and identity politics', *Inference Review* 3:2 (2017), https://inference-review.com/letter/on-class-and-identity-politics (accessed 26 February 2019).
98 W. E. B. Du Bois, *Black Reconstruction in America* (New York: The Free Press, 1992 [1935]); D. R. Roediger, *The Wages of Whiteness* (London: Verso, 1999 [1991]); J. Narayan, 'The wages of whiteness in the absence of wages: racial capitalism, reactionary intercommunalism and the rise of Trumpism', *Third World Quarterly* 38:11 (2017), 2482–500; W. Bottero, 'Class in the 21st century', in K. P. Sveinsson (ed.), *Who Cares about the White Working Class?* (London: Runnymede, 2009), pp. 7–14; D. R. Roediger, *Working Toward Whiteness* (New York: Basic Books, 2005); J. Rhodes, 'The "trouble" with the "white working class": whiteness, class and "groupism"', *Identities* 19:4 (2012), 485–92.

99 J. E. Fox and M. Mogilnicka, 'Pathological integration, or, how East Europeans use racism to become British', *British Journal of Sociology* 70:1 (2017), 5–23.

100 M. James, 'Brexit London: the past, present and the future of racism', *The Sociological Review*, 4 October 2016, www.thesociologicalreview.com/blog/brexit-london-the-past-present-and-future-of-racism-in-the-capital-1.html (accessed 26 February 2019).

101 R. Seymour, 'Is fascism on the rise?', *Lenin's Tomb*, 19 May 2017, www.leninology.co.uk/2017/05/is-fascism-on-rise.html?m=1 (accessed 26 February 2019).

Notes to the Conclusion

1 S. Virdee, 'Racialized capitalism: an account of its contested origins and consolidation', *Sociological Review* 67:1 (2019), 3.

2 R. Seymour, 'The nocturnal side of reason', *Lenin's Tomb*, 20 December 2016, www.leninology.co.uk/2016/12/the-nocturnal-side-of-reason.html (accessed 26 February 2019).

3 R. Williams, *Culture and Society 1780–1950* (New York: Columbia University Press, 1983 [1958]), p. 300.

4 S. Haider, 'The darkness at the end of the tunnel: Artificial Intelligence and neoreaction', *Viewpoint Magazine*, 28 March 2017, www.viewpointmag.com/2017/03/28/the-darkness-at-the-end-of-the-tunnel-artificial-intelligence-and-neoreaction/ (accessed 26 February 2019); A. Nagle, *Kill All Normies: Online Culture Wars from 4chan and Tumblr to Trump and the Alt-right* (London: Zero, 2017); M. Wendling, *Alt-Right: From 4chan to the White House* (London: Pluto Press, 2018).

5 It was, of course, her 2018 essay, 'The Left case against open borders', that saw Nagle fully embrace her role as a slapdash apologist for left nationalism.

6 G. Titley, 'Filter bubble – when scepticism of the mainstream media becomes denial of atrocity', *Wildcat Dispatches* (2016), http://wildcatdispatches.org/2016/12/14/gavan-titley-filter-bubble-how-blanket-distrust-of-the-western-msm-results-in-nothing-more-than-displaced-fidelity-to-its-alternative-mirror-image/ (accessed 26 February 2019).

7 W. Phillips, *This is Why We Can't Have Nice Things: Mapping the Relationship between Online Trolling and Mainstream Culture* (Cambridge, MA: MIT Press, 2015).

8 A. Winter and A. Mondon, 'Articulations of Islamophobia: from the extreme to the mainstream?', *Ethnic and Racial Studies* 40:13 (2017), 2151–79.

9   G. Titley, *Racism and Media* (London: Sage, 2019).
10 J. Dean, *Blog Theory: Feedback and Capture in the Circuits of Drive* (Cambridge: Polity Press, 2010).
11 S. Valluvan, 'What is "post-race" and what does it reveal about contemporary racisms?', *Ethnic and Racial Studies* 39:13 (2016), 2241–51.
12 S. Keskinen, 'Political antagonisms in radical right-wing and anti-immigration rhetoric in Finland', *Nordic Journal of Migration Research* 4:3 (2013), 225–32.
13 J. Burke and D. Smith, 'Donald Trump's land seizures tweet sparks anger in South Africa', *Guardian*, 23 August 2018, www.theguardian.com/us-news/2018/aug/23/trump-orders-close-study-of-south-africa-farmer-killings (accessed 26 February 2019).
14 R. Mason, 'Nigel Farage rows back on call to grant asylum to Syrian refugees', *Guardian*, 30 December 2013, www.theguardian.com/politics/2013/dec/30/nigel-farage-asylum-syrian-refugees-christians (accessed 26 February 2019).
15 G. Titley, 'Swedens of the mind', *Critical Legal Thinking*, 24 February 2017, http://criticallegalthinking.com/2017/02/24/swedens-of-the-mind/ (accessed 26 February 2019).
16 Nagle, *Kill All Normies*, pp. 27–31.
17 R. Orange, '"We're insubordinate": the rural towns at forefront of Swedish populist wave', *Guardian*, 7 September 2018, www.theguardian.com/world/2018/sep/07/were-insubordinate-the-rural-towns-at-forefront-of-swedish-populist-wave (accessed 26 February 2019).
18 S. Ahmed, '"Liberal multiculturalism is the hegemony – it's an empirical fact": a response to Slavoj Žižek', *darkmatter*, 19 February 2008, www.darkmatter101.org/site/2008/02/19/%E2%80%98liberal-multiculturalism-is-the-hegemony-%E2%80%93-its-an-empirical-fact%E2%80%99-a-response-to-slavoj-zizek/ (accessed 26 February 2019).
19 W. Davies, 'The free speech panic: how the right concocted a crisis', *Guardian*, 26 July 2018, www.theguardian.com/news/2018/jul/26/the-free-speech-panic-censorship-how-the-right-concocted-a-crisis (accessed 26 February 2019).
20 E. Durkin, 'Alex Jones claims he's being silenced as bans push him to alternative platforms', *Guardian*, 11 August 2018, www.theguardian.com/us-news/2018/aug/11/alex-jones-claims-hes-being-silenced-as-bans-push-him-to-alternate-platforms (accessed 26 February 2019); Haider, 'The darkness at the end of the tunnel'; Wendling, *Alt-Right*; J. Wilson, 'Burst your bubble: five conservative articles to read as protests stymie Trump', *Guardian*, 9 February 2017, www.theguardian.com/us-news/2017/feb/09/news-bubble-conservative-articles-for-liberals (accessed 26 February 2019).

21 Titley, *Racism and Media*.
22 Z. Tufekci, 'YouTube, the great radicalizer', *New York Times*, 10 March 2018, www.nytimes.com/2018/03/10/opinion/sunday/youtube-politics-radical.html (accessed 26 February 2019). Interestingly, as Tufekci explains, if you watch a couple of Trump rally clips on YouTube, you will be taken into an 'autoplay' web of 'white supremacist rants, Holocaust denials and other disturbing content'. But if you watch some Hillary Clinton and Bernie Sanders content and 'let YouTube's recommender algorithm take [you] wherever it would', you will in quick time come across 9/11 deniers and other purportedly left-inflected conspiracists. And this effect worked for all content, even that which is ostensibly non-political: 'videos about vegetarianism led to videos about veganism. Videos about jogging led to videos about running ultramarathons.'
23 A. Chadwick, *The Hybrid Media System: Politics and Power* (Oxford: Oxford University Press, 2013).
24 P. MacInnes, 'What's up PewdiePie? The troubling content of YouTube's biggest star', *Guardian*, 5 April 2018, www.theguardian.com/tv-and-radio/2018/apr/05/whats-up-pewdiepie-the-troubling-content-of-youtubes-biggest-star (accessed 26 February 2019).
25 J. Russell, 'PewDiePie, the world's most popular YouTuber, is back making more racist comments', *Tech Crunch* (2017), https://techcrunch.com/2017/09/10/pewdiepie-is-back-making-more-racist-comments/?guccounter=1 (accessed 26 February 2019).
26 MacInnes, 'What's up PewdiePie?'.
27 D. Roberts, 'Donald Trump and the rise of tribal epistemology', *Vox*, 19 May 2017, www.vox.com/policy-and-politics/2017/3/22/14762030/donald-trump-tribal-epistemology (accessed 26 February 2019).
28 E. L. Briant, 'Three explanatory essays giving context and analysis to submitted evidence', *UK Parliament: Digital, Culture, Media, and Sport Committee*, 16 April 2018, www.parliament.uk/documents/commons-committees/culture-media-and-sport/Dr-Emma-Briant-Explanatory-Essays.pdf (accessed 22 March 2019). These are the three essays that Emma Briant submitted to the DCMS's 'Fake News Inquiry': these essays cover Cambridge Analytica's techniques in steering social medial feeds, Cambridge Analytica's involvement in Brexit, and the general emergence of a new 'propaganda industry'.
29 B. Tarnoff, 'Donald Trump, Peter Thiel and the death of democracy', *Guardian*, 21 July 2016, www.theguardian.com/technology/2016/jul/21/peter-thiel-republican-convention-speech (accessed 26 February 2019).
30 C. Cadwalladr, 'Follow the data: does a legal document link Brexit campaigns to US billionaire?', *Guardian*, 14 May 2017, www.theguardian

.com/technology/2017/may/14/robert-mercer-cambridge-analytica-leave-eu-referendum-brexit-campaigns#img- (accessed 26 February 2019); C. Cadwalladr, 'Revealed: how US billionaire helped to back Brexit', *Guardian*, 26 February 2017, www.theguardian.com/politics/2017/feb/26/us-billionaire-mercer-helped-back-brexit (accessed 26 February 2019).

31 *Guardian*, 'The Cambridge Analytica Files' (2017–18), www.theguardian.com/news/series/cambridge-analytica-files (accessed 26 February 2019).

32 M. Rosenberg, N. Confessore and C. Cadwalladr, 'How Trump consultants exploited the Facebook data of millions', *New York Times*, 17 May 2018, www.nytimes.com/2018/03/17/us/politics/cambridge-analytica-trump-campaign.html (accessed 26 February 2019).

33 A. Kasprak, 'Code developed by Canadian firm hints at voter "disengagement" efforts in United States', *Snopes*, 12 June 2008, www.snopes.com/news/2018/06/13/code-hints-voter-disengagement-efforts/ (accessed 26 February 2019).

34 Channel 4 News, 'Exposed: undercover secrets of Trump's data firm', 20 March 2018, www.channel4.com/news/exposed-undercover-secrets-of-donald-trump-data-firm-cambridge-analytica (accessed 26 February 2019).

35 C. Cadwalladr, 'Arron Banks, Brexit and the Russia connection', *Guardian*, 16 June 2018, www.theguardian.com/uk-news/2018/jun/16/arron-banks-nigel-farage-leave-brexit-russia-connection (accessed 26 February 2019); J. Jackson, 'Arron Banks launches Breitbart-style site Westmonster', *Guardian*, 19 January 2017, www.theguardian.com/media/2017/jan/19/arron-banks-launches-breitbart-style-site-westmonster#img-1 (accessed 26 February 2019).

36 S. Halpern, 'Cambridge Analytica, Facebook, and the revelations of open secrets', *New Yorker*, 21 March 2018, www.newyorker.com/news/news-desk/cambridge-analytica-facebook-and-the-revelations-of-open-secrets (accessed 26 February 2019).

37 J. Ling, 'Follow the money', *VICE News*, 22 August 2017, https://news.vice.com/en_ca/article/wjz73q/inside-rebel-medias-big-money-anti-islam-crusade (accessed 26 February 2019).

38 Anonymous, '"Alt-right" online poison nearly turned me into a racist', *Guardian*, 28 November 2016, www.theguardian.com/commentisfree/2016/nov/28/alt-right-online-poison-racist-bigot-sam-harris-milo-yiannopoulos-islamophobia (accessed 26 February 2019).

39 R. Dasgupta, 'The demise of the nation state', *Guardian*, 5 April 2018, www.theguardian.com/news/2018/apr/05/demise-of-the-nation-state-rana-dasgupta (accessed 26 February 2019).

40 D. Haraway, 'Anthropocene, Capitalocene, Plantationocene, Chthulucene: making kin', *Environmental Humanities* 6 (2015), 159–65.
41 J. Kynge, C. Campbell, A. Kazmin and F. Bokhari, 'How China rules the waves', *Financial Times*, 12 January 2017, https://ig.ft.com/sites/china-ports/ (accessed 26 February 2019); M. Safi, 'Sri Lanka's "new Dubai": will Chinese-built city suck the life out of Colombo?', *Guardian*, 2 August 2018, www.theguardian.com/cities/2018/aug/02/sri-lanka-new-dubai-chinese-city-colombo (accessed 26 February 2019).
42 S. Žižek, 'Parallax', *London Review of Books* 25:22 (2003), 24, www.lrb.co.uk/v25/n22/slavoj-zizek/parallax (accessed 26 February 2019).
43 A. McClintock, 'Family feuds: gender, nationalism and the family', *Feminist Review* 44 (1993), 67.
44 R. Seymour, *Corbyn: The Strange Rebirth of Radical Politics* (London: Verso, 2017).
45 E. Joyner, 'A new popular leftist movement is gearing up in Germany – but does aufstehen stand a chance?', *Red Pepper*, 4 September 2018, www.redpepper.org.uk/a-new-popular-leftist-movement-is-gearing-up-in-germany-but-does-aufstehen-stand-a-chance/ (accessed 26 February 2019).
46 The case of Diane Abbott is particularly distressing here, revealing appallingly well the intersectional resonance of such vilification. See M. Charles, 'Race, feminism and intersectionality', *Renewal* 26:2 (2018), 64.
47 Davies, 'The free speech panic'.
48 Virdee, 'Racialized capitalism'.
49 C. Bhatt, 'The new xenologies of Europe: civil tensions and mythic pasts', *Journal of Civil Society* 8:3 (2012), 307–26.
50 A. Stille, 'How Matteo Salvini pulled Italy to the far right', *Guardian*, 9 August 2018, www.theguardian.com/news/2018/aug/09/how-matteo-salvini-pulled-italy-to-the-far-right (accessed 26 February 2019).
51 Salvini successfully dropped the 'Nord' from the party's name when rebranding Lega Nord as a national party. How quickly a separatist party can become a fully fledged nationalist party tells us much about how separatism is itself often a matter of repulsing 'constitutive outsides', as opposed to it being a politics of self-affirmation with an internal content of its own.
52 With Five Star's utterly disorganised non-politics (it being entirely an outlet for discontent) rendering it incapable of acting as the ruling coalition's 'senior' partner, Lega has promptly hijacked the national political agenda, and to great acclaim.
53 P. Gilroy, *After Empire: Melancholia or Convivial Culture?* (Abingdon: Routledge, 2004), pp. 154, 157.

54 L. Back and S. Sinha, with C. Bryan, V. Baraku and M. Yemba, *Migrant City* (London: Routledge, 2018).
55 R. Bramwell, *UK Hip-Hop, Grime and the City: The Aesthetics and Ethics of London's Rap Scenes* (London: Routledge, 2015); S. Hall, *City, Street and Citizen* (Abingdon: Routledge, 2012); B. Harries, *Talking Race in Young Adulthood* (Abingdon: Routledge, 2018); E. Jackson, 'Valuing the bowling alley: contestations over the preservation of spaces of everyday urban multiculture in London', *Sociological Review* (2018), https://journals.sagepub.com/doi/abs/10.1177/0038026118772784 (accessed 26 February 2019); M. James, *Urban Multiculture* (Basingstoke: Palgrave Macmillan, 2015).
56 R. Huq, *On the Edge: The Contested Cultures of English Suburbia* (London: Lawrence and Wishart, 2013); H. Jones, S. Neal, G. Mohan, A. Cochrane and K. Bennett, 'Urban multiculture and everyday encounters in semi-public, franchised cafe spaces', *Sociological Review* 63:3 (2015), 644–61; A. Saha and S. Watson, 'Suburban drifts: mundane multiculturalism in Outer London', *Ethnic and Racial Studies* 36:12 (2013), 2016–34.
57 A. Rhys-Taylor, *Food and Multiculture: A Sensory Ethnography of East London* (London: Bloomsbury, 2017), p. 145.
58 J. Kesten, A. Cochrane, G. Mohan and S. Neal, 'Multiculture and community in new city spaces', *Journal of Intercultural Studies* 32:2 (2011), 133–50.
59 S. Neal, K. Bennett, A. Cochrane and G. Mohan, *Lived Experiences of Multiculture* (Abingdon: Routledge, 2018).
60 D. Burdsey, *Race, Place and the Seaside* (London: Palgrave Macmillan, 2016).
61 U. Erel, 'Complex belongings: racialization and migration in a small English city', *Ethnic and Racial Studies* 34:12 (2011), 2048–68; B. Rogaly and K. Qureshi, 'Diversity, urban space and the right to the provincial city', *Identities* 20:4 (2013), 423–37.
62 A. Nayak, 'Purging the nation: race, conviviality and embodied encounters in the lives of British Bangladeshi Muslim young women', *Transactions* 42:2 (2017), 289–302; A. Nayak, *Race, Place and Globalisation: Youth Cultures in a Changing World* (London: Berg, 2003).
63 B. Rogaly, *Stories From a Migrant City: Non-elite Cosmopolitanism and Provincial Urban Citizenship* (Manchester: Manchester University Press, forthcoming).
64 S. Valluvan, 'Conviviality and multiculture', *Young* 24:3 (2016), 205.
65 A. Wise and G. Noble, 'Convivialities: an orientation', *Journal of Intercultural Studies* 37:5 (2017), 425.

66 C. Karner and D. Parker, 'Conviviality and conflict: pluralism, resilience and hope in inner-city Birmingham', *Journal of Ethnic and Migration Studies* 37:3 (2011), 355–72.

67 T. Sealy, 'Multiculturalism, interculturalism, "multiculture" and super-diversity: of zombies, shadows and other ways of being', *Ethnicities* 18:5 (2018), 692–716.

68 www.youtube.com/watch?v=_5k7zAOLiow (accessed 22 March 2019).

69 www.youtube.com/watch?v=kEwv8xOLUI0 (accessed 22 March 2019).

70 M. Charles, 'Grime launches a revolution in youth politics', *The Conversation*, 12 June 2017, https://theconversation.com/grime-launches-a-revolution-in-youth-politics-79236 (accessed 26 February 2019); Bramwell, *UK Hip-Hop, Grime and the City*, pp. 140–1, 146.

71 A. Saha, *Race and the Cultural Industries* (Cambridge: Polity Press, 2018).

72 I am thankful to Adam Elliott-Cooper and Virinder Kalra for drawing my attention to this important reading of the complex intersections of anti-racism, class consciousness and multiculture that the activism around Grenfell made so apparent. See also Robbie Shilliam's concluding chapter for a granular reading of the politics of Grenfell – both the racialised neoliberal politics that precipitated the deadly fire but also the forms of available resistance that Grenfell clarifies vis-à-vis a left political programme. R. Shilliam, *Race and the Undeserving Poor* (Newcastle upon Tyne: Agenda Publishing, 2018), pp. 165–81.

73 L. de Noronha, 'Deportation, racism and multi-status Britain: immigration control and the production of race in the present', *Ethnic and Racial Studies* (forthcoming).

74 Back et al., *Migrant City*.

75 Akala, *Natives: Race and Class in the Ruins of Empire* (London: Two Roads, 2018).

Index

Abbott, Diane 157, 198, 264n.46
Abrahamian, Atossa 2
acculturation 72
Adorno, T. W. 163
'advanced marginality' (Wacquant) 128
Affleck, Ben 86
African governments 53
Ahmed, Riz 75
Ahmed, Sara 74, 190
Akala 207
Alexander, C. 77, 175
Alexander the Great 35
Althusser, Louis 163
'alt-right' discourse 26, 103, 155, 186–7, 190–4
Amis, Martin 142
Anderson, Benedict 13, 32, 38, 216n.40
antisemitism 45, 49
  see also Jewish people
Arendt, Hannah 40–7, 166, 218n.63
Aristotelianism 44
Arnold, Matthew 92
art 81–3
asylum seekers 131, 159
austerity 161, 201
Austria 6, 201
authoritarianism 155–8, 186, 196
Awad, Alma 85

Back, L. 14
Badiou, A. 166
Baker, Julius 173, 204

Balibar, Etienne 14, 39–40, 71, 167, 216n.53
Bangladesh 59, 195
Banks, Aaron 193
Bannon, Steve 193
Barker, Martin 98
Barnett, Anthony 114–15
Bassel, L. 140, 146
Bauman, Z. 69–70, 130–1, 150, 153
Bawer, Bruce 87, 233n.21
belonging and *non-belonging* 5, 13, 34–7, 43, 55
Benjamin, Walter 166
Benoist, Alain 98
Berlusconi, Silvio 63
Beveridge Report (1942) 179
Bhabha, H. K. 40
Bhattacharyya, Gargi 21, 74, 180
Big Narstie 206
Billig, Michael 41, 97, 117
Birmingham 205
blackness and 'black culture',
  pathologisation of 5, 23, 46, 137–41, 151, 158, 247
Blair, Tony (and Blairism) 157–61, 199, 201
Blue Labour 24, 157, 170, 172
Blunkett, David 159
Boccaccio, Giovanni 43
Bonnett, Alastair 164–5, 179
Brah, Avtar 175
Brand, Russell 85

INDEX

Branson, Richard 126
Brexit
   Labour Party's stance on 16–17
   nationalist interpretation of 12
   referendum on (2016) 1–3, 24, 170, 193
Briant, Emma 262n.28
Britannia Unchained 132
British Broadcasting Corporation (BBC) 74
British Empire 110–14, 136
British Legion 116–17
British National Party (BNP) 159
Brito, T. L. 141
Brockway, Fenner 113
'bro-ing' 138
Brown, Wendy 18–19, 93
Brubaker, Rogers 31, 48–50
Buddhism 110, 195
Buffett, Warren 126
Burdsey, Daniel 173, 204
Burke, Edmund 42–3, 95–6
Bush, George W. 93
Butler, Dawn 198
Butler, J. 74
Byron, Lord 83

Caldwell, Christopher 87, 98
Callaghan, James 158
Call the Midwife 105
Cambridge Analytica 193
Cambridge Dictionary 61
Cameron, David 8, 21, 71–2, 91, 143–4, 201–2
capitalism 56, 112, 120, 122, 127, 134–5, 156–7, 160–4, 167–9
Carswell, Douglas 132–3
Casey, Louise and Casey Review, 2016 71–2, 104
Catalonia 20, 56–60
Catholic Church 74
Catholic repression 102
Césaire, Aimé 43, 111, 178–9, 218n.65
Chamayou, G. 119

Champion, Sarah 157, 250
Charles, Monique 206
Chateaubriand, Vicomte de 83
Chatterjee, P. 196–7
Chernilo, D. 32
Chibber, Vivek 165
China 133, 178–9, 195
Christianity 86, 91, 106–10, 120
Christie, Agatha 104
Churchill, Winston (and Churchillism) 62, 114, 120, 136
Church of England 106
citizenship 68, 78
city life 147–53
   habitus of cities 172
civic–ethnic distinction 69
civic nationalism 68–72, 75–6
civilisation and civilisationism 50–2, 55, 91–2
Clark, Kenneth 91–2
Clarke, Kenneth 12
class-based but race-conscious politics 200
class conflict 163, 166
Clinton, Bill 141
Clinton, Hillary 2
Clodius Albinus 101
Collier, Paul 171
Cologne New Year's Eve celebrations (2015–16) 73
colonialism 40, 59, 99–101, 111–15, 135–6, 180
   in reverse 109
commercialism 92
communitarianism 23, 45–6, 66, 157, 182, 188, 190, 203
'community cohesion' thesis 159
company form 135
competition, ethos of 126–7
competitiveness, support for 90
conservatism 18, 89–95, 100, 120
   culture, definition of 92
   dominant strains of 89–90
   ideological positioning of 93–4

INDEX

and neoliberalism 90–5
popular form of 94–5
Conservative Party and Conservative rule 3, 201–2
consumerism and consumer capitalism 148–53
conversion, religious 139
conviviality 205
Corbyn, Jeremy 16, 24–5, 65, 155–7, 183, 198, 201–2, 206
cosmopolitanism 151, 170–3, 205
Costa (chain) 160
Council of Europe 72
Countryfile 22
cricket 92–3
Croatia 195
Cromwell, Oliver 102
Crowder, Steven 191
cultural differences 55–6
cultural studies 18
cultural theory 91

Daily Mail 64, 115
Daily Mirror 115
Daily Telegraph 118
Davidson, Neil 167
Davies, Will 126, 131
Davis, David 136, 160
Dawkins, Richard 73, 85–6
d'Azeglio, Massimo 13
Dean, Jodi 188
decolonisation 59
de Cordova, Marsha 198
Delacroix, Eugène 81–2
demagoguery 3, 72, 203
democratic nationalism 68
Deng Xiaoping 123
Denham, John 157
Denmark 6, 64, 201, 235n.45
de Noronha, L. 214n.24
de Piero, Gloria 157
Desai, R. 241n.3
'deserving' and 'undeserving' poor 177–9
di Santarosa, Santorre 83

Dolar, Mladen 80
'domopolitics' 175
Dorling, Danny 170
Du Bois, W. E. B. 77
Duncan Smith, Iain 131, 133
Durkheim, E. 32, 108, 213n.20

East India Companies 135, 160
'echo-chamber effect' 187–90
economic hardship and uncertainty 9–11
economic migrants 131
The Economist 9, 29
Edward I, King of England 102
El-Enany, N. 66, 135
elites and elitism 62, 92–3
cultural 90
Elliott-Cooper, Adam 227n.30
Emejulu, A. 140, 146
'end of history' thesis 68
English Defence League (EDL) 171
English Labour Network 157
entrepreneurialism 125–7
Epsom 204
'Erdington Conservatism' 170
Escobar, Pablo 126
ethnic coherence 68
ethnic diversity 103–4, 110, 171–4
ethnicity
of foreigners 77
as an identity 42
ethnic minorities 63, 70–2, 99, 103, 107, 113–14, 153, 172–3
religions of 110
'ethno-symbolism' (Anthony Smith) 30
eugenics 178
European Court of Human Rights (ECHR) 3
European Union (EU) 8, 52–3, 69, 129–34, 144–6, 156
Evans, B. 125
exclusionary logics and practices 33–5, 38–9, 42, 45–6
'explanatory nationalism' (Pogge) 81, 239n.77

INDEX

Falklands War (1982) 114, 158
family life 91, 142–3
Fanon, Frantz 44, 75, 109, 218–19n.68
Farage, Nigel 3, 63, 130–1, 133, 155, 160
Farris, Sara 21, 74
fascism 11, 43, 107, 115, 166–9, 253n.41
Febbraro, F. 83
feminism 28, 74, 78, 140
Ferguson, Niall 111
Fichte, J. G. 30
Finland 7, 52, 189
fishing disputes 53
Ford, Rob 171
Formenton, Gianfranco 107
Foucault, Michel 28, 124
Fox, J. E. 145
Fox, Liam 133, 136, 160
France 7, 40, 50–3, 70, 74, 79–81, 86–7, 98, 174
Frankfurt School 163–4
free market ideology 161
free movement of labour 3, 7, 12, 130
free speech 73, 78
French Revolution 42, 44
Freud, Sigmund 19
'friend/enemy' thesis 34
Fukuyama, Francis 4, 122

Game of Thrones 105
Gandhi, Mahatma 92
Garner, Steve 41
Gaullism 69
Gellner, E. 41, 167
gentrification 146–7, 151
Germany 7, 24, 30, 50, 52, 115, 198
Gesellschaft 13
Giddens, Anthony 159
Gilbert, Jeremy 172–6
Gilman, M. E. 141
Gilroy, Paul 14, 22, 33, 38, 47, 54, 64, 110–11, 138–9, 159, 175, 203, 205
Gingrich, Newt 141
Il Giornale 88

Glasman, Lord 170
global financial crisis (2008) 10
globalisation 122, 129
Global South 59, 100, 119, 135–6, 196
Goethe, J. W. 30
Goldberg, David Theo 14, 131–2, 146
Goldsmith, Zac 90–1
Goodfellow, Maya 16
Goodhart, David 24, 65, 100, 138, 171
Goodwin, Matthew 171
Google 191
Gopal, Priyamvada 112–13
Gott, Richard 112
Gove, Michael 133
Gramsci, Antonio 40, 163
Grantchester 105
Gray, John 93–4
Greece 34–5, 53, 58, 62, 82–3
Green, Philip 126
Gregory, D. 119
Greif, Mark 138, 150
Grenfell Tower 155, 206–7
'grooming' 73
Grosrichard, Alain 78–81
Grylls, Bear 116
The Guardian 61
Guha, R. 112

Habermas, Jürgen 20, 69–70
Haider, A. 47
Haider, Shuja 187
halal meat 85
Hall, Stuart 18–19, 50, 123, 157–60, 165–6, 175, 242n.5, 245n.41
'halo-effect' 174
Hannan, Daniel 132
Hanseatic League 39
Harris, Sam 73, 85, 191, 194
Harry, Prince 116
Harry Potter 105
Hatherley, Owen 93, 116
Hayek, F. 94
hegemony 190
Help for Heroes 22, 116–17

Herder, J. G. 30, 54
heritage industry 104
higher education 91–2
Hinduism 110
hip-hop 138
  grime 138, 206
hipsters 149–50
Hitchens, Christopher 73, 85–6
Hitchens, Peter 106
Hitler, Adolf 43, 111
Hobsbawm, Eric 13, 53, 163, 197
Hollinger, D. A. 69
Holocaust, the 115
'homonationalism' (Puar) 74
homophobia 74
hooks, bell 172
Horkheimer, M. 163
Houellebecq, Michel 86–7
housing policy 147
HSBC 126
human capital 131–2
humanitarian intervention 84
humanities, education in 91
human rights 3
Human Rights Act 49
Hungary 7, 52, 195
Huq, Rupa 198, 204

identity politics 47, 91, 235n.44
ideology, definition of 19
Ignatieff, Michael 20, 69–70
'imagined communities' 41
immigration 120, 130, 160
  effect on particular areas 173–6
  see also points system
imperialism 8, 85, 101, 113–15, 119, 135–6, 159, 165
India 59–60, 110, 133, 195
individualism 91
individual responsibility 124–7
Indonesia 195
Ingres, Jean Auguste Dominique 81
integration 71–4, 103–4
'internal outsiders' 48, 51–3

International Monetary Fund (IMF) 53, 123
international relations theory 32
Invictus Games 116
Iraq War 129, 201
Ireland 51, 58–9, 102, 181
  see also Northern Ireland Troubles
Ishaq, Tabinda-Kauser 118
Islam 60, 70, 73–4, 85–7, 107–10
  see also Islamophobia; Muslim communities
Islamism 53, 87
Islamophobia 74–5, 79, 86, 139, 189, 199
Israel 45
Italy 7, 13, 53, 107, 181, 201

Jacobs, Jane 147
James, Malcolm 37, 181
Japan 195
Jenkins, Simon 91
Jewish people 50–1, 62, 101–2, 107, 181, 254n.49
Jobs, Steve 126
Johnson, Boris 63, 133, 136, 160, 185
Jones, Alex 191–2
Jones, Graham 157
Jones, H. 204
Judis, John 11

Kapoor, N. 214n.24
Karner, C. 205
Keenan, S. 66
Keith, Michael 152
Kenya 113
Kertzer, D. J. 53
Kierkegaard, Søren 64
Kipling, Rudyard 50
Kjellberg, Felix (PewDiePie) 191–2
Klein, Naomi 138
Kumar, Deepa 74–5
Kundnani, Arun 21, 76, 78, 93, 231n.1
Kunzru, Hari 149, 152
Kymlicka, Will 70

271

INDEX

Labour Party 16–17, 24, 65, 156–9, 184–5, 199
laïcité principle 40
Lammy, David 157, 198
Land, Nick 191
Leavis, F. R. 92
Lee Kuan Yew 123
'left behind' thesis 24–5, 170
left liberals 108–9
left politics in Britain, future prospects for 207
Leicester 204
Lentin, A. 8, 77, 142
Le Pen, Jean-Marie 100
Le Pen, Marine 3, 7, 155, 162
Letwin, Shirley Robin 125
Lewis, Clive 198
'Lexiter position' 66
liberal democracy 196
liberalism 71, 78, 83–8, 108–9, 127–8
Liddle, Rod 144–5
Little Englanders 158–61
Llobera, Josep 31
Locke, John 102
Louis-Philippe, King of France 128

McClintock, Anne 197
McCrone, David 29
Macedonia 34–5
McGeever, B. 170, 231n.1
MacInnes, Paul 192
McKenzie, L. 170
McRobbie, Angela 140
'Macronisme' 88
Maher, Bill 85–6
Malaysia 56
Malik, Nesrine 17
Malmö 189
Malthus, Thomas 128
Mamdani, Mahmood 42, 75
Marcuse, H. 118, 163
marketisation 92, 123
marriage
 age of 97
support for 91
Marxism 122, 162–4, 167–9, 180
masculinity 81–2, 97, 142, 186, 190
Mason, Paul 156, 162
May, Philip 157
May, Theresa 3, 12, 133, 155, 157, 170
Mbembe, Achille 45–7
Meer, Nasar 59
Meinecke, Friedrich 69
men's rights activists (MRA) 8
Mercer, Robert 193
Merkel, Angela 7–8, 61, 72
middle classes 10, 21, 85, 128, 147–51, 171–2
 petit bourgeois 123, 160–1
Miéville, China 62–3
Miles, Robert 180
militarism 116–20, 159
Milton Keynes 204
minority groups 5, 10, 50–3, 62, 75, 103, 130
 see also ethnic minorities
minority rights 190
Mishra, Pankaj 99–100, 109, 112
misogyny 84
mobility, neoliberal compulsion for 142
modernity 14, 43–4, 84
monarchy 22, 105, 236n.52
Montesquieu, Baron de 50, 80
Morant Bay uprising 112
Mosse, George 14
mothering, as neoliberal ideal 140–1
Müller, Jan-Werner 2, 63–4, 88
multiculture and multiculturalism 25, 72, 103, 107–10, 120, 160, 172–4, 185, 202–6
Murray, Douglas 87
'muscular liberalism' 20–1, 71
Musk, Elon 126
Muslim communities/figure of the Muslim 5, 21, 71–9, 84–8, 108, 120, 139–43, 153, 160
Mussolini, Benito 201
Myanmar 195

272

INDEX

mythmaking 95

Nagle, Angela 2, 187, 190, 260n.5
Nairn, Tom 58
Narayan, Y. 223n.9
national community, ethos of 65
nationalisation of states 43
nationalism 3–20, 29, 33–8, 44–7, 50–6, 107–9; 117–20, 134–6, 146, 149, 153–63, 167–70, 175, 177, 182–3
    challenges irrespective of party political fortunes 185
    'common sense' aspect of 185
    constitutive elements of 20
    debt to conservatism 94
    definition of 4–9, 33–8, 56, 129–30
    ending of 183
    exclusionary nature of 45–6
    French 50
    frenzied forms of 51
    future prospects for 207
    gaps in present account of 186
    gendered 56, 73–4, 97–8
    of groups other than white British 36–8
    and ideology 14, 18
    importance of 8–11
    of the left 177
    liberal, conservative, neoliberal and *communitarian* discourses as part of 15, 67
    moderate 36
    new form of 3–4, 9–15, 18, 162, 170, 184
    and non-belonging 36–7
    overdetermination of 15–16
    and populism 61
    and race 52, 55, 156, 182
    repudiation of 156
    resistance to 16, 18, 184
    resurgence of 194–7
    social alternatives to 203
    as a way of apprehending the world 37
    wide ideological spectrum of 14–15, 18, 67, 89, 182
nation-making 42, 55, 60, 117–18
    mythologies of 50
nations 30–5, 39–43, 48–55
    claims to selfhood 35, 50
    construction of 33
    primordial conception of 30–1, 68
    and race 48–55
    in relation to states 39–43
nation-states 14, 28–35, 42, 69, 85
    exclusionary nature of 33–5, 38–9
    importance of 66
    as the primary territorial units 196
    resistance to the hegemony of 47
    restoration of 195–6
nativism 47, 100, 180, 187, 205
    political 199
Nayak, Anoop 140, 205
Nazi Party 115
Négritude 218–19n.68
Nelson, Fraser 145
neo-anthropology 100
neoliberalism 22–3, 88, 121–54, 156–61, 172, 207
    brashness of 94
    and the consumer city 146–53
    definition of 122–7
    disentangled from conservatism 18, 89–94, 120
    hostility to 200
    seen as a phase of capitalism 122–30
Netflix 29
'new atheism' 85–6
New Labour 159–60
New Republic 141
New Yorker (magazine) 9
'NIMBY' protectionism 90, 93
Nixon, Richard 64
Noble, G. 205
Northern Ireland Troubles 158
Norway 11, 201
nostalgia 22, 52, 84, 104–5, 111–14, 118, 134–6, 156, 159

INDEX

Oakeshott, Michael 96
Obama, Barack 192
Occupy movement 66
Olaloku-Teriba, A. 47
Orientalism 51, 78–9, 83–4, 218–19n.68, 229n.55
  in art 81
Orwell, George 26–7, 118
Osborne, George 91
Osuri, Goldie 59
'othering' 34–5, 50, 55
Ottoman rule 79–82
outsider figures and outsider status 34–7, 55
overdetermination 15–16, 19

Pakistan 59–60, 110, 195
Paltrow, Gwyneth 126
'parallax' concept (Žižek) 195
Parker, D. 205
period drama 22, 104
Peterborough 205
Peterson, Jordan 192
Phillips, Trevor 227n.30
Pie, Jonathan 73
Pinochet, Augusto 123
Pitcher, Ben 66
pluralism 64
Pogge, Thomas 81
points system for immigration control 130–3, 136, 153
Poland 52, 201
political correctness 91
Poor Laws 177
poppy appeal 116–18, 239–40n.86
populism 2–3, 7–8, 57–67, 155, 158–61, 182
  definition of 62–5
  new form of 13
  racial nature of 20
Portes, Jonathan 132
'postcolonial melancholia' (Gilroy) 22, 111
postcolonial theory 59, 110–11

post-ethnic nationalism 70
'post-race' concept 75
poverty, pathologisation of 137–41
Powell, Enoch (and Powellism) 12, 93, 143, 231n.1
'prepolitical uniformity' (Gilroy) 64
progressive nationalism 58–60, 67–70
Puar, J. K. 74
Putin, Vladimir 194–5

Rabinbach, Anson 168
race
  importance of 8
  taxonomies of 48–55
  racial discrimination 76
  racial hierarchies 98–9
racism 16, 66, 88, 103, 131–3, 162, 171, 175, 182, 205
  animalising 51
  cultural 76–8
  new ideology of 98–100
  rationales for 76
  'scientific' 99
  'soft' 160
Rancière, J. 72
Ranger, T. 13
Read, Jason 71
Reagan, Ronald (and Reaganism) 123, 141
Rees-Mogg, Jacob 63, 106
Regnault, Henri 82
Renan, Ernest 32, 68–9, 178
'responsibilisation' 124–7
Rhodes, Cecil 136
Rhys-Taylor, A. 204
rights, faith-based 72
rioting in Britain (2011) 138–9
Robinson, Cedric 40, 112
Rogaly, Ben 173
Rogan, Joe 191, 193
Romanians 145
Romantic expressionism 4
romanticism 30, 68, 81–3, 175, 203
Roma people 5, 23, 144–6, 151

INDEX

Russia 63, 110
Ruth, P. 174
Rydgren, J. 174

Said, Edward 44, 78–81, 99, 218–19n.68
Salvage (magazine) 26
Salvini, Matteo 76–7, 108, 201, 264n.51
Sanders, Bernie 155
Sarkar, Ash 16, 199
Sarkozy, Nicolas 8
Sayer, Derek 173–4
Scandinavia 6
Scarman Report 144
Schmitt, Carl 34, 117, 215n.28
Schwetje, B. 83
Scotland 20, 56–60
Scott, J. 74
Scruton, Roger 91
secessionist movements 56
Second World War 114–19
　period immediately following 116
secularism 85, 108
　hollowing-out of 73
Severus, Septimius 101
sexism 73–4
Seymour, Richard 8, 183, 197
Shaheen, Faiza 198
Shatz, A. 10
Shilliam, Robbie 177–80, 258n.86, 266n.72
Shillman, Robert 193
Shriver, Lionel 109
Singapore 133
slave trade 101
Smith, Anthony 30–1, 69
Snow, Jon 118
social contracts 69
social democracy 16, 52, 59, 88, 156, 158, 180, 198–9, 202, 207
socialism 166, 198, 202
social media 100–1, 186–94
Solomos, J. 14
South Africa 189

sovereignty 58, 196
The Spectator 91
Spiked 8, 73
Spivak, G. C. 56, 74, 97
Sri Lanka 59–60, 110, 195
Standpoint 87
Starkey, David 23, 139
state capitalism 196
statehood 28, 30, 42, 128–9
state-nation and *cultural-nation* distinction 69
Streeck, Wolfgang 2, 65, 171
Subrahmanyam, S. 79
suburbs 152, 204–5
Sugar, Alan 126
Suleiman I 79
The Sun 118
Sweden 6, 76, 174

Taylor, A. 125
television series 104–6
territorial states 39–42
terrorism 189
Tesco 160
Tharoor, Kanishk 29
Thatcher, Margaret (and Thatcherism) 93–5, 123–4, 134, 141, 157–61, 180, 202, 252n.23
Thiel, Peter 193
'Third Way' policies 158–9
'Thomas theorem' 33
Thompson, E. P. 13, 38, 163
The Times 21
Titley, Gavan 8, 77, 142, 189, 191
Toscano, Alberto 168–9, 254n.49
tradition 94–100, 104
　Christian 107, 120
　claims to 95–6
　increased reference to 98
　lapsing of 98
　revision or transposition of 96–7
　stability provided by 95–6
traditionalism 141–2
Triandafyllidou, Anna 34–5

275

INDEX

Trump, Donald 3, 9–10, 63, 98, 126, 162, 169–70, 189, 191, 193
Tufekci, Z. 262n.22
Turkey 52, 83, 195
Tyson, Neil deGrasse 192

United Kingdom Independence Party (UKIP) 3, 193
United States 9–10, 70, 93, 115

'values racism' 21, 78
Varoufakis, Yanis 62
the Vatican 39
Virdee, Satnam 170, 180, 200, 231n.1
visa regulations 133
Vujanic, David 206

Wacquant, L. 128
Wagenknecht, Sahra 24, 198
'war on terror' 49, 116
Washington Consensus 123
Waterhouse, Keith 113
Waters, John 108–9
Watson, S. 204
Weber, Max 32, 50
welfare dependency 124, 137, 145
welfare provision 24, 106–7, 143–4, 160, 164–7, 170, 177–80
Wendling, Mike 187
Westphalian Treaty (1648) 30–1
White, Charlene 118
'white innocence' (Wekker) 238n.75

white majoritarianism 199
'white man's burden' 50, 75
whiteness 94–5, 100–2, 133, 235n.44
whitening the working class 176–82
white supremacy 112–13, 181
Wight, C. 32
William, Prince 116
Williams, Joan 171
Williams, Raymond 38
Windrush 157, 214
Wise, A. 205
Wodehouse, P. G. 104
work ethic 137
workfare 141, 161
working classes 164–5, 170, 173, 200
    whitening of 176–82
World Bank 123
Wright, Patrick 104

xenologies 103
xenophobia 54, 156, 175
xeno-racism 16, 156, 159, 170, 180–1

Yarvin/Moldbug, Curtis 191
Yiannopoulos, Milo 191, 194
Younge, Gary 199
youth culture 199–201
YouTube 191, 194, 206, 262n.22

Zionism 45
Žižek, Slavoj 2, 109, 176, 195
Zukin, Sharon 150–1